Lecture Notes in Computer Science   **10287**

Commenced Publication in 1973
Founding and Former Series Editors:
Gerhard Goos, Juris Hartmanis, and Jan van Leeuwen

More information about this series at http://www.springer.com/series/7409

Vincent G. Duffy (Ed.)

Digital Human Modeling

Applications in Health, Safety, Ergonomics, and Risk Management: Health and Safety

8th International Conference, DHM 2017
Held as Part of HCI International 2017
Vancouver, BC, Canada, July 9–14, 2017
Proceedings, Part II

 Springer

Editor
Vincent G. Duffy
Purdue University
West Lafayette, IN
USA

ISSN 0302-9743   ISSN 1611-3349   (electronic)
Lecture Notes in Computer Science
ISBN 978-3-319-58465-2   ISBN 978-3-319-58466-9   (eBook)
DOI 10.1007/978-3-319-58466-9

Library of Congress Control Number: 2017939545

LNCS Sublibrary: SL3 – Information Systems and Applications, incl. Internet/Web, and HCI

Printed on acid-free paper

This Springer imprint is published by Springer Nature
The registered company is Springer International Publishing AG
The registered company address is: Gewerbestrasse 11, 6330 Cham, Switzerland

Foreword

The 19th International Conference on Human–Computer Interaction, HCI International 2017, was held in Vancouver, Canada, during July 9–14, 2017. The event incorporated the 15 conferences/thematic areas listed on the following page.

A total of 4,340 individuals from academia, research institutes, industry, and governmental agencies from 70 countries submitted contributions, and 1,228 papers have been included in the proceedings. These papers address the latest research and development efforts and highlight the human aspects of design and use of computing systems. The papers thoroughly cover the entire field of human–computer interaction, addressing major advances in knowledge and effective use of computers in a variety of application areas. The volumes constituting the full set of the conference proceedings are listed on the following pages.

I would like to thank the program board chairs and the members of the program boards of all thematic areas and affiliated conferences for their contribution to the highest scientific quality and the overall success of the HCI International 2017 conference.

This conference would not have been possible without the continuous and unwavering support and advice of the founder, Conference General Chair Emeritus and Conference Scientific Advisor Prof. Gavriel Salvendy. For his outstanding efforts, I would like to express my appreciation to the communications chair and editor of *HCI International News*, Dr. Abbas Moallem.

April 2017   Constantine Stephanidis

HCI International 2017 Thematic Areas and Affiliated Conferences

Thematic areas:

- Human–Computer Interaction (HCI 2017)
- Human Interface and the Management of Information (HIMI 2017)

Affiliated conferences:

- 17th International Conference on Engineering Psychology and Cognitive Ergonomics (EPCE 2017)
- 11th International Conference on Universal Access in Human–Computer Interaction (UAHCI 2017)
- 9th International Conference on Virtual, Augmented and Mixed Reality (VAMR 2017)
- 9th International Conference on Cross-Cultural Design (CCD 2017)
- 9th International Conference on Social Computing and Social Media (SCSM 2017)
- 11th International Conference on Augmented Cognition (AC 2017)
- 8th International Conference on Digital Human Modeling and Applications in Health, Safety, Ergonomics and Risk Management (DHM 2017)
- 6th International Conference on Design, User Experience and Usability (DUXU 2017)
- 5th International Conference on Distributed, Ambient and Pervasive Interactions (DAPI 2017)
- 5th International Conference on Human Aspects of Information Security, Privacy and Trust (HAS 2017)
- 4th International Conference on HCI in Business, Government and Organizations (HCIBGO 2017)
- 4th International Conference on Learning and Collaboration Technologies (LCT 2017)
- Third International Conference on Human Aspects of IT for the Aged Population (ITAP 2017)

Conference Proceedings Volumes Full List

1. LNCS 10271, Human–Computer Interaction: User Interface Design, Development and Multimodality (Part I), edited by Masaaki Kurosu
2. LNCS 10272 Human–Computer Interaction: Interaction Contexts (Part II), edited by Masaaki Kurosu
3. LNCS 10273, Human Interface and the Management of Information: Information, Knowledge and Interaction Design (Part I), edited by Sakae Yamamoto
4. LNCS 10274, Human Interface and the Management of Information: Supporting Learning, Decision-Making and Collaboration (Part II), edited by Sakae Yamamoto
5. LNAI 10275, Engineering Psychology and Cognitive Ergonomics: Performance, Emotion and Situation Awareness (Part I), edited by Don Harris
6. LNAI 10276, Engineering Psychology and Cognitive Ergonomics: Cognition and Design (Part II), edited by Don Harris
7. LNCS 10277, Universal Access in Human–Computer Interaction: Design and Development Approaches and Methods (Part I), edited by Margherita Antona and Constantine Stephanidis
8. LNCS 10278, Universal Access in Human–Computer Interaction: Designing Novel Interactions (Part II), edited by Margherita Antona and Constantine Stephanidis
9. LNCS 10279, Universal Access in Human–Computer Interaction: Human and Technological Environments (Part III), edited by Margherita Antona and Constantine Stephanidis
10. LNCS 10280, Virtual, Augmented and Mixed Reality, edited by Stephanie Lackey and Jessie Y.C. Chen
11. LNCS 10281, Cross-Cultural Design, edited by Pei-Luen Patrick Rau
12. LNCS 10282, Social Computing and Social Media: Human Behavior (Part I), edited by Gabriele Meiselwitz
13. LNCS 10283, Social Computing and Social Media: Applications and Analytics (Part II), edited by Gabriele Meiselwitz
14. LNAI 10284, Augmented Cognition: Neurocognition and Machine Learning (Part I), edited by Dylan D. Schmorrow and Cali M. Fidopiastis
15. LNAI 10285, Augmented Cognition: Enhancing Cognition and Behavior in Complex Human Environments (Part II), edited by Dylan D. Schmorrow and Cali M. Fidopiastis
16. LNCS 10286, Digital Human Modeling and Applications in Health, Safety, Ergonomics and Risk Management: Ergonomics and Design (Part I), edited by Vincent G. Duffy
17. LNCS 10287, Digital Human Modeling and Applications in Health, Safety, Ergonomics and Risk Management: Health and Safety (Part II), edited by Vincent G. Duffy
18. LNCS 10288, Design, User Experience, and Usability: Theory, Methodology and Management (Part I), edited by Aaron Marcus and Wentao Wang

Digital Human Modeling and Applications in Health, Safety, Ergonomics and Risk Management

Program Board Chair(s): **Vincent G. Duffy, USA**

- Andre Calero Valdez, Germany
- Eugene Ch'ng, P.R. China
- Elsbeth de Korte, The Netherlands
- Stephen J. Elliott, USA
- Afzal A. Godil, USA
- Ravindra Goonetilleke, Hong Kong, SAR China
- Akihiko Goto, Japan
- Hiroyuki Hamada, Japan
- Dan Högberg, Sweden
- Hui-min Hu, P.R. China
- Satoshi Kanai, Japan
- Noriaki Kuwahara, Japan
- Kang Li, USA
- Lingxi Li, USA
- Jianwei Niu, P.R. China
- Thaneswer Patel, India
- Beatrice V. Podtschaske, USA
- Caterina Rizzi, Italy
- Beatriz Sousa Santos, Portugal
- Nicole Sintov, USA
- Pingbo Tang, USA
- Leonor Teixeira, Portugal
- Renran Tian, USA
- Gentiane Venture, Japan
- Massimiliano Vesci, Italy
- Anita Woll, Norway
- Kuan Yew Wong, Malaysia
- Shuping Xiong, Korea
- James Yang, USA
- Chaoyi Zhao, P.R. China

The full list with the Program Board Chairs and the members of the Program Boards of all thematic areas and affiliated conferences is available online at:

http://www.hci.international/board-members-2017.php

HCI International 2018

The 20th International Conference on Human–Computer Interaction, HCI International 2018, will be held jointly with the affiliated conferences in Las Vegas, NV, USA, at Caesars Palace, July 15–20, 2018. It will cover a broad spectrum of themes related to human–computer interaction, including theoretical issues, methods, tools, processes, and case studies in HCI design, as well as novel interaction techniques, interfaces, and applications. The proceedings will be published by Springer. More information is available on the conference website: http://2018.hci.international/.

General Chair
Prof. Constantine Stephanidis
University of Crete and ICS-FORTH
Heraklion, Crete, Greece
E-mail: general_chair@hcii2018.org

http://2018.hci.international/

Contents – Part II

Health and Aging

Health Data Analytics and Visualization

Design for Safety

Contents – Part I

Smart Human-Centered Service System Design

Clinical and Health Information Systems

Mobile-Application Based Cognitive Behavior Therapy (CBT) for Identifying and Managing Depression and Anxiety

Siva Abhishek Addepally[(✉)] and Saptarshi Purkayastha

School of Informatics and Computing,
Indiana University-Purdue University Indianapolis, Indianapolis, USA
{sivaadde,saptpurk}@iupui.edu

Abstract. Mobile technology is a cost effective and scalable platform for developing a therapeutic intervention. This paper discusses the development of a mobile application for people suffering with depression and anxiety. The application which we have developed is similar to a Cognitive Behavior Therapy (CBT) website, which is freely available on the internet. Past research has shown that CBT delivered over the internet is effective in alleviating the depressive symptoms in users. But, this delivery method is associated with some innate drawbacks, which caused user dropout and reduced adherence to the therapy. To overcome these shortfalls, from web based CBT delivery, a mobile application called MoodTrainer was developed. The application is equipped with mobile specific interventions and CBT modules which aim at delivering a dynamic supportive psychotherapy to the user. The mobile specific interventions using this application ensures that the user is constantly engaged with the application and focused to change the negative thought process. We present MoodTrainer as a self-efficacy tool and virtual CBT that is not meant to replace a clinical caregiver. Rather, it is a supportive tool that can be used to self-monitor, as well as a monitoring aid for clinicians.

Keywords: CBT · Depression · MoodTrainer · mHealth

1 Introduction

Depression and Anxiety are the most common mental disorders which are observed in adults and adolescents. In 2015, it is estimated that 16.1 million adults aged 18 or older in the United States had at least one depressive episode in the past year [1]. According to WHO 2016 fact sheet depression is one of the most common illness worldwide and it effects approximately 350 million people around globe [2]. These depressive disorders are usually associated with an anxiety disorder. Most of the Mental Health Organizations recommend Cognitive Behavior Therapy (CBT) as evidence based approach for the treatment and management of Depression and Anxiety. CBT usually involves a patient and therapist encounters at stipulated intervals, where the patient is required to answer certain questionnaires which asses the patient's mental health status and the severity of the existing disorder. At its core, CBT helps an individual to identify negative thought patterns and replace them by positive ways of thinking [3]. Although

© Springer International Publishing AG 2017
V.G. Duffy (Ed.): DHM 2017, Part II, LNCS 10287, pp. 3–12, 2017.
DOI: 10.1007/978-3-319-58466-9_1

there is effective treatment available, less than half of those affected by it have access to these therapies. The factors which restrict access to such kind of therapies are lack of resources and lack of availability of trained professionals [2].

mHealth has gained more importance with the rapid uptake and utilization of the smartphones, which are powerful and monitor the real-time data of the user [4, 5]. Many researchers have claimed that mHealth is a mechanism which can deliver more effective and more accessible mental health care [6, 7]. Since mobile phones have become an extension of individual's behavior, researchers have shown that behavioral health, which can be considered closely related to mental health, can be greatly affected by the use of smartphones [8]. Smartphone devices run various software applications (mobile apps) which tap the hardware features of the phone and can provide the user with valuable information in a user-friendly format. When these apps are built with mHealth orientation, they can provide patient-specific and user-centered health information which is meaningful, accurate, relevant and up-to-date. By the use of mobile apps, caregivers are able to target the patient, based on their condition and response to treatment [9]. These apps can be built to address a specific area such as to monitor fitness, provide health information, monitor sleep patterns and provide guidance to users for smoking cessation, meeting fitness goals and so on.

With the widespread use of internet technology, the web-based CBT is modified to make use of interactive design, where the user/patient is provided with the series of activities and tasks to be done. By this means of therapy, a larger group of population can access the service without the need of qualified and trained professionals. The major problem associated with this type of care is that the user needs to have access to a computer and internet. Studies demonstrate that this method is effective in improving the knowledge and the prognosis of the mental disorders [10]. But, this method has some drawbacks, such as the poor user interface, no reminders provided by the CBT website to complete the tasks. The other drawback for this type of care delivery is that there is no monitoring of real time data and it relies only on the data entered by the user.

It is also estimated that there are about 6 billion mobile cellular service subscriptions around the globe [11], highlighting that mobile technology has deep and wide penetration in society. Recent research suggests that a user's personality can be attributed to the way they use their mobile phone [12]. This opens an opportunity, where a mobile phone might be the perfect medium to deliver virtual CBT. Apart from delivering CBT, mobile devices can perform functions that can track a user's mental status in real time.

CBT delivered as a smartphone application encompasses all the pitfalls present in the internet mode of delivery. CBT provided in the form of a mobile application has the capability to correlate the user data to the real-time data provided by the smartphone. This allows to monitor the user's status in real time and provide apt information to the user. With the rapidly increasing use of smartphones, users are more reachable and the chances of user dropping out are very low, as it is possible to send notifications and catch the attention of the user to again use the system. Research evidence suggest that CBT delivered via mobile application can have clinically significant improvement in the disease outcomes for depression patients [13].

2 Materials and Methods

We created the MoodTrainer mobile application inspired from a CBT website called MoodGYM (https://moodgym.anu.edu.au). We do not have any association or relation to the MoodGYM website, and only use it as a conceptual base for the intervention that is developed through this mobile application. The effectiveness of MoodGYM for depression and anxiety symptoms in individuals suffering from depression has been demonstrated in several studies [14–16]. Twomey et al. evaluated the effectiveness of the MoodGYM and suggest that CBT delivered by MoodGYM is effective in alleviating the depression symptoms. But, they also highlights that the dropout rate in MoodGYM studies could be a problem [17]. Another systematic review of the computerized CBT delivery methods conducted by Kaltenthaler et al. also highlights that the dropout rates for the different computerized CBT delivery methods are quite high [18]. The high dropout rates for the computerized CBT delivery could be due to usability and accessibility. But a major drawback of the present method of CBT is that it is lacks accessibility features, is not mobile-first and users need to access the CBT using a computer.

To counter these drawbacks, we developed the MoodTrainer mobile app. We developed MoodTrainer with features to track user's behavior in real time and provide timely suggestion for effective results. MoodTrainer tracks user location and asks for responses when they check into an isolated location, detected using Bluetooth beacons and location services. Previous research shows that loneliness can be a risk factor in depression, where loneliness can significantly impact the wellbeing of the individual [19]. With the help of the above-mentioned technologies MoodTrainer tracks the user's movements and isolated behavior. Here, MoodTrainer provides suggestions and recommendations that improve user mood, such as playing their favorite songs or pre-selected motivational quotes.

We conducted a literature review of all the different mobile applications that work as a CBT intervention under depression. In the literature we found 12 papers that discussed use of mobile applications for CBT, out of which 9 papers were opinion or call for research related papers and 3 papers were related to design ideas. There was no research that was related to the implementation/deployment/evaluation of a mHealth app that worked as a virtual CBT. We also searched the Google play store and the Apple app store to search apps (using keywords: mood, depression, anxiety). We found 41 apps in Google play store and 32 apps on the Apple app store that were related to mood and mental health. Most apps were log books or diary about feelings and mood of the user. Few apps went one step forward and allowed relating the times and produce reports that could be shared with clinicians and other users. Only 3 apps – T2 Mood Tracker developed by the National Center for Telehealth & Technology, Cognitive Diary CBT Self-Help by Excel at Life and Pacifa by Pacifica Labs Inc. – were related to evidence-based practices around CBT and mental health research. Most of the other apps were simple user logs which did not use device sensors, reminder/alert systems or paths/challenges that are important for self-help transformation in individuals with depression and anxiety problems. This motivated us to develop the MoodTrainer mobile application that was to be evaluated using a Randomized Controlled Trial, among university students who suffer from depression and anxiety. In this paper, we present the user-interaction (UI) design, user-experience (UX) and feature set that was developed based on the literature findings for evidence-based CBT interventions.

Based on the literature review and use of all the similar applications, we created a requirements specification for each feature with very specific acceptance criteria for each feature. The modular design of the application allowed us to improve the application without affecting any UI element that was already developed and tested. The core UI elements like stylesheet, JavaScript libraries, color schemes were developed and tested at the first cycle of development. The interaction design and UX elements like when to notify, when to change screens, how to showcase progress or alert boxes were unique to each module or feature and these had to be prototyped to test if it made sense for user's workflow and based on their mental state and condition. We used a rapid prototyping methodology to develop the mobile application. Instead of creating paper prototypes, wireframes and then live mockups, we developed the application using HTML pages and deployed them into the mobile devices for testing. Based on the feedback between the researchers, we improved the application through rapid cycles of prototyping, as shown in the Fig. 1.

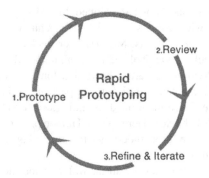

Fig. 1. Rapid prototyping methodology (Color figure online)

The review process involved looking at the requirements document and reviewing if it meets the acceptance criteria. After the review process, we refined, sometimes even the acceptance criteria and started the cycle of development again. This process allowed us to complete development of the application in under 3 months by a single developer.

3 Results

MoodTrainer is a cross-platform, hybrid mobile application, which utilizes web technologies such as HTML, CSS and JavaScript. MoodTrainer is available on Android, iOS, Windows Phone 8.1/10, Blackberry 10, FirefoxOS, LG WebOS and FireOS platforms and we have performed extensive testing on three Android devices, one iOS and two Windows devices. All the three platforms have matured to a level now that there is very little to distinguish between native and hybrid mobile applications that work in an embedded browser view such as WebView for Android or WKWebView for iOS platform. On our testing, we did not notice any differences between native application UX and hybrid mobile UX for the forms, device APIs and notification messages on our application (Figs. 2 and 3).

Fig. 2. The location tracking feature of MoodTrainer.

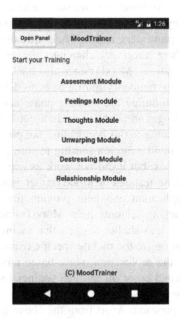

Fig. 3. Modules present in the application for the user.

Various UI screen pages were developed for the application using HTML5. On some pages we utilized advanced HTML5 features such as local storage and geolocation for storing user data and accessing the user location. Local storage is mainly used to store the user responses to the various activities in the app. JQuery Mobile was used to design the UI of the application. Later all the HTML pages and their related JavaScript were imported into NetBeans which was used to create a cordova project. This project was emulated on to a virtual android device to test its functioning of the application. The APK of the above HTML pages was compiled using Apache Cordova and a build release was generated. The generated APK was installed on an android device to check the functionality of the application. The installed application was fast and responsive on different android platforms.

The training aspect of MoodTrainer is like the above listed CBT based intervention apps, which focus on recording data, providing a path for mental health progress and then evaluating and giving feedback to the user to improve their mental condition. We did this in an evidence-based way that has been evaluated for improvements in clinical outcomes. The following are some of the main innovations that make MoodTrainer unique compared to other CBT intervention apps.

MoodTrainer includes a feature which retrieves the user location using native device APIs every few minutes and displays the user location on a map. We utilize the Google maps API and use its mapping functionality to determine nearby locations. Based on user location, we are able to identify if the user is in a remote site, which is less crowded, a trait commonly seen in depressed individuals. When MoodTrainer is able to detect this, we show notifications to either play their favorite mood music that they responded to in the questionnaire or we ask them to go through the mood improvement and self-help questionnaires. In the future, we plan to build a feature where caregivers, clinicians, nurses or friends can be notified and help the user in such situations. MoodTrainer also tracks the user's voice pitch based on the changes in the voice frequency during calls, to detect the user's stress levels. The app observes voice pitch during the learning phase and later watches for changes. When the app detects changes in pitch, it sends a notification to assess user's status. Based on the user's response to this notification, we provide appropriate advice to the user. We also wanted to build a motion-sensing feature using the smartphone's accelerometer to detect agitations, but it did not work as expected and had to be removed from the application. These features of MoodTrainer ensure that the user is continuously engaged with the application and help provide timely and appropriate suggestions. These real-time tracking features help MoodTrainer to provide appropriate responses to the user. Previous studies suggest that mobile application designed focused for depression did not utilize the mobile specific features to provide the user real-time feedback [20]. All of the geolocation, voice-based mood identification and external help features can be turned on or off through settings by the user, so that it does get too intrusive for the user. These innovative features make MoodTrainer unique in delivering CBT for depression. Apart from the above mobile-specific innovations, as a generalized CBT, MoodTrainer navigates the user through a step-by-step, series of modules that analyze the user's level of depression and anxiety (Fig. 4).

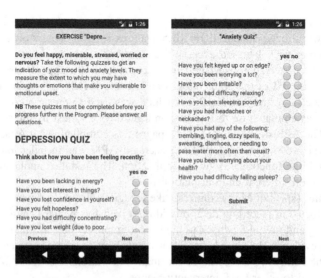

Fig. 4. Represents different questionnaires to evaluate the level of depression and anxiety

The different modules present in the CBT application are:

- **Assessment Module**
  The main motive of this module is to identify the severity of the depression and anxiety symptoms experienced by the users. The user is taken through a series of questionnaires using which the symptoms of the user are classified as mild, moderate and severe. The assessment module is the first module that should be answered by the user, so that assessment and progress path can be created for the user.
- **Feelings Module**
  This module takes the user through a series of tasks which helps the users to identify their feelings and helps them in developing a positive feeling regarding themselves. The feature to associated different songs with different moods may also be done in this module. Depending on the responses in other modules, and assessment of the mood by the application, the associated song will be played.
- **Thoughts Module**
  In this module user walks through a series of activities which aids the user in identifying their negative thoughts and later the user is presented with methods which aid in countering the negative thoughts with positive ones.
- **Unwarping Module**
  This is one of the important module present in this application, the main focus of this module is identifying user's warped thoughts and help them in coming out if the warped thinking.
- **Destressing Module**
  The main goal of this module is to equip the user with the destressing strategies and also help the users in applying these strategies in real life scenarios.
- **Relationship Module**
  This is the final module of the present application; this module mainly focuses on building relationships and suggests the user to look at the Brightside in a relation. This module also analyzes the user's relation with their parents and helps them in having a better relation with their parents.

These modules utilize various scales such which help in assessing the users' thoughts and their current mental state. They are:

- Goldberg Depression and Anxiety scale
- Wrapy Thoughts Quiz
- Pleasant Event Schedule
- Life Whacks Questionnaire
- Measure of parenting Style

Additionally, these modules are equipped with scales that analyze warped thoughts experienced by the user. In advanced modules, the user is asked to perform series of activities that may help in overcoming the warped thoughts. All the above-mentioned modules and features of the application are flexible and the user can enable to disable these features, depending on their comfort level with the trainer. With the use of each module, the user can view their scores and validate their own progress. With these supportive care features, MoodTrainer fulfills the criteria for dynamic supportive psychotherapy. The corner stone of dynamic support therapy is to "be with the patient", which mainly involves interacting with the patient and sharing experiences [21]. The user interaction and responses are logged for the purposes of a real psychologist for feedback.

4   Discussion

While CBT based interventions using mobile phones are not very common, we see that more and more psychologists prefer that their patients start using apps that log behavior and mood. This helps self-management, such as identifying factors that become triggers for mood change, and causes for depressive behavior. The MoodTrainer logs are not supposed to be used by clinicians, but primarily by researchers who want to evaluate the tool, patient activation and patient engagement with the application and how it affects patient outcomes. The secondary user of the logs is the patient. Yet, the more useful thing for the patient is decision support by the virtual CBT based on the questionnaire in the different modules.

The effectiveness of the innovative features in MoodTrainer cannot be commented on until we complete the RCT. But in terms of the ideas and implementation of technologies, we have been able to implement and showcase the useful sensors available in today's smartphones. Being able to use pervasive computing in mental health is the first step towards a new model for CBT and for an all pervasive CBT intervention. While this CBT intervention can work on its own, the best possible use that we see in the foreseeable future is combining MoodTrainer with a telehealth program in mental health. The role of the caregivers and family members should not be dismissed, but this CBT intervention is only complementary to existing behavioral and pharmacological treatments that are available today.

The problem with testing the MoodTrainer application in an RCT is determining the confounding factors such as environmental, case severity and even limited by the way current practices surrounding modern mental health treatments. Unlike other fields of medicine, mental health diagnosis and treatment is quite varied across contexts and needs to be personalized to the patient's mental condition. With a CBT and better ways of logging and decision support, there is a possibility that the personalization can be better targeted.

5   Conclusion

In conclusion, we present MoodTrainer as a self-efficacy tool and virtual CBT that is not meant to replace a clinical caregiver. Rather, it is a supportive tool that can be used to self-monitor, as well as a monitoring aid for clinicians. As there are resource challenges in continuous and direct delivery of CBT, we propose that mobile applications, such as ours, might be the best method for delivering CBT. Delivering CBT via mobile application is cost effective and can also be applied in low resource settings.

References

1. Facts & Statistics | Anxiety and Depression Association of America, ADAA. https://www. adaa.org/about-adaa/press-room/facts-statistics
2. Depression. http://www.who.int/mediacentre/factsheets/fs369/en/
3. Cognitive Behavioral Therapy for Depression. http://www.webmd.com/depression/guide/ cognitive-behavioral-therapy-for-depression#1
4. Mechael, P., Nemser, B., Cosmaciuc, R., Cole-Lewis, H., Ohemeng-Dapaah, S., Dusabe, S., Kaonga, N.N., Namakula, P., Shemsanga, M., Burbach, R., Kanter, A.S.: Capitalizing on the characteristics of mHealth to evaluate its impact. J. Health Commun. **17**, 62–66 (2012)
5. Ling, R.S.: The Mobile Connection: The Cell Phone's Impact on Society. Morgan Kaufmann Publisher, Burlington (2004)
6. Donker, T., Petrie, K., Proudfoot, J., Clarke, J., Birch, M.-R., Christensen, H.: Smartphones for smarter delivery of mental health programs: a systematic review. J. Med. Internet Res. **15**, e247 (2013)
7. Price, M., Yuen, E.K., Goetter, E.M., Herbert, J.D., Forman, E.M., Acierno, R., Ruggiero, K.J.: mHealth: a mechanism to deliver more accessible, more effective mental health care. Clin. Psychol. Psychother. **21**, 427–436 (2014)
8. Luxton, D.D., McCann, R.A., Bush, N.E., Mishkind, M.C., Reger, G.M.: mHealth for mental health: integrating smartphone technology in behavioral healthcare. Prof. Psychol.: Res. Practice **42**, 505 (2011)
9. Sumsion, T.: Client-centred practice in occupational therapy: a guide to implementation. Elsevier Health Sciences, Amsterdam (2006)
10. Christensen, H.: Delivering interventions for depression by using the internet: randomised controlled trial. BMJ **328**, 265 (2004)
11. 2011 ends with almost 6 billion mobile phone subscriptions. https://www.cnet.com/news/ 2011-ends-with-almost-6-billion-mobile-phone-subscriptions/
12. de Montjoye, Y.-A., Quoidbach, J., Robic, F., Pentland, A.: Predicting personality using novel mobile phone-based metrics. In: Greenberg, A.M., Kennedy, W.G., Bos, N.D. (eds.) SBP 2013. LNCS, vol. 7812, pp. 48–55. Springer, Heidelberg (2013). doi:10.1007/978-3-642-37210-0_6
13. Watts, S., Mackenzie, A., Thomas, C., Griskaitis, A., Mewton, L., Williams, A., Andrews, G.: CBT for depression: a pilot RCT comparing mobile phone vs. computer. BMC Psychiatry **13**, 49 (2013)
14. Calear, A.L., Christensen, H., Mackinnon, A., Griffiths, K.M.: Adherence to the MoodGYM program: outcomes and predictors for an adolescent school-based population. J. Affect. Disord. **147**, 338–344 (2013)
15. Schneider, J., Foroushani, P.S., Grime, P., Thornicroft, G.: Acceptability of online self-help to people with depression: users' views of MoodGYM versus informational websites. J. Med. Internet Res. **16**, e90 (2014)
16. Muñoz, R.F., Bunge, E.L., Chen, K., Schueller, S.M., Bravin, J.I., Shaughnessy, E.A., Pérez-Stable, E.J.: Massive open online interventions a novel model for delivering behavioral-health services worldwide. Clin. Psychol. Sci. (2015). doi:10.1177/ 2167702615583840
17. Twomey, C., O'Reilly, G.: Effectiveness of a freely available computerised cognitive behavioural therapy programme (MoodGYM) for depression: meta-analysis. Aust. New Zealand J. Psychiatry **51**, 260–269 (2017)
18. Kaltenthaler, E., Parry, G., Beverley, C., Ferriter, M.: Computerised cognitive-behavioural therapy for depression: systematic review. Br. J. Psychiatry **193**, 181–184 (2008)

19. Cacioppo, J., Hughes, M., Waite, L., Hawkley, L., Thisted, R.: Loneliness as a specific risk factor for depressive symptoms: cross-sectional and longitudinal analyses. Psychol. Aging **21**, 140–151 (2006)
20. Martínez-Pérez, B., de la Torre-Díez, I., López-Coronado, M.: Mobile health applications for the most prevalent conditions by the world health organization: review and analysis. J. Med. Internet Res. **15**, e120 (2013)
21. Viederman, M.: A model for interpretative supportive dynamic psychotherapy. Psychiatry Interpers. Biol. Process. **71**, 349–358 (2008)

The Structure of Clinical Judgment Making Based on Nurse's Visual Observation

Shizuko Hayashi[✉]

Ishikawa Prefectural Nursing University, Kahoku, Ishikawa, Japan
hayashiz@ishikawa-nu.ac.jp

Abstract. To elucidate the structure of nurses' clinical decisions based on visual observation; we established objectives targeting nurses with varying levels of experience. Subjects: Thirty-three nurses. As simulated patient information, written information on an 85-year old inpatient with pneumonia was provided to subjects. Four images of a simulated patient room with the simulated patient in the bed, each image was displayed on the monitor for five seconds. After observation, while confirming the path of line of sight during observing simulated patient room images, which was measured with Talk Eye II, subjects reviewed their thought processes and made an oral report. No significant differences were observed in indices of eye movement based on years of clinical experiences. But, this indicated that potential awareness and peripheral vision might be used to prioritize the order of areas to observe. There were 58 types of observation items, and then divided into the seven categories. From the relationship of included in the thought process, four types of thoughts were extracted. Overall, the proportion of visual observation being reflected in verbal data was 50.4–68.9%. Among nurses with 10 or more years of clinical experience, their visual observation was reflected in verbal data slightly less than among nurses with less clinical experiences. The results of analyses showed the eye movement of nurses, potential awareness and peripheral vision were used to determine the priority of areas for observation. In addition, during the observation of a simulated patient room, and years of clinical experience affected thought type.

Keywords: Eye movement · Clinical experiences · Protocol analysis · Gaze · Verbal report

1 Introduction

Observation is an extremely important nursing activity. Nurses must have the practical ability to quickly understand patients' conditions based on observation and provide necessary support at all times.

Humans use five senses to make observations. Of these five senses, visual information accounts for 83%, therefore playing a very important role in observation. However, vision can also lead to mistakes such as oversights, overlooking, and mistakes. This can therefore harm patients by leading to medical accidents, or cause patients to suffer due to their needs not being noticed. In clinical sites, when nursing students and new nurses observe the same situation as experienced nurses, they may

© Springer International Publishing AG 2017
V.G. Duffy (Ed.): DHM 2017, Part II, LNCS 10287, pp. 13–22, 2017.
DOI: 10.1007/978-3-319-58466-9_2

actually be looking at different things. Even while looking at the same thing, they might come to different conclusions. Observation skills do not only involve looking at a certain thing. Rather, they involve making appropriate judgements based on observation and implementing nursing support.

Previous studies have objectively showed what nurses are looking at using a device that measures eye movements [1–3]. The details of interviews were analyzed to the thought processes of nurses in reaching clinical decisions based on observations [4]. However, no studies have objectively shown nurses' line of sight, and their thoughts and decision-making based on movement of their line of sight.

Therefore, we used a device that tracks eye movements (Talk Eye II) to objectively show the movements of nurses' line of sight and their thoughts based on this visual observation.

2 Study Objectives

To elucidate the structure of nurses' clinical decisions based on visual observation; we established three objectives targeting nurses with varying levels of experience.

(1) To clarify trends in the eye movements of nurses during observing simulated patient room,
(2) To clarify thought process based on nurses' visual observation, and
(3) To clarify the proportion of visually observation of simulated patient room reflected in observed items included in the thought process.

3 Research Methods

Subjects: Thirty-three nurses working at a hospital
    Study procedure:

(1) As simulated patient information, written information on an 85-year old female inpatient with pneumonia was provided to subjects.
(2) Four images of a simulated patient room with the simulated patient in the bed were sequentially shown so that subjects could imagine visiting the hospital room of the simulated patient for observations. Each image was displayed on the monitor for five seconds (Fig. 1).
(3) The eye movements during observation of the simulated patient room images were measured using Talk Eye II.
(4) After observation, while confirming the path of line of sight during observing simulated patient room images, which was measured with Talk Eye II, subjects reviewed their thought processes and made an oral report.

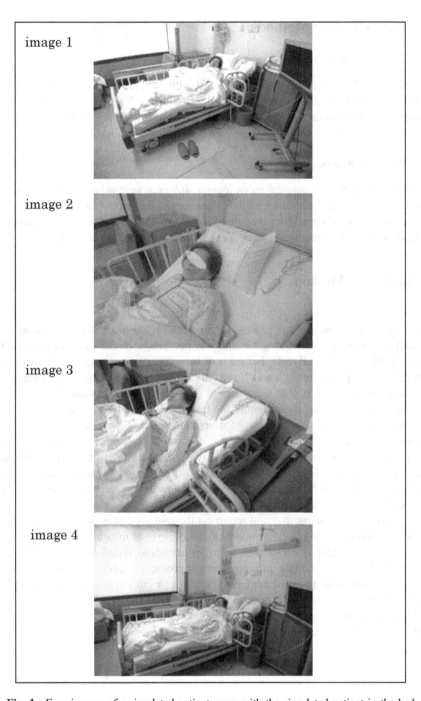

Fig. 1. Four images of a simulated patient room with the simulated patient in the bed

4 Data Collection Method

4.1 Eye Movement Measurements

Movements in the line of sight were measured with Talk Eye II. Gaze was defined as having ocular movement at a velocity of 5 deg/s with eye fixation duration of 100 ms or longer. Data measurement was made with sampling frequency of 30 Hz.

4.2 Thought Processes

After viewing simulated hospital room images, subjects were asked to orally describe their thoughts during observation while reviewing the movement of their line of sight as measured with Talk Eye II in the "think aloud method". We used the retrospective think aloud method whereby subjects speak while reviewing the task [5].

5 Analytical Method

- An arbitrary region analysis processing program (Takei Scientific Instruments Co., Ltd.) was used to set regions for analysis per image in the eye movement data measured using Talk Eye II. For each of four images, we extracted "total gazing time", "gazing time for each area", and "number of people gazing" as measurement indices. In accordance with the situation that each image showed, there were 10 areas in Image I, and nine regions for Images II through IV. Analysis was performed for each of these areas. Measurement indexes were compared in three groups: 1–4 years of clinical experience, 5–9 years of clinical experience, and 10 years or more of clinical experience. "Total gazing time" was analyzed through one-way analysis of variance. "Gazing time for each area" was analyzed through Kruskal-Wallis test. We used SPSS Statistics 20 for statistical analysis and the level of statistical significance was set at 5%.
- We recorded a retrospective oral report on thought processes during image observation while reviewing the movement of line of sight as measured with Talk Eye II using an IC recorder. We then used verbatim records as verbal data. The verbal data were analyzed for thought processes using protocol analysis. Verbal data were classified into four groups based on years of clinical experience: first year, 2–4 years, 5–9 years, and 10 years or more.
- We analyzed the proportion of thought processes in which the visual observation of the simulated hospital room was reflected (Fig. 2).

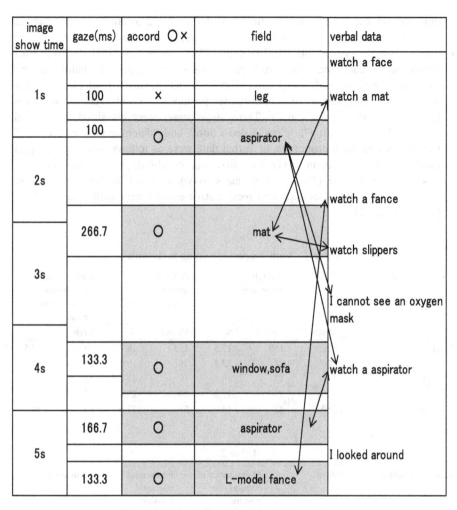

image show time	gaze(ms)	accord O×	field	verbal data
				watch a face
1s	100	×	leg	watch a mat
	100	O	aspirator	
2s				
				watch a fance
3s	266.7	O	mat	watch slippers
				I cannot see an oxygen mask
4s	133.3	O	window,sofa	watch a aspirator
	166.7	O	aspirator	
5s				I looked around
	133.3	O	L-model fance	

Fig. 2. Accord of gaze and verbal (example)

6   Results

- No significant differences were observed in indices of eye movement ("total gazing time", "gazing time for each area", and "number of people gazing") based on years of clinical experiences. However, longer "gazing time for each area" tended to be spent looking at areas of Image I <<suction bottle>>, Image II <<face>>, Image III <<intravenous drip injection site/route>>, and Image IV <<feet/sensor mat>> than at other areas. In addition, in "presence/absence of gaze", the number of people gazing at Image I <<patient's feet/couch>>, Image II <<face>>, Image III <<intravenous drip injection site/route>>, and Image IV <<oxygen mask/central

piping>> tended to be high. This indicated that potential awareness and peripheral vision might be used to prioritize the order of areas to observe.

- There were 58 types of observation items. These were then divided into the following seven categories: <<fall/fall prevention>>, <<oxygen inhalation therapy/suction>>, <<improved living environment under medical treatment>>, <<patient>>, <<maintenance of comfortable posture>>, <<intravenous injection/infusion>>, and <<nurse call>>. Thought processes were classified into "check and initial understanding", "clinical deduction", and "determination of the care". Categories with high proportion of verbal data were as follows: overall <<oxygen inhalation therapy/suction>> (18.7%), first year <<fall/fall prevention>> (23.5%), 2–4 year <<patient>> (18.8%), 5–9 year <<oxygen inhalation therapy/suction>>, and 10 or more years <<improved recuperative environment facilities>> (18.3%) (Tables 1 and 2).

Table 1. Verbal report according to the area

Years of experience		Total	Fall/fall prevention		Oxygen inhalation therapy/suction		Improved living environment under medical treatment	
		Verbal	Verbal	%	Verbal	%	Verbal	%
Total	n = 33	926	160	17.3	**173**	**18.7**	162	17.5
1 years	n = 7	200	**47**	**23.5**	38	19.0	29	14.5
2–4 years	n = 4	101	17	16.8	18	17.8	18	17.8
5–9 years	n = 12	336	53	15.8	**66**	**19.6**	62	18.5
10 years	n = 10	289	43	14.9	51	17.6	**53**	**18.3**

Table 2.

Years of experience		Patient		Maintenance of comfortable posture		Intravenous injection/ infusion		Nurse call	
		Verbal	%	Verbal	%	Verbal	%	Verbal	%
Total	n = 33	75	8.1	114	12.3	139	15.0	103	11.1
1 years	n = 7	15	7.5	20	10.0	27	13.5	24	12.0
2–4 years	n = 4	8	7.9	13	12.9	19	18.8	8	7.9
5–9 years	n = 12	28	8.3	39	11.6	48	14.3	40	11.9
10 years	n = 10	24	8.3	42	14.5	45	15.6	31	10.7

In reference to Tanner [6] "A Research-Based Model of Clinical Judgment in Nursing", from the relationship of "check and initial understanding", "reasoning", and "choice of nursing intervention" included in the thought process, four types of thoughts were extracted: {check and initial understanding type}, {reasoning type}, {choice of nursing intervention type}, and {intuitive choice of nursing intervention type}.

Thought types of the first-year nurses were often {check and initial understanding type}, but nurses with more clinical experience tended to use thought types such as {reasoning type} and {choice of nursing intervention type}.

Among observation categories, <<fall/fall prevention>> was "reasoning" about risk and <<maintenance of comfortable posture>> was "reasoning" about patient's pain; therefore, depending on the type of observation category, content of "reasoning" had different characteristics.

- Overall, the proportion of visual observation being reflected in verbal data was 50.4–68.9%. Based on the years of clinical experience, <<fall/fall prevention>> (67.6%) was most reflected for the first year of experience, while <<fall/fall prevention>> (50.0%) was most reflected for 2–4 years, and (67.6%) for 5–9 years. Rhenius et al. [7], I collated it with the data of thought contents provided by a gaze point and a protocol analysis and confirmed agreement of, 73–98%. Among nurses with 10 or more years of clinical experience, their visual observation was reflected in verbal data slightly less than among nurses with less clinical experiences.

7 Discussion

7.1 Trends in Eye Movement Based on Years of Clinical Experience

No significant differences were noted in the indices of eye movement based on years of clinical experience. Previously, many reports have shown different observation time due to difference in years of clinical experience. In this study, however, as the subjects were shown fairly routine patient situations, observations were able to be made quickly even if they had limited experience. In addition, since patient information was provided prior to displaying the images, subjects likely already had images of important points for observation. Areas gazed up by a high number of subjects are likely to be areas that require particularly careful observation of the displayed images.

However, areas that were gazed up for a short period of time and by a small number of people might be subject to oversights. A particularly small number of nurses gazed at <saturation monitor> in Image I, whereas the number of people gazing at it increased in Image II. As such, there may be appropriate timing for making observations. The existence of such appropriate timing suggests that patterns for patient room observation might already be determined.

In addition, this study set 100 ms or more as the duration of gaze, and there may be a chance that subjects were making observation faster than the set time or making observation through peripheral vision without gazing.

7.2 Thought Processes During Observation

Observation categories obtained from the think aloud method had many speeches on <<oxygen inhalation therapy/suction>>, <<fall/fall prevention>>, <<improved recuperative environment facilities>>, and <<patient>>. In the patient settings in this study, we used an 85-year old elderly patient who was hospitalized for pneumonia. Therefore, in addition to the observation items on respiratory symptoms specialized for pneumonia, observation items for predicting daily activities such as fall risk and fall prevention were noted because of the patient's advanced age.

In this study, subjects made oral reports reviewing their thought processes during image observation while reviewing the movement of line of sight. Visual cognition such as "seeing" by moving line of sight was processed by visual center. Therefore, observation categories with a large amount of verbal data are likely to be observation items of higher priority when observing seniors hospitalized for pneumonia as shown in this study.

7.3 Thought Types During Observation

As types of thought process during observing the patient hospital room, {check and initial understanding type}, {reasoning type}, {choice of nursing intervention type}, and {intuitive choice of nursing intervention type} were extracted.

With {check and initial understanding type}, the thought process was limited to determining position and status of observed contents included in observation categories. In this study, since we did not confirm the meaning of thoughts, we cannot determine whether subjects determined there to be "no abnormality" without thinking further or simply remembered what they saw.

{Reasoning type} is a thought process in which [reasoning] is used to interpret and predict [check and initial understanding]. This process was shown only in 50% or less, and those who showed this type had many years of clinical experience. Furthermore, those who showed thought process of {care determination type} for [care determination] was 10% or less.

Therefore, first-year nurses are limited to the thought process of {check and initial understanding type}, and as the years of clinical experience increased, knowledge and experience become enriched, and nurses started moving onto thought processes of {reasoning type} and {choice of nursing intervention type}. Furthermore, for [reasoning], there were characteristics in content of thought such as risk for patients, stage and degree of symptoms, patient's pain, and prediction of patient's movements. [Reasoning] needs [check and initial understanding] of actual information. Therefore, it is important to first perform [check and initial understanding].

7.4 Relationship Between Eye Movement and Content of Thought

Four categories for those with 10 years or more experience and six categories for those with less experience had gaze consistent with verbal data for observation categories. When gaze and verbal data are consistent, it means that cognitive function worked from visual information. Observation category with the highest consistency was <<intravenous injection/infusion>>, and this should be precisely observed and confirmed regardless of the years of clinical experience. Observation category with low consistency was <<improved recuperative environment facilities>>, where there were many verbal data despite not gazing. For the area of <<improved recuperative environment facilities>>, overall image was understood through peripheral vision other than careful observation.

In terms of years of clinical experience, those with 10 years of experience or more were less consistent, but they might have been using observation with gaze duration of 100 ms or less (the setup value) or peripheral vision. However, with more experience, there could be "complacency" that could lead to mistakes such as "miss" and "oversight".

8   Conclusions

The results of three analyses showed that during the observation of a simulated patient room, as a trend in the eye movement of nurses, potential awareness and peripheral vision were used to determine the priority of areas for observation. In addition, during the observation of a simulated patient room, nurses' [reasoning] for gazing has characteristic, and years of clinical experience affected thought type. Benner and Tannar [8], The expert nurse observes it instantly and shows that I have pattern recognition, similar recognition, common-sense understanding, the practical knowledge that I was an expert of, ability to sense an important point and ability of the rationality that was an expert of with me.

Based on the proportion of areas visually observed by nurses being reflected in verbal data, nurses in their first year thoroughly employed visual observation and performed [check and initial understanding]. However, nurses with 10 years or more experience used peripheral vision for observation and linked this to the thinking process.

Visual observation can lead to oversights, overlooking and mistakes. In order to make appropriate clinical decisions, it is important to make visual observations and to employ one's thinking ability to consider what has been observed. The results of the present study could be useful for examining education methods that encourage the objective presentation of visual observation and subsequent employment of thinking ability.

References

1. Shen, Y.: Evalution of an eye tracking device to increase error recovery by nursing students using human patient, Submitted to the Graduate School of the University of Massachusetts Amhert in partial fulfillment of the requirements for the degree of Master of science in industrial engineering and operations research (2010)
2. Maquard, J.L., Henneman, P.L., He, Z., et al.: Nurses' behaviors and visual scanning patterns may reduce patient identification errors. J. Exp. Psychol. 17(3), 247–256 (2011)
3. Kataoka, J., Sasaki, M., Kanda, K.: Effects of mental workload on nurses' visual behaviors during infusion pump operation. J. Nurs. Sci. 8, 47–56 (2011)
4. Funkesson, K.H., Anbacken, E.M., Ek, A.C.: Nurse's resoning process during care planning talking pressure ulcer prevention as an example a think-aloud study. Int. J. Nurs. Stud. 44(7), 1109–1119 (2007)
5. Ericsson, K.A., Charness, N., Feltovich, P.J., Hoffman, R.R.: The Cambridge Handbook of Expertise and Expert Performance. Cambridge University Press, Cambridge (2006)

6. Tanner, C.A.: Thinking like a nurse: a research-based model of clinical judgment in nursing. J. Nurs. Educ. **45**(6), 204–211 (2006)
7. Rhenius, D., Deffner, G.: Evaluation of concurrent thinking aloud using eye-tracking data. In: 34th Annual Meeting, Proceedings of the Human Factors Society, pp. 1265–1269 (1990)
8. Benner, P., Tanner, C.A.: Clinical judgment: how expert nurses use intuition. Am. J. Nurs. **87** (1), 23–31 (1987)

Towards a Clinical Support System for the Early Diagnosis of Sepsis

Tove Helldin[1]($\boxtimes$), Anna-Karin Pernestig[2], and Diana Tilevik[2]

[1] School of Informatics, University of Skövde, Skövde, Sweden
[2] School of Bioscience, University of Skövde, Skövde, Sweden
{tove.helldin,anna-karin.pernestig,diana.tilevik}@his.se

Abstract. Early and accurate diagnosis of sepsis is critical for patient safety. However, this is a challenging task due to the very general symptoms associated with sepsis, the immaturity of the tools used by the clinicians as well as the time-delays associated with the diagnostic methods used today. This paper explores current literature regarding guidelines for clinical decision support, and support for sepsis diagnosis in particular, together with guidelines extracted from interviews with four clinicians and one biomedical analyst working at a hospital and clinical laboratory in Sweden. The results indicate the need for the development of visual and interactive aids for enabling early and accurate diagnosis of sepsis.

Keywords: Clinical decision support · Sepsis · Guidelines · System transparency · Electronic health record

1 Introduction

Sepsis occurs when the body's response to an infection damages its own tissues and organs. It can lead to shock, multiple organ failures and death, especially if not recognized early and treated promptly. Every hour of delay of appropriate antibiotic therapy increases mortality by 5–10% [3]. Yet, to successfully diagnose sepsis is one of the greatest challenges in critical care. As the symptoms for sepsis are unspecific and similar to other conditions, it remains challenging for the clinician to identify the sepsis patients, especially at an early stage. Moreover, current diagnostic methods, including for example blood cultures, are impaired by a significant time-delay of 1–2 days [33] and/or low sensitivity of 30–40% [5]. This can result in a delay of appropriate patient care, which in turn can lead to a worsen condition for the patient with more severe complications and longer hospitalizations.

To enable early diagnosis of sepsis, research from three fronts are being conducted. One is the development of multimarker panels. Data mining techniques are being utilized for the selection of several subsets of combinations of biological markers and clinical data [26,27], aiding earlier diagnosis, since the biological markers are monitored directly from the patient's blood. The data mining will

© Springer International Publishing AG 2017
V.G. Duffy (Ed.): DHM 2017, Part II, LNCS 10287, pp. 23–35, 2017.
DOI: 10.1007/978-3-319-58466-9_3

provide a classification score for the probability of sepsis as an outcome. This is to be applied, understood and interpreted by the healthcare system facilitating support for clinical decision making. Due to the complexity of sepsis diagnostics, it is imperative to include healthcare personnel in the data analysis process. Therefore, the second main effort focuses on methods for explaining and visualizing results from the data mining process, aiming to increase the interpretability and transparency of the sepsis diagnosis support system. The third focus concerns the more general development of clinical decision support systems (CDSSs) that, based on the collected patient data from physical exams, laboratory results etc., can provide early warnings to the healthcare professionals (see for instance [2]). These systems range from being purely rule-based to using techniques such as artificial neural networks, support vector machines and decision trees to create models suitable for sepsis diagnosis [1,18].

The future of sepsis diagnosis research must, of course, join these efforts, yet they all suffer from their inherent difficulties. The presence of noisy, uncertain and non-linear data aggravates the diagnostic power of the analysis techniques as well as their interpretability. Moreover, CDSSs have not always been positively welcomed in the healthcare sector due to factors such as staff resistance [9,19]. Reasons for the resistance are for example the skepticism regarding the benefits of using such support systems, the imposed changes of their way of working and the lack of transparency of the support system reasoning, i.e. that no information is provided regarding the sources, the strength of the evidence and the reliability of the results generated [9,11,16,19]. Moreover, the inability of such systems to accommodate for clinician input has further been cited as a major reason for the resistance [17].

To facilitate a more easy adoption of a future sepsis diagnosis support system, semi-structured, in-depth interviews with four clinicians and one biomedical analyst have been performed to explore which decision support characteristics are vital for early, efficient and accurate diagnosis of sepsis. The participants were all experts of blood analyses within the field of severe infections and worked at a hospital and clinical laboratory in Sweden. The focus of the interviews was to identify the information needs of the healthcare professionals to make an informed decision as early as possible, the analysis strategies carried out, the challenges associated with diagnosing sepsis and the support tools used today. The results obtained are to be used in the future development of a digital sepsis diagnostic tool. Further, we contrast and compare out results with similar studies of CDSSs in order to contribute with general knowledge of how healthcare professionals can be supported in the process of diagnosing sepsis at an early stage.

The paper is structured as follows: Sect. 2 presents a general overview of CDSSs and guidelines for their implementation, together with research concerning support systems used for diagnosing and treating patients who suffer from sepsis. Section 3 summarizes the study, whereas Sect. 4 presents the results obtained. Section 5 offers a discussion of the work presented, whereas conclusions and directions for future research are presented in Sect. 6.

2 Background

According to Musen et al. [25], a clinical decision support system is any computer program designed to help healthcare professionals make clinical decisions. This broad definition thus comprises any computerized system that can aid its users to, for example, manage clinical information, highlight important information in medical records as well as provide patient-specific recommendations. Berner and La Lande [4] provide an important addition to this definition, arguing that a CDSS must provide guidance to the healthcare professionals at the point of care, thus excluding systems that only provide retrospective analyses of clinical data.

CDSSs can also be described by other means. For example, Metzger and MacDonald [23] have categorized CDSS in terms of when in the clinical process that the support system provides guidance, how active or passive the support system is, the ability of the system to provide adaptable support to the clinical situation, as well as how easy it is for the clinician to access the tool during his/her work flow. Yet another categorization is whether the system is stand-alone or a subsystem of more general electronic health records (EHRs), as well as if the CDSS is knowledge-based or non knowledge-based, i.e. that uses machine learning to generate recommendations [4].

Many of the CDSSs used today stem from research on expert systems, where the aim was to build software that could simulate human thinking through mapping signs, symptoms and laboratory results into probabilistic estimates of different diagnoses [24]. The trend nowadays is rather to develop support systems that assist the clinician in his/her decision making, and where the user is active in the decision making process [4].

2.1 Why and How to Implement CDSS?

Several studies have concluded that clinical decision support can improve clinician performance (see for instance [4,12,14,21]). Positive effects concern, for example, the stronger adherence to relevant guidelines, the cost of care, the reduction of medication errors and decreased rates of potential redundant or inappropriate care [7,10,15]. However, a growing pool of research indicates that the anticipated positive effects are often unrealized, as well as that the impact of introducing the CDSS on the workflow of the clinicians has not been sufficiently evaluated [10,16,32]. For instance, in a survey conducted by Garg et al. [16], it was concluded that in the majority of cases included in their study, the introduction of a CDSS required more time and effort from the users compared with the previously used paper based methods.

Factors obstructing the positive effects of CDSSs are, for example, the failure of the practitioners to use the system, poor usability and integration into the users' workflow, as well as user non-acceptance [16]. For example, positive results have been found in studies where the users were automatically using the system through tight integration with the already established computerized systems used, than when the users had to actively initiate the system [16]. Another factor that might have a negative impact on the acceptance of the users is the anticipated dependence on the systems, eroding the possibilities for independent decision making.

Based on the observed positive and negative effects of introducing CDSSs in the healthcare domain, several researchers have published guidelines for CDSS implementation. For example, Kawamoto et al. [20] examined factors associated with CDSS success across a variety of studies and found four critical factors:

- provide alerts/reminders automatically as part of the workflow,
- provide the suggestions at a time and location where the decisions are being made,
- provide actionable recommendations and
- computerize the entire process.

Berner and La Lande [4] also offer a set of general guidelines for the appropriate implementation and usage of CDSSs:

- assure that users understand the limitations of the system,
- assure that the knowledge base stems from reputable sources (from expert clinicians and/or clinical practice guidelines),
- assure that the system is appropriate for the local site,
- assure that the users are properly trained,
- monitor the proper utilization of the installed CDSS and
- assure that the knowledge base is monitored and maintained.

According to Chaudhry et al. [10] and Berner and La Lande [4], positive results of introducing a new CDSS are most often found in cases where there has been an incremental and local development during several years, led by researchers within the field, and where other computerized support systems are an accepted part of the work environment. Such prerequisites are often not possible to fulfill for most institutions, making it difficult to apply the same development and transition strategies showcased as promoting success. As such, further research is needed where studies of the effectiveness of CDSSs are in focus in order to identify additional design recommendations [4,16].

2.2   CDSS for Sepsis Diagnosis

Due to the complexities associated with sepsis diagnosis and treatment, several researchers have proposed and implemented computerized support tools for such use. For example, Mathe et al. [22], present the *Sepsis Treatment Enhanced through Electronic Protocolization* (Steep) system. This system aids clinicians adhere to regulated treatment plans for sepsis as well as to monitor the patient's status through visual means. The system fetches real-time patient data from the patient's records, and the clinician is able to order medications and procedures through the tool. The system monitors specific lab and vital-signs abnormalities and provides alerts and treatment guidelines, both visually and through electronic messages to the healthcare team, when such values have been measured. However, this tool was developed as a stand-alone tool, requiring active activation of the clinicians and no evaluation of its appropriate usage is provided.

Other tools for diagnosing and classifying patients with sepsis are described in [2,6,28]. Amland and Hahn-Cover [2] describe an alert system integrated into the hospital environment and clinical workflow of the healthcare institution selected for their study. Through a text-based graphical interface, the sepsis criteria measured and their time stamp are displayed. The clinicians are thus provided with the rules applied by the system, as well as how severe the sepsis is. Yet, the study presented in [2] as well as in [6,28] report struggles with designing the algorithms used for the sepsis diagnosis where high sensitivity in the diagnosis process are achieved at the cost of low specificity, setting the arena for potential usability problems associated with too many false positive alarms.

A web-based support system for sepsis treatment is presented in [31], where the healthcare practitioners are guided through the sepsis diagnosis process with the help of rule-based and data-driven logic algorithms, providing patient-adapted treatment instructions. Their research indicate that the healthcare practitioners were more inclined to adhere to the nationally and locally established guidelines for sepsis treatment as well as that their diagnostics improved when using the support system. Moreover, the number of antibiotic-free days increased, together with a shortened time until antibiotics were administered when needed when the system was used. However, no information is given regarding how the actual information was presented to the healthcare professionals, as well as how these users experienced the tool.

The above studies can all provide valuable guidance and inspiration when designing a future CDSS for sepsis diagnosis and treatment at the hospital and laboratories in focus of this study. However, as stated by Chaudhry et al. [10] and Berner and La Lande [4], one observed factor of success is the local development of the tool, where a tight incorporation of the work practices together with early and continuous user involvement can lay the foundation for greater user acceptance and a positive impact on the users' performance.

3   Method

To extract guidelines for the local development of a tool capable of aiding its users to diagnose sepsis, in-depth, semi-structured interviews with five healthcare practitioners were conducted. Of these, one worked as a senior clinician in infectious diseases at a hospital in Sweden. Three worked as laboratory clinicians and one as a biomedical analyst at a clinical laboratory, performing chemical and biomedical analyses of blood samples. The interviewees had an average experience of 17.2 years within their respective field and the interviews took about an hour each to perform. Three were men, two were women. The interviewees were chosen due to their long experience of working with sepsis diagnosis at their respective care unit. They were also selected due to their different roles in the sepsis diagnosis process, where the clinicians and lab analysts work very closely to determine if a patient suffers from sepsis or not.

The hospital selected for the study had approximately 400 000 visiting patients during 2015, of whom around 40 000 were admitted during the same year. Around 8000 blood cultures are done each year at the clinical laboratory and of these close to 4000 patients are suspected to suffer from sepsis (no data is available regarding how many of these patients actually suffer from sepsis or not). All of the interviewees worked with different CDSSs and computerized tools to solve their working tasks. In terms of sepsis diagnosis and treatment, healthcare professionals in Sweden are expected to follow nationally established guidelines together with local protocols. These come in the form of checklists to use during the diagnosis process, as well as a procedure for determining if the patient has sepsis or not through if-else rules.

The questions asked were (translation from Swedish):

- Describe your general working tasks.
- Describe the actions you perform and decisions you make when you suspect that a patient suffers from sepsis.
  - How do you perform these tasks and make these decisions?
  - How do you communicate and collaborate with your colleagues in order to determine if a patient suffers from sepsis or not?
- Do you use any kind of digital support to solve your working tasks?
  - How would you say that these aid you in your work?
  - Which input do you give to this system/which output can it provide to you? In which form?
- Do you use any kind of digital support system to solve your working tasks related to sepsis diagnosis?
- How do you think that the process of diagnosing sepsis could be enhanced in terms of speed and accuracy?

4   Results

Since the interviewees worked at three different care units (i.e. at the department of infectious diseases at the hospital as well as at the clinical chemical lab and the clinical microbiology lab), responsible for different parts of the sepsis diagnosis process, the results will be arranged using a time line of the patient's healthcare process when sepsis is suspected. The results depict the healthcare professionals work tasks from when a patient arrives at the emergency ward, the support systems used and their ideas for the future development of a CDSS (or CDSS competent) to diagnose sepsis at an early stage that would suit well into their current workflow.

4.1   The Process of Detecting Sepsis

Emergency Ward
The ambulance personnel makes a first judgment how seriously ill the patient is and to which healthcare unit the patient should be directed to. If deemed

urgent, the patient is sent to the emergency ward. When the patient arrives at the emergency ward, a nurse creates a digital emergency chart, incorporating all patient parameters measured by the ambulance personnel. This chart is continuously updated with data from new laboratory tests or vital-sign parameters such as the patient's pulse, breathing, blood pressure, mental status and if the patient is in pain. The nurse or clinician further orders a set of routine tests if sepsis is suspected. These are regulated in the national guidelines and in the local hospital regulations. If many or some of the more important parameters indicate that the patient has a severe infection, blood will be withdrawn for blood culture and intravenous antibiotic will be provided immediately. But if there is deemed to be time without venturing the patient's health, lab tests are ordered directly through the EHR system.

The EHR system visually represents data in tabular format. Clinician entries and lab results are displayed in text and numbers. Different tabs present data from different lab tests, and a clinician must often switch between different tabs to collect a full view of a patient's status. There is a possibility to create a personalized view, collecting different lab results in one tab, yet the result is often that the clinician has to scroll through clinical parameter values that do not fit into the same view. If a measured parameter is deemed to fall outside a pre-determined threshold, this value is marked with red font. Yet, the clinician has to actively scroll down to the parameter of interest and look at the color of the value, i.e. there is no alarm or pop-up message available to aid the clinician. The clinician in infectious diseases interviewed argued that values not falling within the accepted interval should be visualized and interacted with in a better way than just by marking the text red in the text-based EHR system used. Moreover, s/he argued that the users of the system should be presented with an aggregated view of the test results to better grasp the complete status of the patient. Further, the clinician in infectious diseases argued that some decision support rules should be incorporated into the EHR system that set off an alarm when a clinical parameter value/the aggregation of clinical parameter values that might indicate sepsis have been fulfilled. Since few clinicians are infection specialists, sepsis can quite easily be missed for something else - for example, the signs of a heart attack might as well be due to sepsis. Such rules could minimize the risk of missing such important findings in the data. According to the clinician, this should preferably come in the form of a pop-out dialogue box, presenting the important findings in the data, what it can indicate as well as what the next step in the treatment process should be.

The clinician in infectious diseases further stressed the importance of being able to compare the measured clinical parameters of each patient, and to detecting trends and possible effects of recommended treatments, functions that are not supported by the EHR system used today. Such functionality could have a possible effect on the clinician's decision making, where s/he can easily see the status of a patient in one and the same view.

The clinician in infectious diseases interviewed argued for the importance of developing decision support systems of this kind for ensuring patient safety.

S/he stressed the importance of the system having a supporting role, indicating important findings and recommending actions to make sure that the patients receive treatment fast. Important is also that the users of such system receives appropriate training and is able to interact with the system in a good way. Also important is the fact that the clinicians know the rules and methods behind the recommendations, that they follow the national and local guidelines, and that it makes its users aware of interesting findings.

Clinical Chemical and Microbiology Laboratory

When lab tests are ordered by the hospital personnel, blood samples are withdrawn from the patient and delivered to the clinical lab either manually or by using the tube system at the current hospital. Depending on the tests ordered, either the clinical chemical lab or the clinical microbiology lab professionals are in charge of the tests. At the clinical chemical lab, most of the analysis is done automatically. The whole process of receiving blood samples in tubes, to the analysis and reporting of the results back to the clinician is today fully automatic. For all tests, there are reference intervals indicating normal/abnormal values. These threshold values are updated if new research or guidelines are to be executed. If a measured value does not fall within this reference interval, an alarm is set off and manual analysis is carried out. In order for this process to work, meticulous controls of the clinical lab machines are carried out. Despite the high level of automation, the chemical analysts interviewed claimed that as they work as consultants to the clinicians, it is of utmost importance that they have knowledge of what the different tests indicate, as well as that they are able to perform manual analyses in the case of, for example, machine malfunction or if a test result is inconclusive.

Manual analyses at the clinical chemical lab are mostly performed in the form of protein profile analyses that can determine which type of bacteria is causing the sepsis, however such analyses are not common (in about 1% of the cases). Here, images of proteins are manually analyzed and the results are reported back to the clinician via the EHR and through oral communication with the clinician in charge of the patient's care.

At the clinical microbiology lab, more manual work is conducted. A first analysis is performed using a dedicated machine that every 10th minute investigates if bacteria have started to grow in the blood cultures or not. When the bacteria has reached a certain density of growth, an audio and visual alarm is set off. The blood cultures are then analyzed manually in a microscope where the analyst is able to make a first judgment regarding the type of bacteria found. Here, the analyst uses his/her expert knowledge and looks for the color, shape, groupings etc. of the bacteria found. If more specific results are sought for, blood culturing are followed by subculture on agar plates for subsequent phenotypic identification. Manual and automatic pattern analysis is made of the bacteria in order to detect patterns, aggregate findings, etc. to determine which species of bacteria that has been found. Yet this process takes several hours, time often not available in the case of sepsis.

The lab analysts argued for an appropriate level of CDSS automation, where the analyst is still kept in the loop. As such, the support systems should be a natural component of the workflow, acting as support and have an advisory role, aiding the analysts to recall important parameters and values. Such support would also aid the analysts if manual control is needed, delimiting the risk of alienating them from the tasks conducted. Moreover, the analysts argued that the CDSS should be designed to delimit the tedious manual workload of, for example, updating the patient's EHR with lab data, as has been the case with some support systems used. Further, the system should provide appropriate alarms, based on national and local guidelines, where the reason for the alarm is explicitly presented, i.e. which parameter threshold values have been met? Which evidence point towards a certain diagnosis, and which do not?

Despite the increasing level of sophisticated automation at the laboratory, one of the laboratory clinicians argued for constant and increased communication with the hospital clinicians, together with continuous updates of the patient's status to keep the patient in focus, not the numbers in a lab report. This was also stressed by the microbiological analyst participating in the study, who argued that a closer collaboration between the clinical lab personnel and the hospital clinicians could improve the accuracy of the diagnoses made. Due to their specialized knowledge of different bacteria and their antibiotic resistance, additional, more specified, information could be provided to the hospital clinicians. However, such collaboration would demand that also the laboratory personnel has access to the patient EHR data, which is not the case today. Moreover, since most of the lab results are automatically sent to the hospital clinicians when ready, the clinicians can receive many different lab reports, which sometimes contain inconclusive results. If incrementally aggregating the lab results, the lab personnel could use their expertise to aid the hospital clinicians to make a more accurate decision regarding the patient's treatment.

5   Discussion

Apparent during the interviews was the fact that the clinicians and lab analysts have to deal with large amounts of data to solve their tasks. For the hospital clinicians, measured parameters must be manually processed, and the national and local guidelines remembered, often during time-critical and stressful situations. Moreover, since the symptoms of sepsis are quite general, the clinicians must have such guidelines in mind even when sepsis is not their main hypothesis regarding the patient's status. Junior clinicians might follow the strategy to order every test available, resulting in even more, and perhaps irrelevant, data to include in the analysis process, thus aggravating the clinician's decision making. Additionally, the number of laboratory tests ordered at hospitals often increase in a much faster pace than the recruitment of clinicians, adding to their workload and feeding the risk of overlooking important lab results [8].

According to Stadler et al. [30], the increasing usage of EHRs has lead to a dramatic increase and availability of digital healthcare data. Such data, presented in a comprehensive manner, can aid a clinician to get a quick view of the patient's current and past status. If not, the sheer amount of data feeds the possibility of overlooking or misinterpreting the data. As further argued by Stadler et al. [30], the incorporation of interactive visualizations within the EHR systems should be investigated, where for example dashboards can be used to convey the information contained within the EHR. To incorporate visualizations of patient vital-sign parameters, individual lab results, together with an aggregation of the patient data to create a comprehensive view of the patient's status could provide a basis for the support needed in order to diagnose sepsis at an early stage. Such information should not only be available to the hospital clinicians, but also to the lab personnel, enabling them to provide their expertise into the decision making process. Yet, even though the usage of dashboards as analytic tools is growing, their use with EHR data is still in its infancy [30].

The interviewees were all accustomed to using computerized support tools in their work and saw their increasingly important role within the healthcare sector as an information and support provider. The clinician in infectious diseases stressed the importance of using CDSSs as support in the decision making process, rather than as a means of performing analytical tasks fully automatically. Such support should come in the form of process and action advice, together with highlighting or through other means communicating important information based on an expert knowledge-base relevant for the tasks at hand. A commonly referenced description of different levels of automation is the one proposed by Sheridan and Verplank [29] where ten levels describe the task allocation between the human and the automation (from low to high). As stated by Cummings [13], higher levels of automation is often the best solution when automating tasks that require no flexibility in decision-making and with a low probability of system failure. Yet, the higher levels might not be suitable in time-critical domains where there are many external and changing constraints due to the possibility of imperfect and unreliable automation. From the scale, the CDSS to be used for the clinician's diagnosis of sepsis should offer a set of decision/action alternatives, suggest the most probable ailment, and execute suggestions such as lab orders if the clinician approves to. Of course, in the lab, the automation can be higher, implying that the automation executes its tasks automatically, and only informs the analysts if there is something wrong with the test, or if the parameter values are out of range, however always informing its users of its knowledge-base and rules. As such, the developers of the CDSS should always have the importance of system transparency in mind.

In addition to the more general guidelines presented in Sect. 2.1, this study has resulted in the identification of guidelines for the development of a CDSS for sepsis diagnosis:

- adjust the level of automation in accordance with the healthcare practitioners' tasks and workflow,
- visually aggregate the information regarding the patient's status in the EHR, possibly through the usage of dashboards,
- enable interactive means of investigating the patient data,

- provide visual and audio warnings to the healthcare practitioners when an important parameter value/the aggregation of parameter values falls outside the reference interval,
- enable a close collaboration between the lab personnel and the hospital clinicians and
- enable the healthcare practitioners to inspect the knowledge base of the CDSS and the evidence supporting its recommendations.

5.1 Limitations of the Study

The results obtained from the interviews performed as well as the literature study made should be used as input to a second follow-up study where additional practitioners from the hospital and lab departments are represented. Since most of the manual decision making is performed by the hospital clinicians, additional interviews and observations must be performed together with this particular user group. A broader literature study of CDSSs used for other diagnoses and treatments should also be performed to identify additional important guidelines for the development of the support tool for sepsis diagnosis.

6   Conclusions and Future Work

Research for continuously making the sepsis diagnosis process as fast as possible is vital. More and more demands are put on healthcare practitioners, where increased effectiveness and improved patient care is required. The amount of data has increased in a much faster pace than the number of clinicians, increasing the risk of missing important analytical results, even if the systems used demand electronic verification. This study has focused on extracting general guidelines to be applied during the development process of a CDSS to be used for sepsis diagnosis. A follow-up study with additional participants from the healthcare domain is planned to extract further requirements to be used when implementing a first prototype of the CDSS. Additional work is also needed in terms of investigating how the analysis results from new lab tests should be visualized and interacted with to ensure their transparency.

Acknowledgment. This study was supported by research grants from the Swedish Knowledge Foundation. We would like to thank the study participants for their valuable input and feedback.

References

1. Alder, M.N., Lindsell, C.J., Wong, H.R.: The pediatric sepsis biomarker risk model: potential implications for sepsis therapy and biology. Expert Rev. Anti-Infect. Ther. **12**, 809–816 (2014)
2. Amland, R.C., Hahn-Cover, K.E.: Clinical decision support for early recognition of sepsis. Am. J. Med. Qual. **31**(2), 103–110 (2016)

3. Bauer, M., Reinhart, K.: Molecular diagnostics of sepsis? Where are we today? Int. J. Med. Microbiol. **300**(6), 411–413 (2010)
4. Berner, E.S., La Lande, T.J.: Overview of clinical decision support systems. In: Berner, E.S. (ed.) Clinical Decision Support Systems, pp. 1–17. Springer, New York (2016)
5. Bochud, P.Y., Bonten, M., Marchetti, O., Calandra, T.: Antimicrobial therapy for patients with severe sepsis and septic shock: an evidence-based review. Crit. Care Med. **32**(11), S495–S512 (2004)
6. Brandt, B.N., Gartner, A.B., Moncure, M., Cannon, C.M., Carlton, E., Cleek, C., Wittkopp, C., Simpson, S.Q.: Identifying severe sepsis via electronic surveillance. Am. J. Med. Qual. **30**(6), 559–565 (2015)
7. Buising, K.L., Thursky, K.A., Black, J.F., MacGregor, L., Street, A.C., Kennedy, M.P., Brown, G.V.: Improving antibiotic prescribing for adults with community acquired pneumonia: does a computerised decision support system achieve more than academic detailing alone? - A time series analysis. BMC Med. Inform. Decis. Mak. **8**(1), 35 (2008)
8. Callen, J., Georgiou, A., Li, J., Westbrook, J.I.: The safety implications of missed test results for hospitalised patients: a systematic review. Qual. Saf. Health Care **20**(2), 194–199 (2011)
9. Carroll, C., Marsden, P., Soden, P., Naylor, E., New, J., Dornan, T.: Involving users in the design and usability evaluation of a clinical decision support system. Comput. Methods Programs Biomed. **69**(2), 123–135 (2002)
10. Chaudhry, B., Wang, J., Wu, S., Maglione, M., Mojica, W., Roth, E., Morton, S.C., Shekelle, P.G.: Systematic review: impact of health information technology on quality, efficiency, and costs of medical care. Ann. Intern. Med. **144**(10), 742–752 (2006)
11. Clancy, C.M., Cronin, K.: Evidence-based decision making: global evidence, local decisions. Health Aff. **24**(1), 151–162 (2005)
12. Cresswell, K., Majeed, A., Bates, D.W., Sheikh, A.: Computerised decision support systems for healthcare professionals: an interpretative review. J. Innov. Health Inform. **20**(2), 115–128 (2013)
13. Cummings, M.: Automation bias in intelligent time critical decision support systems. In: AIAA 1st Intelligent Systems Technical Conference, p. 6313 (2004)
14. Doolan, D.F., Bates, D.W., James, B.C.: The use of computers for clinical care: a case series of advanced US sites. J. Am. Med. Inform. Assoc. **10**(1), 94–107 (2003)
15. Evans, R.S., Pestotnik, S.L., Classen, D.C., Clemmer, T.P., Weaver, L.K., Orme Jr., J.F., Lloyd, J.F., Burke, J.P.: A computer-assisted management program for antibiotics and other antiinfective agents. N. Engl. J. Med. **338**(4), 232–238 (1998)
16. Garg, A.X., Adhikari, N.K., McDonald, H., Rosas-Arellano, M.P., Devereaux, P., Beyene, J., Sam, J., Haynes, R.B.: Effects of computerized clinical decision support systems on practitioner performance and patient outcomes: a systematic review. JAMA **293**(10), 1223–1238 (2005)
17. Gremy, F., Degoulet, P.: Assessment of health information technology: which questions for which systems? Proposal for a taxonomy. Med. Inform. **18**(3), 185–193 (1993)
18. Gultepe, E., Green, J.P., Nguyen, H., Adams, J., Albertson, T., Tagkopoulos, I.: From vital signs to clinical outcomes for patients with sepsis: a machine learning basis for a clinical decision support system. J. Am. Med. Inform. Assoc. **21**(2), 315–325 (2014)

19. Horsky, J., Schiff, G.D., Johnston, D., Mercincavage, L., Bell, D., Middleton, B.: Interface design principles for usable decision support: a targeted review of best practices for clinical prescribing interventions. J. Biomed. Inform. **45**(6), 1202–1216 (2012)
20. Kawamoto, K., Houlihan, C.A., Balas, E.A., Lobach, D.F.: Improving clinical practice using clinical decision support systems: a systematic review of trials to identify features critical to success. BMJ **330**(7494), 765 (2005)
21. Kharbanda, A.B., Madhok, M., Krause, E., Vazquez-Benitez, G., Kharbanda, E.O., Mize, W., Schmeling, D.: Implementation of electronic clinical decision support for pediatric appendicitis. Pediatrics **137**(5), e20151745 (2016)
22. Mathe, J.L., Martin, J.B., Miller, P., Ledeczi, A., Weavind, L.M., Nadas, A., Miller, A., Maron, D.J., Sztipanovits, J.: A model-integrated, guideline-driven, clinical decision-support system. IEEE Softw. **26**(4), 54–61 (2009)
23. Metzger, J., MacDonald, K.: Clinical Decision Support for the Independent Physician Practice. California Healthcare Foundation, Oakland (2002)
24. Miller, R.A.: Medical diagnostic decision support systems - past, present, and future. J. Am. Med. Inform. Assoc. **1**(1), 8–27 (1994)
25. Musen, M.A., Middleton, B., Greenes, R.A.: Clinical decision-support systems. In: Shortliffe, E.H., Cimino, J.J. (eds.) Biomedical Informatics, pp. 643–674. Springer, London (2014)
26. Pierrakos, C., Vincent, J.L.: Sepsis biomarkers: a review. Crit. Care **14**(1), 1 (2010)
27. Sankar, V., Webster, N.R.: Clinical application of sepsis biomarkers. J. Anesth. **27**(2), 269–283 (2013)
28. Sawyer, A.M., Deal, E.N., Labelle, A.J., Witt, C., Thiel, S.W., Heard, K., Reichley, R.M., Micek, S.T., Kollef, M.H.: Implementation of a real-time computerized sepsis alert in nonintensive care unit patients. Crit. Care Med. **39**(3), 469–473 (2011)
29. Sheridan, T.B., Verplank, W.L.: Human and computer control of undersea teleoperators. Technical report, DTIC Document (1978)
30. Stadler, J.G., Donlon, K., Siewert, J.D., Franken, T., Lewis, N.E.: Improving the efficiency and ease of healthcare analysis through use of data visualization dashboards. Big Data **4**(2), 129–135 (2016)
31. Tafelski, S., Nachtigall, I., Deja, M., Tamarkin, A., Trefzer, T., Halle, E., Wernecke, K., Spies, C.: Computer-assisted decision support for changing practice in severe sepsis and septic shock. J. Int. Med. Res. **38**(5), 1605–1616 (2010)
32. Van de Velde, S., Roshanov, P., Kortteisto, T., Kunnamo, I., Aertgeerts, B., Vandvik, P.O., Flottorp, S.: Tailoring implementation strategies for evidence-based recommendations using computerised clinical decision support systems: protocol for the development of the guides tools. Implement. Sci. **11**(1), 29 (2016)
33. Ziegler, R., Johnscher, I., Martus, P., Lenhardt, D., Just, H.M.: Controlled clinical laboratory comparison of two supplemented aerobic and anaerobic media used in automated blood culture systems to detect bloodstream infections. J. Clin. Microbiol. **36**(3), 657–661 (1998)

APSEN: Pre-screening Tool for Sleep Apnea in a Home Environment

Varun Kanal$^{(\boxtimes)}$, Maher Abujelala, Srujana Gattupalli, Vassilis Athitsos,
and Fillia Makedon

Computer Science and Engineering Department, University of Texas at Arlington,
Arlington, TX, USA
{varunajay.kanal,athitsos,makedon}@uta.edu,
{maher.abujelala,srujana.gattupalli}@mavs.uta.edu

Abstract. This paper describes the APSEN system, a pre-screening tool for detecting sleep apnea in a home environment. The system was designed and evaluated in two parts; the apnea detection using SpO_2 and the posture detection using IR images. The two parts can work together or independently. During the preliminary study, the apnea detection algorithm was evaluated using an online database, and the right algorithms for detecting the sleep posture were determined. In the overnight study, both of the subsystems were tested on 10 subjects. The average accuracy for the apnea detection algorithm was 71.51% for apnea conditions, and 98.68% for normal conditions. For the posture detection algorithms, during the overnight study, the average accuracies are 74.91% and 89.71% for SVM and CNN, respectively. The results represented in the paper indicate that the APSEN system could be used to detect apnea and postural apnea in a home environment.

Keywords: Apnea · Posture detection · Physiological data · Oximeter · Smartwatch · Kinect · Machine learning · SVM · CNN · Pre-screening tool

1 Introduction

Sleep apnea is a breathing disorder wherein the person's breathing is reduced or completely ceased during sleep. An estimated 17% of adults suffer from mild to severe sleep related breathing disorders [1]. Due to this cessation there is an imbalance in the CO_2 O_2 levels in the body, leading to changes in many physiological signals. According to one report, in 2015, in United States, an approximately $150B loss was incurred due to undiagnosed apnea [2].

1.1 Types of Apnea

There are three main types of Apnea: Central, Obstructive and Mixed:

Central. Central sleep apnea (CSA) occurs when the muscles responsible for breathing fail to function as intended [3].

© Springer International Publishing AG 2017
V.G. Duffy (Ed.): DHM 2017, Part II, LNCS 10287, pp. 36–51, 2017.
DOI: 10.1007/978-3-319-58466-9_4

Obstructive. Obstructive sleep apnea (OSA) occurs when there is an excessive relaxation of the soft pallet which closes the upper airway [4]. Along with this the position of the tongue also plays a role.

Mixed. Mixed sleep apnea (Complex sleep apnea) occurs when both CSA and OSA happen in the same apnea episode [5].

1.2 Influence of Position

One of the pathogenesis of obstructive sleep apnea is the excessive relaxation of the soft pallet. This leads to a collapse of the upper airway. When there is an excessive relaxation, gravity assists in this collapse [6]. When the subject lies on their back, gravity acts on the already loose soft pallet and closes the airway, causing apnea. One of the therapies for managing apnea is positional therapy. In this the subjects are conditioned to sleep on their side instead of on their back [7]. This reduces the apnea severity as the gravity is no longer helping in the collapse in the airway. This does not stop the apnea completely but helps manage it.

1.3 Diagnosis of Sleep Apnea

The gold standard for the diagnosis of sleep apnea is an overnight polysomnography (PSG) [8]. During PSG a subject sleeps in a lab setting while they are observed for eight hours. During this time, multiple sensors are attached to the subject, recording their many physiological signals. Some of the signals recorded are electrocardiogram (ECG/EKG), electroencephalogram (EEG), electrooculogram (EOG), oxygen saturation (SpO$_2$) and electromyogram (EMG), among others. The subject is also recorded using a camera and a microphone.

The most common treatment for OSA is Continuous Positive Airway Pressure machine (CPAP). This machine provides high pressure air to the upper airway to stop it from collapsing. Other alternatives include surgery, oral appliances and behavioral and positional therapy. Most oral appliances to manage OSA manipulate the position of the mandible and/or the tongue in order to prevent upper airway collapse. Behavioral therapy may be employed to motivate weight loss and to reduce body mass index (BMI). In positional therapy the patient is encouraged to sleep in a non-supine position.

1.4 Previous Work

There are devices already in the market to detect apnea in a home environment. ARES is one such device [9]. This system is designed as a headband with multiple sensors that record physiological data from the subject. The system records SpO$_2$, Pulse Rate, Airflow, Snoring (microphone) and Head Movement and Position (accelerometers). Along with this the system is also accompanied with an online tool that uses a questionnaire to find more details about the subjects. Questions like body type, symptoms of daytime drowsiness and snoring, among others, are recorded to help detect apnea. Another system, ApneaLink Air, designed by ResMed, is a home sleep testing device [10]. This device uses a chest band with a central control box on the band which connects to and contains multiple sensors. This device records respiratory effort, pulse, oxygen saturation, nasal flow and snoring. These signals are used to determine apnea.

Burgos *et al.* designed a real-time apnea detection system. This system uses a PDA as a UI and as a control center for the system [11]. They designed a classifier to recognize the area under the curve for SpO_2 signals. With this they recognized apnea events. Al-Mardini *et al.* also designed a sleep apnea detection system that utilizes smartphones [12]. They used three sensors to help detect apnea: an oximeter to measure SaO_2, a microphone to record respiratory effort, and an accelerometer to detect movement. Their criteria to detect apnea was to measure the drop in SaO_2. If the drop was greater than 4% then an apnea event was recorded. Another condition was added that the event should last for more than 10 s. They studied this device on 15 subjects some who were diagnosed with sleep apnea and some who were healthy with no symptoms. They found that their system gave an accuracy of 100% for correctly identifying apnea and 85.7% for correctly identifying the absence of apnea. Samy *et al.* designed a framework to predict OSA by conducting a daytime non-intrusive test [13]. They used multimodal data collection including physiological signals like blood pressure and heart rate. Along with this they also recorded sleep quality, sleepiness, psychological and contextual conditions by asking them to fill out a questionnaire. They used machine learning algorithms to classify apnea. They used Support Vector Machine (SVM) and K-Nearest-Neighbors (KNN) for classification. They recorded an overall accuracy of 79.8% for SVM and 75.1% for KNN.

1.5   Need for APSEN

PSG is an expensive test, although the expenses may vary according to the place where the study takes place. According to one website the cost is around $3500 (before insurance) in technical fees alone [14]. The subjects are attached with multiple sensors. This may make some subjects a little uncomfortable and affect the quality of their sleep. Moreover, the subjects sleep in a lab setting which does not capture the conditions in which they sleep at home. This may lead to an underestimation of apnea severity.

In this paper an apnea detection system is proposed. This system uses easily available and inexpensive sensors to detect apnea and postural apnea. This system is dubbed 'APSEN' for short. It can detect apnea and correlate it with the subject's sleeping position to determine postural apnea. The system will provide the user with an indication of when the apnea occurs, historical patterns, and real-time feedback when the apnea condition becomes severe. This system is intended to be a pre-screening tool, not a full substitute for a PSG. If the system suspects that the subject has apnea, a full PSG test is recommended to the subject.

2   System Setup

The APSEN system was designed to work in a natural home setup. This system is intended to be used by the user in the comfort of their own home. There are three main equipment required for the system: a bluetooth oximeter (Nonin II 9560), a smartwatch (Microsoft Band 2), and an IR camera (Kinect V2). The system setup is illustrated in Fig. 1, and it is explained in detail in a YouTube video[1]. The system is designed in two parts. The first part uses the oximeter to detect apnea, while the second part uses the Kinect to detect the sleeping posture. These two parts can be used together or independently during the night. The APSEN system architecture is shown in Fig. 2. The main apnea detection depends on the oximeter data. The other sensors are not mandatory. Therefore, if the subject can afford it or has only the oximeter available this system is still usable. Although without the smartwatch the subject will not receive real-time feedback, they will still receive a summary report at the end of the use.

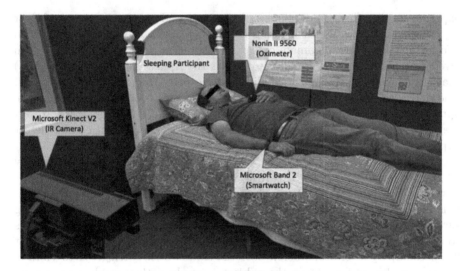

Fig. 1. System setup

2.1   Apnea Detection

The apnea detection subsystem depends upon the SpO_2 data received from the bluetooth oximeter. The main functionalities of this subsystem are to detect apnea, send notifications, and prepare a sleep summary at the end of the experiment. The GUI is displayed in Fig. 3. At the start of the experiment the subjects wear the oximeter on the index finger of their left hand and the smartwatch on their wrist of their right hand. Before the subject goes to bed, they have to connect with either or both the oximeter and the smartwatch. At the end of the

---
[1] https://youtu.be/9pM8ZCSE8Eg.

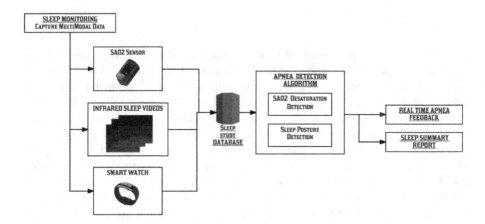

Fig. 2. The APSEN system architecture

experiment, they have to disconnect the sensors and see the summary of their apnea events, if any, which includes how many apnea events they had, when and for how long, the maximum oxygen desaturation and the minimum oxygen level at each apnea event. Finally, it displays the Apnea-Hypopnea Index (AHI) that states whether the apnea condition is *Normal, Mild, Moderate or Severe*. The AHI is calculated as the average number of apnea events per hour [15]. The apnea condition is labeled as *Normal* if AHI < 5, *Mild* if 5 ≤ AHI < 15, *Moderate* if 15 ≤ AHI < 30, and *Severe* if AHI ≥ 30. Since the system cannot detect hypopnea, this index is an estimation.

The apnea detection algorithm works in a similar manner as described by Al-Mardini *et al.* [12]. It tracks when the current SpO_2 value decreases. If this desaturation is at least 4% (e.g. decreasing from 97% to 93.12% or below) then it is marked as an apnea episode. An additional fail safe is added by making sure that this desaturation lasts for at least 10 seconds. The apnea episode is considered 'finished' when the SpO_2 increases again and saturates for at least 2 s. If the SpO_2 level drops below 80% the smartwatch is triggered to vibrate, waking up the subject. Once the subject is awoken, they would take a deep breath, restarting the respiration cycle. The subsystem records all the data in a local database with a name chosen by the subject for each recording. So if the subject stops or pauses the experiment for any reason such as to go to the rest room, they can come back and resume the system or enter the name of the recording to continue saving the data in the same database. This subsystem visualizes apnea events in real-time by highlighting the area in the SpO_2 graph that represents apnea episodes (see Fig. 3). It also displays apnea information on the top-right corner of the interface. To make sure the SpO_2 desaturation reaches the apnea threshold, 4%, there is a slight delay in showing the apnea information; however, it does not affect the calculation of the apnea length. The real-time visualization is very beneficial if there is someone observing the subject, like a family member. This observer can add comments in the interface about

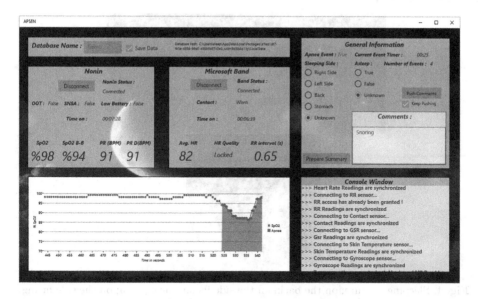

Fig. 3. The apnea detection GUI

the subject, for example if the subject was snoring. If the subject is not using an IR camera, the observer can use this interface to mark the subject's sleeping position.

One of the complications of the bluetooth oximeter is that it disconnects or falls from the finger if the subject makes excessive hand movements. In that case, the system will beep 5 or 6 times with an interval of 2 s. It will then close the communication with the oximeter. This subsystem is designed using Universal Windows Platform (UWP) running on the Windows 10 operating system. We chose to use UWP in particular because it can run on any laptop, phone or tablet running Windows 10 [16]. During the experiment, this interface was tested on a laptop running Windows 10; however, the interface can be changed to work on both phones and tablets as well.

2.2 Posture Recognition

This part of the system records and classifies the position in which the subject sleeps. This subsystem was based on a previous work done in our lab [17]. The setup utilizes a Kinect V2 camera. Out of all the modes the Kinect provides, only IR data is recorded. IR data was chosen as the system is intended to be recorded in a normal home environment when the subject is sleeping. Moreover, IR data is a gray scale image; therefore, it is only a 2 dimensional matrix which reduces the load on the input side of the system. This also reduces the computation required to process the images. Three postures were considered; the subject laying on the back (Supine), on the side facing the camera, and on the side facing away from

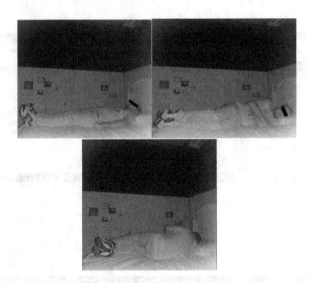

Fig. 4. Sleeping posture; on the back, on the side facing the camera; on the side facing away from the camera

the camera as shown in Fig. 4. The subsystem was designed to work without blankets or quilts as that would lower the accuracy in identifying the posture.

This subsystem was designed in MATLAB. Kinect V2 was connected to MATLAB using Kin2, a toolbox designed by Terven and Córdova-Esparza [18]. Principle Component Analysis (PCA) was performed on the IR images. This was done to get the essential patterns of the data [19]. To classify the posture, Support Vector Machine (SVM) was utilized. MATLAB's inbuilt SVM function does not support classification for more than two classes. Therefore, LIBSVM, a package designed by Chang and Lin, was utilized [20]. We also explore the classification performance provided by a deep learning network on our problem of sleep posture recognition. Deep learning has demonstrated remarkable performance in problems related to classification and regression. In recent times, the use of deep learning has been facilitated due to the available computation capabilities and the rise of GPUs. To this end, we performed experiments by using a Convolutional Neural Network framework to classify the three sleep postures. We used the CaffeNet architecture [21] and pre-trained it on 1.2M image ILSVRC-2012 dataset [22] which is an ImageNet subset. This pre-training is required to avoid overfitting and to build a powerful model. We have fine-tuned the model to accept IR data as input and perform classification on the three posture classes. In the back end of the system, these recognition networks can be swapped.

Furthermore, the GUI shown in Fig. 5 was developed to record and store the image of the subjects while they are sleeping, at a sample rate of 1 frame per second. It has a window that displays the images in real-time. If the subject would like to get up from the bed to drink water or use the restroom, they

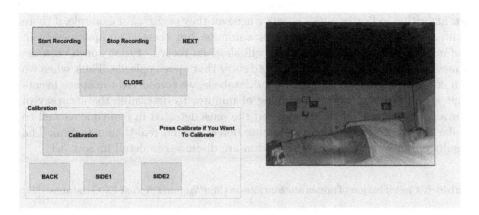

Fig. 5. The posture detection GUI

can pause the system. The subjects can also calibrate the posture detection subsystem to get higher accuracy. The lower part of the GUI walks the subject through the calibration steps. The subject would first lie on their back and press the BACK button. The system would then record and store the images. Next when prompted the subject would lie on their side facing the camera and press the SIDE1 button. After this when prompted the subject would lie on their side facing away from the camera and press the SIDE2 button. At the end of the session the subject would be directed to a window which analyzes the images and displays the historical pattern of the sleeping posture. This historical pattern can be used to identify postural apnea by looking up the sleeping posture while the subject was in the apnea state.

2.3 Experiments

Preliminary Study: In this project, we do not have access to subjects with known apnea conditions. Therefore, we are using Apnea-ECG database provided on *Physionet*[2], an online research resource for complex physiologic signals. The purpose of using this database is to be able to evaluate our algorithm on SpO_2 data with apnea annotations marked by a sleep expert [23,24]. The database has 30 training recordings for ECG data and apnea annotations; however, only 8 recordings include SpO_2 data, which we used to evaluate our apnea detection algorithm. These recordings are classified as *Apnea* (4 recordings), *Borderline* (1 recording), and *Control* (3 recordings) as described in Table 1. The apnea annotations from the *Physionet* only mark apnea at the beginning of each minute (one annotation per minute), which is different from our real-time algorithm (multiple annotations per minute). In other words, *Physionet* database indicates that apnea was in progress at the beginning of the next one-minute interval, whereas

---

[2] https://physionet.org/physiobank/database/apnea-ecg/.

our algorithm indicates apnea events whenever they occur[3]. For example, if there is no apnea event during the start of a minute, but there is an apnea event in the middle of it, then the database will show no record of that apnea episode; however, our real-time algorithm would show that apnea episode. Thus, when we ran our algorithm using the *Physionet* database, we considered the apnea events that are in progress at the beginning of minutes to determine the accuracy of our algorithm, and we also considered the ones detected in real-time as well to make a comparison between per minute detection and real-time detection. The results of our apnea detection algorithm are discussed in detail in Sect. 3.1.

Table 1. Classification of apnea annotations in the *Physionet* Apnea-ECG database [23]

Class	Description
Apnea	"Contain at least one hour with an apnea index of 10 or more, and at least 100 min with apnea during the recording."
Borderline	"Contain at least one hour with an apnea index of 5 or more, and between 5 and 99 min with apnea during the recording."
Control	"Contain fewer than 5 min with apnea during the recording."

During the preliminary study we collected 900 IR images each from 10 participants (7 males, 3 females). This data was collected while they performed the three sleep postures under consideration (300 frames per sleep pose). The purpose of this preliminary data was to prove that IR images can be used to detect sleeping posture, and to figure out the right algorithm to develop and tune. The machine learning classifiers used to do the sleep posture recognition with the preliminary data are: *K-Nearest Neighbor (KNN), Support Vector Machine (SVM) with linear kernel, and Convolutional neural network (CNN).* This was done to identify a suitable algorithm for posture detection using IR images. This work was a continuation of the work performed in our lab [17]. The results of the machine learning classifiers were promising and they are described in detail in Sect. 3.2. The 10 participants were divided into two groups: 'Training' and 'Testing'. The Training group had seven participants with 6300 data points in total. The Testing group had three participants with 2700 data points in total. There was an equal number of data points for each posture. As described in Sect. 2.2 PCA was performed on each data point to get the essential pattern of the data. This was then used as a data point of the classification algorithms. Accuracy was calculated as the number of 'Hits' or correct classification out of the total number of data points. Accuracy for CNN model on our dataset is calculated after every 100th epoch. We trained our CNN infrared image posture recognition model for 1000 epochs.

---

[3] https://physionet.org/physiobank/database/apnea-ecg/annotations.shtml.

Overnight Study: Although the purpose of our system is to create an apnea pre-screening tool for use in a home environment, the overnight experiment took place in simulated apartment setup we have in our lab as seen in Fig. 1. The reason for that is to be able to make sure the oximeter is connected at all times, and to mark the ground truth position of the subject in order to evaluate the accuracy of our posture detection algorithms. Ten male subjects between the ages of 24 and 31 were part of this overnight study. Each subject came to our lab around their bedtime, signed the IRB Protocol (2017-0276), wore the sensors (oximeter and smartwatch), interacted with the GUIs and connected the sensors, and went to bed. At the end of the overnight experiment, the subjects interacted with the GUIs again and filled out a survey. The survey has some demographical questions and questions about the subject's experience with the system setup. The survey data are discussed in detail in Sect. 3.3.

Data from these ten subjects was used to create an SVM model. Some subjects did not sleep in one of the positions throughout the night. Therefore the calibration data was added to the dataset to make sure all postures were represented for each subject. For the ease of computation, at the maximum 500 images were considered per posture per subject. Therefore in total, at the maximum, each subject would have 1500 images. To validate the model created from this method, a K- Fold Cross-Validation was performed on the dataset. A 5 Fold Cross-Validation method was considered. The results for this are shown in the Sect. 3.2. As described previously, PCA was performed on the data set and accuracy was calculated as the number of 'Hits' out of the total number of data points. This cross-validation data was also used to make a CNN model. The accuracy of this system was calculated after every 20 epochs. We trained our system for 1000 epochs.

3   Results

This section discusses the results of the apnea detection algorithm and posture detection algorithms in both the preliminary and the overnight study, in addition to user surveys.

3.1   Apnea Detection

Preliminary Study Results: As mentioned in Sect. 2.3, the apnea detection algorithm is evaluated based on the annotations provided on the *Physionet* website. Table 2 shows the full results of our detection algorithm when apnea episodes were considered both at the beginning of the minute and in total (real-time). For the data label A represents data collected from actual apnea subjects, B represents borderline cases and C represents control subjects. Row 8 in Table 2 shows the accuracy of our algorithm when considering true positive and true negative matchings of apnea episodes at the beginning of minutes to be between 83.20% (A01) and 54.40% (A04) with a mean of 71.51% for *Apena* class recordings. This means that our algorithm has an average accuracy of 71.51% for detecting

Table 2. Apnea detection algorithm accuracy

Row	Description	A01	A02	A03	A04	B01	C01	C02	C03
1	Total no. of calculated apnea episodes using our algorithm (multiple annotations per minute)	586	644	427	499	6	2	10	0
2	Total no. of annotated apnea episodes from *Physionet* (1 annotation per minute)	470	420	246	453	19	0	1	0
3	Total no. of calculated apnea episodes using our algorithm (1 annotation per minute)	392	277	217	233	4	1	3	0
4	Total no. of apnea episodes matching in both *Physionet* and our algorithm (1 annotation per minute)	390 out of 470	260 out of 420	185 out of 246	231 out of 453	1 out of 19	0 out of 0	0 out of 1	0 out of 0
5	Total no. of 'no apnea' episodes from *Physionet* (1 annotation per minute)	18	107	272	38	467	483	500	453
6	Total no. of calculated 'no apnea' episodes using our algorithm (1 annotation per minute)	96	250	301	258	482	482	498	453
7	Total no. of 'no apnea' episodes matching in both *Physionet* and our algorithm (1 annotation per minute)	16 out of 18	90 out of 107	240 out of 272	36 out of 38	464 out of 467	482 out of 483	497 out of 500	453 out of 453
8	Our algorithm accuracy (1 annotation per minute)	83.20 %	66.41 %	82.05 %	54.40 %	95.70 %	99.80 %	99.20 %	100 %
9	Calculated AHI from *Physionet* annotations (1 annotation per minute)	57.79	47.82	28.49	55.36	2.35	0.00	0.12	0.00
10	Calculated AHI from our algorithm (1 annotation per minute)	48.20	31.54	25.14	28.47	0.49	0.12	0.36	0.00
11	Calculated AHI from our algorithm (multiple annotations per minute)	72.05	73.32	49.46	60.98	0.74	0.25	1.20	0.00

apnea episodes at the beginning of minutes for people who have apnea. A04 has the lowest accuracy (54.40%, row 8) and its calculated AHI from annotations is 55.36 (row 9). The AHI estimation for A04 from our algorithm ranges between 28.47 (row 10) and 60.98 (row 11). Thus, our algorithm was able to detect that the subject has at least moderate apnea. Considering that our system is an apnea pre-screening tool and not apnea diagnosis tool, our algorithm can be considered successful in notifying the subjects when it is highly recommended that they consult a sleep expert, which is when the apnea condition is at least mild (AHI > 5). In the rest of the data (B01, C01, C02 and C03), the minimum accuracy achieved is 95.70% (B01, row 8), and the average accuracy is 98.68%. In these recordings (B01, C01, C02 and C03), both the calculated AHI from annotations (row 9) and from our algorithm (row 10 and 11) do not exceed 5, which indicates that the subjects have a normal AHI and they do not need to consult a sleep expert. These findings can indicate that our algorithm can detect apnea conditions with moderate accuracy in cases of severe apnea conditions and higher accuracy in case of normal conditions. Although it gives a moderate accuracy in severe apnea condition, the AHI was still high suggesting that the subject should still visit a sleep expert.

Overnight Study Results: The 10 subjects of the overnight experiment produced around 55 h of recordings (minimum of 2.62 h, maximum of 7.89 h, mean of 5.5 h). The calculated AHI values ranged between 0 and 1.88 (mean of 0.29) which indicates that the subjects were healthy. These results indicate that the apnea detection algorithm did a satisfiable job of detecting apnea in both preliminary data and overnight study data. Although some apnea events were recorded in the overnight study data, none of the participants reported that they had a known apnea condition. The AHI for the subjects who had apnea episodes were low enough to be classified in the *Normal* category.

3.2 Posture Recognition

Preliminary Study Results: First SVM and KNN were performed on the preliminary data. The results for this is tabulated in Table 3. The accuracy for KNN was 65.67% while the accuracy for SVM is 79.14%. With a high accuracy of 79.14% it was proved that SVM could be used for classifying sleeping posture using IR data as an input. Moreover, it was also observed that SVM is more suitable to classify sleeping posture than KNN. The experiments for CNN were performed by training the model for 1000 epochs. The preliminary test dataset accuracy obtained for the CNN model trained for 500 iterations was 92%. It shows that it is sufficient to train the model for those many epochs as after that it can be prone to overfitting. Test data accuracy from models trained at different epochs are shown in Table 4.

Table 3. KNN and SVM accuracy with preliminary data

	KNN	SVM
Accuracy (%)	65.67	79.14

Overnight Study Results: The IR data collected from the subjects during the overnight study was used to create an SVM and a CNN model. As both

Table 4. CNN model accuracy with preliminary data

Iteration	0	100	200	300	400	500	600	700	800	900	1000
Accuracy (%)	33.48	71.76	88.83	77.52	77.76	92.11	83.25	83.92	87.50	88.20	88.46

Table 5. 5 fold SVM accuracy

Folds no.	1	2	3	4	5	Mean
Accuracy (%)	64.05	78.12	87.81	73.05	71.53	74.91

these models proved to be a suitable classification algorithms in the preliminary study, they were used to create a model using the overnight study dataset. The data collected during the preliminary study gives an ideal scenario of the sleeping posture. While the data collected during the overnight study gives an actual indication of the sleeping posture. Table 5 shows the accuracy of the SVM model created using the 5 Fold method. The highest accuracy observed using this method was 87.81%. On an average the accuracy of this model was 74.91%. These results support the decision of using SVM for the classification of sleep posture. Table 6 shows the results of the CNN for the same overnight study. The same 5 fold method was used to create and validate the CNN model. The table shows the highest accuracy for each of the folds. As observed, the highest accuracy found using the 5 fold method was 99.84% and the mean accuracy was 89.71%. These results validate the use of both CNN and SVM for the analysis of the sleep posture. The results shown to subjects during the overnight study for the posture detection subsystem was calculated from the SVM model, created from the preliminary dataset.

3.3 User Surveys Analysis

At the end of the experiment, the subjects were asked to interact with the GUIs to run the posture detection algorithm on the collected IR images and to check the sleep summary report. After that, the subjects filled out a survey about their experience of using our system. Figure 6 shows that 40% of the participants found that the sensors are uncomfortable. In particular, the subjects had no issue with the smartwatch, but they found the oximeter pressing on their finger uncomfortable. There are products available in the market, for example a wrist worn oximeter the WristOx2 by Nonin, which could be used to increase the comfort level. 40% of the subjects did not feel very comfortable being recorded

Table 6. 5 fold CNN model accuracy with overnight experiment data

Fold no.	1	2	3	4	5	Mean
Accuracy (%)	95.99	94.77	99.84	74.11	83.83	89.71

while they are asleep. The study conducted was observed to make sure that it ran smoothly, this may have contributed to the discomfort. In actual use cases there might be no observer. This may improve the comfort level of the subjects. 70% of the subjects found that sleeping on the bed without a blanket or a comforter was acceptable for the purposes of the study. All the participants found that our GUIs and the sleep report were both easy to use and understand.

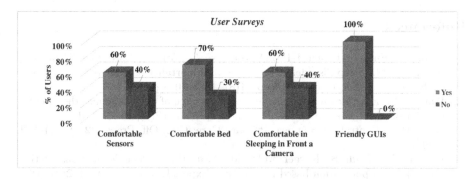

Fig. 6. User surveys analysis

4 Conclusion and Future Work

In this paper we described a system that was created for pre-screening sleep apnea in a home environment. The system was designed and evaluated in two parts; the apnea detection using SpO_2 and the posture detection using IR images. From the results from the preliminary study it can be observed that our apnea detection algorithm identifies apnea with a high accuracy. From the results of both preliminary and the overnight study, it can also be observed that the posture recognition algorithm gives a high accuracy using both SVM and CNN models. Therefore this system could be used to detect apnea and postural apnea in a home environment.

There were some limitations to the study, like the fact that the subjects considered for the overnight study did not have a known apnea condition. As a future work, the APSEN system can be tested on subjects with known or expected apnea condition. The posture detection algorithms can be tuned to address the subject's concern of sleeping without blankets or comforter. No criteria for Body Mass Index (BMI) was considered while recruiting subjects for the overnight study. As obesity is a factor in pathogenesis of sleep apnea [25] in future studies we would like to include subjects with varying BMI to get a more accurate indication of actual apnea condition. It should also recognize the sleep postures in real-time and save them in the same database as the oximeter and the smartwatch. Integrating real-time posture detection in the system would help provide the subject with more meaningful notifications during severe apnea conditions, such as: 'sleep on your side'. We would also like to test our posture detection algorithm on different backgrounds, which might affect the quality of our recordings.

Acknowledgments. This work was supported in part by the National Science Foundation under award numbers 1338118, 1405985, 1565328, and 1055062.

References

1. Young, T., Finn, L., Peppard, P.E., Szklo-Coxe, M., Austin, D., Nieto, F.J., Stubbs, R., Hla, K.M.: Sleep disordered breathing and mortality: eighteen-year follow-up of the Wisconsin sleep cohort. Sleep **31**(8), 1071–1078 (2008)
2. Watson, N.: Health care savings: the economic value of diagnostic and therapeutic care for obstructive sleep apnea. J. Clin. Sleep Med. **12**(8), 10–12 (2016)
3. Badr, M.S.: Central sleep apnea. Primary Care: Clin. Off. Pract. **32**(2), 361–374 (2005)
4. Lee, W., Nagubadi, S., Kryger, M.H., Mokhlesi, B.: Epidemiology of obstructive sleep apnea: a population-based perspective. Expert Rev. Respir. Med. **2**(3), 349–364 (2008)
5. Guilleminault, C., Korobkin, R., Winkle, R.: A review of 50 children with obstructive sleep apnea syndrome. Lung **159**, 275–287 (1981)
6. Eiseman, N.A., Westover, M.B., Ellenbogen, J.M., Bianchi, M.T.: The impact of body posture and sleep stages on sleep apnea severity in adults. J. Clin. Sleep Med. **8**(6), 655–666 (2012)
7. Oksenberg, A., Silverberg, D., Offenbach, D., Arons, E.: Positional therapy for obstructive sleep apnea patients: a 6-month follow-up study. Laryngoscope **116**(11), 1995–2000 (2006)
8. Blackwell, T., Redline, S., Ancoli-Israel, S., Schneider, J.L., Surovec, S., Johnson, N.L., Cauley, J.A., Stone, K.L.: Comparison of sleep parameters from actigraphy and polysomnography in older women: the SOF study. Sleep **31**(2), 283–291 (2008)
9. SleepMed: Unparalleled insight starts with the ARES^{TM}. http://www.sleepmedinc.com/at-home
10. ResMed: ApneaLink Air^{TM}. http://www.resmed.com/us/en/healthcare-professional/products/diagnostics/apnealink-air.html
11. Burgos, A., Goñi, A., Illarramendi, A., Bermúdez, J.: Real-time detection of apneas on a PDA. IEEE Trans. Inf Technol. Biomed. **14**(4), 995–1002 (2010)
12. Al-Mardini, M., Aloul, F., Sagahyroon, A., Al-Husseini, L.: Classifying obstructive sleep apnea using smartphones. J. Biomed. Inform. **52**, 251–259 (2014)
13. Samy, L., Macey, P.M., Alshurafa, N., Sarrafzadeh, M.: An automated framework for predicting obstructive sleep apnea using a brief, daytime, non-intrusive test procedure. In: Proceedings of the 8th ACM International Conference on PErvasive Technologies Related to Assistive Environments, pp. 70:1–70:8 (2015)
14. Phillips, K.: Center, Alaska Sleep Education: How Much Does a Sleep Study Cost? (Rates, Fees, & Discounts). http://www.alaskasleep.com/blog/costs-sleep-studies-rates-fees-discounts
15. Tsai, W.H., Flemons, W.W., Whitelaw, W.A., Remmers, J.E.: A comparison of apnea–hypopnea indices derived from different definitions of hypopnea. Am. J. Respir. Crit. Care Med. **159**(1), 43–48 (1999)

16. Microsoft Dev Center: What's a Universal Windows Platform (UWP) app? https://docs.microsoft.com/en-us/windows/uwp/get-started/whats-a-uwp
17. Metsis, V., Kosmopoulos, D., Athitsos, V., Makedon, F.: Non-invasive analysis of sleep patterns via multimodal sensor input. Pers. Ubiquit. Comput. **18**(1), 19–26 (2014)
18. Terven, J.R., Córdova-Esparza, D.M.: Kin2. a kinect 2 toolbox for MATLAB. Sci. Comput. Program. **130**, 97–106 (2016)
19. Wold, S., Esbensen, K., Geladi, P.: Principal component analysis. Chemometr. Intell. Lab. Syst. **2**(1–3), 35–52 (1987)
20. Chang, C.C., Lin, C.J.: LIBSVM: a library for support vector machines. ACM Trans. Intell. Syst. Technol. **2**(3), 27:1–27:27 (2011)
21. Jia, Y., Shelhamer, E., Donahue, J., Karayev, S., Long, J., Girshick, R., Guadarrama, S., Darrell, T.: Caffe: convolutional architecture for fast feature embedding. In: Proceedings of the ACM International Conference on Multimedia, MM 2014, Orlando, FL, USA, 03–07 November 2014
22. Russakovsky, O., Deng, J., Su, H., Krause, J., Satheesh, S., Ma, S., Huang, Z., Karpathy, A., Khosla, A., Bernstein, M.S., Berg, A.C., Li, F.: Imagenet large scale visual recognition challenge. Int. J. Comput. Vis. **115**(3), 211–252 (2015)
23. Goldberger, A.L., Amaral, L.A., Glass, L., Hausdorff, J.M., Ivanov, P.C., Mark, R.G., Mietus, J.E., Moody, G.B., Peng, C.K., Stanley, H.E.: PhysioBank, PhysioToolkit, and PhysioNet: components of a new research resource for complex physiologic signals. Circulation **101**(23), e215–e220 (2000). [Circulation Electronic Pages]. http://circ.ahajournals.org/content/101/23/e215.full
24. Penzel, T., Moody, G.B., Mark, R.G., Goldberger, A.L., Peter, J.H.: The apnea-ECG database. In: Computers in Cardiology 2000, pp. 255–258. IEEE (2000)
25. Eckert, D.J., Malhotra, A.: Pathophysiology of adult obstructive sleep apnea. Proc. Am. Thorac. Soc. **5**(2), 144–153 (2008)

Tacit Process for Obtaining Nursing Skills
Focusing on Nurse's Sense of Patients Close to Death

Jukai Maeda[1](✉), Yasuko Kitajima[1], Masako Yamashita[1], and Yuki Tsuji[2]

[1] Tokyo Ariake University of Medical and Health Sciences,
2-9-1 Ariake, Koto, Tokyo 135-0063, Japan
{jukai,kitajima,yamashita}@tau.ac.jp
[2] Tokoha University, 1-30 Mizuochicho Aoi, Shizuoka 420-0831, Japan
yuki.ty18@gmail.com

Abstract. In Japan, it is no secret among nurses that some hospital nurses can sense that a patient is close to death in spite of there being no obvious changes. However, no empirical data about this phenomenon have ever been compiled. The purpose of this study is to clarify the characteristics of nurses with such ability. A questionnaire survey was given to 262 nurses anonymously during November 2013. The items to be asked in the questionnaire were whether or not they had ever sensed a patients' being close to death as a dependent variable, and their charcteristics as independent variables. 143 nurses were responded. The mean age of the respondents was 50.2. 47 respondents responded "yes", and 92 responded "no" to the question, "whether they had ever sensed that a patient was close to death without obvious changes in their vital signs". As a result of chi-square test, significantly relevant to this variable were "educational background (BScN and Junior College)", and "possessed license (RN and LPN)". The t-test showed that a significant difference was noticed in years of experience as an RN between "yes" and "no" groups. These results suggest that the ability to sense patients' coming close to the end of life without the presence of obviously objective signs depends not on their natural abilities, but on their experience. Of course, we must consider that these responses were based on self-report, so the issues such as confirmation or hindsight bias related to heuristics may take place. However, the frequency of nurses who self-reported they were able to sense patients close to death without any obvious changes shows something more than just a rumor among nurses.

Keywords: Expertization · Heuristics · Nursing skill · Tacit knowing · Tacit knowledge

1 Introduction

In Japan, as in many other countries, persons who have received a certain amount of education at a nursing educational institution are allowed to take the national examination for nurses. The curriculum to become a nurse is determined by the

© Springer International Publishing AG 2017
V.G. Duffy (Ed.): DHM 2017, Part II, LNCS 10287, pp. 52–60, 2017.
DOI: 10.1007/978-3-319-58466-9_5

Ministry of Health, Labour and Welfare, and it includes not only knowledge relating to nursing, but fundamental nursing skills such as helping patients in their daily lives and helping doctors in medical exams, as well as practice in hospitals, etc. Only those who pass this curriculum with a certain level of success can graduate the nursing educational institution and take the national examination for nurses.

The fact that nursing skills education is organized within the school education means that on the other hand, in the instructor-student framework it goes without saying that the skills instructors have obtained can be transferred to the students. According to a survey by the Japanese Nursing Association, out of 103 fundamental nursing skills there were only 4 of the skills regarding which 7 out of 10 or more of the new nursing graduates answered that they could "do by themselves" at the time of starting work. We believe that this fact suggests a need to review methods of teaching nursing skills, as well as a need to rethink the premise that nursing skills are capable of being transferred.

One basis for this idea is that there are cases of nurses who can sense that patients in the hospital are near death in spite of there being no changes which are obvious to anyone such as lowered blood pressure and weakened respiration. "The ability to know when a person is near death", which is well known in clinical settings, is obviously not something to be studied in nursing curriculum and is not part of the education, nor are there textbooks which handle it. Therefore, if this skill does indeed exist, it is not a skill which has been acquired by being taught by someone else, but can rather be called a skill which is tacitly acquired by oneself.

This skill is fundamentally connected with the "tacit knowledge" which was proposed by Polanyi [2]. If it can be confirmed that there exists a skill which nurses acquire tacitly without learning it from an instructor, we can anticipate a basis for creating a new methodology for nursing education which doesn't presume transmission from an instructor. "The ability to know when a patient will die" is not a topic for discussion in traditional curriculum based upon transfer of knowledge, so it can be called a superior subject inasmuch as it allows one to refute the argument that acquired skills are acquired by being transferred.

Considering the above, the goal of this research is to clarify the existence of the skill to know that hospitalized patients are near death as well as the process by which it is acquired. This paper will clarify the existence of nurses who know when patients are near death in spite of clear indicative changes, as well as independent variables that relate to the cultivation of this skill.

2   Method

2.1   Study Framework

In this research we conduct an analysis based upon the framework of nurses collecting some kind of data from patients or their surroundings and then processing that data and using the results to make clinical judgment that "the patient's death is near". We would like to emphasize the fact that this is in no way premised upon such things as a sixth sense or sense of foreboding on the parts of the nurse.

As shown in Fig. 1, nurses collect data from a patient. The collected data are processed to form or organize information using the nurse's knowledge. The relationship among data, information, and knowledge is based on Blum's definition [1]. We will never observe nurses' information processing directly unless they give details in words. However, such types of skills as predicting patient death without obvious changes in vital signs are difficult to explain how they become to know. So, in this study, we focus on nurse's clinical judgment as a conclusion of such information processing. In fact, we know some nurses utilize the information that patient was close to death. For instance, to inform the patient's family so as to come to the hospital, to share the information with other nurses, to check if the patient has a will for DNAR, and to locate physician in charge are done on the basis of their clinical judgment.

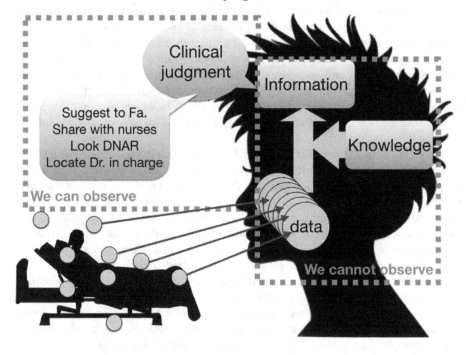

Fig. 1. Framework of information processing by nurses

2.2 Subjects

In Japan there are 4 nursing qualifications (registered nurse, practical nurse, midwife, and public health nurse). The parent set comprises persons holding one of those qualifications. The subjects of this survey were 43 trainees who were taking a certified nurse manager training lecture given by the researcher, 99 teaching staff and graduate students participating in an FD workshop of a nursing university, and 120 nursing staff from a psychiatric hospital who gave their cooperation, for a total of 262 subjects. The time of the survey was November 2013.

2.3 Data Collection

A questionnaire survey was given to the subjects anonymously. In the workshop, the questionnaire was passed out to the participants, who submitted them at the end of the training or answered via a web form containing the same contents. In the hospital, we had the head nurse pass out and collect the questionnaires and had them answered in a week.

2.4 Questionnaire Items

The subjects were asked questions necessary to know their characteristics such age, sex, and other population statistics items, as well as the licenses they held (registered nurse, practical nurse, midwife, and public health nurse) and the number of years experience in each license. They were also asked whether or not they had ever sensed that patients in the hospital are near death in spite of there being no changes which are obvious to anyone, and if so, their feelings at that time. Furthermore, they were asked if there were any other nurses who could make such predictions, and if so, they were asked to list characteristics they shared in common with said nurses, etc.

2.5 Analysis

With a dependent variable of "whether or not they had ever sensed that patients in the hospital are near death in spite of there being no obvious changes", and independent variables of "age", "sex", "marriage status", "possessed licenses", "number of children", "number of children", and "number of years experience in each license, they were asked regarding each independent variable based upon the relative level of measurement, and we investigated regarding significant relations between two variables using chi-square test (and Fisher's exact test) or the Student's t-test. We also investigated variables predicting the existence of awareness of patients' being near death within the independent variables via logistic regression. We set the standard for significance for each of these tests at 5% (two-tails test).

2.6 Ethical Considerations

Before the research, we received approval from the ethics committees of the universities to which the researchers belong, and implemented the research as per the approved plan (approval number: Ariake University of Medical and Health Sciences ethics approval no. 75).

3 Results

3.1 Characteristics of the Respondents

Responses were received from 143 persons (54.6%). The age group distribution of the respondents was shown in Fig. 2. The mean age of the respondents was 50.2 ($SD = 13.1$), while the lowest value was 20 and the highest 72. Regarding nominal measurements, as shown in Table 1, there were 117 women, 17 men, 79 staff nurses, 16 senior staff nurses, 12 head nurses, one director nurse, and 21 faculty members of nursing. As for the possessed licenses (multiple answers allowed), there were 89 RNs, 79 LPNs, 14 midwives, and 13 public health nurses. The educational backgrounds for acquiring nursing qualifications were 56 from 3-year diploma courses, 53 from LPN schools, 23 from BScN programs, and 5 from junior colleges. The mean number of years of experience per each license was 21.8 ($SD = 14.1$) for practical nurses, 16.6 ($SD = 11.2$) for nurses, 13.7 ($SD = 10.8$) for midwives, and 1.3 ($SD = 3.0$) for public health nurses, and the overall average number of years of experience was 20.7 ($SD = 12.6$).

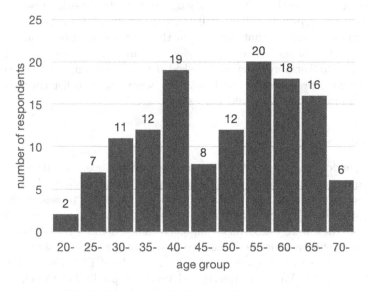

Fig. 2. Age group distribution of respondents

3.2 The Relation Between Experience of Awareness of Death and Each Variable

47 respondents (33.8%) responded "yes" and 92 (66.2%) responded "no" to whether they had ever sensed that patients in the hospital were near death in spite of there being no obvious changes, while 4 respondents did not answer.

Table 1 shows the t-test results regarding relations between experience of patient's death perception without apparent changes in vital signs, and each continuous variable. A significant relation was only noticed in number of years of experience as a registered nurse (RN). No test results indicating a relationship with number of years experience with other licenses, age, number of children, were found.

Table 1. Relation between experience of patient's death perception without apparent changes in vitals and continuous variables

Variables		Experience of Pt. death perception								t	p^a	d^b
		Yes				No						
		n	M	SD	95%Cl	n	M	SD	95%Cl			
Age		45	48.7	12.0	[45.1, 52.3]	92	50.9	13.6	[48.0, 53.8]	0.91	.3621	0.17
Number of children		35	1.9	1.2	[1.44, 2.27]	78	1.5	1.1	[1.26, 1.74]	−1.58	.1180	0.31
Years of experience	LPN	47	6.7	13.2	[2.79, 10.5]	92	11.0	14.6	[8.01, 14.1]	1.73	.0868	0.31
	RN	47	13.7	12.3	[10.1, 17.3]	92	6.3	10.3	[4.18, 8.43]	−3.75	.0003	0.65
	MW	47	0.2	1.5	[−0.22, 0.64]	92	1.7	5.9	[0.46, 2.91]	1.67	.0964	0.34
	PHN	47	0.0	0.1	[−0.01, 0.06]	92	0.0	0.4	[−0.04, 0.13]	0.33	.7424	0.07
	Whole career	44	21.8	12.7	[17.9, 25.6]	87	20.1	12.6	[17.4, 22.7]	−0.73	.4663	0.14

[a] Two-tailed Student's t-test, [b] Effect Size (Cohen's d)

Next, Table 2 shows the relation between the dependant variable and each categorical variable. No relation was seen between the variables by sex and marriage status. However, a significantly larger number of nurses who had graduated universities or junior colleges compared to nurses who had graduated trade schools, as well as a significantly larger number of nurses with nursing licenses compared to those who did not, answered "yes" to whether they had ever sensed that patients in the hospital are near death in spite of there being no obvious changes.

4   Discussion

The concept of tacit knowledge was proposed by Polanyi [2] and became widely known in Japan as well due to Nonaka [3,4]. When we conducted this survey, as a result of searching literatures including the word "tacit knowledge", using the Japan Medical Abstracts Society Web (www.jamas.or.jp), a major medical paper database in Japan, there were 12 original articles since 2005, 12 meeting minutes since 2003, and 12 expositions since 2006, suggesting that research dealing with tacit knowledge in the nursing field had only just begun. Leading research regarding tacit knowledge in the nursing field deals with "drawing blood", "information gathering", and other skills which nurses are supposed

Table 2. Relation between experience of patient's death perception without apparent changes in vitals and categorical variables

	Variables	n	Experience of Pt. death perception		
			Yes	No	P value
Sex	Female	117	43	70	[a].0527
	Male	17	2	15	
Marital status	Not married	27	10	16	[b].6478
	Married	96	29	65	
	Divorced/separated	15	6	9	
Job title	Staff nurse	79	23	54	[b].2578
	Chief nurse	16	8	8	
	Head nurse	12	6	6	
	Director of nursing	1	1	0	
	Nurse educator	21	7	13	
	Others (Grad. students etc.)	11	2	8	
License (RN)	Yes	89	37	48	[a].0031
	No		10	44	
License (LPN)	Yes	79	19	60	[a].0067
	No		28	32	
License (MW)	Yes	13	1	12	[a].0603
	No		46	80	
License (PHN)	Yes	14	7	5	[a].1059
	No		40	87	
Education	Diploma (LPN)	53	10	43	[b].0022
	Diploma (RN)	56	21	34	
	BScN/Associate degree	28	15	11	

Note. RN = Registered Nurse. LPN = Licensed Practice Nurse. MW = Nurse Midwife. PHN = Public Health Nurse.
[a]Two-tailed Fisher's exact test.
[b]Two-tailed chi-square test.

to possess—that is to say skills which are established by education within the teacher-student framework—and their purpose is to create explicit knowledge from the tacit knowledge which exists therein. We believe this is problematic in two ways. The first is that nursing research which advocates the explication of tacit knowledge is being conducted based upon the idea that changing tacit knowledge to explicit knowledge will make it a skill which can be transferred, based on the premise that "skills can be transferred". The second is that the focus has been shifted from how this kind of tacit knowledge is acquired in the first place to the changing of the acquired "skill called tacit knowledge" into explicit knowledge. In such cases, in addition to the issue of it not having been made clear whether skills which have been made into explicit knowledge can be transferred through this "explicit knowledge", there is also the issue of it being impossible to discern whether this skill was acquired by the transfer of whether it was acquired via one's own experience.

The position of this research is that there exist knowledge and skills which cannot be transferred. "Knowing when a patient will die", which this research covers, is not recognized as a skill which should be acquired as a nurse, and of course, it has never been taught at nursing schools. Therefore, if this skill is acquired a posteriori, it can be said that it was not learned from teachers or senior nurses, but rather naturally through genuine experience of the nurses' own. The reason why it is called "tacit knowledge" is that it was acquired tacitly, and the nurses with such skills cannot say verbally what it is. The results of this questionnaire survey shows that those who had experienced sensing that patients are near death without any changes in vital signs were uniquely the "registered nurses" with more years of experience, suggest that experience is important in predicting patients' being near death. This is also supported by the fact that there is a significantly larger number of persons who can make such predictions among those with registered nurse than those without it. So why do registered nurse and years of experience as a registered nurse increase the ability to sense a patient being near death more than other nursing qualifications and experience? This is a matter of speculation, but it would seem that experience caring for dying patients is important. Midwives mainly deal with births, which is the opposite of death. The main role of public health nurses is the improvement of public health, so they do not come across individual deaths very much. Under Japanese law, practical nurses are able to conduct the same work as registered nurses, but the local rules of hospitals and medical facilities often impose restrictions upon them such as not being able to work at night shifts or work as leaders. These things suggest that there is a limitation for licensed practical nurses to the "experience", and that limit may hinder their acquisition of the ability to sense dying patients without changes in visible signs. In order to verify these, it is necessary to collect further empirical data and gather more information regarding the existence of ability to sense, e.g. number of dying patients they caring for in the past, or hospital departments they worked in.

An interesting phenomenon is the fact that it became clear that more persons who received nursing education in universities or junior colleges can significantly sense a patient being near death. University and junior college graduates possess registered nurse without exception. Until now, new graduate registered nurses from higher education often received criticism that "they have knowledge not along with skills". However, it is easy to imagine that, within the nurses who have done training which not only accumulated knowledge but creates it, there are not a few nurses who accumulate experience as knowledge in a clinical setting or create new knowledge from their experience. The number of BScN nurses in Japan will be increasing in the future due to the increase of nursing universities.

We believe that it is worthwhile to consider the construction of a body of nursing knowledge which considers their individual characteristics.

There were not a few nurses who self-reported they were able to sense patients close to death without any changes obvious to anyone. This frequency shows something more than just a rumor. However, still, there is no denying that it is a product of their cognitive bias such as confirmation bias or hindsight bias. Brabland et al. [5] conducted a cohort study to evaluate if nurses and physicians could accurately predict mortality of acutely admitted patients, just using their clinical intuition. The study clarified To avoid cognitive biases, it will be necessary for us to obtain prospective data as well as retrospective data like presented on this paper.

5   Conclusion

As a result of a questionnaire survey for nurses;

- 47 out of 143 nurses self-reported that they had ever sensed hospitalized patients were close to death without apparent changes in their vital signs.
- Presence or absence of the experience depended on the tyoe of nursing lisence obtained, years of experience, and educational background statistically.
- There was a tendency that a person with a long experience as an RN (registered nurse) had experiences to sense patients close to death.
- Also, RNs who graduated from university or junior college tended to have the experiences.
- Prospective study will be desirable to reduce cognitive bias of participants.

Acknowledgments. This research was supported by JSPS KAKENHI Grant Number 25670931 and 15K11485.

References

1. Blum, B.I.: Clinical information systems-a review. W. J. Med. **145**(6), 791–797 (1986)
2. Polanyi, M.: Personal Knowledge: Towards a Post-Critical Philosophy. The University of Chicago Press, Chicago (1958)
3. Nonaka, I.: The Knowledge-Creating Company. Harvard Business Review. Harvard Business Publishing, Boston (1990). November–December, pp. 96–104
4. Nonaka, I., Takeuchi, H.: The Knowledge Creating Company. Oxford University Press, New York (1995)
5. Brabrand, M., Hallas, J., Knudsen, T.: Nurses and physicians in a medical admission unit can accurately predict mortality of acutely admitted patients: a prospective cohort study. PloS One **9**(7), e101739-1–e101739-7 (2014). doi:10.1371/journal.pone.0101739

Conversion of JPG Image into DICOM Image Format with One Click Tagging

Olakunle Oladiran[1]([⊠]), Judy Gichoya[2], and Saptarshi Purkayastha[1]

[1] School of Informatics and Computing,
Indiana University-Purdue University Indianapolis, Indianapolis, USA
{ooladira, saptpurk}@iupui.edu
[2] Indiana University School of Medicine, Indianapolis, USA
jgichoya@iupui.edu

Abstract. DICOM images are the centerpiece of radiological imaging. They contain a lot of metadata information about the patient, procedure, sequence of images, device and location. To modify, annotate or simply anonymize images for distribution, we often need to convert DICOM images to another format like jpeg since there are a number of image manipulation tools available for jpeg images compared to DICOM. As part of a research at our institution to customize radiology images to assess cognitive ability of multiple user groups, we created an open-source tool called Jpg2DicomTags, which is able to extract DICOM metadata tags, convert images to lossless jpg that can be manipulated and subsequently reconvert jpg images to DICOM by adding back the metadata tags. This tool provides a simple, easy to use user-interface for a tedious manual task that providers, researchers and patients might often need to do.

Keywords: Medical informatics · Radiology informatics · DICOM · Image manipulation

1 Introduction

A lot of research has been conducted on radiological reporting to determine how patients can be actively involved in their own healthcare delivery [1]. This includes improving patient understanding of the need for certain procedures, understanding own disease/condition, improving communication with clinicians and family members as well as improving participation in treatment. Recommendation from these studies have called for focus on patient education, and ways to improve patient's understanding of their radiological images [2, 6]. Moreover, it is imperative that radiological reporting moves from being radiologist-centric to being patient-centric through better use of patient's capabilities and establishing better fit with the cognitive abilities of the patients [3].

1.1 Background

Over the years, radiology informatics efforts have focused on improving imaging based on the cognitive abilities of the radiologist [6]. However, more recently there has been

© Springer International Publishing AG 2017
V.G. Duffy (Ed.): DHM 2017, Part II, LNCS 10287, pp. 61–70, 2017.
DOI: 10.1007/978-3-319-58466-9_6

clamoring for patients to be more actively involved in their healthcare, which begs the question - how do we represent images and radiology reports for consumption by patients? [5]. Thus, tools, image viewers and reporting verbiage need to be adapted for consumption by patients. Some researchers have developed methods, primarily in the patient portal space, but most have only provided high-level concepts without creating tools that implement those concepts into practice [4]. The aim of our study and the developed tool that we report in this paper is to support the ways in which radiology images can be fit with the cognitive abilities of patients, regardless of their level of education, socio-economic background and medical literacy.

1.2   Purpose

The metadata in Digital Imaging and Communications in Medicine (DICOM) images contains information about patient identification, imaging equipment, health facility, provider and procedure performed. Moreover, DICOM stores the sequential order in which the images were captured and this information is used by image viewers for image display. If these images are transformed in anyway, it is important to preserve the metadata information, in order to protect the integrity of the radiology images to support accurate clinical diagnosis disease under study. DICOM metadata is standardized and well adopted with a number of viewers that can understand the embedded XML tags from DICOM images. One of the goals of our research is to maintain the metadata information in the images during interconversion between DICOM and JPG, as this would let us keep all the metadata information that is embedded in the DICOM image.

2   Related Work

One of the research conducted to solve a problem usually encountered in radiology reporting was based on patient education [4]. The authors developed a portal system to extract salient findings from reports and place them where patients can read. However, the authors focused a little less on the level of education of the consumers and also the simplicity of the reports to the barest minimum. We decided to build on this to present information on the images that can be easily assessable to the consumers.

Ujare and Baviskar performed research to convert DICOM images to other formats which are usually smaller in size [1]. The authors designed and developed a framework to extract patient information from a DICOM image and save it in a separate text file. The authors were more concerned about size reduction for ease of transfer rather than metadata preservation, which is relevant for batch processing. So, we extended the concept of information extraction to metadata reintegration into the images, after we edited images in a way that enhanced a user's understanding of the images presented to them.

3   Method

3.1   Problems and Challenges

As part of our research on 'Customizing Radiology Images to Improve Patient-Provider-Radiologist Communication' (Imaging 3.0), we labeled and colored certain parts of the radiology images (See Fig. 1) that are important to make observations related to the patient problem. Our study site is at a large tertiary hospital in central Indiana with over million outpatient visits each year, with many patients coming from low and middle income groups. This site was appropriate for our study, since it has patients with low medical literacy, but also has highly trained staff like nurses, physicians and radiologists from one of the largest medical schools in the US. As part of the study, we needed to customize images that fit the cognitive abilities of the three selected user groups – patients, referring physicians and radiologists. These three user groups were interviewed using a cognitive fit theory based semi-structured interview guide. To conduct the interviews and capture the effects of customized images on the user group's interpretation of the images, we needed a tool that will allow easy manipulation of radiology images. For the tool, our approach was to export the DICOM images from the Picture Archiving and Communication System (PACS), convert them into JPG format, then label/color the images either manually or automatically using image processing software and convert it back to DICOM images. These manipulated images can then be viewed in any DICOM viewer used by radiologists, physicians or patients.

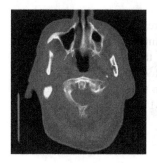 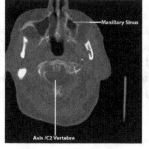 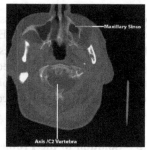

Original DICOM Image   Modified image in JPG   Reconverted DICOM

Fig. 1. The CT head were edited and was uploaded as a DICOM image in a DICOM viewer.

Although, we currently have applications that perform similar tasks, such as J2D, the limitation of such applications is that, when used to convert DICOM to JPG, the images lose metadata information like seriesID, instanceID, patient demographics etc. Therefore, these converted images do not appear in correct series or order. Many converters do not always maintain the same fidelity or image encoding as the original image in the DICOM format. The DICOM standard part 3.5 2016e Data Structures and Encoding specifies the encoding of pixel, overlay and waveform data. Section 8.2 of part 3.5 also defines Native or Encapsulated Format Encoding, such as JPEG image

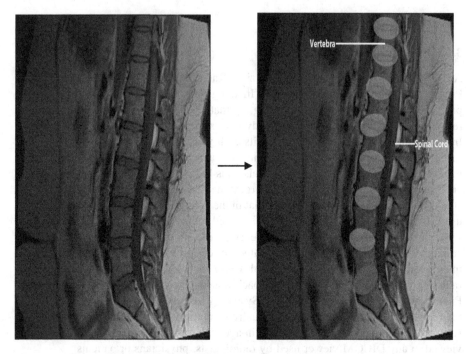

Fig. 2. Enhanced JPEG image prepared in photoshop

compression, RLE compression, JPEG-LS image compression, JPEG 2000 image compression, MPEG2, MPEG-4 AVC/H.264 video compression and lately even HEVC/H.265 video compression. The actual quality of the radiology image/video depends on this encapsulated format. Most conversion tools support only a single encapsulation format, most often with a lossy compression format. With the lack of a good converter, we developed a simple, yet novel DICOM image converter.

3.2 Solution to the Problem

We developed a Java SE application called Jpg2DicomTags, which facilitates conversion of DICOM to JPG and back to DICOM while retaining the metadata of the original DICOM image. The converted files are saved in the same folder as that of the JPG and can be viewed as a series of a single study in a DICOM viewer. We use the batch processing technique for selecting all original and modified images, and copying the tags back to the modified DICOM. Apart from this, it also provides the feature of converting a file from any valid encapsulation format to DICOM file format. The application does not require prior training, since it is a single screen interface (See Fig. 3), can be integrated with any Radiology Information System (RIS) or Electronic Health Record (EHR) system and works with all known DICOM – little endian or big endian file formats. We tested the converted DICOM images with Orthanc, dcm4chee, RadiANT, Horos, Osirix and MicroDicom viewers and PACS servers. We also tested

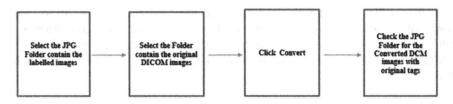

Fig. 3. Conversion of labelled JPG to DICOM with original tags.

the converted images to be accessed using Web Access to DICOM Objects (WADO) specification on browsers including on tablet and mobile devices. Our primary interface for the multi-user group interviews was on a tablet computer and a DICOM viewer, streaming images from a PACS server over WADO.

In order to have a near-accurate understanding of radiological images, we needed to enhance the images to aid participant's ability to interpret and be able to have a clear understanding of what is being shown to them. We started by exporting de-identified imaging studies from a proprietary PACS system at our research site. We then deployed the images creating fake patients on a PACS system that supports WADO standard called Orthanc [7]. We needed to use the DICOM web plugin with Orthanc to support our use-case. We selected different modalities of radiology images to ensure that our study covered a wide range of procedures. We selected 5 Magnetic Resonance Imaging (MRI) studies (Lumber spine – AX T1 TSE, T2 TSE, SAG STIR, SAG T1 TSE and SAG T2 TSE) with about 12 images in each study and 2 Computed Tomography (CT) – HEAD BONE and HEAD WO, one CHEST X-ray and one Ultrasound USG of the abdomen.

These images of the sample procedures used were still in DICOM format and the metadata tags were still intact. This is expected to support the associated batch processing activities used to guide participant's understanding of the study regardless of their level of education.

Following the selection of the samples, we needed to convert the DICOM images to plain jpeg, so that the image can be easily edited using automated or manual image processing software applications. To measure any visible change in the participants' cognitive abilities for our study, we needed to edit images. The correct ordering of the images from a study to show the progression of the affected parts of the body is important to convey meaning and make accurate medical interpretation of a radiology study. This is the main reason why the metadata tags have to be retained when we modified the images. However, retaining the tags during image-conversion was a major challenge. Although jpeg images also have metadata, since we could not find an application that currently performs that task, we had to go through a long process which resulted in the development of Jpg2DicomTags application.

3.3   Image Conversion Process

Jpg2DicomTags is able to recognize the encapsulated encoding of the image and extract the image data into JPEG 2000 lossless format. This extraction process helps keep the fidelity of the image after the image has been enhanced or edited using commonly available image processing software. We initially used MicroDicom, a DICOM viewer with an image-conversion capability to convert the images from DICOM to a JPEG format. We then modified the JPEG images using Adobe Photoshop.

3.4   Image Enhancement Process

Participants of the Cognitive-Fit study vary based on familiarity with clinical images, so we needed to enhance the images to be easily understood by anyone regardless of their level of education. Enhancing the images was also done to measure the improvement on the participants' cognitive ability by asking relevant questions. These questions were asked intermittently after the original and the enhanced images were shown to the participants (Fig. 2).

The next phase was the labeling and highlighting process using Adobe Photoshop. We started by labelling the images to show the affected part of the body it came from. We also used color-coding method to distinguish between the area on the image that was affected from the area that clinically unaffected. These steps were conducted on every image of the selected study procedures that we used for the research, while we maintained the serial identification assigned when the images were converted to JPEG. In the later phases of the study, we are automating the manual process by referring to the radiology report that has been interpreted by a radiology. We are using natural language processing and machine learning techniques to locate areas of interest that need to be labelled and colored automatically.

3.5   Development of Jpg2DicomTags Application

Following the completion of the image-enhancing process, we needed to convert the images back to DICOM format which would enable us to reintegrate the metadata into the images. DICOM viewers with conversion capabilities such as MicroDicom, and some other applications such as J2D were initially considered for this task. However, these applications were limited in their functionalities and could not retain the metadata information of the original DICOM images.

Jpg2DicomTags is licensed under the Apache License v2 because we believe that such a tool should be widely available for integration with viewers and PACS systems. The application was developed to support one-click tagging of a whole study during the conversion stage. The basic functionality of the application is to convert a JPEG format back to a DICOM format with the original tags added to the modified images in a study.

3.6   JPEG Format to DICOM Format Conversion Process

We used the application to perform the conversion process and it took us just about four steps to complete:

1. The application was initiated to reveal a user interface with options of choosing the folders containing both the modified study in .JPG format and the original. DCM format.
2. We selected the first option to locate the folder containing the newly-modified study.
3. We also selected the second option to locate the directory of the folder containing the original DICOM folder.
4. We converted the images by clicking the 'Convert' button on the interface of the application.

After the action was completed, the modified images in DICOM format was saved automatically in the same folder as the JPEG folder. These newly saved DICOM images inherited the tags from the original DICOM study which allowed the study to be well arranged so as for the consumers to view it in the correct order and also for other DICOM compatible application to read it in the correct order (Fig. 4).

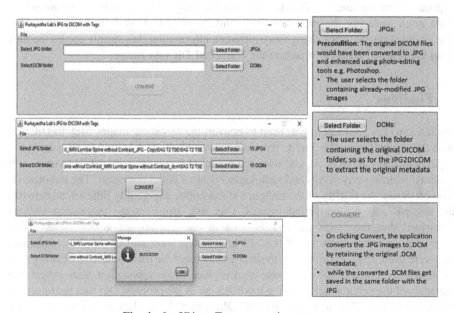

Fig. 4. Jpg2DicomTags conversion process

3.7   Comparative Analysis of the Tools

The following Table 1 shows the advantages that Jpg2DicomTags has over other tools.

Two-way Conversion: Tool converts from JPG to DICOM and DICOM to JPG. There are some tools that can only convert one-way, which results in loss of metadata information.

Table 1. Comparison of different features in jpg and DICOM conversion tools

Features	Comparative analysis of the tools			
	RadiANT	J2D	MicroDicom	Jpg2Dicomtags
Two-way conversion	✓	✓	✓	✓
Converts DICOM to. dcm	`		✓	✓
Retains resolution			✓	✓
One-click tagging				✓
No brand customization				✓

DICOM to.dcm: Allows the tool to convert DICOM files without.dcm file extension for easy recognition by other viewers. Jpg2DicomTags can rename files, as well as encapsulate valid formats with DICOM metadata.

One-Click Tagging: allows tagging of a series of instances into a single study in one click.

Brand Customization: Many other tools produce a watermark of the name of application on the images. This is either on the image data itself or in the metadata, most often replacing the metadata device information such as from MRI machines. Jpg2DicomTags does not change any metadata information, but simply copies the tags from the original DICOM image to the converted DICOM image.

4 Findings

Jpg2DicomTags application was used to convert the modified images back to DICOM with the original tags added to it. We have converted all the exported images using the Jpg2DicomTags application, and used the modified images in over 30 interviews with patients, referring physicians and radiologists using a tablet computer. The radiologists who often rate the fidelity of the images did not notice any quality differences between the original and the converted images. Our tests using image processing toolkits confirmed that there was no loss of data in the conversion process, with 100% pixel-to-pixel match between all the 112 images that were part of the four modalities that were used. Jpg2Dicom is able to successfully meet the main objective of being able to accurately convert the.jpg image to.dcm files. The application also injects the metadata of the original.dcm into the modified.jpg in the process. Our unit tests verified that there was 100% match in all the DICOM tags and metadata information between the 112 original and converted images. The performance of the application was excellent. The conversion process for all the 112 images took less than 2 s on a 2.0 Ghz Intel i3, 4 GB RAM desktop computer. The binary size of the application is under 3 Kb and only requires the Java Runtime Environment (JRE) v6 and higher. We also observed the application can handle as many images in a batch as possible. The criteria for the batch processing to begin is that, the count of the original DICOM images must coincide with the modified.jpg images.

Furthermore, it was observed that resolution of the images remains the same during the conversion from one format to the other. Most of the other applications capable of converting to or from DICOM format usually reduce the quality of the images in the process. However, Jpg2DicomTags retains the original quality and also leaves the images plain without any unwanted customization.

The converted images were tested with Orthanc, dcm4chee, RadiANT, Horos, Osirix and Microdicom viewers and PACS servers to examine any deviation from the original DICOM images. Our experience is that the tool works perfectly as expected. Therefore, it can be concluded that images converted with Jpg2DicomTags will be compatible with most viewers and PACS servers. The accuracy of the application is an important feature to be exploited in both research-based and clinical-based settings.

5   Discussion

Jpg2DicomTags was deliberately created as a single, one-click application so that it can be integrated with other tools such as DICOM viewers and PACS systems. In the process of developing this application, we realized that there is clearly a dearth of usable tools that can convert DICOM images in a simple and useful way. There are a number of DICOM manipulation software libraries, APIs and even software as a service (SaaS). Yet, most of these do not have a usable application that can be integrated easily with existing systems in the regular workflow of users. We also chose to develop the software application in Java, so that it was platform-independent and could be used on multiple platforms.

Jpg2DicomTags also has a few limitations. Firstly, it cannot work with video encapsulation formats such mpeg, which are also used in radiology. Since our modalities and use-case focused on the most common type of radiology modalities, we only work with images. Similarly, the tool is not able to process 3D images or audio that is used by the DICOM format. Secondly, the tool cannot use streaming data to convert data on the fly. It is designed to work in batch processing mode, primarily because our use-case was meant to work with batch data. Besides some rare edge cases, we don't see the need for a tool that does conversion and manipulation of the images to be able to perform conversion using streaming data source.

5.1   Contributions to Human Computer Interaction

This research serves as a template on which consumers' cognitive abilities can be examined to determine their preferences for radiology images. The process of preserving the metadata of DICOM images is a cog in a wheel of automated radiological reporting, which may be the next generation of reporting using more complex concept such as machine learning and analytics to determine patient's preferences and present images to patient's that can be easily understood.

6   Conclusion and Future Work

6.1   Future Opportunity of the Tool

In future, we will integrate the editing features such as labeling, overview on hovering on sections of the images and also coloring in the same viewer/editor while retaining the metadata during the process of conversion. We will release the tool as a plugin that can be integrated with multiple DICOM viewers and we hope that further research can be conducted in this field by anyone who is interested in improving radiology reporting procedures.

References

1. Ujgare, S.N., Baviskar, S.P.: Conversion of DICOM image into JPEG, BMP and PNG image format. Int. J. Comput. Appl. **62**(11), 0975–8887 (2013)
2. Mangano, M.D., Rahman, A., Choy, G., Sahani, D.V., Boland, G.W., Gunn, A.J.: Radiologists' role in the communication of imaging examination results to patients: perceptions and preferences of patients. AJR Am. J. Roentgenol. **203**(5), 1034–1039 (2014). doi:10.2214/ajr.14.12470
3. Johnson, A.J., Easterling, D., Williams, L.S., Glover, S., Frankel, R.M.: Insight from patients for radiologists: improving our reporting systems. J. Am. Coll. Radiol. **6**(11), 786–794 (2009). doi:10.1016/j.jacr.2009.07.010
4. Arnold, C.W., McNamara, M., El-Saden, S., Chen, S., Taira, R.K., Bui, A.A.: Imaging informatics for consumer health: towards a radiology patient portal. J. Am. Med. Inform. Assoc. **20**(6), 1028–1036 (2013). https://www.ncbi.nlm.nih.gov/pmc/articles/PMC3822110/pdf/amiajnl-2012-001457.pdf. doi:10.1136/amiajnl-2012-001457
5. Jacob, J.: Consumer access to health care information: its effect on the physician-patient relationship. Alaska Med. **44**(4), 75–82 (2002)
6. Koehring, A., Foo, J.L., Miyano, G., Lobe, T., Winer, E.: A framework for interactive visualization of digital medical images. J. Laparoendosc. Adv. Surg. Tech. A **18**(5), 697–706 (2008). doi:10.1089/lap.2007.0240
7. Orthanc in a nutshell. http://www.orthanc-server.com/static.php?page=about

Eye Movement Differences Between Novices and Expert Surgeons in Laparoscopic Surgery Simulator

Hisanori Shiomi[1(✉)], Kazuaki Yamashiro[3], Kouichirou Murakami[2],
Hiroyuki Ohta[2], Tomoko Ota[4], Yuki Miyamoto[4], Yuka Takai[3],
Akihiko Goto[3], Hiroyuki Hamada[5], and Masaji Tani[2]

[1] Nagahama Red Cross Hospital, Nagahama, Shiga, Japan
shiomi@belle.shiga-med.ac.jp
[2] Shiga University of Medical Science, Otsu, Shiga, Japan
{emkami,hohta,mtani}@belle.shiga-med.ac.jp
[3] Osaka Sangyo University, Daito/Osaka, Japan
k.yamashiro546@gmail.com,
{takai,gotoh}@ise.osaka-sandai.ac.jp
[4] Chuo Business Group, Osaka, Japan
tomoko_ota_cbg@yahoo.co.jp, miyamoto.yuki12@gmail.com
[5] Kyoto Institute of Technology, Kyoto, Japan
hhamada@kit.ac.jp

Abstract. Laparoscopic surgery is thought to be more difficult to acquire the surgical technique compared with conventional one. Eye movement differences between novices and experts have been shown in the various fields. However, a few papers compared the eye gaze movement behavior of novice and expert surgeons during performance of a laparoscopic surgery task with a simulator. The examinee operated the same case of the laparoscopic cholecystectomy of the simulator, and the eye movement detection method was a pupil corneal reflection method. The expert operator showed economical hand and eye movement compared with novices. Once their act change to a camera operator, their gaze behavior seemed to change to the trainer's one. The medical students improved to shorten the duration time in procedure in one week of training, however, the gaging pattern did not change. Using this eye tracking system, the new educational system can be established to train the medical student, novice surgeon, and also expert surgeons as trainer.

Keywords: Surgical training · Laparoscopic surgery · Eye-tracking

1 Introduction

Laparoscopic surgery has been developed from 1990s, rapidly. Compared with the conventional open operation, it is characterized to use video system during hand-eye co-ordination, and thought to be more difficult to acquire the surgical technique [1].

Eye movement differences between novices and experts have been shown in the various fields, such as pilots and radiologists [2, 3]. Thus, the domain knowledge and

© Springer International Publishing AG 2017
V.G. Duffy (Ed.): DHM 2017, Part II, LNCS 10287, pp. 71–78, 2017.
DOI: 10.1007/978-3-319-58466-9_7

experience affect the performance and eye movement on the related task. So far, a few papers compared the eye gaze movement behavior of novice and expert surgeons during performance of a laparoscopic surgery task with a simulator. Here we describe the hand motion and eye movement analysis during operation of laparoscopic cholecystectomy on simulator

2   Method

The examinee operated the same case of the laparoscopic cholecystectomy of the simulator, LapVR, according to the guidance of the software. The eye movement was measured by TalkEyeII (Takei Scientific Instruments) and EMR ACTUS (nac Image Technology Inc.). The eye movement detection method was a pupil corneal reflection method, and the detection rate was 60 Hz. The surgery contents were devided into 5 parts; dissection of the triangle of Calot and identification of the cystic duct and the cystic artery (step 1), clipping and cut of the cystic duct (step 2), clipping and cut of the cystic artery (step 3), dissecting of the gallbladder away from the gallbladder bed (step 4), removing the specimen and irrigate the abdominal cavity, if necessary (step 5). The movement of the operator's hands was analyzed from the video. The simulation was done in two settings, conducted by the solo operator and with a camera operator wearing the eye tracking glasses.

2.1   Experiment 1

The expert and novice surgeons operated cholecystectomy on the simulator with same scenario. Their eye movement was analyzed as described above. Also, their touch field of both hands were analyzed by the video.

2.2   Experiment 2

Four stuff surgeons demonstrated laparoscopic cholecystectomy using the simulator, and they explained their procedure at the same time. Twenty-three medical students did same scenario, and the stuff surgeon instructed them. The trainer's talking was recorded with video, and analyzed its contents. The contents were categorized into four elements, procedure, how to use surgical instrument, how to use the simulator, and how to deal with intraoperative complication. The two factors, procedure and how to use the surgical instruments, were divided into several elements, such as, organs, surgical forceps, handling, and directions, and their combination.

3   Result

3.1   Experience 1

In step 1, the operative field is relatively narrow, and the right hand of the novices touched the triangle of Calot, and the left hand the neck of the gallbladder, mainly.

Their left hand grasped and released the gallbladder, frequently (Fig. 1a). However, most of the period, their right hand touched nothing, because they encountered the complication, such as bleeding (Fig. 1b). In step 2 and 3, the operator needs to change their right hand's operative instrument at least 4 times (Fig. 1c). The novices gazed the tip of the forceps, when they insert it. In step 4, the operative field enlarged compared with step 1, 2, and 3. The novices gazed their right hand for longer time than gallbladder (Fig. 1d).

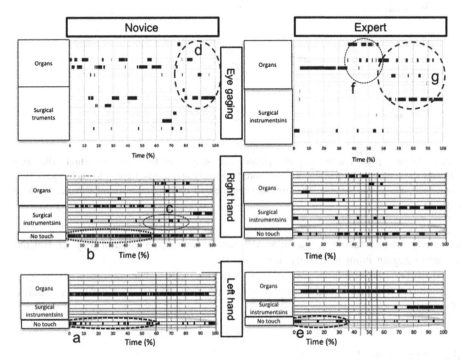

Fig. 1. The gaging pattern and the movement of left and right hand of stuff surgeon and novice surgeon. Novice's left hand grasped and released the gallbladder, frequently (a). However, most of the period, their right hand touched nothing, because they encountered the complication, such as bleeding (b). In step 2 and 3, the operator needs to change their right hand's operative instrument at least 4 times (c). The novices gazed the tip of the forceps, when they insert it. In step 4, the operative field enlarged compared with step 1, 2, and 3. The novices gazed their right hand for longer time than gallbladder (d).

On the other hand, the expert surgeon gazed the triangle of Calot in step 1. They once grasped the gallbladder, their left hand did not release it (Fig. 1e). In step 2 and 3, the expert gazed the target organ such as cystic duct and cystic artery, not the tip of the surgical instrument they insert (Fig. 1f). In step 4, the expert looked right hand (forceps) and the grasped gallbladder one after another. (Fig. 1g).

During the simulation of the novice surgeon as an operator, the gaging point of both novice and stuff surgeon as a scopist. The gaging point of stuff surgeon was then

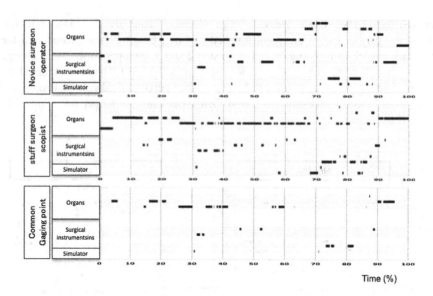

Fig. 2. Gaging pattern difference of operator and scopist in the same operation. The stuff surgeon's eye movement pattern showed more frequently coming and going to each organ, as if novice surgeon as an operator. The stuff surgeon focused on surgical instrument more, when he acted as a scopist.

discretely, and its pattern was similar with that of the novice surgeon (Fig. 2). But the common gaging point were only 32%.

However, the common gaging point was only 32%. The gaging point of stuff surgeon as an operator and a scopist was quite different, even in the same scenario (Fig. 3).

3.2   Experience 2

In the step 2, the duration from insertion of the forceps to reaching to the target organ with right hand was analyzed. The average time in second time was 13.3 s and significantly shorter than that in first time, 22.4 s (p < 0.05, Fig. 4).

Figure 5 shows the gaging pattern to organ, such as gallbladder, cystic duct, and cystic artery, and forceps. The stuff surgeon finished step 2 in a short time, and the gaging pattern were well organized. The gaging pattern of medical students were various. Medical student A gaged organ and forceps in longer time as stuff surgeon and the times that his gaging points come and go were more frequent. The gaging point of student B showed coming and going ceaselessly. Most students reduced their time in step 2, however its gaging pattern did not change (Fig. 6).

The content of teaching was investigated from the video and the stuff surgeon explain his procedure more, but fewer in how to use surgical instrument and how to deal with complication, such as bleeding and bile leakage (Fig. 7).

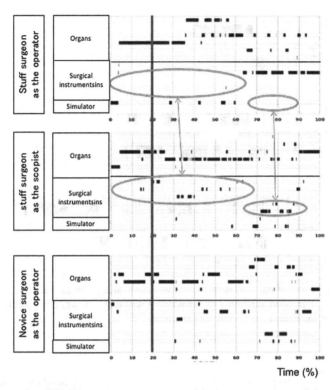

Fig. 3. Gaging pattern difference of stuff surgeon as as operator and a scopist. The stuff surgeon's eye movement pattern as a scopist showed more frequently coming and going to each organ and surgical instruments, as if novice surgeon as an operator.

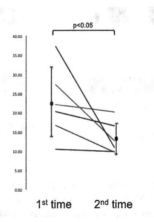

Fig. 4. The duration time of reaching the objective organs by the surgical instrument from insertion into the abdominal cavity. At 1st time, the time was 22.4 s in average, but reduced to 13.3 s, significantly ($p < 0.05$).

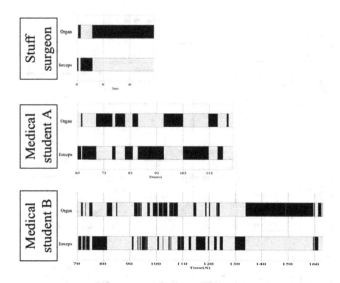

Fig. 5. Gaging pattern of the stuff surgeon, and two medical students in the step 2, clipping and cut of the cystic duct. Stuff surgeon's eye movement was reduced, while the medical students' were unified but frequent, or discretely and frequent.

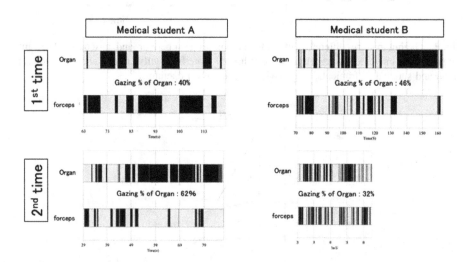

Fig. 6. Gaging pattern of the medical students during their operation on the simulator in 1st time and 2nd time. Organ contains gallbladder, bile duct, cystic duct, cystic artery, and liver. Forceps means various surgical instrument such as grasper, scissors, and dissector.

In detail, the stuff surgeon explained more about anatomy, but taught to medical students focusing on the direction and handling of organ movement (Fig. 8).

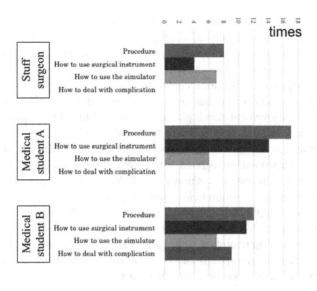

Fig. 7. The contents of explanation during operation of the stuff surgeon himself and guidance during medical student's operation.

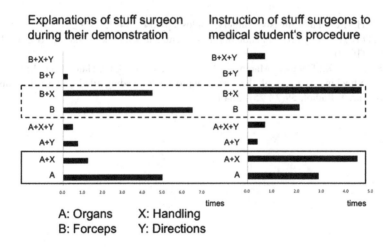

Fig. 8. Explanation details from the video during the stuff surgeon's demonstration and instruction during the medical student's procedure on the simulator. Stuff surgeon explained much about anatomy in their demonstration, but more focused in directions of organs or forceps.

4 Discussion

In this study, differences of gaze behavior and hand movement in various level of surgeon were analyzed using laparoscopic surgery simulator. The expert operator showed economical hand and eye movement compared with novices. Once their act change to a camera operator, their gaze behavior seemed to change to the trainer's one. However, its coherence was only 32% (Fig. 2). The expert surgeon (stuff surgeon) gaged to surgical instrument more, when they act as a scopist, suggesting that they made sure the operation had done safely.

From the analysis of medical students, the time of the surgical procedure were easily shortened in a short period, but the eye movement did not make more efficient at the same time. Eye movement development may more difficult to acquire than that of simple task in laparoscopic surgery. From these data, it is suggested that the gaging pattern may be a new indicator to show proficiency level of each surgeon.

When expert surgeon demonstrated their operation and guidance it at the same time, they focused more on the anatomy of cholecystectomy, not how to use the instrument, how to make operation field to move organs using forceps, and how to deal with intraoperative complication. In actual surgery, such information is more important, but a few surgical textbook and text videos show successful cases. Also, the content of teaching during operation were various in each medical student. From these points, the new educational system can be established to train the medical student, novice surgeon, and also expert surgeons as trainer.

References

1. Fuchs, K.H.: Minimally invasive surgery. Endoscopy **34**, 154–159 (2002)
2. Ballard, D.H.: Hand-eye coordination during sequential tasks. Philos. Trans. R. Soc. Biol. Sci. **337**, 331 (1992)
3. Ellis, S.M., Hu, X., Dempere-Marco, L., Yang, G.Z., Wells, A.U., Hansell, D.M.: CT of the lungs: eye-tracking analysis of the visual approach to reading tiled and stacked display formats. Eur. J. Radiol. **59**(2), 257–264 (2006)

Evaluation Methods to Support Health Information Systems Development: A Framework Supported in Literature and Practical Experience

Leonor Teixeira[1,3(✉)], Beatriz Sousa Santos[2,3], Vasco Saavedra[1],
and Carlos Ferreira[1,3]

[1] Department of Economics, Management and Industrial Engineering,
University of Aveiro, Aveiro, Portugal
{lteixeira,vsaavedra,carlosf}@ua.pt
[2] Department of Electronics, Telecommunications and Informatics,
University of Aveiro, Aveiro, Portugal
bss@ua.pt
[3] Institute of Electronics and Informatics Engineering of Aveiro (IEETA),
Aveiro, Portugal

Abstract. Given the diversity and complexity of the Health Information Systems (HIS), and taking into account the impact of this type of systems in the clinical performance and patient outcome, a rigorous evaluation process in the system development life cycle (SDLC) is extremely important. An effective evaluation during development not only promotes the quality of the final solution, but also ensures motivated users, error-free systems, and can even establish good practices to minimize costs in future developments. However, the HIS evaluation is a difficult process due to the complex nature of the health care domain, the objects being evaluated, as well as the comprehensiveness of the concept of the evaluation itself. The present work intends to explore, based on a literature review, the main methods of HIS evaluation to support the development, identifying in which stage of the SDLC these methods can be applied. Additionally, this work discusses the reasons for the evaluation of such systems, illustrating these issues with two real case studies of HIS implementations, in which some of the methods were successfully applied.

Keywords: Health Information System · Evaluation methods · SDLC · Formative · Summative · User-centred

1 Introduction

The concept of Health Information Systems (HIS) comprehends the widest range of information technologies used in healthcare systems to assist healthcare organisations in order to gather and process data, as well as disseminate information. This type of systems have the potential to increase efficiency and, at the same time, saving considerable amounts of health expenditure [1]. Actually, HIS incorporate a variety of different types of systems, such as: patient information systems, clinical information

© Springer International Publishing AG 2017
V.G. Duffy (Ed.): DHM 2017, Part II, LNCS 10287, pp. 79–90, 2017.
DOI: 10.1007/978-3-319-58466-9_8

systems, clinical decision support systems, administrative systems, radiology information systems, pharmacy information systems, laboratory information systems, hospital information systems, among others aimed for information management [2].

Given the diversity and complexity of HIS, and taking into account that the goal of this type of systems is to improve the clinical performance and patient outcome, assuring the quality, effectiveness and efficiency of health services, a rigorous evaluation to get the most benefits out of an HIS is extremely important.

However, the HIS evaluation is a difficult process due to the complex nature of the health care domain and the objects to be evaluated [3], as well as the comprehensiveness of the concept of evaluation itself [4]. The evaluation of HIS involves the assessment of the application and its impact on the organizational environment in which it is implemented, determining the systems effectiveness and efficiency, level of user's satisfaction, the systems' usability level, as well as the weaknesses and strengths of these systems.

Regarding the evaluation itself, there are different evaluation perspectives, taking into account different motivations and involving different stakeholders. The very definition of HIS evaluation differs in the literature, according to the focus given to the study. Some evaluation approaches are focusing on economic criteria [5–7], and others on user-oriented criteria [8–10].

One of the definitions that meets the most consensus is presented by Ammenwerth et al. [11] that defines HIS evaluation as "the act of measuring or exploring properties of a HIS in planning, development, implementation, and operation, the result of which informs a decision to be made concerning that systems in a specific context". Another important study about HIS evaluation that tries to address some questions (*who*, *what*, *how*, *when* and *why*) related with evaluation activities and that integrates technological, human, social and organisational issues, was presented by Yusof et al. [12]. According to theses authors, the evaluation seeks to answer five questions: *why* (objective of the evaluation); *who* (stakeholders and their needs and perspectives); *when* (phase in the system development life cycle - SDLC); *what* (focus of evaluation); and, *how* (methods used in evaluation).

Despite the large body of literature on HIS evaluation and the emergence of different guidelines to reduce the complexity of the evaluation of HIS, the reality shows difficulties related to these evaluations, particularly in terms of the methods to be used and phases of the SDLC in which they should be applied.

Thus, this work aims to explore, based on the literature review, the main methods of HIS evaluation to support the development, identifying in which stage of the SDLC which methods can be applied. It is intended that this work covers the whole life cycle of HIS with emphasis on the formative process, from the requirements analysis to development. Additionally, this work discusses the reasons for the evaluation of such systems, and the issues discussed will be illustrated using two real case studies on the implementation of HIS, in which some of the methods were successfully applied.

2   Theoretical Background

2.1   Health Information Systems and the Importance of an Evaluation Process

The role of HIS in medical practice has changed significantly over the past 5 decades. Initially, and as in other types of sectors, the technologies were developed to support the operationalization of administrative functions, increasing work efficiency and reducing operative costs. Currently HIS are used to support any area in the health organisations, with a particular relevance in the management of the patient's clinical information, thus having a great impact on clinical practice and on the communication between healthcare providers and their patients [13].

Nonetheless, for an HIS to reach its maximum potential, it should: (i) be designed and implemented effectively, (ii) be accepted and properly adopted by its potential users, (iii) benefits the system where it is inserted, taking into account the purpose for which it was developed. In this context, the evaluation of HIS becomes an extremely important activity, as it allows to measure, characterize and predict the level of success of the HIS in the context of clinical practice. As in any other area, it is difficult to know the real benefits and the impact of an IS in its environment, without going through an evaluation process.

In the real world, the evaluation process by itself is quite comprehensive, and may have different objectives, be driven by different interest groups or even be supported by different theories. In practice, and taking into account the vast literature on the subject, there are different types of evaluation, which can be classified into one of two major groups: (i) a process that ensures that the product under evaluation meets the requirements and needs of information, satisfies the organizational objectives, is free of bugs, resulting in a functional product, usable, and well accepted by potential users [9, 10]; (ii) a process that allows determining the impact of the product in the sector, thus providing a set of benefits to the environment where it is inserted, measured in terms of costs, quality of service, work efficiency and patient safety [14–16].

Although these evaluation processes have a relationship of dependency (since the result of the former will in some way influence the result of the latter), evaluation studies are often conducted by different interest groups, sometimes even in different research disciplines. In the first case we can find this type of studies in areas related to Software Engineering and Usability Engineering. In the second case, this type of study is often conducted by researchers in the areas of Social Sciences in order to understand certain economic, social or cultural phenomena.

2.2   System Development Life Cycle Focused Evaluation

The HIS are complex systems [3]. However, given the impact these systems have on a healthcare context, they are classified into the group of systems with 'zero tolerance' to failures. Thus, SDLC focused evaluation emerges as a powerful tool to be used, not only to minimize the possibility of failure, but also to ensure that technologies are enabled to fulfil their potential in improving care, reducing cost and increasing efficiency [17]. Evaluation allows to understand how and under what conditions HIS work, and determine the safety and effectiveness of the system [1], at the same time as it allows to collect evidences about the good practices, effects and impacts of the technologies.

Studies related to the evaluation of technologies using the most diverse techniques have been performed since 1960's [11]. In the case of HIS, most of these studies started by focusing on how these technologies are related to professionals, management and user involvement, coming later to integrate issues related with lessons learned with the process of HIS development [18]. From the 1980s studies related to user acceptance and adoption technologies in health care organizations began to appear [18].

Regarding evaluation in the HIS development, some reference studies have appeared in the last two decades; the Kaplan and Shaw' [19] study is noteworthy as it presents a review of how aspects related to people, social and organizational issues have been considered in HIS evaluations, emphasizing the importance of using evaluation mechanisms during the whole SDLC. Nykänen and Kaipio [18] also state that the focus of HIS evaluation changes during its life cycle, being that in the implementation phase evaluation often addresses technical aspects, but with a completed system the evaluation focuses on impact on quality of service and on patient care. Gremy et al. [20] and Kushniruk [9] also present frameworks that support the evaluation along the SDLC. While the former highlight the role of humans in the five step evaluation process, i.e., conception, preparation of machine, execution of the program, output, and general impact; the framework proposed by Kushniruk [9], considers the evaluation process as an iterative process, using qualitative methods in different stages of a SDLC. Ammenwerth and De Keizer [5] found interesting developments in evaluation research in a period of 20 years (1982–2002), prevailing in these studies the explanatory research and quantitative methods.

It should be noted that in the last two decades, there have been many evaluation studies that focused on the users' perspective and the usability of the systems, due to the recognition of the importance of good usability of HIS and its impact on the health care practice [9, 21]. The evaluation with focus on usability techniques during the development process has also aroused the interest of many researchers in this area of knowledge [9, 10, 22].

In general, HIS evaluation is related with the human, technology and context of utilization. However, it is complex and represents a major challenge due to the complex nature of the health care domain and the object to be evaluated [3]. In order to minimize this difficulty, several studies have appeared with proposals of HIS evaluation frameworks, taking into account human, social, organizational, and cultural aspects [2, 12, 19, 23, 24]. The study by Yusofa et al. [2] presents the analysis of some HIS evaluation frameworks, concluding that "these frameworks complement each other in that they each evaluate different aspects of HIS pertinent to human, organizational and technological factors", and "not provide explicit evaluation categories to the evaluator". Andargoli et al. [7] also present an interesting review of the literature on evaluation frameworks, classifying them in: (i) SDLC focused; (ii) generic; (iii) social relationships focused, and (iv) behavioural focused evaluation frameworks. Based on this study, the authors conclude that, although there are several frameworks, there seems to be a lack of consensus regarding *what* to evaluate, *when* to carry out the evaluation, and *how* to conduct the evaluation.

In another perspective, and according to Symons [25], an effective evaluation of an Information System (IS) requires a comprehensive understanding of the interaction between *content, processes* and *context*. *Content* refers to the characteristics of the technology in study; *Context* refers to the environment in which the implementation takes place; and *Process* is the way through which the implementation is conducted. The Content, Context, Process (CCP) model was originally proposed by Pettigrew [26] in the scope of management and organizational change. Later, this model was adapted by Symons [25] for the IS evaluation, currently being used by several other authors to overcome the limitations of the generic frameworks of IS evaluation, since the CCP model represents a flexible solution that can easily be extended to any problem and application domain.

Some authors attempted to accommodate in a single model the answer to *what, how, when, why and who* questions, and the CCP framework. The *Content* dimension of the model refers to a particular area under examination and is concerned with the subject of evaluation – *what*. The *process* dimension focuses on questions of *when* evaluation takes place, and *how* evaluation is performed. The *Context* dimension aims to capture *why* evaluation is carried out and *who* is involved in the evaluation. [6, 7].

3   Methods and Tools to Evaluate HIS in Development Life Cycle

Regarding the evaluation methods in the HIS development, some studies argue that the best ones emerged from the Cognitive Sciences and Engineering of the Human Factor and can be applied at any phase of the SDLC (formative evaluation), or even in the final stage after the developed product (summative evaluation) [6, 17, 18, 23, 27, 28]. This argument is not oblivious to the fact that all Interactive Information System (IIS) that are designed to be used by people must meet all their needs and expectations as, if not, it may lead to dissatisfaction and consequently to the rejection of the product. If on one hand the IIS is characterized as a functional product that exists to help solving a problem within an organization and allowing increased organizational efficiency, on the other, the IIS without the user component does not make sense, and thus the user emerges as one of the central elements in the context of IISs.

The framework described in Fig. 1, supported in the models of Stockdale and Standing [6] and Andargoli et al. [7], maps the answers to *what, how, when, why* and *who* questions into the CCP model.

Comparing with the previous models presented by Stockdale and Standing [6] and by Andargoli et al. [7], this framework adds the order in which the answers to the questions *"what, how, when, why* and *who"* must be found.

Before any evaluation process, the motivation must be found, i.e., the reason that led to the need for the evaluation. Thus, the answer to the *why* question should be the starting point, since it represents the reason which the evaluation will be done. Given this motivation, we should look at how to achieve that motivation through content, i.e. by answering the '*what* to evaluate'. Taking into account the content, it is possible to

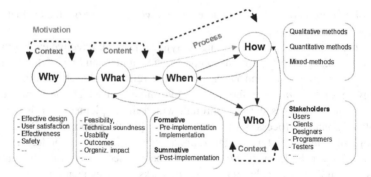

Fig. 1. Framework mapping the answer to *what, how, when, why* and *who* into the CCP model

identify the process, namely, at which stage the evaluation product should be performed (*when*), *how* this evaluation should be accomplished in terms of the methods to be used, as well as, which stakeholders should be involved in the evaluation process (*who*). It should be noted that the stakeholders to be involved heavily depends on the evaluation phase and the method chosen for this evaluation.

Thus, the models to be used in an evaluation process (*how*) are determined by the phase to be evaluated (*when*), by the type of evaluation to be performed (*what*), which in turn depends on the objective that is in the origin of the evaluation (*why*).

As mentioned there are formative and summative approaches containing different evaluation measures, some of them focusing on economic criteria and others on user-oriented criteria. While formative evaluation aims to provide feedback to the designers and programmers and is focused on the user-oriented criteria, the summative evaluation is concerned with assessing the outcome after the technology is completed, and usually can focus on either user-oriented or economic criteria. In particular case of formative evaluation, it is important to collect measurements during the pre-implementation stage to establish a basis for comparison, and during the implementation to evaluate changes and make adjustments into the process.

Focusing on user-oriented methods, these can be used in the scope of a formative evaluation to ensure that the product under development takes into account the needs of the users, and also in the context of a summative evaluation, to ensure that the final product conforms to the pre-defined specifications and matches the users' expectations in terms of usability.

Regarding the evaluation methods, several tools classified in qualitative, quantitative and mixed-methods are available [7, 17, 29].

Table 1 presents some of the most used methods in the context of HIS evaluation, having the ones that combine several techniques presented better results. These methods can be used in the different phases of SDLC.

Figure 2 presents the most appropriate methods for each development phase, although any of them can be used in a combined approach at different stages of development.

Table 1. Most used methods and tools to evaluate HIS in SDLC

When (phase)		*How* (methods and tools)
Formative evaluation	Pre-implementation	- Workflow
	Implementation	- Job analysis
Summative evaluation	Post-implementation	- Documentation analysis
		- Task analysis
		- Observation
		- Ethnography
		- Interviews
		- Questionnaires
		- Focus groups
		- Heuristic evaluation
		- Prototype
		- Usability testing
		- Cognitive walkthroughs
		- Video analysis
		- Logging
		- Randomized trials
		- Cost-effectiveness analyses
		- Cost-benefit analyses

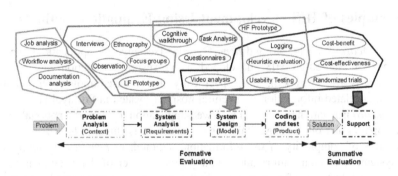

Fig. 2. Main methods and tools used in HIS development

In order to understand the problem – **problem analysis phase** –, it is necessary to be aware of the processes and the activities involved. In this stage the workflow analysis and job analysis represents the most suitable methods.

The requirements analysis stage – **system analysis** –, which also arises in a pre-liminary stage of development, requires the knowledge of the user's tasks, their needs, as well as the understanding of the users' mental model. During this stage, several methods can be applied, from traditional social sciences (such as observation, interviews, focus groups, ethnography, and questionnaire) to methods that evaluate socio-cognitive aspects (such as task analysis, video analysis, and cognitive walkthroughs using low-fidelity prototype) [9, 10, 30].

In the project stage – **system design phase** –, the evaluation techniques are particularly useful because they ensure that the model includes all the requirements described in the system specification. In this phase (and since the representation is abstract, usually in UML or another graphic representation language), the method of prototyping (low-fidelity and/or high-fidelity prototype), coupled with methods from usability engineering, such as usability tests and heuristic evaluation, are the most suitable for evaluation [31]. The questionnaire could also be used in conjunction with usability tests, as well as task analysis, video analysis, and cognitive walkthroughs to validate the mental model.

In the development stage – **coding and test phase** –, the same techniques used in the project phase are used, and at this stage the low-fidelity prototype is no longer necessary, since all the tests can already be executed using components or the final product (evolutionary prototype or high-fidelity prototype).

Finally, after the product is developed – **support** –, we have the usability tests, video analysis, heuristic evaluation, and logging (in field studies) to ensure that the product is usable, correctly used and well accepted by the user community. Field studies are evaluation studies that usually occurs in natural settings to know how people interact with technology in the real world [32], and is widely used with the logging method. From an economic perspective, we have randomized trials, cost-effectiveness analyzes and cost-benefit analyzes techniques.

4   Examples of HIS Development Using Evaluation Methods

The *hemo@care* (see Fig. 3a) and *hemo@record* (see Fig. 3b) applications represent two types of web-based HIS, developed using several evaluation methods. The *hemo@care* is a local system, more specifically, a web-based application to manage haemophilia-related information in a central hospital located in Portugal [13, 33]. The *hemo@record* is a national system, i.e., a web-application to support a national registry of haemophilia and other congenital coagulopathies in Portugal [34–36].

In terms of complexity of the information, although of *hemo@care* represents a local system, it contains information with a greater level of detail comparing with *hemo@record*. In terms of requirements, in the case of the former, and because it is a local system, the requirements were collected in a single hospital, involving clinicians,

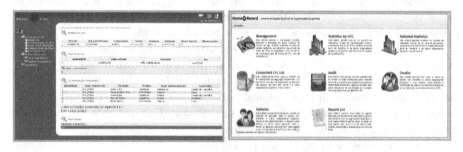

Fig. 3   (a) Hemo@care (b) Hemo@record

nurses and people with hemophilia (PWH). In the later, as it represents a national system for the exclusive use of clinicians, the requirements have been collected from a group of clinicians that work in hemophilia care from several hospitals located in different Portuguese cities.

Given the particularities of each system, the evaluation methods used in the development process of each one were different.

In order to **understand the problem** context in the case of *hemo@care*, workflow analysis techniques complemented with documentation analysis were used [10]. Since *hemo@record* did not fit into the specific organizational system, the understanding of the problem component was performed using benchmarking techniques, analyzing several national registration systems that were already successfully implemented in other countries [37].

Regarding the **requirements elicitation**, techniques such as documentation analysis, direct observation, ethnography, focus group, interviews, and task analysis were used, following a triangular approach [8, 10, 30]. The task analysis method was particularly useful for understanding the user's mental model, in a complex requirements elicitation context [30]. In the particular case of *hemo@record*, the focus group was the technique that most contributed to the final result, being the meetings mediated with the help of a collaborative prototype [31]. The usage of a prototype at this stage promoted the requirements elicitation, and at the same time assisted in the conversion of implicit knowledge (user experience) in explicit knowledge (documented knowledge).

At the **design and development phase**, in the case of *hemo@care*, evolutionary prototyping and task analysis were the tools that most stood out, and were complemented with heuristic evaluation, usability tests and questionnaire. Regarding the task analysis in this stage, it allowed to validate the functionalities previously found and simultaneously allowed to understand the user mental model in order to find the best sequence to present information within the scope of the functionality. For *hemo@record*, the methods which provided better results were the prototyping through mock-ups [31], as well as the heuristic evaluation. The prototype in this stage allowed validate de functionalities previously identified and find new requirements.

It should be noted that in both cases the application development processes followed an iterative and incremental approach.

The experience of the development of these two HIS allowed us to conclude that, given the nature of the problem and the type of HIS, we should carefully choose the evaluation techniques to support the development of technology. This is justified by the fact that the same techniques can provide different results according to the type of system, so it is necessary to adjust the method to the problem in study.

5   Summary and Conclusions

Evaluation of HIS development is a very important procedure to determine the impact of technology, as well as to assure the quality of the final solution.

Moreover, besides the importance of HIS evaluation, the challenge of an evaluation process is greatly due to the complex nature of the health care domain, the objects to be evaluated, and the comprehensiveness of the concept of evaluation itself. The literature reports the lack of consideration of some evaluation aspects in HIS development, more specifically in terms of the methods to be used and phases of the SDLC in which these methods should be applied.

The present work described a study that explored the main methods of HIS evaluation to support the development, identifying in which stage of the SDLC these methods can be applied. Additionally, this work presented the reasons for the evaluation of such systems, illustrating these issues with the example of two real case studies of HIS implementations, in which some of the methods were successfully applied.

From this investigation emerged a proposal of a framework that portrays the mapping of the five evaluation questions – *what, how, when, why* and *who* – in the Content, Context, Process (CCP) model, highlighting the order in which those questions should be answered. Additionally, a model based on literature review and fine-tuned with the results of the practical experience from implementing two HIS – *hemo@care* and *hemo@record* – that assists in the choice of the evaluation method according to the SDLC phase, was proposed.

Regarding the evaluation methods at each stage of the SDLC, the contextual methods that involve the user in his/her work environment, such as workflow analysis and job analysis, direct observation, ethnography and on-site interviews for the phases of problem understanding and requirement analysis should be highlighted. In the project phase, the prototyping technique represents a good alternative to simulate real scenarios, and presents excellent results when used in conjunction with usability tests and heuristic evaluation. Also the task analysis technique is an important method in the project phase to aid in the understanding of the mental model and the conversion of tacit knowledge in explicit knowledge. In the development phase, although it makes sense to use the same techniques used in the design phase, high-fidelity prototypes, more specifically evolutionary prototypes, developed with the same technology as the final solution should be preferred.

Finally, it is important to note that the complete evaluation process should take into account an iterative and incremental development approach, thus allowing the possibility to detect and correct previous failures.

Acknowledgments. This work is funded by National Funds through FCT - Foundation for Science and Technology, in the context of the project PEst-OE/EEI/UI0127/2014.

References

1. Sligo, J., Gauld, R., Roberts, V., Villa, L.: A literature review for large-scale health information system project planning, implementation and evaluation. Int. J. Med. Inform. **97**, 86–97 (2017)
2. Yusof, M.M., Papazafeiropoulou, A., Paul, R.J., Stergioulas, L.K.: Investigating evaluation frameworks for health information systems. Int. J. Med. Inform. **77**, 377–385 (2008)
3. Alalwany, H., Alshawi, S.: The rationale of e-health evaluation: the case of NHS Direct. Int. J. Bus. Inf. Syst. **9**, 484–497 (2012)
4. Ammenwerth, E., Gräber, S., Herrmann, G., Bürkle, T., König, J.: Evaluation of health information systems - problems and challenges. Int. J. Med. Inform. **71**, 125–135 (2003)

5. Ammenwerth, E., De Keizer, N.: An inventory of evaluation studies of information technology in health care: trends in evaluation research 1982–2002. Methods Inf. Med. **44**, 44–56 (2005)

6. Stockdale, R., Standing, C.: An interpretive approach to evaluating information systems: a content, context, process framework. Eur. J. Oper. Res. **173**, 1090–1102 (2006)

7. Andargoli, A., Scheepers, H., Rajendran, D., Sohal, A.: Health information systems evaluation frameworks: a systematic review. Int. J. Med. Inform. **97**, 195–209 (2017)

8. Teixeira, L., Saavedra, V., Ferreira, C., Santos, B.S.: Using participatory design in a health information system. In: Conference Proceedings on IEEE Engineering Medicine and Biology Society 2011, pp. 5339–5342 (2011)

9. Kushniruk, A.: Evaluation in the design of health information systems: application of approaches emerging from usability engineering. Comput. Biol. Med. **32**, 141–149 (2002)

10. Teixeira, L., Ferreira, C., Santos, B.S.: User-centered requirements engineering in health information systems: a study in the hemophilia field. Comput. Methods Programs Biomed. **106**, 160–174 (2012)

11. Ammenwerth, E., Brender, J., Nykänen, P., Prokosch, H.U., Rigby, M., Talmon, J.: Visions and strategies to improve evaluation of health information systems: reflections and lessons based on the HIS-EVAL workshop in Innsbruck. Int. J. Med. Inform. **73**, 479–491 (2004)

12. Yusof, M.M., Kuljis, J., Papazafeiropoulou, A., Stergioulas, L.K.: An evaluation framework for health information systems: human, organization and technology-fit factors (HOT-fit). Int. J. Med. Inform. **77**, 386–398 (2008)

13. Teixeira, L., Ferreira, C., Santos, B.S., Martins, N.: Modeling a web-based information system for managing clinical information in hemophilia care. In: Annual International Conference of the IEEE Engineering in Medicine and Biology Society. IEEE Engineering in Medicine and Biology Society, pp. 2610–2613 (2006)

14. Westbrook, J.I., Braithwaite, J., Iedema, R., Coiera, E.W.: Evaluating the impact of information communication technologies on complex organizational systems: a multi-disciplinary, multi-method framework. Medinfo **11**, 1323–1327 (2004)

15. Wyatt, J.C., Wyatt, S.M.: When and how to evaluate health information systems? Int. J. Med. Inform. **69**, 251–259 (2003)

16. Renkema, T., Berghout, E.: Methodologies for information systems investment evaluation: a comparative review. Inf. Softw. Technol. **39**, 1–13 (1997)

17. Cresswell, K.: Evaluation of implementation of health IT. In: Evidence-Based Health Informatics, pp. 206–219 (2016)

18. Nykänen, P., Kaipio, J.: Quality of health IT evaluations. In: Evidence-Based Health Informatics, pp. 291–303 (2016)

19. Kaplan, B., Shaw, N.: Future directions in evaluation research: people, organizational, and social issues. Methods Inf. Med. **43**, 215–231 (2004)

20. Gremy, F., Fessler, J., Bonnin, M.: Information systems evaluation and subjectivity. Int. J. Med. Inform. **56**, 13–23 (1999)

21. Van Gennip, E.M.S.J., Talmon, J.: Assessment and evaluation of information technologies. IOS Press, Amsterdam (1995)

22. Sohaib, O., Khan, K.: Integrating usability engineering and agile software development: a literature review. In: 2010 International Conference on Computer Design and Applications (ICCDA), pp. V2-32–V2-38 (2010)

23. Grant, A., Plante, I.: The TEAM methodology for the evaluation of information systems in biomedicine. Comput. Biol. Med. **32**, 195–207 (2002)

24. Shaw, N.T.: "CHEATS": a generic information communication technology (ICT) evaluation framework. Comput. Biol. Med. **32**, 209–220 (2002)

25. Symons, V.J.: A review of information systems evaluation: content, context and process. Eur. J. Inf. Syst. **1**, 205–212 (1991)
26. Pettigrew, A.M.: Contextualist research and the study of organizational change processes. In: Mumford, E., Hirschheim, R., Fitzgerald, G., Wood-Harper, A.T. (eds.) Research Methods in Information Systems, pp. 53–72. North Holland, New York (1985)
27. Yusof, M.M., Paul, R.J., Stergioulas, L.: Health information systems evaluation: a focus on clinical decision supports system. Stud. Health Technol. Inform. **116**, 855–860 (2005)
28. Kay, S.: Evaluation of health information systems : beyond efficiency and effectiveness. Comput. Biol. Med. **32**, 111–112 (2002)
29. Ahmadian, L., Salehi Nejad, S., Khajouei, R.: Evaluation methods used on health information systems (HISs) in Iran and the effects of HISs on Iranian healthcare: a systematic review. Int. J. Med. Inform. **84**, 444–453 (2015)
30. Teixeira, L., Ferreira, C., Santos, B.S.: Using task analysis to improve the requirements elicitation in health information system. In: 29th Annual International Conference of the IEEE Engineering in Medicine and Biology Society, EMBS 2007, pp. 3669–3672 (2007)
31. Teixeira, L., Saavedra, V., Ferreira, C., Simões, J., Sousa Santos, B.: Requirements engineering using mockups and prototyping tools: developing an healthcare web-application. In: Yamamoto, S. (ed.) HCI International, pp. 652–663. Springer International Publishing Switzerland, Creta (2014)
32. Preece, J., Sharp, H., Rogers, Y.: Interaction Design: Beyond Human-Computer Interaction. Wiley, Glasgow (2015)
33. Teixeira, L., Saavedra, V., Ferreira, C., Santos, B.S.: Improving the management of chronic diseases using web-based technologies: an application in hemophilia care. In: 2010 Annual International Conference of the IEEE Engineering in Medicine and Biology Society, EMBC 2010 (2010)
34. Teixeira, L., Saavedra, V., Ferreira, C., Santos, B.S.: Web platform to support the Portuguese national registry of haemophilia and other inherited blood disorders. Int. J. Web Portals. **7**, 65–80 (2015)
35. Teixeira, L., Ferreira, C., Ieeta, D.: Registo Nacional de Pacientes com Hemofilia e outras Coagulopatias Congénitas : o sistema Português National Patient Registry with Hemophilia and other Congenital Coagulopathies : the Portuguese system. In: 10th Iberian Conference on Information Systems and Technologies (CISTI), pp. 1–6 (2015)
36. Teixeira, L., Saavedra, V., Simões, J.P., Santos, B.S., Ferreira, C.: The Portuguese national registry for hemophilia: developing of a web-based technological solution. Procedia Comput. Sci. **64**, 1248–1255 (2015)
37. Teixeira, L., Saavedra, V., Sousa Santos, B., Ferreira, C.: Portuguese Haemophilia Registry. Set of variables for a computerized solution. Hamostaseologie (2016, in press)

Software Requirements Engineering in Digital Healthcare: A Case Study of the Diagnosis and Monitoring of Autism Spectrum Disorders in Children in the UK's National Health Service

Catherine Tryfona[✉], Tom Crick, Ana Calderon, and Simon Thorne

Cardiff Metropolitan University, Cardiff, UK
{ctryfona, tcrick, acalderon, sthorne}@cardiffmet.ac.uk

Abstract. A major issue in designing digital healthcare software solutions is ensuring they meet the clinical needs and requirements of key services, as well as the expectations of various healthcare professionals. Modern software requirements engineering must be adapted to cater for this demand; we argue that traditional (and popular) requirements engineering processes – particularly in relation to the elicitation and validation of key requirements – may not be the most appropriate within the context of a multi-disciplinary team of healthcare professionals. Successful software requirements engineering is vital in ensuring that digital healthcare solutions fulfill expectations and meet the clinical needs; we thus propose that new methods of gathering requirements in the 'third space' are needed. This paper draws on a case study of the multi-disciplinary team of healthcare professionals involved in the diagnosis and support of autism spectrum disorders (ASD) in young children within the UK's National Health Service (NHS). It is worth noting that, in the context of our case study, requirements engineering is an iterative process and requires the input of numerous stakeholders from often stretched and fragmented services.

Keywords: Autism spectrum disorder · M-Health · User behaviour analysis · Software engineering · Requirements engineering

1 Introduction

Digital health can best be regarded as an encompassing term covering a wide range of ICTs applied to healthcare, wellness and ambient-assisted living [1]. It is a rapidly progressing field and, while spending on pharmaceuticals has declined recently, global spending on ICT in healthcare is predicted to have grown to 18 billion Euros by 2017. Digital healthcare initiatives, especially the virtualisation of healthcare, is high on the agenda of most national governments within European, with a view to managing resources and budgets [2], particularly in response to growing and aging populations. According to Thummler [1] the growth of the digital health industry has been rapid in recent years, facilitated by a move towards distributed patient-centered care, where the need for physical contact between patients and professionals is reduced.

© Springer International Publishing AG 2017
V.G. Duffy (Ed.): DHM 2017, Part II, LNCS 10287, pp. 91–98, 2017.
DOI: 10.1007/978-3-319-58466-9_9

Mobile health (m-health) refers more specifically to mobile computing, medical sensor and communication technologies for health [3]. According to Istepanian [4], the concept of m-health was first introduced in 2003 and has since been of increasing importance in key areas of healthcare policy, including wellbeing, disease management and diagnostics. Given that mobile technologies have become increasingly common-place in the everyday lives of the population and more accessible in terms of cost [5], the use of these technologies present a potentially affordable technological solution to epidemiological and health-based challenges.

2   User Behaviour Analysis Software and the Diagnosis and Monitoring of Autism Spectrum Disorders Within the UK's National Health Service

According to the UK's National Autistic Society, approximately 700,000 people in the UK are living with autism, with many remaining undiagnosed and unsupported [6]. Whilst the average age of diagnosis of autism has reduced [7], early intervention remains key to improving prognosis. Given the importance of early diagnosis and with estimates of prevalence being between 1 in 68 and 1 in 88 children [8], accurate and effective identification of ASD in young children remains a pressing public health issue [9]. As there is currently no single biological marker or test to diagnose autism, cases in the NHS are typically discussed at multi-disciplinary panel meetings, during which a number of healthcare professionals, including speech and language therapists, pedia-tricians and psychologists, will present their findings based on their interactions and observations of the child (Fig. 1). Where there is agreement amongst the majority, a diagnosis of autism may be reached [10].

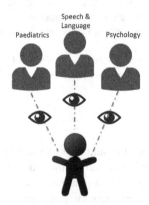

Fig. 1. The diagnosis of ASD within the NHS

The accuracy and stability of a diagnosis is dependent, therefore, on reliable and comprehensive information being obtained from multiple sources [11]. It is not a process without difficulties, however, particularly when observing children under 36 months [9], as it relies heavily on snap-shot observations and accurate reporting. Within the NHS, there is considerable pressure on resources, meaning that the period of time between appointments is increasing. This can result in a subsequent delay in achieving a diagnosis, which is usually necessary for families and schools to be able to access many support services. The ability to gather evidence between appointments, both at home and within an educational setting, therefore, may provide a valuable way to hasten the diagnosis process and reduce pressure on stretched publicly funded healthcare services [5]. Consequently, there is an emerging area of research and a number of recent initiatives in using mobile technology to collect evidence to support the diagnostic process and the ongoing observation of autism in children, with a view to identifying support strategies and managing their effectiveness [12–14].

The wide availability of touchscreen technology means that children are now able to interact with computing devices from a much earlier age. User-behaviour analysis tools such as Harimata [12] claim to be able to collect data about how the user, in this case, the child, interacts with the device in terms of physical gestures or games designed specifically to detect possible signs of autism [5, 13]. Similarly, m-health software solutions such as NODA [13] can be used to guide the parent or care-giver through the collection of video evidence of behaviours within the home or educational setting, which can then be uploaded via a wireless communication link and subsequently evaluated by a health-care professional in advance of an appointment (Fig. 2) [12].

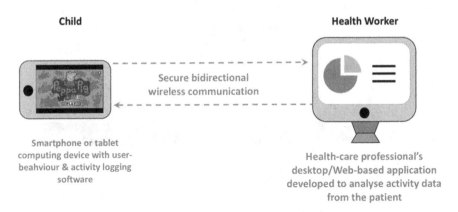

Fig. 2. Communication link between mobile device and healthcare professional

Although critical evaluation of the effectiveness of such software products falls outside of the scope of this paper, such m-health solutions offer a number of potential benefits, including:

- A reduction in expenditure for appointment times,
- A reduction in the number of appointments needed to secure a diagnosis,
- The ability to collect evidence outside of the health care professional's office.

In order for these software products to support the National Health Service, it is vital that the user-requirements engineering processes effectively capture the unique and evolving needs of the various professionals working within a dynamic organisation such as the NHS [5].

3 Requirements Engineering and Semantics

Software requirements are those properties a software solution must exhibit in order to address an organizational problem that the software solution aims to address [15]. Requirements engineering aims to bridge the gap between the social and technical worlds [1] and is a critical part of the software engineering process. Any errors at this stage of the software development process may result in negative effects on subsequent states of the project and a reduction in quality of the final software product [16]. Consequently, requirements engineering has become a well-established discipline, with a range of techniques and approaches having been developed over time [17], the popularity of many fluctuating in response to evaluation of their effectiveness and the evolving nature of the domains within which they are deployed.

Requirements engineering can be simply described as having two broad sub-disciplines of Requirements Management and Requirements Development (Fig. 3), which can be further broken down [18] as:

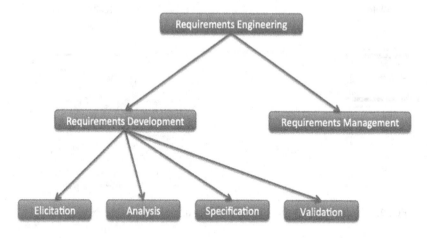

Fig. 3. Requirements Engineering (Wiegers and Beatty 2013) [18]

- Elicitation: activities associated with discovering requirements (e.g. stakeholder discussion, document analysis and prototyping).
- Analysis: striving for a more precise understanding of each requirement and representing sets of requirements in various ways.
- Specification: representing and storing the collected requirements knowledge in an organized manner.
- Validation: confirmation that the requirements information will enable the development of a solution that meets stakeholder requirements.

Requirements management describes activities including:

- A review of approved functional and non-functional requirements.
- Evaluating the impact of proposed requirements changes and the incorporation of approved changes to the project in a controlled manner.
- Ensuring the project plans match requirements as they evolve.
- Tracing and tracking specific requirements within the project, including source code, design and tests.

4 Requirements Engineering Within Digital Health

Whilst digital health solutions demonstrate considerable potential for supporting healthcare professionals in patient-centred work [19], this is dependent on information systems and software solutions meeting the specific needs of clinical staff based within complex health organisations. The deployment of poorly designed systems within the context of healthcare can result in a failure to realise the anticipated benefits of digital health solutions, the squandering of already pressured financial resources and, potentially, the compromise of patient safety [17, 19]. For software engineers, then, the highly specialised nature of healthcare and the critically important nature of digital healthcare solutions in ensuring patient welfare, can present unique challenges at this critical phase of the software development process.

Given these challenges and the need for robust requirements engineering processes, there is increasing call from the various funding agencies in North America and Europe for industry-university collaboration project proposals on multidisciplinary research in to ways in which healthcare agencies are able to draw on the technological and financial benefits associated with digital health solutions [1, 17]. The European Union, however, recognise the need for further research in to Requirement Engineering strategies in order to ensure that digital health projects meet the robust standards that are required to ensure acceptance and adoption of new technologies [1, 2]. As is the case with other domains, requirements engineers may well encounter healthcare professionals or managers within the health service sectors who have different understandings and attitudes towards technology. Robust requirements engineering processes are more likely to result successful implementation of software solutions, increasing the likelihood of the adoption of new technologies.

The highly regulated aspect of digital health can, at least in part, be attributed to the need for consideration of legal and ethical issues surrounding responsibility towards patient safety, along with confidentiality, data protection and data security. Consequently, the software requirements process must ensure compliance and compatibility with the various EU directives and ISO standards that govern these concerns [24].

We suggest that user-behaviour analysis software to support the diagnosis of autism spectrum disorders presents a unique and useful case study for research in to requirements engineering processes. In the absence of a single biological marker to identify ASDs, diagnosis is dependent on a portfolio of evidence, which is then evaluated by a multidisciplinary team of healthcare professionals before a consensus is reached regarding a diagnosis. Furthermore, understanding of autism is continually evolving, with new diagnostic criteria and definitions of ASD and sub-categories of the condition being published as recently as 2013 [20–22]. The requirements engineering processes, therefore, should be iterative in nature and accommodate changes in clinical needs, criteria and knowledge. Whilst securing an accurate diagnosis of ASD is of paramount importance, there is less scope to compromise a patient's physical safety in the case of error.

4.1 The Trend Towards Participatory Design and Stakeholder Involvement

Given the specialised and highly-regulated nature of the healthcare sector, it could be argued that methods of requirements engineering that draw on regular input from stakeholders are the most likely to be beneficial to the requirements engineering process, particularly during the first and critical phase of elicitation. Fricker et al. [23] conducted a survey on the software requirements engineering processes of software projects from multiple domains during 2012. There were 419 valid respondents and multiple answers were possible where more than one method was used. Requirements elicitation processes included:

- Workshops (79% of respondents)
- System Archeology (70% of respondents)
- Requirements Reuse (64% of respondents)
- Interviews (63% of respondents)
- Document Analysis (50% of respondents)
- Creativity (Workshops, idea castings, idea databases) (44% of respondents)
- Surveys (12%)
- Data Mining (6%)
- Other (3%)

Although this survey included development projects from multiple domains, the results highlight the current popularity of stakeholder involvement in the requirements engineering process.

Within the context of digital health solutions to support the diagnosis of ASD in young children, however, the coordination of multidisciplinary teams with distinct organizational features can be challenging. Furthermore, time is a resource under considerable pressure, and so there may be little time to devote to interviews, workshops and other participatory methods of eliciting and validating requirements.

A small window of opportunity may exist in the regular cross-disciplinary meetings that occur, where paediatrics, psychology and speech and language therapy meet to discuss individual patients and agree on diagnoses where appropriate. These meetings are likely to have busy agendas and therefore may lend themselves to more esoteric methods of requirements elicitation such as observation.

Sørby [19] proposes that observation as a method of requirements elicitation might be carried our by medical students who are a natural feature of clinical appointments. Sørby goes on to suggest that students are likely to possess sufficient domain knowledge, whilst being able to devote more time and motivation to facilitate digital health projects. Within the context of the diagnosis of ASD, students are a frequently presence in appointments within the various stakeholder health services. Whilst this presents an interesting solution, it requires further exploration to evaluate its effectiveness within the context of the UK's NHS.

5 Conclusions

There is a growing emphasis on digital health solutions to support changing healthcare models, with an increasing emphasis on patient-centred and patient-devolved healthcare. The relatively accessible cost of mobile technology such as smartphones and tablet computers, make m-health solutions a particularly interesting area of research and development. Despite the established nature of requirements engineering as a discipline, there is so far limited research specifically in to the requirements engineering within the domain of healthcare, where it could be argued that its success is critically important, with the potential for stretched finances to be squandered and patient safety to be compromised by poorly implemented software solutions.

We propose that further research in requirements engineering processes for healthcare is required and suggest that the development of user-beahviour analysis software to support the diagnosis of autism spectrum disorders in the NHS presents an interesting case study for such research. As this autism spectrum disorders require the intervention and observation of a multi-disciplinary team of healthcare professionals within a stretched public health service, novel methodologies can be explored within a complex organisational structure whilst supporting a pressing public health issue. It is likely that a mixed-methods approach to eliciting, modeling and managing software requirements will be required, including a return to methods that have since fallen out of favour (e.g. observation and surveys) in combination with novel approaches that emerge from this interesting field of research.

References

1. Thummler, C.: Digital Health. In: Fricker, S., Thummler, C., Gavras, A. (eds.) Requirements Engineering for Digital Health. London, pp. 1–22 (2015)
2. Commission, E.: Health, Demographic Change and Wellbeing. European Commission: Horizon 2020 (2015). http://ec.europa.eu/programmes/horizon2020/en/h2020-section/health-demographic-change-and-wellbeing. Accessed 20 Apr 2015
3. Alepis, E., Lambrinidis, C.: M-health: supporting automated diagnosis and electronic health records. SpringerPlus 2(1), 103–111 (2013). doi:10.1186/2193-1801-2-103
4. Istepanian, R.S.H.: m-health : a decade of evolution and impact on services and global health (2010)
5. Tryfona, C., Oatley, G., Calderon, A., Thorne, S.: M-health solutions to support the National Health Service in the diagnosis and monitoring of autism spectrum disorders in young children. In: Antona, M., Stephanidis, C. (eds.) UAHCI 2016. LNCS, vol. 9739, pp. 249–256. Springer, Cham (2016). doi:10.1007/978-3-319-40238-3_24
6. National Autistic Society (2015). http://www.autism.org.uk/about.aspx. Accessed 28 Feb 2016

7. Corsello, C.: Diagnositic instruments in autistic spectrum disorders. In: Volkmar, F.R. (ed.) Encyclopedia of Autism Spectrum Disorders, pp. 919–926. Springer, Heidelberg (2013)
8. Centers for Disease Control and Pre. Autism Spectrum Disorder (ASD) (2015). http://www.cdc.gov/ncbddd/autism/facts.html. Accessed 25 Apr 2015
9. Taylor, C.M., Vehorn, A., Noble, H., Weitlauf, A.S., Warren, Z.E.: Brief report: can metrics of reporting bias enhance early autism screening measures? J. Autism Dev. Dis. 44, 2375–2380 (2014). doi:10.1007/s10803-014-2099-5
10. Filipek, P.A., et al.: The screening and diagnosis of autistic spectrum disorders. J. Autism Dev. Dis. 29(6), 439–484 (1999)
11. Bishop, S., Luyster, R., Richler, J., Lord, C.: Diagnostic assessments. In: Chawarska, K., Klin, A., Volkmar, F. (eds.) Autism Spectrum Disorders in Infants and Toddlers, pp. 23–43. New York (2008)
12. Abowd, G.: Pilot evaluation of a novel telemedicine platform to support diagnostic assessment for autism spectrum disorder. In: ITASD 2014 Paris Conference, Paris (2014)
13. Anzulewicz, A.: HARIMATA-Embracing mobile devices for early diagnosis of autism spectrum disorders. In: ITASD 2014 Paris Conference, France (2014). http://www.dailymotion.com/video/x27j03l_harimata-embracing-mobile-devices-for-early-diagnosis-of-autism-spectrum-disorders_webcam
14. Billeci, L.: Eye-tracking technology to assess joint attention deficit in children with autism spectrum disorders. In: ITASD 2014 Paris Conference, France (2014). http://www.dailymotion.com/video/x27izmy_eye-tracking-technology-to-assess-joint-attention-deficit-in-children-with-autism-spectrum-disorders_webcam
15. BSI Standards. PD ISO/BSI Standards Publication Software Engineering—Guide to the Software Engineering Body of Knowledge (SWEBOK) (2016)
16. Loniewski, G., Insfrán Pelozo, C.E.: OpenUP/MDRE: A Model-Driven Requirements Engineering Approach for Health-Care Systems. Valencia University (2011)
17. Gorschek, T., Tempero, E., Angelis, L.: On the use of software design models in software development practice: an empirical investigation. J. Syst. Softw. 95, 176–193 (2014). doi:10.1016/j.jss.2014.03.082
18. Wiegers, K., Beatty, J.: Software Requirements, 3rd edn. Microsoft Press, Washington (2013)
19. Sørby, I.D.: Observing and analysing clinicians' information and communication behaviour: an approach to requirements engineering for mobile health information systems (2007)
20. NHS: Asperger's not in DSM-5 mental health manual (2012). http://www.nhs.uk/news/2012/12December/Pages/Aspergers-dropped-from-mental-health-manual-DSM-5.aspx. Accessed 24 Apr 2015
21. Ousley, O., Cermak, T.: Autism spectrum disorder: defining dimensions and subgroups. Curr. Dev. Dis. Rep. 1, 20–28 (2013). http://link.springer.com/10.1007/s40474-013-0003-1
22. Boucenna, S., et al.: Interactive technologies for autistic children: a review. Cognitive Computation 6, 722–740 (2014)
23. Fricker, S.: Requirements engineering: best practice. In: Fricker, S., Thummler, C., Gavras, A. (eds.) Requirements Engineering for Digital Health, pp. 25–43. Springer, New York (2015)
24. Bourquard, K., Gall, F., Cousin, P.: Standards for interoperability in digital health: selection and implementation in an eHealth project. In: Fricker, S.A., Thümmler, C., Gavras, A. (eds.) Requirements Engineering for Digital Health, pp. 95–115. Springer, Cham (2015). doi:10.1007/978-3-319-09798-5_5

Compare the Receiver Operating Characteristic (ROC) and Linear Discriminant Analysis (LDA) for Acromegaly Detection by Three-Dimensional Facial Measurements

Ming-Hsu Wang[1], Bi-Hui Chen[2], and Wen-Ko Chiou[1(✉)]

[1] Graduate School of Management, Chang Gung University, Tao-Yuan, Taiwan
wkchiu@mail.cgu.edu.tw
[2] Department of Business Administration, Chihlee University of Technology,
New Taipei City, Taiwan

Abstract. Excessive growth hormone secretion will result in acromegaly affect metabolic function. Patients with acromegaly is 2–4 times greater risk of death than the normal. Early diagnosis is the key follow-up treatment of acromegaly. The clinical diagnosis is based on typical acromegaly the face and body features, endocrine and radiological. However, acromegaly diagnosis is still quite deferred. Typical acromegaly, with the symptoms and appearance, the physician can diagnose. Obvious early symptoms, diagnosis is not easy. As imaging technology advances, one after another to explore the diagnosis of acromegaly, however, did not the size of the stereoscopic 3D image. The aim of this study is to compare the compare the Receiver operating characteristic (ROC) and discriminant analysis for acromegaly detection by three dimensional facial measurements. To explore the difference of detection rate between the two analysis methods. The result shows that the accuracies of three categories from the univariate discriminant analysis, the lateral angles displayed the highest accuracy between all three categories in the female but the lowest rate for the ROC analysis. However, the lateral angles displayed the lowest accuracy between all three categories in the male and the lowest rate for the ROC analysis. The lateral angles, calculated from the two prominent variables, made a larger difference than the other two categories. From the result, it shows that the accuracy difference analysis between the two analysis methods in both genders. The difference could come from the different operation of the analysis methods. It could use the different analysis method to analyze the different facial dimensions for the acromegaly detection in the future and increase the accuracy for disease detection.

Keywords: Acromegaly · Receiver operating characteristic · Discriminant analysis

1 Introduction

Acromegaly is a rare disease, with an estimated incidence of three to four cases per million population per year, and a prevalence of between 40 and 70 cases per million [1–6]. Excess growth hormone (GH) and the resultant elevations of insulin-like growth

© Springer International Publishing AG 2017
V.G. Duffy (Ed.): DHM 2017, Part II, LNCS 10287, pp. 99–107, 2017.
DOI: 10.1007/978-3-319-58466-9_10

factor (IGF-I), the biochemical hallmarks of this disease [7, 8], produce its characteristic multisystem, often disfiguring, physical manifestations as well as its clinically significant comorbidities including diabetes mellitus (DM), hypertension (HTN), arthritis, sleep apnoea and cardiovascular disease [9–14]. The mortality is two to four times higher than the general population, and is predominantly due to vascular, metabolic, and pulmonary comorbidities [15–17]. The effectiveness of treating acromegaly patients, like many other diseases, is heavily dependent upon how early it is detected [18]. Therefore, early recognition is considered key to achieve a high rate of treatment success [10, 19] and avoiding long-term comorbidities. Increased awareness by healthcare professionals, especially primary care physicians, of acromegaly presentations is needed. Educational programs should be targeted at early recognition of acromegaly, with the hope that these will lead to earlier diagnosis. However, acromegaly has long been known for its insidious nature and long delay from onset of symptoms to diagnosis [20–22].

Although the mean age of disease occurrence is 32 years old, the mean age at diagnosis is 39–42 years old, and most series report a delay in the diagnosis of 7–10 years from the onset of signs and symptoms [23]. The clinical characteristics at diagnosis of patients with acromegaly did not change from 1981 to 2006, suggesting that clinical recognition of acromegaly has not significantly improved over the last 25 years. The reasons why acromegaly has traditionally been under-recognized are unclear, but could include its slowly progressive course allowing its changes to go un-noticed by the patient, family members or physicians, as well as the overlap of many of its comorbidities with common disorders. As effective therapies, can now prevent disease progression and return lifespan to normal, early recognition of acromegaly is essential [16, 24]. Recent developments including highly sensitive biochemical markers, both GH and IGF-I [25, 26], and MRI scans to identify small tumors are available for diagnosing acromegaly.

The most common problem leading to the diagnosis was acral changes (24%) [27]. And, in this photograph appeared recently in the New England Journal of Medicine as one of the journal's periodic "Medical Mysteries" with the caption, "Which twin is the patient?" [28]. The changes of the face could be a key factor for acromegaly diagnosis. Previous studies have shown that face classification software using regular two-dimensional (2D) photographs allow distinguishing between different genetic syndromes [29–31]. And an attempt has been made to recognize acromegaly by a computer program using a morphable model that establishes a three-dimensional model from a regular 2D photograph [32]. Acromegaly can be detected by computer software using photographs of the face. Classification accuracy by software is higher than by medical experts or general internists, particularly in patients with mild features of acromegaly. It is a promising tool to help detecting acromegaly [33]. If a patient's appearance suggests that he or she may have the disease, additional laboratory blood tests may be performed to confirm its presence or absence. Because these tests are expensive and time consuming, it would clearly be valuable to have an inexpensive and automatic prescreening method. Early detection is important in treating the disease successfully, but it is often missed because the signs are subtle and the condition is rare. Since many of the symptoms of the disease, such as swelling of the nose and growth of the jaw, affect facial appearance, the disease can be detected by experts (endocrinologists, for example) in many cases from a normal frontal photograph of a person.

However, identification methods and tracking facial changes in the early stages of acromegaly, by patients or family members, could be an important issue for promoting early disease diagnosis and treatment. The aim of this study is to compare the compare the Receiver operating characteristic (ROC) and discriminant analysis for acromegaly detection by three-dimensional facial measurements. To explore the difference of detection rate between the two analysis methods.

2 Methods

2.1 Samples

A group of patients with acromegaly was compared with a healthy control group. Eleven facial soft tissues measurements were collected. The study group consisted of 70 patients with acromegaly (35 females with ages ranging between 34–64 years with a mean age of 44.7 years; and 35 men aged between 28–67 years with a mean age of 43.5 years) who were admitted to the Chang Gung Memorial Hospital, Linkou, Taiwan between 2012 and 2014. All subjects participating in this cross-sectional study were Taiwanese and reside in the Taiwan. All patients with acromegaly were diagnosed on the basis of relevant clinical features including a mean GH level > 5 ng/mL, plasma IGF-I level greater than the average age/sex-matched levels, or a nadir GH > 1 ng/mL after a 75-gm oral glucose tolerance test (OGTT). And the control group comprised of 140 healthy adults (70 women with ages ranging between 28–41 years with a mean age of 30.5 years and 70 men with aged between 29–43 years with a mean age of 30.9 years). Controls were matched by gender to the acromegaly patient group at twice the sample size of those with the disease. Control subjects were volunteers from Chang Gung Memorial Hospitals.

2.2 3D Facial Measurements

All examinations were conducted using standardized protocols and trained staff gathered the data. Three-dimensional (3D) facial data was collected via a 3D camera system (LT3D FaceCam EXII) (Fig. 1).

Participating subjects sat in front of a white background and 3D facial stereo photographs were taken with the subject's head positioned in a cephalostand oriented on the Frankfort horizontal plane. Thirteen landmarks (Fig. 2) were digitalized. Eleven variables from the three categories were selected and applied, including five frontal widths, three lateral depths and three lateral angular measurements. All linear dimensions were measured from point-to-point (i.e., facial width -zy-zy). The angles measured were given in triple abbreviations (i.e., nasofrontal angle -g-n-prn). All measurements were collected and calculated by the one well-trained researcher.

Fig. 1. 3D face camera system and experiment space set-up

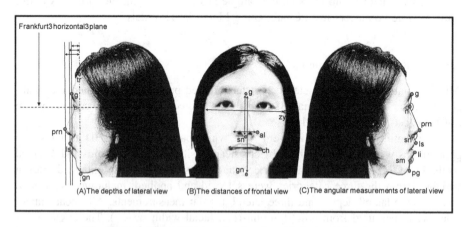

Fig. 2. Definition of thirteen landmarks and eleven dimensions

2.3   Statistical Analysis

The discriminant function equations were constructed in two ways by using each variable using univariate methods. All accuracies of discriminant equations were obtained by cross-validated classification. Receiver operating characteristic (ROC) curves were used to select the most sensitive and specific facial measurements (cutoff values) for detecting acromegaly. The statistical software packages used for this study were SPSS version 20 (SPSS Inc., Chicago, IL, USA).

3   Results and Discussion

Compare the average accuracy between both genders, higher accuracy for the discriminant analysis than the ROC analysis, besides the lateral view width. It shows that the difference accuracy between the two analysis methods. And the lateral view angle shows the lowest accuracy from the ROC in both genders.

The result in the Table 1 shows that the accuracies of three categories from the univariate discriminant analysis, the lateral angles displayed the highest accuracy between all three categories in the female but the lowest rate for the ROC analysis. However, the lateral angles displayed the lowest accuracy between all three categories in the male and the lowest rate for the ROC analysis. The lateral angles, calculated from the two prominent variables, made a larger difference than the other two categories. Furthermore, the angles could be calculated by the relative point-to-point from the 2D lateral image without the real dimensional measurements [34].

Table 1. Average detection rate of ROC and LDA in both genders

Measurement category	Females		Males	
	ROC	LDA	ROC	LDA
Frontal view width	70%	67%	90%*	88%
Lateral view distance	60%	69%	58%	82%
Lateral view angle	14%*	78%	20%*	70%

*ROC: receiver operating characteristic *LDA: linear discriminant analysis

ROC graphs are a very useful tool for visualizing and evaluating classifiers. They are able to provide a richer measure of classification performance than scalar measures such as accuracy, error rate or error cost. [35]. An ROC curve is a two-dimensional depiction of classifier performance. To compare classifiers, we may want to reduce ROC performance to a single scalar value representing expected performance. A common method is to calculate the area under the ROC curve, abbreviated AUC. Since the AUC is a portion of the area of the unit square, its value will always be between 0 and 1.0. However, because random guessing produces the diagonal line between (0, 0) and (1, 1), which has an area of 0.5, no realistic classifier should have an AUC less than 0.5 [36].

When using normalized units, the area under the curve (often referred to as simply the AUC) is equal to the probability that a classifier will rank a randomly chosen positive instance higher than a randomly chosen negative one (assuming 'positive' ranks higher than 'negative'). This can be seen as follows: the area under the curve is given by (the integral boundaries are reversed as large T has a lower value on the x-axis).

$$A = \int_{\infty}^{-\infty} \text{TPR}(T)\text{FPR}'(T)\,dT = \int_{-\infty}^{\infty} \int_{-\infty}^{\infty} I(T' > T) f_1(T') f_0(T)\,dT'\,dT = P(X_1 > X_0)$$

where X_1 is the score for a positive instance and X_0 is the score for a negative instance.

It can further be shown that the AUC is closely related to the Mann–Whitney U, which tests whether positives are ranked higher than negatives. It is also equivalent to the Wilcoxon test of ranks.

$$G_1 = 1 - \sum_{k=1}^{n}(X_k - X_{k-1})(Y_k + Y_{k-1})$$

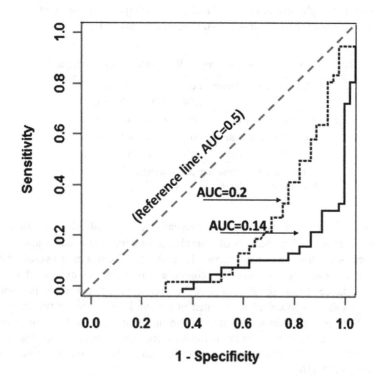

Fig. 3. ROC curve for the lateral view angle (AUC: Females = 0.14; Males = 0.2)

Linear discriminant analysis [37] is a well-known scheme for feature extraction and dimension reduction. For many applications, such as face recognition, all scatter matrices in question can be singular since the data is from a very high-dimensional space, and in general, the dimension exceeds the number of data points. This is known as the undersampled or singularity problem [38].

Compare the two analysis methods, discriminant analysis shows the more consistent accuracy than the ROC analysis in three measurement categories. For the gender comparison, shows the higher accuracy for the males than the females.

About the limitation of this study, facial appearance may vary from one ethnic population to another one. Therefore, the data obtained from a special population (Taiwanese) couldn't be generalized. It could be the limitation that the standard cut-off measurements wouldn't be possible for all ethnic populations. It will be an important issue to compare the acromegaly facial measurements for different ethnic populations in the future study (Fig. 3).

4 Conclusion

From the result, it shows that the accuracy difference analysis between the two analysis methods in both genders. The difference could come from the different operation of the analysis methods. Linear discriminant analysis shows the consistent AUC from 67–78% for females, and 70–88% for males. ROC analysis shows the AUC from 14–70% for females, and 20–90% for males. It could use the different analysis method to analyze the different facial dimensions for the acromegaly detection in the future and increase the accuracy for disease detection.

Acknowledgement. This project was funded by the Ministry of Science and Technology of the Republic of China, Taiwan, under grant no. (MOST 103-2221-E-182-050-MY3). The authors, therefore, acknowledge with thanks the Ministry of Science and Technology of the Republic of China for financial support.

References

1. Alexander, L., Appleton, D., Hall, R., Ross, W.M.: Epidemiology of acromegaly in the newcastle region. Clin. Endocrinol. (Oxf) **12**(1), 71–79 (1980)
2. Bengtsson, B.A., Eden, S., Ernest, I., Oden, A.: Epidemiology and long term survival in acromegaly. Acta. Med. Scand. **223**, 327–335 (1988)
3. Ritchie, C.M., Atkinson, A.B., Kennedy, A.L., et al.: Ascertainment and natural history of treated acromegaly in Northern Ireland. Ulster. Med. J. **59**, 55–62 (1990)
4. Extabe, J., Gaztambide, S., Latorre, P., Vazquez, J.A.: Acromegaly: an epidemiological study. J. Endocrinol. Invest. **16**(3), 181–187 (1993)
5. Holdaway, I.M., Rajasoorya, C.: Epidemiology of acromegaly. Pituitary **2**(1), 29–41 (1999)
6. Daly, A.F., Petrossians, P., Beckers, A.: An overview of the epidemiology and genetics of acromegaly. J. Endocrinol. Invest. **28**, 67–69 (2005)
7. Melmed, S.: Medical progress: acromegaly. N. Engl. J. Med. **355**, 2558–2573 (2006)

8. Freda, P.U.: Current concepts in the biochemical assessment of the patient with acromegaly. Growth Horm. IGF Res. **13**, 171–184 (2003)
9. Beauregard, C., Truong, U., Hardy, J., et al.: Long-term outcome and mortality after transsphenoidal adenomectomy for acromegaly. Clin. Endocrinol. (Oxf) **58**, 86–91 (2003)
10. Mestron, A., Webb, S.M., Astorga, R., et al.: Epidemiology, clinical characteristics, outcome, morbidity and mortality in acromegaly based on the Spanish acromegaly registry. Eur. J. Endocrinol. **151**, 439–446 (2004)
11. Swearingen, B., Barker, F.G., Katznelson, L., et al.: Longterm mortality after transsphenoidal surgery and adjunctive therapy for acromegaly. J. Clin. Endocrinol. Metab. **83**, 3419–3426 (1998)
12. Ezzat, S., Strom, C., Melmed, S., et al.: Colon polyps in acromegaly. Ann. Internal Med. **114**, 754–755 (1991)
13. Ron, E., Gridley, G., Hrubec, Z., et al.: Acromegaly and gastrointestinal cancer. Cancer **68**, 1673–1677 (1991)
14. Colao, A., Vitale, G., Pivonello, R., et al.: The heart: an endorgan of GH action. Eur. J. Endocrinol. **151**, 93–101 (2004)
15. Rajasoorya, C., Holdaway, I.M., Wrightson, P., et al.: Determinants of clinical outcome and survival in acromegaly. Clin. Endocrinol. **41**, 95–102 (1994)
16. Bates, A.S., Van't Hoff, W., Jones, J.M., et al.: An audit of outcome in acromegaly. Q. J. Med. **86**, 293–299 (1993)
17. Colao, A., Cuocolo, A., Marzullo, P., et al.: Is the acromegalic cardiomyopathy reversible? Effect of 5-year normalization of growth hormone and insulinlike growth factor I levels on cardiac performance. J. Clin. Endocrinol. Metab. **86**, 1551–1557 (2001)
18. Freda, P.U.: Advances in the diagnosis of acromegaly. Endocrinologist **10**, 237–244 (2000)
19. Clemmons, D.R., Chihara, K., Freda, P.U., et al.: Optimizing control of acromegaly: integrating a growth hormone receptor antagonist into the treatment algorithm. J. Clin. Endocrinol. Metab. **88**, 4759–4767 (2003)
20. Pearce, J.M.: Pituitary tumours and acromegaly (Pierre Marie's disease). J. Neurol. Neurosurg. Psychiatry **73**, 394 (2004)
21. Nabarro, J.D.: Acromegaly. Clin. Endocrinol. **26**, 481–512 (1987)
22. Molitch, M.E.: Clinical manifestations of acromegaly. Endocrinol. Metab. Clin. North Am. **21**, 597–614 (1994)
23. Nabarro, J.D.: Management of acromegaly. J. Clin. Pathol. **1**, 62–67 (1976)
24. Kauppinen-Makelin, R., Sane, T., Reunanen, A., et al.: A nationwide survey of mortality in acromegaly. J. Clin. Endocrinol. Metab. **90**, 4081–4086 (2005)
25. Freda, P.U., Post, K.D., Powell, J.S., et al.: Evaluation of disease status with sensitive measures of growth hormone secretion in 60 postoperative patients with acromegaly. J. Clin. Endocrinal. Metab. **83**, 3808–3816 (1998)
26. Freda, P.U., Reyes, C.M., Nuruzzaman, A.T.: Basal and glucose-suppressed GH levels less than 1 µg/L in newly diagnosed acromegaly. Pituitary **6**, 175–180 (2003)
27. Nachtigall, L., Delgado, A., Swearingen, B., et al.: Changing patterns in diagnosis and therapy of acromegaly over two decades. J. Clin. Endocrinol. Metab. **93**, 2035–2041 (2008)
28. Nieuwlaat, W.A., Pieters, G.: A medical mystery– which twin is the patient? N. Engl. J. Med. **351**, 68 (2004)
29. Loos, H.S., Wieczorek, D., Würtz, R.P., et al.: Computer-based recognition of dysmorphic faces. Eur. J. Hum. Genet. **11**, 555–560 (2003)
30. Boehringer, S., Vollmar, T., Tasse, C., et al.: Syndrome identification based on 2D analysis software. Eur. J. Hum. Genet. **14**, 1082–1089 (2006)

31. Vollmar, T., Maus, B., Wurtz, R.P., et al.: Impact of geometry and viewing angle on classification accuracy of 2D based analysis of dysmorphicfaces. Eur. J. Med. Genet. **51**, 44–53 (2008)

32. Learned-Miller, E., Lu, Q., Paisley, A., Trainer, P., Blanz, V., Dedden, K., Miller, R.: Detecting acromegaly: screening for disease with a morphable model. In: Larsen, R., Nielsen, M., Sporring, J. (eds.) MICCAI 2006. LNCS, vol. 4191, pp. 495–503. Springer, Heidelberg (2006). doi:10.1007/11866763_61

33. Schneider, H.J., Kosilek, R.P., Günther, M., et al.: A novel approach to the detection of acromegaly: accuracy of diagnosis by automatic face classification. J. Clin. Endocrinol. Metab. **96**, 2074–2080 (2006)

34. Bishara, S.E., Cummins, D.M., Jorgensen, G.J., Jakobsen, J.R., et al.: A computer assisted photogrammetric analysis of soft tissue changes after orthodontic treatment Part I: methodology and reliability. Am. J. Orthod. Dentofacial. Orthop. **107**, 633–639 (1995)

35. Fawcett, T.: An introduction to ROC analysis. Pattern Recogn. Lett. **27**(8), 861–874 (2006)

36. Hanley, J.A., McNeil, B.J.: The meaning and use of the area under a receiver operating characteristic (ROC) curve. Radiology **143**, 29–36 (1982)

37. Fukunaga, K.: Introduction to Statistical Pattern Classification. Academic Press, San Diego (1990)

38. Krzanowski, W.J., Jonathan, P., McCarthy, W.V., Thomas, M.R.: Discriminant analysis with singular covariance matrices: methods and applications to spectroscopic data. Appl. Stat. **44**, 101–115 (1995)

Evaluation of Functionality and Usability on Diabetes Mobile Applications: A Systematic Literature Review

Qing Ye[1,2], Suzanne A. Boren[1,2], Uzma Khan[3],
and Min Soon Kim[1,2(✉)]

[1] University of Missouri Informatics Institute, University of Missouri-Columbia,
Columbia, Missouri, USA
kimms@health.missouri.edu
[2] Department of Health Management and Informatics, School of Medicine,
University of Missouri-Columbia, Columbia, Missouri, USA
[3] Department of Medicine, School of Medicine,
University of Missouri-Columbia, Columbia, Missouri, USA

Abstract. *Objective:* To systematically review the studies related to the functionality and usability evaluation of diabetes mobile apps. *Method:* We searched three electronic databases: PubMed, Scopus, and Cochrane. The search terms used were "mobile app", "mobile application", "diabetes", and "evaluation". We limited the articles to those that were written in English and published from January 1, 2006 to October 4, 2016. *Results:* There were seven articles focused on type 1 diabetes, two articles focused on type 2 diabetes, two articles focused on both type 1 and type 2 diabetes, nine articles focused on diabetes that authors did not state specific type. With regard to types of evaluation, only one study reported solely on functionality, seven studies reported usability, and twelve studies reported both functionality and usability. The methods used for evaluations included survey, interview, laboratory testing, user testing, questionnaire, expert evaluation, and heuristic evaluation. *Conclusion*: Future studies should consider the standard evaluation methods for evaluate functionality and usability of diabetes self-management (DSM) apps.

Keywords: Diabetes · Functionality · Mobile applications · Usability

1 Introduction

Diabetes Self-Management. Diabetes mellitus is a group of metabolic diseases characterized by chronic hyperglycemia [1]. In 2014, there were 29.1 million Americans with diabetes, including 8.1 million people who were undiagnosed [2]. Diabetes self-management education is a process of educating patient the knowledge of diabetes to improve their self-management behaviors [3]. Several studies suggested through appropriate diabetes self-management, diabetic patients can improve the long-term health outcomes [2, 4–7].

Diabetes Self-Management Applications (Apps). Mobile health is defined as "mobile computing, medical sensor, and communications technologies" that can improve

© Springer International Publishing AG 2017
V.G. Duffy (Ed.): DHM 2017, Part II, LNCS 10287, pp. 108–116, 2017.
DOI: 10.1007/978-3-319-58466-9_11

chronic disease care outside hospitals [8]. In recent years, there has been a rapid development of health apps for smartphones and tablets. Based on the report of IMS Institute for Healthcare Informatics, there were almost 165,000 health apps in 2015 [9]. With this increase in health apps there has also been an increase in the number of apps designed specifically for diabetic patients. In 2013, researchers searched Google Play, App iTunes, and BlackBerry World app stores. They found 1,812 diabetes-related apps [10]. DSM apps are tools on smartphones or tablets designed to help diabetic patients to achieve behavioral changes [11]. DSM apps provide functions, including monitoring carbohydrate intake, exercise, and blood sugar level.

According to the International Standards Organization (ISO 9241-11), usability is defined as "the extent to which a product can be used by specified users to achieve specified goals with effectiveness, efficiency, and satisfaction in a specified context of use" [12]. Usability testing is defined as "a systematic way of observing actual users trying out a product and collecting information about the specific ways in which the product is easy or difficult for them" [13]. Zhang et al. indicated "Usability testing is a mandatory process to ensure that a mobile application is practical, effective, and easy to use, especially from a user's perspective [14]. The results of less attention to usability may include "frustrated users and decreased efficiency coupled with increased cost [15].

However, limited research and review have been conducted on the functionality and usability evaluation of these apps. The purpose of this review was to systematically review the studies related to the functionality and usability evaluation of diabetes mobile apps.

2 Method

Data Sources. In October 2016, we searched three electronic databases: PubMed, Scopus, and Cochrane. The search terms used were "mobile app", "mobile application", "diabetes", and "evaluation". We limited the articles to those that were written in English and published from January 1, 2006 to October 4, 2016.

Inclusion Criteria. The inclusion criteria were any research related to evaluation on functionality or usability of diabetes applications.

Study Selection and Data Extraction. We reviewed the titles and abstracts of identified articles. Based on the inclusion criteria, eligible articles were included for full-text review. We collected data from eligible articles, the object of study, diabetes types, study sample, sample size, numbers of apps used in the study, evaluation types (functionality or/and usability), evaluation methods, findings of evaluation, app types (native or web-based app), app platforms (e.g., iOS, Android), device, and evidence-based guidelines used for developing the app.

3   Results

Study Selection. Out of 200 articles, we identified 20 articles as eligible for our systematical literature review (Fig. 1). There were 13 articles from PubMed and 7 articles from Scopus.

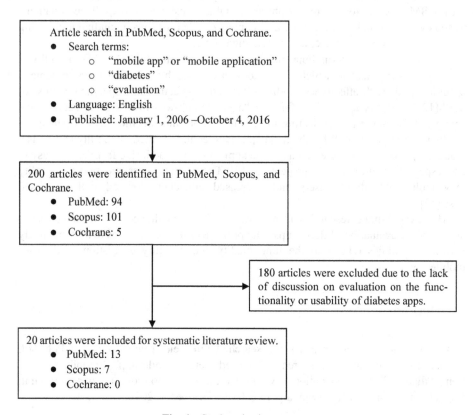

Fig. 1. Study selection process

Description of Included Studies. Table 1 shows the summary of functionality and usability studies on diabetes mobile applications. The publication years ranged from 2008 to 2016. There were seven articles focused on type 1 diabetes [16–22], two articles focused on type 2 diabetes [23, 24], two articles focused on both type 1 and type 2 diabetes [25, 26], and nine articles did not report specific diabetes types [11, 27–34]. Thirteen studies evaluated one in-house mobile app [16, 17, 19–21, 23–30] and seven studies evaluated two or more apps developed by others [11, 18, 22, 31–34]. The number of apps for evaluation ranged from one to 656. Sample size for evaluation ranged from five to 123 subjects. The study sample types included adolescents [16–18], adults [19, 20, 24–28, 30], elderly people [23].

Table 1. Summary of functionality and usability studies on diabetes mobile applications. DMT: Diabetes Mellitus Type, F: Functionality, U: Usability, N: Native app, W: Web app, NR: No reported, N/A: Not applicable, ADA: American Diabetes Association, JDS: Japan Diabetes Society.

Author year	DMT, study sample	Evaluation sample size	Number of apps	Evaluation types (F/U)	Evaluation methods	App types (N, W)	App platforms	Development guidelines
Padman et al. 2013 [16]	1, Adolescents	8	1	F, U	survey	NR	Android	NR
Cafazzo et al. 2012 [17]	1, Adolescents	20	1	U	laboratory testing; interview	NR	iOS	NR
Froisland et al. 2012 [18]	1, Adolescents	12	2	F, U	user testing; interview; questionnaire	1 N, 1 W	Android	NR
Diouri et al. 2015 [19]	1, Adults	10	1	U	user testing; questionnaire	NR	Android	NR
Lloyd et al. 2015 [25]	1 and 2, Adults	5	1	U	user testing; survey	NR	Android	ADA
Arsand et al. 2015 [26]	1 and 2, Adults	6	1	F, U	user testing; questionnaire	NR	Pebble	NR
Domhardt et al.2015 [27]	NR, Adults	6	1	F, U	laboratory testing; questionnaire	NR	Android	NR
Sultan et al. 2009 [28]	NR, Adults	15	1	U	user testing; questionnaire; heuristic evaluation	NR	Windows	NR
Preuveneers et al. 2008 [20]	1, Adults	43	1	F, U	questionnaire; laboratory testing	NR	Windows	NR
Rollo et al. 2011 [23]	2, Elderly people	10	1	U	user testing; questionnaire	NR	NR	NR
Waki et al. 2015 [24]	2, Adults	5	1	F, U	interview	NR	Android	JDS
Jabar et al. 2013 [29]	NR, N/A	1	1	U	expert evaluation	W	Android	NR

(continued)

Table 1. (*continued*)

Author year	DMT, study sample	Evaluation sample size	Number of apps	Evaluation types (F/U)	Evaluation methods	App types (N, W)	App platforms	Development guidelines
Anthimopoulos et al. 2015 [21]	1, N/A	24	1	F	laboratory testing	NR	Android	NR
Garcia-Zapirain et al. 2016 [30]	NR, Adults	123	1	U	survey	W	NR	NR
Caburnay et al. 2015 [31]	NR, N/A	110	110	F, U	expert evaluation	NR	iOS	NR
Arnhold et al. (2014) [11]	NR, N/A	N/A	656 apps for Functionality; 66 apps for Usability	F, U	expert evaluation	NR	iOS and Android	NR
Martin et al. (2011) [32]	NR, N/A	8	8	F, U	user testing; heuristic evaluation; expert evaluation	NR	iOS	NR
Demidowich et al. (2012) [33]	NR, N/A	42	42	F, U	expert evaluation	NR	Android	NR
Whitlock et al. (2012) [34]	NR, N/A	3	3	F, U	user testing; heuristic evaluation	NR	iOS	NR
Garcia et al. (2011) [22]	1, N/A	N/A	15	F, U	user testing; heuristic evaluation; expert evaluation	NR	Android, iOS, and Blackberry	NR

Types of Evaluation and Evaluation Methods. With regard to types of evaluation, only one study reported solely on functionality [21], seven studies reported usability [17, 19, 23, 25, 28–30], and twelve studies reported both functionality and usability [11, 16, 18, 20, 22, 24, 26, 27, 31–34]. The methods used for evaluations included survey [16, 25, 30], interview [17, 18, 24], laboratory testing [17, 20, 21, 27], user testing [18, 19, 22, 23, 25, 26, 28, 32, 34], questionnaire [18–20, 23, 26–28], expert evaluation [11, 22, 29, 31–33], and heuristic evaluation [22, 28, 32, 34].

Apps Types and Platforms. Out of thirteen studies that evaluated in-house mobile app, two apps were implemented as web-based mobile apps [29, 30]. The other eleven studies did not report app types [16, 17, 19–21, 23–28].

With regard to the platforms, eleven studies used Android platform [11, 16, 18, 19, 21, 22, 24, 25, 27, 29, 33], six studies used iOS platform [11, 17, 22, 31, 32, 34], two studies used Windows platform [20, 28], one study used Blackberry platform [22], and one study used the Pebble (smartwatch) platform [26]. Two studies did not report the platform types on which the apps developed [23, 30].

Diabetes Guidelines for Developing Apps. Even though evidence-based guidelines guide effective app development [35], only two studies reported the evidence-based guidelines used when the apps were developed [24, 25]. The other eleven studies which developed apps did not report the guidelines for app development [16, 17, 19–21, 23, 26–30].

4 Discussion and Conclusion

This study showed only six studies reported on usability. Usability plays an important role helping users to complete a task successfully with minimal cognitive load [36, 37]. This study revealed that only two studies provided the information about the diabetes guidelines for app development. It is not certain whether the studies used diabetes guidelines but failed to report them, or they did not consider using guideline when developing DSM apps. This result is consistent with the findings from several functionality studies on diabetes apps. Our team had conducted functionality analysis of current diabetes apps to investigate the presence of evidence-based guidelines while developing apps [38]. There were 168 diabetes eligible apps from iOS and Google Play included in the study. The functionality of each app was coded according to the validated AADE7 Self-Care Behaviors™ by the American Association of Diabetes Educators. The results showed very few apps followed the AADE7 Self-Care Behaviors™ guideline. Similarly, Chomutare et al., analyzed the functions of 101 DSM apps from Apple iPhone, Google Android, BlackBerry, and Nokia Symbian [35]. The study found that features of diabetes apps on the online market did not follow evidence-based guidelines either [35].

This study showed that most studies used triangular methodologies for functionality and usability evaluation, which was encouraging because mixed methods can reveal more comprehensive usability problems that a single method may not detect [39]. We also found lack of consistency in reporting evaluation findings that some studies did not provide scientific details on study subjects, such as level of prior mobile app experience, health literacy, and education level, which would influence the results evaluation outcomes. For future app development and evaluation, systematic and consistent reporting guideline including the methodical and scientific details should be used to inform research community.

Limitations of the Study. Our study has limitations. First, we did not consider the clinical outcomes of the diabetes apps because we were interested in evaluation methods. The clinical outcomes may provide additional information on the intervention effect that may be influenced by the functionality or usability. Second, we only included studies that were published in English in our review. Inclusion of the literature published in a language other than English should have expanded the pool of literature.

References

1. Maniam, A., Dhillon, J.S.: Barriers to the effective use of diabetes self-management applications. In: The 3rd National Graduate Conference (NatGrad 2015). Universiti Tenaga Nasional, Putrajaya Campus (2015)
2. National Diabetes Statistics Report: Estimates of Diabetes and Its Burden in the United States. Centers for Disease Control and Prevention (2014)
3. Norris, S.L., Lau, J., Smith, S.J., Schmid, C.H., Engelgau, M.M.: Self-management education for adults with type 2 diabetes: a meta-analysis of the effect on glycemic control. Diabetes Care **25**(7), 1159–1171 (2002)
4. Whitlock, L.A., McLaughlin, A.C., Harris, M., Bradshaw, J.: The design of mobile technology to support diabetes self-management in older adults. In: Zhou, J., Salvendy, G. (eds.) DUXU 2015. LNCS, vol. 9194, pp. 211–221. Springer, Cham (2015). doi:10.1007/978-3-319-20913-5_20
5. Diabetes Prevention Program Research Group: The Diabetes Prevention Program (DPP): description of lifestyle intervention. Diabetes Care **25**(12), 2165–2171 (2002)
6. Suhl, E., Bonsignore, P.: Diabetes self-management education for older adults: general principles and practical application. Diab. Spectr. **19**(4), 234–240 (2006)
7. Lindstrom, J., Louheranta, A., Mannelin, M., Rastas, M., Salminen, V., Eriksson, J., Uusitupa, M., Tuomilehto, J.: The finnish diabetes prevention study (dps): lifestyle intervention and 3-year results on diet and physical activity. Diabetes Care **26**(12), 3230–3236 (2003)
8. Eng, D.S., Lee, J.M.: The promise and peril of mobile health applications for diabetes and endocrinology. Pediatr. Diab. **14**(4), 231–238 (2013)
9. Aitken, M.: Patient Adoption of mHealth Use, Evidence and Remaining Barriers to Mainstream Acceptance (2015)
10. Martinez-Perez, B., de la Torre-Diez, I., Lopez-Coronado, M.: Mobile health applications for the most prevalent conditions by the World Health Organization: review and analysis. J. Med. Internet Res. **15**(6), e120 (2013)
11. Arnhold, M., Quade, M., Kirch, W.: Mobile applications for diabetics: a systematic review and expert-based usability evaluation considering the special requirements of diabetes patients age 50 years or older. J. Med. Internet Res. **16**(4), e104 (2014)
12. ISO 9241-11: Ergonomic Requirements for Office Work with Visual Display Terminals (VDTs): Part 11: Guidance on Usability. 1 ed. 1998: International Organization for Standardization. 22

13. Dumas, J.F., Redish, J.C.: A Practical Guide to Usability Testing, p. 412. Greenwood Publishing Group Inc., Westport (1993)
14. Zhang, D., Adipat, B.: Challenges, Methodologies, and Issues in the Usability Testing of Mobile Applications. Int. J. Hum.-Comput. Interact. 18(3), 293–308 (2005)
15. Yen, P.Y., Bakken, S.: Review of health information technology usability study methodologies. J. Am. Med. Inform. Assoc. 19(3), 413–422 (2012)
16. Padman, R., Jaladi, S., Kim, S., Kumar, S., Orbeta, P., Rudolph, K., Tran, T.: An evaluation framework and a pilot study of a mobile platform for diabetes self-management: insights from Pediatric users. Stud. Health Technol. Inform. 192, 333–337 (2013)
17. Cafazzo, J.A., Casselman, M., Hamming, N., Katzman, D.K., Palmert, M.R.: Design of an mHealth app for the self-management of adolescent type 1 diabetes: a pilot study. J. Med. Internet Res. 14(3), e70 (2012)
18. Froisland, D.H., Arsand, E., Skarderud, F.: Improving diabetes care for young people with type 1 diabetes through visual learning on mobile phones: mixed-methods study. J. Med. Internet Res. 14(4), e111 (2012)
19. Diouri, O., Place, J., Traverso, M., Georgescu, V., Picot, M.C., Renard, E.: Development of a smartphone application to capture carbohydrate, lipid, and protein contents of daily food: need for integration in artificial pancreas for patients with type 1 diabetes? J. Diab. Sci. Technol. 9(6), 1170–1174 (2015)
20. Preuveneers, D., Berbers, Y.: Mobile phones assisting with health self-care: a diabetes case study. In: MobileHCI 2008 - Proceedings of the 10th International Conference on Human-Computer Interaction with Mobile Devices and Services (2008)
21. Anthimopoulos, M., Dehais, J., Shevchik, S., Ransford, B.H., Duke, D., Diem, P., Mougiakakou, S.: Computer vision-based carbohydrate estimation for type 1 patients with diabetes using smartphones. J. Diab. Sci. Technol. 9(3), 507–515 (2015)
22. Garcia, E., Martin, C., Garcia, A., Harrison, R., Flood, D.: Systematic Analysis of Mobile Diabetes Management Applications on Different Platforms. In: Holzinger, A., Simonic,K.-M. (eds.) USAB 2011. LNCS, vol. 7058, pp. 379–396. Springer, Heidelberg (2011). doi:10.1007/978-3-642-25364-5_27
23. Rollo, M.E., Ash, S., Lyons-Wall, P., Russell, A.: Trial of a mobile phone method for recording dietary intake in adults with type 2 diabetes: evaluation and implications for future applications. J. Telemed. Telecare 17(6), 318–323 (2011)
24. Waki, K., Aizawa, K., Kato, S., Fujita, H., Lee, H., Kobayashi, H., Ogawa, M., Mouri, K., Kadowaki, T., Ohe, K.: DialBetics with a multimedia food recording tool, FoodLog: smartphone-based self-management for type 2 diabetes. J. Diab. Sci. Technol. 9(3), 534–540 (2015)
25. Lloyd, B., Groat, D., Cook, C.B., Kaufman, D., Grando, A.: iDECIDE: A mobile application for insulin dosing using an evidence based equation to account for patient preferences. Stud. Health Technol. Inform. 216, 93–97 (2015)
26. Arsand, E., Muzny, M., Bradway, M., Muzik, J., Hartvigsen, G.: Performance of the first combined smartwatch and smartphone diabetes diary application study. J. Diab. Sci. Technol. 9(3), 556–563 (2015)
27. Domhardt, M., Tiefengrabner, M., Dinic, R., Fotschl, U., Oostingh, G.J., Stutz, T., Stechemesser, L., Weitgasser, R., Ginzinger, S.W.: Training of carbohydrate estimation for people with diabetes using mobile augmented reality. J. Diab. Sci. Technol. 9(3), 516–524 (2015)
28. Sultan, S., Mohan, P.: How to interact: evaluating the interface between mobile healthcare systems and the monitoring of blood sugar and blood pressure. In: 2009 6th Annual International Conference on Mobile and Ubiquitous Systems: Networking and Services, MobiQuitous 2009 (2009)

29. Jabar, M.A., Azmi, M.F., Sidi, F.: Integration of mobile and web application: an implementation of diabetic management system. J. Theor. Appl. Inf. Technol. **55**(2), 168–173 (2013)

30. Garcia-Zapirain, B., de la Torre Diez, I., Sainz de Abajo, B., Lopez-Coronado, M.: Development, technical, and user evaluation of a web mobile application for self-control of diabetes. Telemed. J. E- Health **22**(9), 778–785 (2016)

31. Caburnay, C.A., Graff, K., Harris, J.K., McQueen, A., Smith, M., Fairchild, M., Kreuter, M. W.: Evaluating diabetes mobile applications for health literate designs and functionality. Prev. Chronic Dis. **12**, E61 (2015)

32. Martin, C., Flood, D., Sutton, D., Aldea, A., Harrison, R., Waite, M.: A Systematic Evaluation of Mobile Applications for Diabetes Management. In: Campos, P., Graham, N., Jorge, J., Nunes, N., Palanque, P., Winckler, M. (eds.) INTERACT 2011. LNCS, vol. 6949, pp. 466–469. Springer, Heidelberg (2011). doi:10.1007/978-3-642-23768-3_59

33. Demidowich, A.P., Lu, K., Tamler, R., Bloomgarden, Z.: An evaluation of diabetes self-management applications for Android smartphones. J. Telemed. Telecare **18**(4), 235–238 (2012)

34. Whitlock, L.A., McLaughlin, A.C: Identifying usability problems of blood glucose tracking apps for older adult users. In: Proceedings of the Human Factors and Ergonomics Society (2012)

35. Chomutare, T., Fernandez-Luque, L., Arsand, E., Hartvigsen, G.: Features of mobile diabetes applications: review of the literature and analysis of current applications compared against evidence-based guidelines. J. Med. Internet Res. **13**(3), e65 (2011)

36. Issa, T., Isaias, P.: Usability and Human Computer Interaction (HCI). In: Issa, T., Isaias, P. (eds.) Sustainable Design, pp. 19–36. Springer, Heidelberg (2015)

37. Nielsen, J.: Usability 101: Introduction to Usability. (2012). [cited 2017 February 9, 2017]. https://www.nngroup.com/articles/usability-101-introduction-to-usability/

38. Kim, M.S., Ye, Q., Khan, U., Boren, S.A.: Developing a mobile application to improve diabetic patients' self-care behaviors: a functionality analysis. AMIA 2016 Annual Symposium (2016)

39. Lyles, C.R., Sarkar, U., Osborn, C.Y.: Getting a technology-based diabetes intervention ready for prime time: a review of usability testing studies. Curr. Diab. Rep. **14**(10), 534 (2014)

Health and Aging

Abductive Cognitive Support
for (Semantic) Dementia Persons

Akinori Abe[1,2(✉)]

[1] Division of Behavioral Science, Faculty of Letters, Chiba University,
1-33 Yayoi-cho, Inage-ku, Chiba 263-8522, Japan
ave@ultimaVI.arc.net.my, ave@chiba-u.jp
[2] Dwango Artificial Intelligence Laboratory, Tokyo, Japan

Abstract. Previously, I introduced the concept of affordance to support dementia persons. Limited merits of affordance for supporting dementia persons are pointed out by Bozeat and Hodges. In addition, after the extension of Gibson's concept of affordance, it is mainly applied to the interface design. Based on the concept of affordance by Gibson, I proposed a dementia person support mechanism in which functions or meanings of things can be suggested. It is based on abduction framework and performed under the context of chance discovery to determine affordance. That is, the suggestion is not offered explicitly. I showed my assumption that complex situation can be transformed to a combination of simple situations and necessity of develop a mechanism to transform complex situation to a combination of simple situations. In addition I discussed it as curation in chance discovery. Thus the framework can be realized by the introduction of shikake's concept. A shikake is a trigger to start a certain action or to change person's mind and behaviour. As a result of the action, all or part of problem will be solved. It sometimes is not the person's will. In this paper, I will discuss the support of dementia persons as an installation of shikake in the environment. By the installation of shikake dementia persons can be implicitly guided to behave properly. It can be regarded as a proper selection of affordance by a proper curation. I will also discuss this type of issue from the viewpoint of the first-person research and information design.

1 Introduction

Recently according to the long life of us, it has been pointed out that one of the serious problem is dementia. Dementia is the progressive decline in cognitive function, such as memory, attention, language, and problem solving, due to damage or disease in the body beyond what might be expected from normal aging. For such dementia person it is difficult to understand several things. Accordingly it is necessary to support such person to understand things to have daily lives. Limited merits of affordance for supporting persons with dementia are pointed out by Bozeat and Hodges (Bozeat et al. 2002; Hodges et al. 2000).

Previously, I introduced the concept of affordance to support persons with dementia (Abe 2009, 2012b), in which functions of things can be suggested as

© Springer International Publishing AG 2017
V.G. Duffy (Ed.): DHM 2017, Part II, LNCS 10287, pp. 119–131, 2017.
DOI: 10.1007/978-3-319-58466-9_12

a similar or related things. It is based on abductive framework and performed under the context of chance discovery to determine affordance. However it is rather difficult to determine affordance even for normal persons. I proposed the introduction of curation (Abe 2014) for affordance selection. In addition much more useful or better system can be considered for affordance selection. For that in this paper a concept of shikake can be introduced. A shikake is a trigger to start a certain action or to change person's mind and behaviour. As a result of the action, all or part of problem will be solved. In this paper, the support of persons with dementia as an installation of shikake in the environment will be discussed. By the installation of shikake, persons with dementia can be implicitly guided to behave properly. It can be regarded as a proper selection of affordance.

This paper mainly introduces the abduction and affordance paradigm to obtain the meaning of an object. The meaning of an object will be abduced with the guidance of affordance.

2   Affordance and Abduction

The followings are explained in several places and times. However, for the HCII conference I have not fully explained yet. I will give an introduction of abduction and related logics for the understanding the following discussions.

2.1   Affordance

Gibson ecologically introduced the concept of affordance for perceptional phenomena (Gibson 1977, 1979). It emphasizes the environmental information available in extended spatial and temporal pattern in optic arrays, for guiding the behaviours of animals, and for specifying ecological events. Thus Gibson defined the affordance of something as "a specific combination of the properties of its substance and its surfaces taken with reference to an animal." For instance, the affordance of climbing a stair step in a bipedal fashion has been described in terms of the height of a stair riser taken with reference to a person's leg length (Warren 1984). That is, if a stair riser is less than 88% of a person's leg length, then that means that the person can climb that stair. On the other hand, if a stair riser is greater than 88% of the person's leg length, then that means that the person cannot climb that stair, at least not in a bipedal fashion. For that Jones pointed out that "it should be noted also that this is true regardless of whether the person is aware of the relation between his or her leg length and the stair riser's height, which suggests further that the meaning is not internally constructed and stored but rather is inherent in the person's environment system" (Jones 2003).

Since Gibson's introduction, affordance has been widely discussed, and the other perspective and extensions have been added, for instance by Norman

(Norman 1988). Especially, it has been effectively introduced to interface designs after several extensions. However, this paper will not deal with this aspect of affordance.

2.2   Abduction and Chance Discovery

Abduction. In this section, as an incomplete knowledge reasoning (reasoning dealing with incomplete knowledge), In the following, I briefly explain incomplete logical reasoning systems—induction, and abduction.

Peirce characterized abduction and induction as follows (Peirce 1955):

- Abduction is an operation for adopting an explanatory hypothesis, which is subject to certain conditions, and that in pure abduction, there can never be justification for accepting the hypothesis other than through interrogation.
  Inference for (novel) discovery
- Induction is an operation for testing a hypothesis by experiment, and if it is true, an observation made under certain conditions ought to have certain results.
  Inference for classification and learning, which are (generalized) discovery

Thus although abduction and induction are categorized into an incomplete knowledge reasoning and can discover something "new." In fact, something abduction discovers are rather different from those which induction discovers. If we need to discover general tendencies or classification induction will be better. On the other hand, if we need to discover something rare or novel, abduction will be better. In the following a computational abduction, which is hypothetical reasoning will be illustrated.

Hypothetical Reasoning. Abduction is usually used to find the reason or explanation (set of hypotheses) in a logical way to explain an observation. For instance, the inference mechanism of Theorist (Poole et al. 1987) that explains an observation (O) by a consistent and minimal hypotheses set (h) selected from a set of hypotheses (H) is shown as followings.

$$F \nvdash O. \quad (O \text{ can not be explained by only } F.) \tag{1}$$

$$F \cup h \vdash O. \quad (O \text{ can be explained by } F \text{ and } h.) \tag{2}$$

$$F \cup h \nvdash \square. \quad (F \text{ and } h \text{ is consistent.}) \tag{3}$$

Where F is a fact (background knowledge) and $\square$ is an empty clause. A hypothesis set (h) is selected from a hypothesis base ($h \in H$).

Chance Discovery. It is important to deal with rare or novel phenomena which might lead us to risk or beneficial opportunity in the future. This type of activity is called as chance discovery. A chance is defined as *"a novel or rare event/situation that can be conceived either as an opportunity or a risk in the future"* (Ohsawa and McBurney 2003). It is rather difficult to discover a chance by usual statistical strategies. Abduction and analogy (Abductive Analogical

Reasoning (Abe 2000) which can be regarded as an extension of CMS (Reiter and de Kleer 1987) was adopted to perform chance discovery (Abe 2003a,b). Where chance discovery is regarded as and characterized as an explanatory reasoning for the unknown or unfamiliar observations. A chance is therefore defined as followings:

1. **Chance** is a set of unknown hypotheses. Therefore, explanation of an observation is not influenced by it. Accordingly, a possible observation that should be explained cannot be explained. In this case, a hypotheses base or a knowledge base lacks necessary hypotheses. Therefore, it is necessary to generate missing hypotheses. Missing hypotheses are characterized as chance.
2. **Chance** itself is a set of known facts, but it is unknown how to use them to explain an observation. That is, a certain set of rules is missing. Accordingly, an observation cannot be explained by the facts. Since rules are usually generated by inductive ways, rules that are different from the trend cannot be generated. In this case, rules are generated by abductive methods, so trends are not considered. Abductively generated rules are characterized as chance.

3   Dementia and Its Care

3.1   Dementia

Dementia is the progressive decline in cognitive function, such as memory, attention, language, and problem solving, due to damage or disease in the body or brain beyond what might be expected from normal aging. In the later stages, persons with dementia will not be able to recognize time (day of the week, day of the month, and year etc.), place, and person. Phenomena due to aging and dementia are quite different. For instance, for memory, aged person does not forget all of his/her experiences, on the other hand, persons with dementia forgets whole of his/her experiences. Dementia is roughly categorized to cortical and subcortical. For instance, several types of cortical dementia are reported such as Alzheimer's disease. Except for the treatable types, there is no cure to dementia, although scientists are progressing in making a type of medication that will slow down the process of dementia. For instance, for the medication of Alzheimer, actions such as cheerful communication and proper stimulation are recommend for slowing down (Kasama 1997). In addition, some studies have found that music therapy which stimulates emotion as well as brain may be useful in helping patients with dementia (Aldridge 2000). Alternative therapies are also discussed for the care of Alzheimer's disease and dementia (Cafalu 2005a,b).

3.2   Dementia Care

Bozeat and Hodges analyzed the feature of mapping between objects and their meaning for a person with semantic dementia from four factors—affordance, presence of recipient, familiarity, and problem solving (Bozeat et al. 2002; Hodges et al. 2000). They showed very important and interesting results. For instance, they pointed out that "as a group, the patients did not achieve better performance on a subset of affordable objects when use of these was compared with a familiarity-matched subset of objects lacking such affordances. This absence of a general group benefit applied both to overall use and to the specific component of use afforded by the object's structure.[...] it became clear that there was a reliable benefit of affordance on the specific components of use, but only for the most impaired patients." They also pointed out that "[t]he impact of recipient, like affordance, was found to be modulated by the degree of semantic impairment. The patients with a moderate level of conceptual impairment demonstrated significantly better use with the recipient present, whereas the patients with mild and severe impairment showed no effect. [...] It was not surprising, therefore, to find that familiarity also influenced performance on object use assessments."

These observations and analyses show that proper affordance might give a certain support to persons with dementia for understanding (meanings of) objects. In the following section, their observations are considered to develop the dementia person support system.

4   Dementia Care Inspired by Affordance

In this section I discuss how to present or suggest hidden information in dementia care situation. Such hidden information can be presented as certain stimuli in several situations, for instance a group house for dementia persons. Perhaps it will be rather difficult to prepare such stimuli in a general situations. Because it will be difficult to prepare a special function in such a general situations. Anyway, as shown in the previous section, even for a person with dementia, if he/she receives certain stimuli, he/she sometimes achieve the better performance. The problem is that what type of stimulus will be better to present and how to make it recognize. Actually such stimulus should be "afforded (selected from an environment)" by the user. That is, it can be regarded as an "affordance" in an environment. Accordingly I will introduce the concept of affordance to a dementia care system. Proper affordance might give a certain support to persons with dementia in understanding (the meanings of) objects.

For affordance, according to the Gibson's definition, an *Object* is observed and affordance is selected in the environment to understand its meaning. In addition, we can give a certain meaning to the *Object* explicitly or implicitly. Though meaning actually should exist inside of the *Object*, in this framework meaning is explicitly described for the logical formalization[1]. That is, the meaning should be observed and the affordance functions as a type of link to *Objects*. When the meaning is fixed, the affordance determination situation will be logically described as follows:

$$F \cup Object \cup affordance \models meaning \tag{4}$$

$$F \cup Object \cup affordance \not\models \Box \tag{5}$$

---

[1] This logical formation was defined by the author (Abe 2009, 2012b).

The above formalization is described based on the formalization of Theorist (Poole et al. 1987) which is a hypothetical reasoning (abduction). F is so called facts which involves fundamental knowledge in the world. The generated (selected) affordance is consistent with F and *Object* (Eq. (5)). Then *Object* is given meaning (the *Object*'s meaning can be understood) as an explanation by affordance and abduction.

Thus in this framework affordance can be regarded as a hypothesis set. Consistent affordance (Eq. (5)) can be selected in the environment (hypothesis base) to explain meaning. In addition, for understanding subset of or similar afforded objects (*Object'*), the affordance determination situation will be logically described as follows:

$$F \cup Object \cup Object' \cup M \cup affordance \models meaning \qquad (6)$$

The above logical descriptions can be illustrated in Fig. 1. In fact, the above description is based on Goebel's formalization of analogy (Goebel 1989). M is a mapping function from *Object* to *Object'*. That is, to understand the same meaning of the subset of or similar afforded objects, an additional mapping function M is required. Thus if M can be determined and the usage of *Object* is known, *Object'* can also be understood. For normal persons, M is easy to understand. However, for persons with dementia, it is pointed out that it is rather difficult to understand and determine M. Then the issue becomes how to suggest a mapping function M as an additional hypothesis.

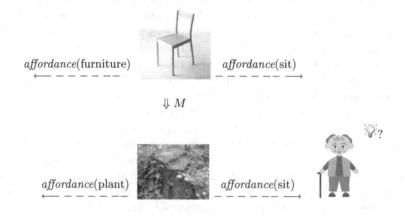

Fig. 1. Affordance: communication between human and environment

In the following sections, I will discuss the above problem.

5   Shikake

5.1   What is a Shikake?

According to Matsumura's definition (Matsumura 2013), a shikake is an embodied trigger for behaviour change to solve social or personal issues. As a result of the action, all or part of problem will be solved. It may not sometimes be the person's will. Matsumura continues that the shikake should be properly designed. That is, the relationship between a problem to solve and a trigger to action should be properly designed.

In addition, Matsumura uses a keyword "affordance" to explain such a trigger. His affordance is based on Norman's one (Norman 1988), accordingly it may be different from Gibson's one. However, in the followings, discussion will be conducted based on Gibson's one. Because our affordance is based on Gibson's affordance.

5.2   Shikakeology

Shikake. Key concepts shown in chance discovery are very similar to those in shikakeology. In fact, a chance is a rare and novel event. In addition, hidden or potential events are mainly dealt with in chance discovery. A chance itself is not easy to discover, because it is usually hidden or out of our scope. A shikake should sometimes easy to discover, because it functions as a trigger. Without being found out, any shikake cannot function. However, the shikake itself may not easy to be understood.

An example of a (n implicit) shikake is, for instance, hidden Mickey (Fig. 2) in the Disney Land. In order to discover the hidden Mickey, people run around the Disney Land. During searching, they may discover other interesting things. Of course, when they can find the hidden Mickey, they will be happy. Thus hidden character functions as a trigger to such activities (search and run). By this trigger (shikake), they can enjoy the Disney Land more than a simple tour in the Disney Land. Even if they cannot find it, they will come back to the Disney Land again to find it. A shikake also has such an effect, but in this paper such an effect will not be considered.

In the followings I will explain the relationships between shikake and curation, affordance, and chance which I use in the framework of the support system for dementia person.

Shikake and Curation. Curation in chance discovery (Abe 2010, 2012a) can be regarded as a strategy of the information display[2]. A shikake can also be regarded as a strategy to lead us information. In the usual curation, information display is designed for audience to understand information easily. Then the curator's

---

[2] Of course there are a "general" curation in museums and e-Science Data Curation (Lord and MacDonald 2003). However, in this paper, only curation in chance discovery will be considered.

Fig. 2. Hidden Mickey

knowledge can be transferred to audience by his/her curation. By a shikake, the staff will not directly transfer his/her knowledge to the audience, but by a trigger of shikake, their knowledge will be transferred to the audience. Thus a shikake will be provided in some case in curation.

Shikake and Affordance. From the viewpoint of the concept of affordance, a shikake is in an environment and offers a certain guidance for affordance selection. When we can collect the affordance properly, the shikake functions properly and we can proceed to the next stage. A shikake is a type of controller for the affordance selection. By being aware of a shikake, we can be lead to proper affordance source to collect it. For instance, if people are aware of any affordance from a hidden Mickey which is a shikake, we can collect proper affordance which shows that a hidden Mickey is, for instance, very interesting and enjoyable. That is, they can select a proper affordance according to their better benefit. Thus shikake can be explained by the concept of affordance.

Shikake and Chance. A shikake exists in an environment, and if it is applied to us we can change or proceed our activity directions for the better future. A chance will be exist in an environment, and by discovering it we can proceed to the better future. Thus the curated environment can be regarded as an environment equipped with a shikake. According to the policy of chance discovery, curation will be performed implicitly. A shikake can be either explicitly or implicitly placed. For an implicit placement, a chance and a shikake have a certain relationship. Because the above type of strategy is explained by affordance selection. That is, in the environment, a shikake exists and the shikake is a certain pointer for the proper selection of affordance. A shikake does not coincide with a chance but it can help in chance discovery. Of course, in chance discovery, any shikake cannot be explicit.

In the next section, a support system for dementia person will be discussed from the aspect of a shikake.

6 Introduction of a Shikake to Dementia Support System

In the previous section, I discussed the support system for dementia person in which affordance is selected to obtain meaning or function of things. I discussed the difficulty of the affordance selection even for normal persons, and pointed out that the issue becomes how to suggest a mapping function M as an additional hypothesis. M is an additional mapping function. As Bozeat and Hodges suggested, feature of mapping between objects and their meaning for a person with semantic dementia are affordance, presence of recipient, familiarity, and problem solving Thus a mapping system is very important to extend or change existing information to information on unknown world based on familiarity of more than two things. If a mapping function from the familiar world to unknown world is properly provided, it is rather easy to guess the meaning in the unknown world. In order to recognize the mapping function, it is necessary to introduce a certain system such as curation or a shikake to guess such a function. In this section, one of the solutions will be shown as an introduction of a shikake.

As explained in the above, a shikake is defined as an embodied trigger for behaviour change to solve social or personal issues. In addition, as discussed in the previous section, a shikake should sometimes easy to discover, because it functions as a trigger, but the shikake itself may not easy to understand. In addition, by a shikake, the staff will not directly transfer his/her knowledge to the audience, but by a trigger of shikake, their knowledge will be transferred to the audience. Thus the feature of a shikake is suitable for suggestion of a mapping function M.

Then a shikake can be included in the formulae shown in the previous section.

$$F \cup Object \cup Object' \cup M \cup affordance \models meaning \tag{7}$$

can be transformed as follows:

$$F \cup Object \cup Object' \cup shikake \cup affordance \models meaning \tag{8}$$

$$F \cup Object \cup affordance \not\models \Box \tag{9}$$

Accordingly a shikake can function as a the other object with mapping function. $Object' \cup shikake$ means that $Object'$ is a shikake to select a proper affordance for guessing the meaning or function of $Object$. For instance, if somebody does not understand the meaning or usage of a folding bed, a folding wallet can be placed near the folding bed or shown to the user. Perhaps it will be better to show the wallet in an unfolding style. If he/she close and open a folding wallet, he/she can understand how to use the folding bed. That is, they can select an affordance as folding from the bed. In this case, showing a folding wallet can be a shikake to understand (select an affordance) the function of a folding bed. If the user is aware of the similarity between a folding bed and a folding wallet, he/she can understand the function of a folding bed. In this case, a folding wallet can be shown implicitly, for instance it is placed on a floor as if it were dropped by somebody. This shikake mechanism is described in Fig. 3.

The shape of the folding wallet can become a trigger to understand the usage of a folding bed. It may be rather different from the hidden Mickey. However, both can be a trigger to the next action. For the hidden Mickey, it functions as a search object to be found. For the folding wallet, it functions as a reference object to understand the similar thing. For an example, the similar relationship is shown. However, other relationships or functions can be considered to prepare a shikake.

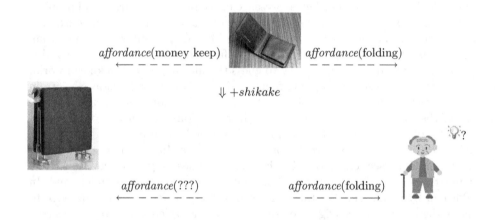

Fig. 3. Shikake: a key to the better affordance selection

Thus if we consider the existence of a shikake, affordance will be selected more easily and properly. Because a shikake functions as a hint to select the better affordance.

In the above, a shikake as an object is shown. However, the other type of shikake can be considered. For instance there are lot of sentences in the world for the proper guidance of human's activities. For instance, instead of "caution!!" in a certain place such a phrase as "Watch your right side to check the existence running cars." is frequently placed near a crosswalk (without a signal). This type of phrase will be effective for the person in hurry. In fact this type of a shikake will not understood by a semantic dementia person. However, a certain phrase can be function as a shikake even for the person with dementia. For instance in the above case, if you say "after reading book, please close the book" to the person with dementia, they can understand how to fold the bed.

Tadaki studied curation system which tries to control visitors focus to art works (Tadaki and Abe 2017). She conducted several shikake instrations to determine which type of shikake will function better. The result can be extended to use in the support system for the persons with dementia. The showing strategy of labels (a shikake introducing to the meaning of the object) will be considered as a good curation.

In several places (shops), music is very effectively used for avoiding shoplifting (Beckerman 2015). In fact, this type of shikake is frequently used, but for the our case, can it be used as a shikake? If it is possible, it will be very useful. But I do not think it can be used for our purpose. Because the sound is an invisible object. Therefore it is rather difficult to place a certain sound as a shikake. Perhaps a special sound may stimulate the brain to fire a certain place for reminding meanings. For this case, though this idea is very interesting, but since I'm not a brain scientist, I will not deal with this solution. In fact as shown above, music therapy will stimulates emotion as well as brain (Aldridge 2000). This type of sound effect will be used in several situations.

The concept of information design is very important in the presentation. In fact, it can be regarded as a special case of curation. Thus it can be discussed in the context of shikake. In the book edited by Robert Jacobson (Jacobson 1999), Roger Whitehouse discussed the uniqueness of individual perception. He tested several designs in several situations. He pointed out that "[m]ost importantly, we began to understand how easy it is to disenfranchise individuals simply by not perceiving and correctly interpreting the most basic facts about their needs." Then he pointed out that "[a]s designer, we need to be conscious of, accept, and embrace the notion of unique perceptual abilities and respond generously to the needs it implies." It can also be discussed in the context of the first-person research (Suwa and Hori 2015). In the first-person research, all matters (objects, behaviour etc.) are subjectively observed and analysed. Thus we cannot generalize all matters.

For the first-person, Jocene Vallack pointed out (Vallack 2010) that "the first-person experiences undergo a metamorphosis and become universal insights. The process occurs though one's solo journey into the epoche[3], beyond which lie the eternal forms of existence." That is, the status of research will change from subjective to intersubjective and therefore universal. Thus according to his thought. if we continue the first-person research, it will become a universai research. However, it will not so easy for our aim. Because our target is person with dementia. It will be more difficult. We should stay in the first-person research to conduct the tailor-made support.

Thus there are lot of matters to consider when we design a support system for persons with dementia.

7   Conclusions

In this paper, a series of the support systems for persons with dementia inspired by affordance are reviewed. In addition, a shikake is introduced to supplement the affordance selection in a dementia support system. A shikake is a trigger to start a certain action or to change person's mind and behaviour. In this paper,

---

[3] Jocene Vallack defined epoche as "incubation period.".

a shikake is used as a part (hint) of a mapping function between an unfamiliar thing and a familiar thing. A familiar thing is offered as a shikake to select proper affordance.

In this paper only a theory and a simple example are shown. In the next paper, experiments with the support system for persons with dementia inspired by affordance and shikake installed system will be reported.

In addition, I discussed several aspects of shikake in this paper. These aspects should be considered in the next support system.

References

Abe, A.: Abductive analogical reasoning. Syst. Comput. Jpn. **31**(1), 11–19 (2000)

Abe, A.: The role of abduction in chance discovery. New Gener. Comput. **21**(1), 61–71 (2003a)

Abe, A.: Abduction and analogy in chance discovery. In: Ohsawa, Y., McBurney, P. (eds.) Chance Discovery, pp. 231–248. Springer, Heidelberg (2003b)

Abe, A.: Cognitive chance discovery. In: Stephanidis, C. (ed.) UAHCI 2009. LNCS, vol. 5614, pp. 315–323. Springer, Heidelberg (2009). doi:10.1007/978-3-642-02707-9_36

Abe, A.: Curation in chance discovery. In: Proceedings of ICDM 2010 5th International Workshop on Chance Discovery, pp. 793–799 (2010)

Abe, A.: Curation in chance discovery. In: Ohsawa, Y., Abe, A. (eds.) Advances in Chance Discovery. SCI, vol. 423, pp. 1–18. Springer, Heidelberg (2012a)

Abe, A.: Cognitive chance discovery: from abduction to affordance. In: Magnani, L., Li, L. (eds.) Philosophy and Cognitive Science. SAPERE, vol. 2, pp. 155–172. Springer, Heidelberg (2012b)

Abe, A.: Cognitive chance discovery: from abduction to affordance and curation. Int. J. Cogn. Inf. Nat. Intell. (IJCINI) **8**(2), 47–59 (2014)

Aldridge, D.: Music Therapy in Dementia Care. Jessica Kingsley Publishers, London (2000)

Beckerman, J.: The Sonic Boom. Mariner Book, New York (2015)

Bozeat, S., Ralph, M.A.L., Patterson, K., Hodges, J.R.: When objects lose their meaning: waht happens to their use? Cogn. Affecgtive Behav. Neurosci. **2**(3), 236–251 (2002)

Cafalu, C.A.: The role of alternative therapies in the management of Alzheimer's disease and dementia, Part I. Ann. Long-Term Care **13**(7), 34–41 (2005a)

Cafalu, C.A.: The role of alternative therapies in the management of Alzheimer's disease and dementia, Part II. Ann. Long-Term Care **13**(8), 33–39 (2005b)

Gibson, J.J.: The theory of affordances. In: Shaw, R., Bransford, J. (eds.) Perceiving, Acting, and Knowing (1977)

Gibson, J.J.: The Ecological Approach to Visual Perception. Houghton Mifflin, Boston (1979)

Goebel, R.: A sketch of analogy as reasoning with equality hypotheses. In: Jantke, K.P. (ed.) AII 1989. LNCS (LNAI), vol. 397, pp. 243–253. Springer, Heidelberg (1989). doi:10.1007/3-540-51734-0_65

Hodges, J.R., Bozeat, S., Ralph, M.A.L., Patterson, K., Spatt, J.: The role of conceptual knowledge in object use evidence from semantic dementia. Brain **123**, 1913–1925 (2000)

Jacobson, R. (ed.): Information Design. MIT Press, Cambridge (1999)

Jones, K.S.: What is an affordance? Ecol. Psychol. **15**(2), 107–114 (2003)

Kasama, A.: Dementia. http://www.inetmie.or.jp/~kasamie/dementia.html. Accessed 9 Feb 2016

Lord, P., MacDonald, A.: e-Science Curation Report (2003)

Matsumura, N.: A shikake as an embodied trigger for behavior change. In: Proceedings of AAAI 2013 Spring Symposium on Shikakelology, pp. 62–67 (2013)

Norman, D.: The Design of Everyday Things. Addison Wesley, Boston (1988)

Ohsawa, Y., McBurney, P. (eds.): Chance Discovery. Springer, Heidelberg (2003)

Peirce, C.S.: Abduction and induction. In: Philosophical Writings of Peirce, chap. 11, pp. 150–156. Dover (1955)

Poole, D., Goebel, R., Aleliunas, R.: Theorist: a logical reasoning system for defaults and diagnosis. In: Cercone, N.J., McCalla, G. (eds.) The Knowledge Frontier: Essays in the Representation of Knowledge, pp. 331–352. Springer, Heidelberg (1987)

Reiter, R., de Kleer, J.: Foundation of assumption-based truth maintenance systems: preliminary report. In: Proceedings of AAAI 1987, pp. 183–188 (1987)

Suwa, M., Hori, K. (eds.): An Introduction of First-Person Research. Kindai-Kagaku-sha, Tokyo (2015). (in Japanese)

Tadaki, K., Abe, A.: A study of a shikae in museums–from the viewpoint of captions in art museums. In: Proceedings of the 31th Annual Conference of the Japanese Society for Artificial Intelligence 2017, 4B1-OS-23a-5 (2017)

Vallack, J.: Subtextual phenomenology: a methodology for valid, first-person research. Electron. J. Bus. Res. Methods **8**(2), 109–112 (2010)

Warren, W.H.: Perceiving affordances: visual guidance of stair-climbing. J. Exp. Psychol. Hum. Percept. Perform. **10**, 683–703 (1984)

Age and Computer Skill Level Difference in Aging-Centered Design: A Case Study of a Social Type Website

Wen-Yu Chao[1(✉)], Qing-Xing Qu[1,3], Le Zhang[1], and Vincent G. Duffy[1,2]

[1] School of Industrial Engineering, Purdue University, West Lafayette, USA
chaow@purdue.edu
[2] School of Agriculture and Biological Engineering, Purdue University, West Lafayette, USA
[3] Department of Industrial Engineering, Northeastern University, Shenyang, People's Republic of China

Abstract. According to the estimation of US Census Bureau, the age demographic will change from 13 percent of the population aged 65 and older in 2010 to 19 percent in 2030 [1]. With the fast growing number of elderly population, designers may be driven by market to consider an aging-centered design. However, the real challenge of aging-centered design may not only be the preference or interest by age difference but also the technology gap of using computer.

From the user testing results of a project on human-centered website design for elderly, we found out that elderly have lower performance than young people with a lower efficiency and a higher error rate. However, the difference wasn't shown with a statistical significance because there's a big in-between-group variance in elderly group. During the user testing process, an inconsistency of computer experience and skill level difference between elder users has been shown in their behavior. Some elderly with more computer experience show strong confidence in performing tasks independently and some totally rely on the guidance of experimenter. This result implies aging may not be the only factor affects user's behavior in aging-centered design.

In this paper, we planned a 2 by 2 factorial experiment. Our goal is to carefully examine the effects of each factor and their interactions. From the experiment, we expect to have 2 key findings: (1) Computer skill level difference affects the performance and it is confounded with the age factor. (2) Users' subjective perceived value of the website will affect users' subjective rating of usability.

By this experiment, we could confirm that aging is not the only factor that prevents us from applying a universal design to different age groups. The emphasis on of aging-centered design may be highlighting the technology gap in between elderly.

Keywords: User-centered design · Usability · User behavior · User mental model · Aging-centered design

© Springer International Publishing AG 2017
V.G. Duffy (Ed.): DHM 2017, Part II, LNCS 10287, pp. 132–141, 2017.
DOI: 10.1007/978-3-319-58466-9_13

1   Introduction

According to the estimation of US Census Bureau, the age structure will change from 13 percent of the population aged 65 and older in 2010 to 19 percent in 2030 [1]. As our reliance on Internet has got stronger in nowadays world, the number of senior web users has also grown. In the future, the senior citizen population would potentially become the main demographic of website users. And thus, web designer will be driven by market to consider a user-centered design of website for senior citizen group.

User-centered design (UCD) is an approach and also a design philosophy to put users at the center of all design decisions during an iterative design process. The idea could be implemented by continuously probing the users' needs and modifying the design based on users' physical and psychological capabilities and recognized individual differences by their demographic. The tools in the design process include user research, prototyping, and user testing [2]. In this paper, user-centered design for senior web users will be called as Aging-Centered Website Design since the aging group would be the target users in this context.

For facilitating Aging-Centered Website Design, several kinds of user research and user testing have been done to explore the physical and psychological limitations of aging group. Psychological findings on aging and their abilities have shown, elder people vary a lot in their behavior by many reasons, such as vision and hearing impairment, decline in working memory, and learning effects [3–6]. Hawthorn has further pointed out that the studies of abilities of elder people should include controls of education, eyesight, medication and especially, training effects [6].

Nielsen has conducted usability studies with 75 senior web users whose age is above 65. He has found out significant differences between elder and younger webs users in quantitative user testing metrics such as task completion time, error and success rate. In over all, senior web users are slower and they may make more mistakes [7]. There are many other studies have shown the similar results [4, 8–10]. Except the findings of age difference in the performance of using websites, age difference has also shown in attitude toward using computers, and thus it affects user mental models [11]. The real challenge of Aging-Centered Website Design may not only be the age difference between elderly and younger adults, but also the technology gap in between elderly and other age groups.

Richard Hodes, the Director of the National Institute on Aging, indicated at SPRY conference that the technology gap affecting older adults and difficulties in using search engines and navigating the Web have left elders hesitant about using the Internet [5]. More and more studies have also found age and prior experience differences of using technologies in performance, user behavior, human computer interactions, and attitude toward computers [8, 9, 12–14].

However, seldom do the practitioners of user experience (UX) evaluation consider the prior experience differences and use it as a control in user testing of their Aging-Centered Design project [15–18]. In this paper, we proposed a scientific study of the user testing for an Aging-Centered Website Design project. The study is consisted of 2 research models: a 2 by 2 factorial experiment to test the effects and the interaction of age and computer skill level; and a structural equation model to describe the causal relationships between age, computer skill level, usability and perceived value. The study results would imply that using these two factors as controls in user testing could help designer better understand the user behavior and the user mental model of aging group.

The organization of this paper is as follows: Sect. 2 presents an Aging-Centered Website Design project which is used as the research object in the proposed study; Sect. 3 introduces the hypotheses and research models and Sect. 4 details the experimental design and experiment procedures, testing setting of the proposed study; Sect. 5 would be discussions and conclusion is in Sect. 6.

2   An Aging-Centered Website Design Project: Care and Share

The Care & Share project is a Aging-Centered Website Design project that was done in a Fall 2016 course, CGT512 in Purdue university for participating in 2017 HCI student design competition. The goal of this design project is to solve the social isolation problem for both senior citizens and international students. The design idea is to create a website to bring seniors and international students together by volunteer services and social events. The main functions of the website are: seniors post social events or volunteer service request on the website, and students can search the interested events to join.

The first author in this paper was responsible for planning and conducting user research, usability testing and user feedback sessions for this project. In this project, we found out that elderly have lower performance than young people with a lower efficiency and a higher error rate. However, the difference wasn't shown with a statistical significance while there was a large in-between-group variance in elderly group. During the user testing process for the low-fidelity prototypes, an inconsistency of computer skill level difference between elder users was shown. Some elderly with more experience of using computer show strong confidence in performing tasks independently and some totally rely on the guidance of experimenter. This result implies aging may not be the only factor affects user's behavior in ageing-centered design.

Another interesting finding is user's subjective rating of website usability may be affected by their perception of the website value, especially for elder people. During our testing process, the elder testers found this website may bring value to their social life, so they may have tended to give a better subjective rating to the website usability.

3   Hypotheses and Research Model

Based on the literature review and previous findings from an aging-centered design project, we formed four hypotheses as shown below:

Hypothesis 1: There is an interaction between age and computer skill levels in website user testing results including task completion time (TCT), error rate (ER), subjective usability scale (SUS), perceived value (PV).

Hypothesis 2: Age affects website user testing results (including TCT, ER, SUS, PV).

Hypothesis 3: Computer skill levels affects website user testing results.

Hypothesis 4: Website usability testing results and consumer Perceived Value of the website would be related variables.

In this study, we proposed 2 research models to test above hypotheses. The first one was built by a 2 by 2 factorial experiment structure as shown in Fig. 1 and will be analyzed by DOE analysis method. In this model, hypothesis 1 will be tested by H1; hypothesis 2 will be tested by H2–H5; and hypothesis 3 will be tested by H6–H9.

The second one is a causal relationship model as shown in Fig. 2, and it will be analyzed by Structure Equation Modeling method [19]. In this structural model, hypothesis 2 will be tested by H11–H12; hypothesis 3 is tested by H13–H14; and hypothesis 4 is tested by H15.

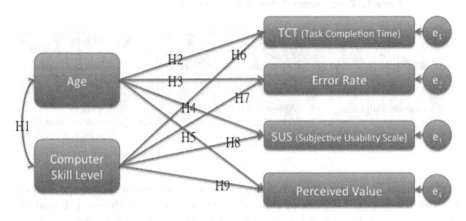

Fig. 1. Path diagram for the proposed 2^2 factorial experiment.

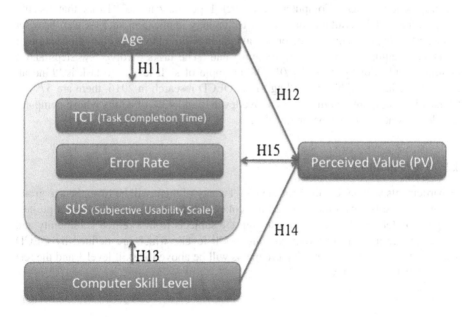

Fig. 2. Path diagram for the proposed causal relationship model.

4   Methodology

4.1   Experimental Design (DOE)

We designed a 2 by 2 factorial experiment to test the main effects of age and computer skill level and their interaction to the website user testing results. Two factors and their levels are as shown in the Table 1.

Table 1. Experimental design of age and computer skill level effects.

Factors	Higher Level	Lower Level
Age	Above 65	College Students
Computer Skill Level	Above skill level 1	Skill level 1 (including those below level 1)

The higher level of age factor is defined as those senior citizens whose age is above 65, which follows the US census Bureau's definition of senior citizens [1]. And the lower level of age factor is the group of college students whose age is around 18–22.

The criterion of categorizing higher and lower levels of the computer skill level factor is based on the definition of Organization for Economic Co-operation and Development (OECD). Computer skill level 1 people can do "Tasks that usually required the widely available or familiar technology application such as web browser and email software. There is little or no navigation required to access the information or commands required to solve the problem." and "The tasks involve few steps and a minimal number of operators" [20]. The example of skill level one task is "Find all emails from John Smith". According to the OECD research in 2016, there are 57% of adults whose computer skill level is above level 1, and 43% of adults whose computer skill level is at level 1 or below level 1.

4.2   Participants

40 participants will be recruited for the test. Twenty of them will be from the age group which is above 65. And the other 20 are college students. We will perform a pre-test designed by OECD definition for selecting the subjects from a retired community and Purdue university with different computer skill levels, which are defined by OECD research. For each age group, 10 participants will be above the skill level 1 and the rest will be level 1 and below level 1.

4.3 Research Object

This study will simulate the user testing during human-centered design process, so the research object will be the prototypes of the website in Care & Share project. The example of the website homepage prototype is as shown in the figure below (Fig. 3).

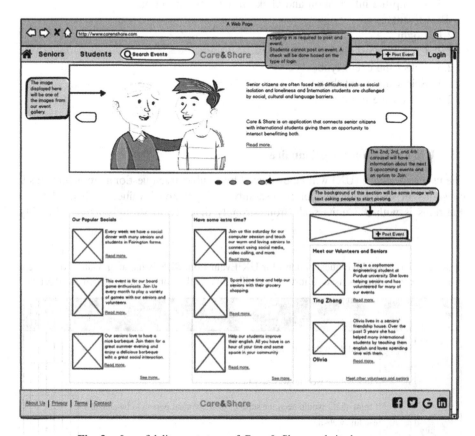

Fig. 3. Low-fidelity prototype of Care & Share website homepage.

4.4 Experiment Procedures

The moderator will firstly introduce the project idea and the main features of the website, and then the test scenario will be introduced. The test scenario assumes users are using the website for the first time. They will first need to sign up and review consent procedures before performing any further tasks.

And then we will run the Cognitive Walkthrough [21] to collect testing metrics, including task completion time and error rate. The participants will be told to finish a task without knowing the detailed steps of the task. Participants will be asked to Think Aloud by Nielsen's protocol [22] when carrying out the task, while the observer taking notes. The test will be paused after they complete a task to record the completion time, and the moderator will judge the success in finishing the subtask. Below are the two tasks the participants will perform during the test:

1. Sign up
   1.1 Click on login button
   1.2 Click on sign up via email
   1.3 Fill up the information and click on the sign up button
2. Post Events
   2.1 Login
   2.2 Click on Post Events
   2.3 Select the event type
   2.4 Select the event theme
   2.5 Fill up the information

4.5 UX Evaluation Questionnaire

The user experience (UX) will be evaluated by a subjective questionnaire, which has 9 questions in two main categories, usability and perceived value. Each of those 9 questions is with a 7 units scale from strongly disagree to strongly agree. Usability

Table 2. The subjective questionnaire for UX Evaluation. SUS is the abbreviation of System Usability Scale, which is used to test the usability; PV is the abbreviation of Perceived Value.

Construct	Item	Measurement	1	2	3	4	5	6	7
Usability	SUS1	I found the website unnecessarily complex.							
	SUS2	I thought the website was easy to use.							
	SUS3	I think that I would need the support of a technical person to be able to use this website.							
	SUS4	I thought there was too much inconsistency in this website.							
	SUS5	I would imagine that most people would learn to use this website very quickly.							
	SUS6	I felt very confident using the website.							
Perceived Value	PV1	I think this service would add values to my life.							
	PV2	This website is worth for me to sacrifice some time and efforts.							
	PV3	I think that I would like to use this website frequently.							

questions were adopted based on the system usability scale (SUS) questions which are designed by Brooke [23]. And for testing users' subjective feeling of the website service, we choose 3 perceived value questions from the E-S-QUAL. E-S-QUAL is a multiple-item scale for assessing electronic service quality, designed by Parasuraman et al. [24]. E-S-QUAL tests user's subjective feeling in many different perspectives, including usability and customer satisfaction [25–28]. However, since the research object is the website prototypes, not the final product, we just have selected a subset of questions from the specific factor to do the test (Table 2).

5   Discussion

Previous studies often used "prior computer experience" to indicate the familiarity. Czaja et al. firstly defined the previous computer experience by the self-rating from a 5 point-scale (0–6 months, 6 months–1 year, 1–3 years, 3–5 years, or more than 5 years) [8]. Kang and Yoon summed up several 5 point-scale questions to represent the background knowledge, including the previous experience and frequency of use [13]. However, there's a gap between experience and familiarity. In the proposed study, we will directly measure the computer skill level with a standardized test by the definition of OECD, which could be a more objective measurement rather than self-report. Since we have also found in our previous user testing that it's hard for some elder users to recall and precisely describe their computer experience.

In the proposed study, we will consider age and computer skill level as predictors and user testing results as response so we could systematically examine the effects, interactions and the causal relationships between each variable. In many previous studies, the main goal is to compare the age difference, so the prior computer experience knowledge is just a control in experiment or it will be examined by ANCOVA [8, 13, 14]. Although the effect of prior computer experience could be seen but it's hard for us to examine the interactions between age and prior computer experience.

With the real application for the use testing of an aging-design project, we expect to see the following 2 results in our proposed study: (1) Computer skill level difference affects the performance and it is confounded with the age factor. (2) Users' subjective perceived value of the website will affect users' subjective rating of usability.

6   Conclusion and Future Work

A factorial experiment to investigate the effects of age and computer skill level to the website user testing results had been proposed in this paper. In the proposed study, two research models were built to test 4 hypotheses, including the factorial experiment and structural equation modeling. This study would validate the findings in previous studies that elder people vary by prior computer experience [6]. This study implies computer skill level should be controlled in the user testing of the aging-centered website design project. Additionally, after user testing, the difference of user mental models of elderly and college students about their perceptions of the website service quality can be learned, which may provide designer a better understanding of different user groups.

Acknowledgement. This work was an extension of an aging-centered website design project in the Fall 2016 course, CGT512, in Purdue University. Authors are grateful for the course instructor, Dr. Mihaela Vorvoreanu, and the project team members, Wenjie Wu and Ankit Batheja.

References

1. U. S. D. of C. Bureau of the Census, An Aging Nation: The Older Population in the United States (2014). http://www.census.gov/library/publications/2014/demo/p25-1140.html. Accessed 08 Feb 2017
2. Norman, D.A., Draper, S.W.: User Centered System Design; New Perspectives on Human-Computer Interaction. L. Erlbaum Associates Inc., Mahwah (1986)
3. Botwinick, J., Storandt, M.: Memory, related functions and age, vol. viii. Charles C Thomas, Oxford (1974)
4. Kelley, C.L., Charness, N.: Issues in training older adults to use computers. Behav. Inf. Technol. **14**(2), 107–120 (1995)
5. Kline, D.W., Scialfa, C.T.: Sensory and perceptual functioning: basic research and human factors implications. In: Fisk, A.D., Rogers, W.A. (eds.) Handbook of Human Factors and the Older Adult, pp. 27–54. Academic Press, San Diego (1997)
6. Hawthorn, D.: Possible implications of aging for interface designers. Interact. Comput. **12** (5), 507–528 (2000)
7. Nielsen, J.: Usability for Senior Citizens, 28 May 2013. https://www.nngroup.com/articles/usability-for-senior-citizens/. Accessed 09 Feb 2017
8. Czaja, S.J., Sharit, J.: Age differences in the performance of computer-based work, **8**(1) 59–67 (1993)
9. Czaja, S.J., Sharit, J., Ownby, R., Roth, D.L.: Examining age differences in performance of a complex information search and retrieval task, **16**(4) 564–579 (2001)
10. Wagner, N., Hassanein, K., Head, M.: Computers in human behavior computer use by older adults: a multi-disciplinary review. Comput. Hum. Behav. **26**(5), 870–882 (2010)
11. Czaja, S.J., Shark, J.: Age differences in attitudes toward computers, **53**(5) 329–340 (1998)
12. Beier, M.E., Ackerman, P.L.: Age, ability, and the role of prior knowledge on the acquisition of new domain knowledge : promising results in a real-world learning environment, **20**(2) 341–355 (2005)
13. Kang, N.E., Yoon, W.C.: Age- and experience-related user behavior differences in the use of complicated electronic devices. Int. J. Hum.-Comput. Stud. **66**(6), 425–437 (2008)
14. O'brien, M.A., Rogers, W.A., Fisk, A.D.: Understanding age and technology experience differences in use of prior knowledge for everyday technology interactions. ACM Trans. Access Comput. **4**(2), 9:1–9:27 (2012)
15. Castilla, D., et al.: Process of design and usability evaluation of a telepsychology web and virtual reality system for the elderly: butler, **71**, 350–362 (2013)
16. Kurniawan, S.: Research-derived web design guidelines for older people, pp. 129–135 (2005)
17. Lee, C.: User-centered system design in an aging society : an integrated study on technology adoption by, no. 2010 (2014)
18. Silva, P.A., Nunes, F.: 3 × 7 usability testing guidelines for older adults, vol. 2, pp. 1–8 (2010)
19. Joseph, H., Hult, T., Ringle, C., Sarstedt, M.: A Primer on Partial Least Squares Structural Equation Modeling (PLS-SEM). SAGE Publications, Thousand Oaks (2016)

20. OECD, Skills Matter. Paris: Organisation for Economic Co-operation and Development (2016)
21. Wharton, C., Rieman, J., Lewis, C., Polson, P.: The cognitive walkthrough method: a practitioner's guide. In: Nielsen, J., Mack, R.L. (eds.) Usability Inspection Methods, pp. 105–140. Wiley Inc. (1994)
22. Nielsen, J.: Usability Engineering. Morgan Kaufmann Publishers Inc., Burlington (1993)
23. Brooke, J.: SUS-A quick and dirty usability scale. Usability Eval. Ind. 189(194), 4–7 (1996)
24. Parasuraman, A., Zeithaml, V.A., Malhotra, A.: E-S-QUAL: a multiple-item scale for assessing electronic service quality. J. Serv. Res. 7(3), 213–233 (2005)
25. Bai, B., Law, R., Wen, I.: The impact of website quality on customer satisfaction and purchase intentions: evidence from Chinese online visitors. Int. J. Hosp. Manag. 27(3), 391–402 (2008)
26. Drury, C.G.: Integrating service quality and human factors. In: Salvendy, G., Karwowski, W. (eds.) Introduction to Service Engineering, pp. 433–443. Wiley Inc. (2009)
27. Kettinger, W.J., Lee, C.C.: Perceived service quality and user satisfaction with the information services function*. Decis. Sci. 25(5–6), 737–766 (1994)
28. Kuo, Y., Wu, C., Deng, W.: Computers in human behavior the relationships among service quality, perceived value, customer satisfaction, and post-purchase intention in mobile value-added services. Comput. Hum. Behav. 25(4), 887–896 (2009)

Application and Effect of Media Therapy to the Recreational Activities at Group Homes Reduction of Spiritual Pain of Elderly People with Dementia

Teruko Doi[1](✉) and Noriaki Kuwahara[2]

[1] TM Medical Service, DOI Clinic, Kyoto Institute of Technology,
Nagaoka, Nagaokakyo, Japan
mialuna.conme.pino@gmail.com
[2] Kyoto Institute of Technology, Kyoto, Japan
nkuwahar@kit.ac.jp

Abstract. At group home "Terado", improvement of quality of lives of the elderly suffered from dementia is being attempted through a method called Media Therapy using interactive digital photo albums in order to achieve enjoyable days and realization of individuality in their lives. In Media Therapy, we utilize an interactive digital photo album that is a collection of photographs and videos of the personal history and life story of a resident with dementia. This album is used for several sessions where the resident watches this album projected on a screen with the people involved such as his/her family, the care staff, his/her regular doctor, nurse or occupational therapist, and enjoy a casual conversation while viewing the video. As a result, the resident displayed mental calmness during the implementation of Media Therapy. Moreover, by sharing the life history of the resident, the care staff also displayed improvement in their care skill and grew confidence toward care work. Judging from both subjective opinions and objective data, there was clear improvement in the quality of care. In this study, we report the result of applying this Media Therapy to the team care of care staff, which is necessary in the frontline care work. The interactive digital photo album produced for Media Therapy was used for the daily recreation at the group home, which involved not only the resident for whom the album was produced, but also other residents of the facility. Reduction of BPSD (behavioral and psychological symptom of dementia), which is difficult to treat through dementia care, was observed. This is inferred to have resulted from the change in the relationship between the dementia patient and the care staff, and the patient and other residents. Through the power of human relationship, the hardship of the dementia patient was alleviated, and resulted in the reduction of BPSD. Based on this observation, we focused on the relationship between the caregiver and care receiver, and discussed the method for constructing the relationship between them, which is the basis of care work.

Keywords: Media Therapy · Dementia · Recreation · PDCA cycle · Spiritual pain

© Springer International Publishing AG 2017
V.G. Duffy (Ed.): DHM 2017, Part II, LNCS 10287, pp. 142–149, 2017.
DOI: 10.1007/978-3-319-58466-9_14

1 Introduction

Japan is now entering the high level of aging society that is internationally unprecedented.

The percentage of people above 65 years old in the total population is increasing, and it reached one in four people in 2015. Therefore establishment of high quality care that supports the dignity of the elderly people is an urgent task. Especially, it can hardly be said that the dignity of elderly dementia patients is properly protected at home or care facilities.

Group home is a facility where the elderly people with dementia symptoms who face difficulties in living due to illness or disability live together independently with supports from specialized staff, with each resident taking up a role, such as cooking or cleaning, based on his/her abilities.

(Handbook for Dementia Group Home, 2006, Akashi-shi, Hyogo Prefecture)

We believe that the most important aspect in managing a group home is the corporate philosophy. "Every day with a smile on everyone, achieving your own life": The "smile" mentioned in this motto means not only the smiles of the elderly people who receive care, but also include the smiles of the care staff who administer care work to the elderly. Care is a people-centered service where individuals interact directly with one another. Unless the care staff conducts their duties without stress, it is impossible to operate a high-quality group home that cherishes the dignity of the elderly people with dementia.

In this study, we will discuss the method of a recreation that reduces and removes the spiritual pain of the elderly people with dementia, using the example of Media Therapy which is a recreation that leads to the care burden reduction of the care staff.

2 Approach of Teruko Doi Laboratory

At Teruko Doi Laboratory, we are engaged in these projects.

- Education, training, instruction and organization of workshops related to medical treatment and care.
- Research and study related to dementia care.
- Research and study related to medical treatment and care.
- Training and dispatching of animal therapy, supplying temporary labor force and training of therapists.

The philosophy of group home "Terada" that was established in 2011 is thus: "Achieve every day with a smile on everyone and realization of individual life through the collaboration between medical treatment and care". At "Terado", various recreations for practicing person-centered care are carried out in order to cherish the dignity of the elderly people with dementia and offer them days that are full of smiles. These daily recreations include animal therapies such as dog therapy, horse therapy and aqua therapy, garden therapy that involves growing flowers, fruit trees and vegetables, and practice of Japanese traditional culture such as tea ceremony and flower arrangement.

The pictures below show the views from a tea ceremony practice (HCII 2015).

And these pictures below were taken during a flower arrangement practice (AHFE2014).

Views from the Flower Arrangement Practice.

3 Spiritual Pain

Hisayuki Murata ["Hisayuki Murata, 2011, Spiritual Pain and Its Care in Patients with Terminal Cancer, Journal of the Japan Society of Pain Clinicians, **18**(1), 1–8", "Hisayuki Murata, 2003, Spiritual Pain of Terminal Cancer Patients, Its Care Assessment and Construction of a Conceptual Framework for Its Care, Journal of Japanese Society for Palliative Medicine, **5**(2), 157–165"] claimed that the human existence has three dimensions, namely existence in time, relational existence and autonomous existence, and defined spiritual pain as the pain that caused by the disappearance of the meaning of self-existence. This definition was made from the view that care is for mitigating and reducing the suffering of another person, and if possible removes it. Moreover, he made following further definitions. "Meaninglessness and purposelessness of life" caused by the disappearance of future for a person with terminal cancer or incurable disease who is facing imminent death is defined as spiritual pain of time. Anxiety of the self-loss due to losing relationships with others caused by incapability of communications because of terminal cancer or dementia is defined as relational spiritual pain. And "worthlessness, dependence and meaninglessness" caused by losing independence and productivity due to terminal cancer, incurable disease or dementia is defined as spiritual pain of autonomy.

The difficulty and suffering of dementia patients is categorized into this spiritual pain. Therefore, it is demanded on the frontline care work to mitigate and reduce the spiritual pain, and if possible remove it. In order to realize such care, it is necessary for the dementia patient to feel that he/she is accepted by others. In other words, change in the sense of value of the patient is necessary. As a concrete method, we propose careful listening for understanding the suffering of the patient and making him/her feel understood. Moreover, by analyzing the conversation record from the listening, it is possible to evaluate whether the change in the sense of value of the patient was achieved.

It can be said that Murata [Hisayuki Murata, 1994, Idea of Care and Interpersonal Support–From the Frontline of Terminal Care and Welfare–, Kawashima Shoten] proposes a more concrete care methodology compared to person-centered care. However, due to the limitation in time, to practice listening/conversation record analysis during the frontline care work is extremely difficult for the care staff who are busy with the daily care work. Moreover, it is not directly covered by the elderly care insurance. Due to these reasons, its introduction to facilities is not progressing.

4 PDCA Cycle

In this study, we distinguished between "Group Recreation" and "Individual Recreation" among the recreational activities. Moreover, we separated the group recreations into two types: one is mainly engaged in interactions with others, and the other is mainly based on the individual and independent engagements.

The main purpose of the group recreation that emphasizes the interaction with others is to create mutual trust between the care staff and the patients. On the other hand, the main purpose of the group recreation that emphasizes the independent engagement of each person is to regain his/her awareness of personal role in the local community and recover pride.

Finally, the purpose of the individual recreation is to involve the family of the patient and regain mutual familial love and feeling of gratitude, and moreover to deepen the trust with the care staff.

Recreation Design as Care

	Group Recreation		Individual Recreation
	Mainly engaged with interaction with others	Mainly based on independent engagement	Mainly engaged with interaction with family.
	Creation of mutual trust with the care staff.	Regain the former roles in local community and pride.	Both the family and the patient regain love and gratitude toward each other. Deepening of trust with the care staff.
Planning (P)	(1) Understand Dementia (Identification of core symptoms and BPSD)		
	(2) Recreation that helps gaining understanding from the family.		
	(3) Recreation that can be enjoyed together with the care staff.		
	(4) Recreation that incorporates the past experiences of the patient.		
	(5) Using real tools (Teacher, equipment, set-up of the situation, appropriate clothing)		
	(6) Producing extraordinary space and experience.		
	(7) Conducting in the limited framework regarding purpose and time.		
	(8) Prior understanding of the personal information of the patient (character, personal history).		
	(9) Recreation based on Japanese tradition.		
	(10) Prior understanding of physical conditions of the patient.		
Implementation (D)	(1) Understand Dementia (Identification of core symptoms and BPSD)		
	(2) Using real tools (Teacher, equipment, set-up of the situation, appropriate clothing)		
	(3) Producing extraordinary space and experience.		
	(4) Conducting in the limited framework regarding purpose and time.		
	(5) Prior understanding of the personal information of the patient (character, personal history).		
	(6) Prior understanding of physical conditions of the patient.		

It is important to plan, implement, evaluate the effect and adjust according to the evaluation these recreations for the dementia patients with symptoms such as memory disorder, disorientation and decline in judgment ability. This is commonly called PDCA cycle, as shown in Fig. 1. PDCA cycle is a method proposed by Deming that continuously improve work by repeating the following four steps: Plan → Do → Check → Act.

As stated above, it can hardly be said that the methodology for concretely plan (P) and implement (D) recreations as dementia care is established today. Even in person-centered care, which is a progressive initiative in dementia care, planning (P) and implementation (D) is the responsibility of each care worker, though evaluation (C) is defined in detail as DCM. Therefore in this study, based on the approaches for dementia care at the group home so far, we summarized the recreation purposes and points to be noted in the table, regarding planning (P) and implementation (D) of recreations as methodology.

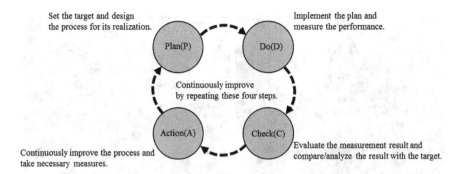

Set the target and design the process for its realization.

Implement the plan and measure the performance.

Plan(P)

Do(D)

Continuously improve by repeating these four steps.

Action(A)

Check(C)

Continuously improve the process and take necessary measures.

Evaluate the measurement result and compare/analyze the result with the target.

Fig. 1. Diagram of PDCA Cycle Proposed by William Edwards Deming

5 Application to Media Therapy

At group home "Terado", Media Therapy is being implemented as an individual recreation, for reducing the spiritual pain of a patient and improve his/her relationship with the family and the care staff.

- Case Example of Media Therapy.

The subject is Mrs. K, a woman in her 80s. She displays strong BPSD, and the elderly care insurance assessed her nursing care level as level 4. She worked as a maternity nurse from when she was 18 until she was 53. After her son and daughter became independent, she lived only with her husband. She is strong-willed and competitive, but also compassionate and full of motherly affection. She revers men and feels highly dependent on her husband, presumably because of her generation.

We held six sessions covering the following periods in her life.

1. From childhood to adolescence.
2. Wedding and the early days in her marriage.
3. Her 20s and 30s with her children growing up.
4. Early in her 40s, an overseas trip with her daughter.
5. Late in her 40s when she felt fulfilled both in her work and at home.
6. In her 50s and later, traveled with her husband after retirement.

Views from the Media Therapy

The following results were observed:

- By including the episodes that brought smile on her face during the Media Therapy, such as how she met her husband or stories from her work, to the everyday communication, the relationship between the subject and the care staff improved.
- The son, who never visited her because he could not accept the dementia of his mother and thought she was as good as dead, regained his forgotten love and gratitude toward his mother when he saw her crying and laughing during the Media Therapy.
- Her BPSD was reduced, judging from the following signs. The reversal of day and night was solved. The complaints about anxiety during the nighttime and the confusion caused by paranoia were reduced.

They are changes toward a good direction that leads to bringing back smile on her face.

It can be inferred that the relational spiritual pain was reduced through the Media Therapy using an interactive video that allows the patient to share her life with the family and care staff, discuss it and be in the same place.

6 Conclusion

A person with dementia possesses personal history of 70 to 80 years. It is his/her own story and it is precious because it is absolutely unique in the world. We infer that by sharing this story between the elderly person with dementia, his/her family and the care staff and discuss it among these three parties during the Media Therapy, the relational spiritual pain defined in the support model, namely the anxiety of losing relationship with others, was cared.

Care is to reduce and remove suffering through the power of human relationship. Recreations for the elderly people with dementia who are suffering from symptoms such as memory disorder, disorientation and decline in judgment ability must be more ingenious than the recreations for healthy people in order to reach and engage with the elderly people with dementia. During the implementation of recreations, the care staff was aware of PDCA cycle. Especially the points of consideration in planning (P) and implementation (D) were compiled.

In order to bring smiles not only to the patient but his/her family and the care staff in the frontline of dementia care, we will continuously evaluate the effect brought by utilizing ICT.

Investigation of Quantification of the Suitable Photos for Conversation Assistance for Elderly and Youth

Miyuki Iwamoto[✉], Noriaki Kuwahara, and Kazunari Morimoto

Kyoto Institute of Technology, Kyoto, Japan
cabotine.six.stars@gmail.com

Abstract. The aging of Japan is proceeding at an unprecedented rate in the world, and the aging rate is very high. As the aging society advances and the living environment changes, the environment surrounding the elderly is also changing. Along with then, various social problems are caused. For example, a syndrome of shut itself up of the elderly may be mentioned. "Housebound" is to spend most of the living space and the living time in the house, resulting in the disuse of cognitive functions and further the opportunities and motivation for activities such as going out and interpersonal contact decreasing. In addition, there are elderly who are shut itself do need various support and nursing care in many cases.

As for prevention, it is not only to increase the frequency of outings but also to revitalize all aspects of life of elderly by playing a role in society.

Thus, in order to prevent the decline of cognitive function, it is thought that the connection with society becomes increasingly important. While the younger generations are accordingly expected to be talking partners for aged people, there is a problem in that they are unfamiliar with how to communicate with the elderly because so many of them grew up in small families without grandfathers or grandmothers. We examined the differences in the mental burden and the quality of communication between patients and caregivers/volunteers when they used photos as communication support content in order to find the best medium for communication. We revealed that what category is the more ideal as the contents but we did not mention the photos in the category. We will investigate the differences in the mental states and communication quality of elderly people and their younger conversation partners when photos are used to support communication, and quantification the best medium for this purpose.

Keywords: Elderly · Reminiscence videos · Dementia · Conversation

1 Introduction

The aging of Japan is proceeding at an unprecedented rate in the world, and the aging rate is very high [1]. There are increased nuclear families, and the time spent by elderly and young people together is decreasing. As the aging society advances and the living environment changes, the environment surrounding the elderly is also changing. Along with then, various social problems are caused. For example, a syndrome of shut itself up of the elderly may be mentioned.

V.G. Duffy (Ed.): DHM 2017, Part II, LNCS 10287, pp. 150–160, 2017.
DOI: 10.1007/978-3-319-58466-9_15

"Housebound" is to spend most of the living space and the living time in the house, resulting in the disuse of cognitive functions and further the opportunities and motivation for activities such as going out and interpersonal contact decreasing. A live tend to shut itself means that roles in the community and society decrease, and the frequency of going out is low. The factors that lead to a syndrome of shut itself can be cited three factors of physical, psychological, social and environmental. These three factors are considered to be related to each other (Fig. 1) [2].

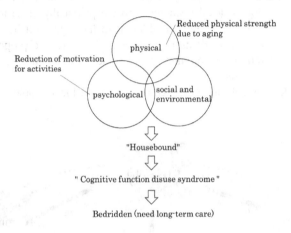

Fig. 1. Factors and position of housebound

In addition, there are elderly who are shut itself do need various support and nursing care in many cases. For example, the elderly who are not trying to actively participate in social activities is thought to increase the risk of developing dementia. Therefore, syndrome of shut itself may risk of dementia. As for prevention, it is not only to increase the frequency of outings but also to revitalize all aspects of life of elderly by playing a role in society.

Cognitive function is to acquire information from the outside through the five senses, to understand the current situation, to recognize it, to cause some kind of reaction. For example, it is memorizing or talking. People are always in this state except when they are asleep. However, due to aging, visual and auditory functions generally degrade, so often it will incorrectly recognize information from the outside. For example, it is a mistake or a mistake.

In addition, the cognitive function of the elderly is characterized by large individual differences. This is considered to be influenced by socio-cultural factors (Education, occupation, hobby, exercise, etc.) in addition to the intrinsic factor (Genetic, stress, physical condition, mental state etc.). As one of methods for preventing dementia and cognitive decline, it is attention to activate physical activity in everyday life [3].

Thus, in order to prevent the decline of cognitive function, it is thought that the connection with society becomes increasingly important.

Aiming to realize a society where elderly people can live with peace of mind, a wide variety of watching services are provided. The watching service is a service that watches everyday living for old couples and old singles, responds promptly if they have abnormal situation occurs, and provides peace of mind for families and the elderly. In addition, a mechanism to monitor the elderly by cooperation of private (local residents), administrative and medical is developed. It has expected them as neighbors to watch over the elderly people, that is, proximity and everyday life. The information gained through such a network between residents is conveyed to specialized agencies, so that prompt response can be made.

As we have said as was mentioned above, as a way to watch over the elderly, we believe that cooperation of local residents who are physically close to each other is indispensable. However, at present it is difficult to have ties and bonds because the mental distance with local residents is far away. Therefore, we propose a watching system with consideration for community and society by communicating with reference to the reminiscence method.

This is a style in which families, medical care staff, local people surround elderly people (Fig. 2).

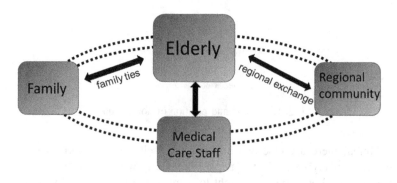

Fig. 2. Watching the elderly to suggest

In order to implement this watching system, cooperation of local residents is indispensable. In order to gain the cooperation of local residents, it efforts that they do not feel the burden of exchanges with the elderly become necessary. Their numbers are insufficient to meet the current needs. While the younger generations are accordingly expected to be talking partners for aged people, there is a problem in that they are unfamiliar with how to communicate with the elderly because so many of them grew up in small families without grandfathers or grandmothers. The 20th century is the era of change, and the era largely changes in the first half, the middle stage, the second half. Therefore, it is difficult to find common points of conversation with each other. Furthermore, it is difficult to find a common topic between the elderly born in the first half and the young born in the second half. Therefore, in order to provide topics and to have a smooth conversation, it is necessary to provide content that does not feel burdens or dissatisfactions for elderly people and young people.

We examined the differences in the mental burden and the quality of communication between patients and caregivers/volunteers when they used photos as communication support content in order to find the best medium for communication.

We revealed that what category is the more ideal as the contents but we did not mention the photos in the category.

We will investigate the differences in the mental states and communication quality of elderly people and their younger conversation partners when photos are used to support communication, and quantification the best medium for this purpose.

2 Experiment

2.1 Summary

In the face-to-face conversation between the elderly and the young adults, we examined the influence on the continuation of the conversation for each photographic image and whether the burden is felt during the conversation.

We have already done the evaluation for each category, and as a result. We conducted experiments in 5 categories [4]. The categories used for conversation were "Food" "Play" "Event" "Home Appearance", "Lives during the Showa Era".

We set a time limit of 10 min per category and did a conversation without limiting the time for each photograph. When I judged that the conversation was interrupted, I presented a new photo. The experiment is 10 min per category.

A camera (line-of-sight device) had used to capture the expressions of the elderly patients throughout the sessions. The expressions of the elderly were then analyzed from the video recordings.

Whether young people are accustomed to conversation with the elderly or not familiar with the degree of burden and whether there is a time difference for each photograph by not restricting the conversation time in one picture, Also, it was aimed to verify whether there is a relationship between time difference and emotion.

2.2 Evaluation Item

The participants in the study answered a series of questions in the form of a 5-stage subjective evaluation after each conversation. For the questionnaire, in addition to the questions we asked in the experiments we have conducted up to now, we asked whether a sense of burden was felt during the 10 min of conversation. The experiment's results show these subjective evaluations (the questionnaires, and also the young adults' degree of burden from the "stress check sheet"). The proportion of the conversation during which they were smiling was measured for the elderly patients.

As for the subjects, one young adult interviewed five elderly and estimated an average of the mental load he or she felt, excluding personal compatibilities. The young adult indicated the degree of mental load felt on the stress check sheet (Fig. 3) every minute.

The stress check sheet represented facial expressions on a 1-7-scale, with the face corresponding to "1" meaning that there was an absence of any burden (stress) to continue the conversation, and the face corresponding to "7" meaning that the person felt a great deal of burden. A camera was used to capture the resident's expressions and actions throughout the sessions. We compared these to see which photographs brought

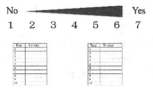

Fig. 3. Stress check sheet

him or her pleasure or joy. Facial expressions were correlated with emotions analyzed in a previous study [5].

2.3 Subject

The partners were 8 students of 23–25 years old. They grew up in a family of nuclear families and is not used to conversation with the elderly.

The elderly were 5 senior ladies and 1 senior man of ages from 84 to 96 suffering mild dementia.

2.4 Experiment Environment

The layout of the experiment is shown in Figs. 4 and 5 below.

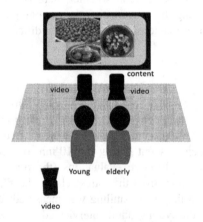

Fig. 4. The layout of the experimental environment

We borrowed a room in the nursing home, in which we placed chairs side by side.

We used a laptop PC in which photos categorized as explained above were up-loaded to support a 10 min conversation.

We carried out checks on the degree of burden felt through the conversation by the students.

Fig. 5. Experimental environment.

2.5   Expression Analysis

The expressions of the elderly were analyzed from the video recordings. Analysis of facial expressions of older people analyzed images of facial expressions that had been caught in 1 min for each photograph in the previous experiments but in this experiment the expression images of one category for ten minutes are framed every second, Frame images for the number of conversation hours for each piece of content photograph were classified by their respective pictures and analyzed using the frame images. By making it into a frame, it is possible to delete facial expressions of parts other than conversation in the video, and it can be thought that picture and emotion can be related more.

In this expression analysis, we evaluated the "degree of smile" on a frame-by-frame basis. We defined 0% as an expressionless state in which there was no smiling at all, and 100% as a state of the highest laughter. We used the highest degree of smile expressed as the result for each photograph displayed.

2.6   Experimental Methods

The experiment was carried out as follows.

① Young people and elderly people sit next to each other in front of the television screen.
② Shoot the face of young people and elderly people with video camera.
③ Display the photo image on the TV monitor.
④ Start conversation.
⑤ The conversation will automatically change 1 min for each photo. Maximum 10 photos (10 photos per category)
⑥ Young people change the picture and simultaneously measure the stress of the conversation every minute.
⑦ Fill out the stress check sheet.
⑧ Perform 1 to 6 in each category.

The above was done for young people for five elderly people.
We talked two categories to one elderly person.

We prepared 10 photos for each of the categories of "Food," "Event," "Play," "lives during the Showa Era," and "Home appearance," which were shown during the flow of the conversation.

The partner student indicated the degree of mental load he or she felt on the stress check board every minute. The stress check sheet was hidden from the patient's eyes. Our purpose was to check the mental load of the partner in the conversation, not to expose their complaints to the elderly. Thus, the partner could point at a value without worrying about offending the elderly patient, enabling them to judge honestly. The sheet was sometimes shown in the middle of their conversation but they continued to talk while pointing at the applicable value on a minutely basis. They then answered the questions on the questionnaire through the 5-stage subjective evaluation each time after the experiment. A camera (Positive/negative) was used to capture the expressions of the elderly patients throughout the sessions. The expressions of the elderly were finally analyzed from the video recordings.

3   Results

The results of the experiment described in Sect. 2.6 are shown below. Figure 6 shows the amount of stress accumulated for each photo image category.

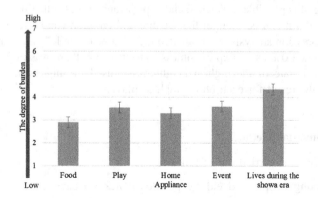

Fig. 6. Stress levels based on image type

The horizontal axis represents each category, and the vertical axis represents the accumulation on the numerical stress check sheet. This is a comparison of the young adults stress levels in case for each category of photos which is a comparison of the burden felt to continue the conversation as the conversation support content. Only the younger subjects' mental stress levels are shown.

The most stress was experienced when images depicting "Lives during the Showa Era" were shown. In the "Events" "Play" we found that there was almost the same degree of burden (stress). We found that food is the least stressful category.

Figure 7 shows an average of the degree of smile of elderly people by category, and is classified into cases of subject A and subject B. The horizontal axis represents each

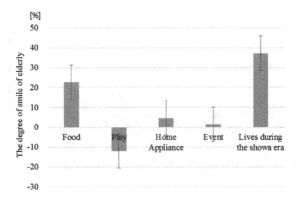

Fig. 7. The results of the expression analysis

category, and the vertical axis represents the degree of smile of the elderly. The degree of smile represents the negative area from 0 to −100, and the positive area is expressed from 0 to 100.

"Food" "Lives during the showa era" category has higher smile degrees of elderly people than other categories. On the other hand, in the category of "Play", "Home Appliance", "Event", it was found that the degree of smile was about the same.

Figures 8, 9, 10, 11 and 12 show the relationship between the degree of smile of elderly people per photograph and the degree of burden of young people for each category. The horizontal axis shows each picture, and the vertical axis shows that the bar graph shows the degree of smile of elderly people, and the line graph shows the degree of burden of young people. The degree of smile of elderly people represents negative areas by 0 to −100, and positive areas are represented by 0 to 100. In addition, the degree of burden of young people represents the score of the stress check sheet (1: feel no stress ⇔ 7: feel the stress).

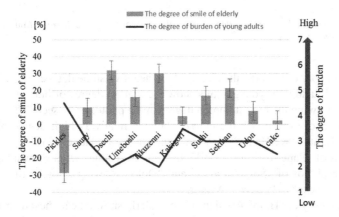

Fig. 8. Relationship between the degree of smile of elderly and the degree of burden of young adults (Food)

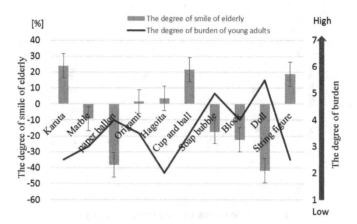

Fig. 9. Relationship between the degree of smile of elderly and the degree of burden of young adults (Play)

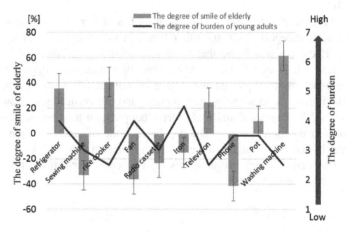

Fig. 10. Relationship between the degree of smile of elderly and the degree of burden of young adults (Home Appliance)

In the category of "Food", the elderly show negative smile degree only with picture of "pickles". In addition, young adults show the highest degree of burden in the photo of "pickle", showing the lowest burden degree in the photos of "Osechi" "Chikuzenni".

In the category of "play", the elderly shows a relatively high degree of smile in photos of "Karuta" "Kendama" "Ayatori", and shows a relatively low degree of smile in the photos of "Paper balloon" "Doll". In addition, young adults show a high degree of burden in photos of "Soap bubbles" and "Doll", showing a low burden degree in pictures of "Karuta" "Hagoita" "Ayatori".

In the category of "Home Appliance", the elderly shows the highest degree of smile in the photo of "washing machine" and shows the lowest degree of smile in the photo of "Phone". In addition, young adults show the highest degree of burden in the photo of

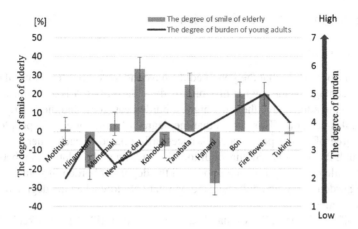

Fig. 11. Relationship between the degree of smile of elderly and the degree of burden of young adults (Event)

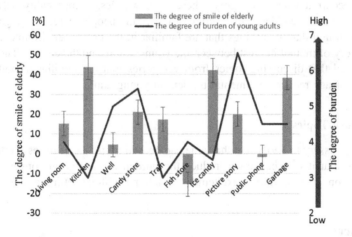

Fig. 12. Relationship between the degree of smile of elderly and the degree of burden of young adults (Lives during of Showa Era)

"Iron", showing the lowest burden degree in the photo of "rice cooker", "Television" and "washing machine".

In the category of "event", the elderly shows the highest degree of smile in the photo of "New Year day" and shows the lowest degree of smile in the photo of "Hanami". In addition, young adults show the highest degree of burden in the photo of "Fire flower", and show the lowest burden degree in the photo "Mochituki".

In the category of "Lives during of Showa Era", the elderly show a relatively high degree of smile in photos of "Kitchen" "Ice candy" and "Garbage", showing only a low degree of smile in the photo of "Fish store". In addition, young adults show the highest degree of burden in the photo of "picture story" and show the lowest burden degree in the photos of "Kitchen" "Train".

4 Conclusion and Future Topics

4.1 Conclusion

The category of "Food" that the young adults have the lowest burden shows the second highest percentage of the degree of smile of the elderly, but "Lives of during Showa Era" that young adults have the most highest burden category, and the elderly have the highest smiles category. This shows that the degree of smile of elderly people and the burden degree of young people are not necessarily related to each other.

Although it can not be said unconditionally, looking at the relationship between the degree of smile of elderly for each photo and the degree of burden of young adults, the degree of burden of young adults tends to be relatively low when the degree of smile of elderly is high.

"Osechi" "Chikuzenni" "Karuta" "Kendama" "Ayatori" "Rice cooker" "Washing machine" "New Year day" "Kitchen" "Ice candy", the burden of young adults is low, the degree of smile of the elderly was high, it is considered to be a photograph which is comparatively suitable as content. In all evaluation, it was found that when the conversation occurred with a cate-gory where there was less commonality between the young people and the elderly, the burden of the young people increases. Regardless of age, it was found that with things that are familiar in the present environment that can be a category of mutual interest between the young adults and the elderly. Therefore, it is considered that discussing topics from categories that are familiar to both groups regardless of age reduces the mental burden on young adults.

4.2 Future Topics

It will be necessary to verify that the same can be said in more categories. Furthermore, we believe that it is necessary to reduce the burden of silence on conversation and change of conversation during excitement by talking without setting a time limit.

References

1. A Overview Ministry of Health, Labour and Welfare, a 12-year Heisei version of Annual Report on Health and Welfare, the aging of the world, the Ministry of Health, Labour and Welfare website (online)
2. Where to get. http://www1.mhlw.go.jp/wp/wp00_4/chapt-a5.html detail_recog.html. Accessed 13 Jan 2012
3. Takuuchi Takahito: Retracted, confined syndrome. Nursing care prevention training text. Social Insurance Research Institute, Tokyo, pp. 128–140 (2001)
4. Lautenschlager, N.T., Cox, K.L., Flicker, L., Foster, J.K., van Bockxmeer, F.M., Xiao, J., Greenop, K.R., Almeida, O.P.: Effect of physical activity on cognitive function in older adults at risk for Alzheimer disease: a randomized trial. JAMA 300, 1027–1037 (2008)
5. Miyuki, I., Noriaki, K., Kazunari, M.: The relationship between conversation skill and feeling of load on youth in communicate with elderly persons using video image and photographs. In: ACIT 2014 (2014)
6. Tomomi, O., Mariko, T., Mariko, A., Naoko, K., Yukikazu, S.: Expression analysis-comparison of the characteristics of the facial expression, Proposed by Ekman (2010)

Generating Personalized Dialogue Towards Daily Counseling System for Home Dementia Care

Seiji Sakakibara[1]([envelope]), Sachio Saiki[1], Masahide Nakamura[1],
and Kiyoshi Yasuda[2]

[1] Graduate School of System Informatics Kobe University,
1-1 Rokkodai, Kobe, Nada, Japan
sakakibara@ai.cs.kobe-u.ac.jp, sachio@carp.kobe-u.ac.jp,
masa-n@cs.kobe-u.ac.jp
[2] Chiba Rosai Hospital, 2-16 Tatsumidai-higashi, Ichihara, Japan
fwkk5911@mb.infoweb.ne.jp

Abstract. The dementia counseling is a dementia care that cures physiologically unstable situation of a person with dementia, through receptive and attentive conversations. A person with dementia should receive the counseling as often as possible. However, it is difficult for a limited number of caregivers to spare sufficient time and effort. This motivated us to exploit the virtual agent technology we are developing, for implementing daily dementia counseling system at home. However, our previous system relies on static dialogue scripts. Therefore, it is difficult to realize person-centered conversations that are essential to the dementia counseling. In this paper, we propose a method that dynamically generates personalized dialogues for individual people with dementia. The proposed method extensively uses life history and linked open data (LOD). More specifically, we obtain the life history of a user based on The Center Method, then the system choose appropriate conversation considering the history. During the conversation, the system finds new information in LOD relevant to the response and uses it to develop further conversation. We also implement a prototype to show practical feasibility of the proposed method.

1 Introduction

Japan is currently entering a hyper-aging society. The Japanese Ministry of Health, Labour and Welfare estimates that the number of elderly people over the age of 65 will increase to 36.57 million, which is 30.3% of the total population [2]. Due to the increase of the elderly, more and more people will suffer from *dementia*. The number of people with dementia grows to 7 million in 2025, which is one-fifth of all elderly. Thus, assistive methods and technologies for preventing, nursing and supporting people with dementia are strongly required.

The *person-centered care* [6] is an ideal principle for dementia care, where caregivers understand individual situations of people with dementia, and

© Springer International Publishing AG 2017
V.G. Duffy (Ed.): DHM 2017, Part II, LNCS 10287, pp. 161–172, 2017.
DOI: 10.1007/978-3-319-58466-9_16

provide personalized support and care for them. Among various ways of the person-centered care, this paper especially focuses on the *dementia counseling* [8,11]. Due to BPSD (behavioral and psychological symptoms of dementia), people with dementia often fall into psychologically unstable modes, including fear, sad and anger. The dementia counseling is a care that cures such unstable situations through receptive and attentive conversations. Preferably, any person with dementia should receive the counseling as often as possible. However, it is unreasonable to consult a professional doctor or therapist every day. Also, even for caregivers at home (e.g., family), the time and effort spent on the counseling are quite limited since they have many other supports to do.

We have been studying an assistive technology, called *Virtual Care Giver (VCG)* [10], that supports elderly people at home by using the virtual agent (VA) technology. The VA is an animated chat-bot software with speech recognition and synthesis technologies. Through a PC screen, a user can talk to the VA who behaves like a human being. Integrated with smart home and cloud services, the VCG provides information, communication and assistive services for elderly at home. The VCG can become a companion for a user regardless of time, and it never gets tired. Therefore, we consider that the VCG is a very promising technology for the daily dementia counseling at home.

However, we have found it difficult to apply the current version of VCG to the dementia counseling. To perform effective counseling, a counselor carefully chooses appropriate conversation topics for individual people with dementia. It should reflect the personal situation, including the life history, the current living, hobby and preference, and so on. However, the VCG currently relies on a static *playscript* for what VA should speak to a user. The playscript must be programmed by a service developer, and thus the contents of the conversation is almost fixed before the counseling. To adapt individual people with dementia, the developer has to write many different scripts reflecting their situations. This causes much development effort.

Our long-term goal is to develop a system that provides daily dementia counseling for people with dementia living at home. Especially in this paper, we propose an efficient method that can dynamically generate personalized dialogues for every person with dementia. More specifically, we develop the method with the following three approaches.

- A1: Extracting life history with Center Method
- A2: Expanding conversation with linked open data (LOD)
- A3: Generating personalized dialogues using life history and LOD

As for A1, we propose a method where a system obtains the personal background of a user (i.e., person with dementia) based on his/her *life history*. The life history is personal information of a person with dementia about how he/she has been living so far. It includes birthplace, family, school, work, reminiscence, hobby and so on. In the proposed method, the system obtains user's life history from the given care management sheets of the *Center Method* [9], or by asking questions so that the user fills data items of the sheets. In A2, we propose a method that can expand and enrich simple conversation, according to the response from the user. Specifically, when a user answers a word, the system tries to find other relevant words by exploiting the *Linked Open Data (LOD)* [1], and uses the new words for the next conversation. In A3, we propose a mechanism that dynamically generates personalized dialogues using the life history and the LOD. For this, we use *dialogue templates*, which specify common outlines of conversations. During run-time, the system chooses a dialogue template, and fills it with personal topics obtained from the life history and the LOD to build a personalized dialogue.

Based on A1, A2 and A3, we develop a prototype of the daily counseling system. The prototype system provides personalized dialogue based on birthplace of a user. First, the system asks user's birthplace. Then, using LOD, the system finds a specialty associated with the birthplace and generates a new question with the specialty. Thus, we can see that the prototype system can provide personalized dialogues without pre-defined playscript. Thus, the proposed method can contribute significantly to the daily counseling system for people with dementia.

2   Preliminary

2.1   Home Demantia Care

With the increase of elderly people, the number of people with dementia grows accordingly. Many facilities of welfare and nursing care suffer from chronic shortage of workers. The number of job openings is increasing year by year (as of Dec. 2016) [5]. The number of nursing home is not sufficient against the number of applicants, who are over 524,000 elderly people. The Japanese government starts to encourage *home care* rather than building new facilities. It is more and more important to consider quality of life of elderly, and to support their independent life at home.

As symptoms of dementia vary greatly from one person to another, the *person-centered care* [6] is considered as an ideal principle of dementia care. In the principle, one must respect every patient as a human being, understand the patient from his/her perspective, and provide a tailor-made care for the patient.

2.2   Dementia Counseling

The *dementia counseling* is a non-drug treatment for people with dementia. A caregiver relieves patients in a psychologically unstable condition through receptive and attentive conversations. The caregiver should take appropriate topics and conversation attitudes carefully, based on the principle of person-centered care [8,11].

The counseling has effects of removing fear, stimulating positive feeling via long-term memory, keeping good condition, giving vitality for life, and so on. In the communication, attitudes of accept, sympathize and listen are important. The dementia counseling is normally operated by a professional counselor and a speech therapist. However, more casual (but practical) counseling can be performed by a family caregiver.

Fig. 1. Screen shot of virtual care giver

Preferably, the dementia counseling should be performed on a daily basis. However, it is expensive to receive professional treatment every day. It is also difficult for a family caregiver to spare sufficient time and effort just for the counseling. Thus, in reality, it is quite challenging to achieve daily and on-demand dementia counseling.

2.3 Virtual Care Giver [10]

Our research group has been studying smart services that exploit the *virtual agent (VA)* technology to assist elderly people at home. In a project, we are developing a system, called *Virtual Care Giver (VCG)* [10], where the VA integrates smart home and cloud services to provide home care.

Figure 1 shows a screen shot of VCG. The VA appears in the left. The VA is an animated human-like chatbot program, implemented with the speech recognition and synthesize technologies. A user can interact with the VA via voice. Connected with behaviors of the VA, the VCG can display supplementary texts, pictures and movies in a Web browser, as shown in the right side of the figure. Using VCG, we have implemented elderly care services, such as daily greeting, routine reminder, and favorite song movie. The VCG can be an accompany of a user regardless of time, and it never gets tired. Therefore, the VCG is a quite promising and realistic solution for the daily dementia counseling.

However, we have found it difficult to apply the VCG directly to the daily dementia care. Currently, every conversation of VCG relies on a *playscript*. The playscript is written as a program by a service developer, and it must be prepared before execution of the care scenario. During run-time, the VCG chooses a designated script and starts conversation. On the other hand, the dementia counseling requires person-centered topics and conversation attitudes. Therefore, to adapt individual people with dementia, the developer has to write the enormous number of playscripts to cover all possible situations.

2.4   The Center Method [9]

The *Center Method* [9] is known as a practical tool to support person-centered dementia care. The method provides a pack of sheets (forms), where every person with dementia (or caregiver) writes personal circumstances in the sheets. The sheets are shared by his/her surrounding people to consider person-centered treatments. The method aims to cover the following five categories:

- **(A) Basic Profile:** describes the basic profile, degree of independence, conditions of disease to grasp the current situation of the person.
- **(B) Life:** describes preferences and histories of the way of life and environment most important for the person.
- **(C) Mind and Body:** objectively summarizes physical or mental problems that the person wants to be supported.
- **(D) Focus:** identifies what the person can do and know based on clinical observation.
- **(E) Care Plan Introduction:** creates a preferred care plan based on topics identified from A to D.

There are 16 sheets within the above five categories. One can start with even a single sheet. Filling personal information in the sheets reveals ideas and possibilities useful for the person-centered care.

2.5   Linked Open Data

Linked Open Data (LOD) is a technology of sharing open data, where the published data is linked on the Web. LOD is represented in RDF (Resource Description Framework), which describes every data as a machine-readable Web resource. RDF specifies every resource as a *triple* of subject, predicate, and object. Figure 2 shows a schematic representation of an RDF data model. In the figure, an oval represents a resource, a rectangle represents a literal (constant value), and an arrow represents a predicate. This example describes two facts: "the area of Tokyo is 2,188 km^2" and "The country where Tokyo exists is Japan". Since every data is referred by URI, a resource can be *linked* with other relevant resources. For a given original concept, linked data across different domains allow machine processing to derive various associated concepts automatically. Famous LOD datasets include *DBpedia*, which is LOD version created from Wikipedia. Some LOD publish a *SPARQL endpoint*, which allows a client to query RDF in the SPARQL query language. If no SPARQL endpoint is available, a client downloads whole dataset as a file, or uses WebAPI to obtain data in designated format.

3   Generating Personalized Dialogue for People with Dementia

3.1   Goal and Approach

The goal of this paper is to propose a method that generates person-centered dialogues essential for daily dementia counseling. When we let a system provide a

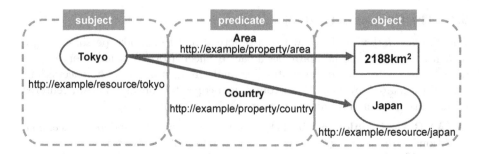

Fig. 2. Graph representing RDF

dementia counseling, we have to consider carefully what topics should be appropriate. Due to the memory impairment, which is the core symptom of dementia, the person forgets recent events and information quite easily. Therefore, even if the system asks about timely news or recent topics, the person would not be able to follow the conversation. This would lead to the loss of confidence or physiological anxiety of the person.

Moreover, the system should behave attentively according to what the person says. For example, suppose that the system asks a person with dementia about his/her birthplace. Depending on the person, of course, the answer varies like Hiroshima, Okayama, Tokyo or so on. In our previous VCG (see Sect. 2.3), the developer had to prepare playscripts that cover all possible birthplaces. Moreover, to expand the conversation associated with the birthplace, further scripts are needed. So, it is quite expensive for the developer to write such a lot of playscripts in advance.

To cope with the challenge, we take the following three approaches.

- **A1: Extracting life history with Center Method**
- **A2: Expanding conversation with linked open data (LOD)**
- **A3: Generating personalized dialogues using life history and LOD**

3.2   A1: Extracting Life History with Center Method

For an effective dementia counseling, it is essential to affect the long-term memory of a person with dementia. Therefore, we propose to choose topics of counseling based on *life history* of the person. The life history refers to information about how the person has been living so far, which includes birthplace, family, school, work, reminiscence, hobby, and so on. Compared to timely news, the life history is more robust information in the long-term memory. Also, the person can easily explain it, since it is his/her own history. Moreover, the life history represents unchangeable *facts*, which can be easily managed by the system.

To extract the personal life history, we extensively use four sheets from the Life category of the Center Method (see Sect. 2.4).

(Sheet B-1) My Family: describes family of the person with dementia.
(Sheet B-2) My History: describes history and records of life of the person.

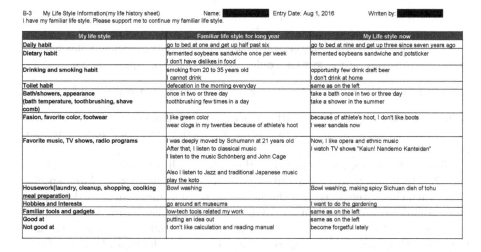

B-3   My Life Style Information(my life history sheet)   Name: ▮▮▮▮▮▮   Entry Date: Aug 1, 2016   Written by: ▮▮▮▮▮▮
I have my familiar life style. Please support me to continue my familiar life style.

My life style	Familiar life style for long year	My Life style now
Daily habit	go to bed at one and get up half past six	go to bed at nine and get up three since seven years ago
Dietary habit	fermented soybeans sandwiche once per week I don't have dislikes in food	fermented soybeans sandwiche and potsticker
Drinking and smoking habit	smoking from 20 to 35 years old I cannot drink	opportunity few drink draft beer I don't drink at home
Toilet habit	defecation in the morning everyday	same as on the left
Bath/showers, appearance (bath temperature, toothbrushing, shave comb)	once in two or three day toothbrushing few times in a day	take a bath once in two or three day take a shower in the summer
Fasion, favorite color, footwear	I like green color wear clogs in my twenties because of athlete's hoot	because of athlete's hoot, I don't like boots I wear sandals now
Favorite music, TV shows, radio programs	I was deeply moved by Schumann at 21 years old After that, I listen to classical music I listen to the music Schönberg and John Cage Also I listen to Jazz and traditional Japanese music play the koto	Now, I like opera and ethnic music I watch TV shows "Kaiun! Nandemo Kanteidan"
Housework(laundry, cleanup, shopping, coolking meal preparation)	Bowl washing	Bowl washing, making spicy Sichuan dish of tohu
Hobbies and interests	go around art museums	I want to do the gardening
Familiar tools and gadgets	low-tech tools related my work	same as on the left
Good at Not good at	putting an idea out I don't like calculation and reading manual	same as on the left become forgetful lately

Fig. 3. Example of sheet B-3 - my history

(Sheet B-3) My Style: describes preferred life style of the person.
(Sheet B-4) My Living: describes preferred living environment of the person.

Figure 3 shows an example of Sheet B-3. We can see the personal life style like the dietary habit, favorite music, what he is good/bad at, and so on.

Using the life history information derived from the above sheets, the system finds a clue to the person-centered conversation in the dementia care.

To extract the life history information, we consider two methods. The first method is that a user (person with dementia or caregiver) manually fills the Sheets B-1 to B-4 and the system operator registers the information to the system. This method would cause expensive effort for the user to fill many data items in the sheets.

The second method is that the virtual agent (VA) interactively asks the person with dementia to fill the sheet. The VA asks questions like "Where were you born?", "What did you do for living?", "What is your favorite music?". The person answers each question via voice. Although this method takes time, the system can create opportunity of conversations, in addition to the acquisition of the life history.

3.3   A2: Expanding Conversation with Linked Open Data

"A system asks a question, then a person with dementia answers it. The system moves to the next question." Such mechanical dialogues make the dementia counseling boring. For example, consider the following dialogue where the VA tries to extract the life history (as mentioned in A1).

VA: "Where were you born?", Person: "I was born in Hiroshima."

If the conversation just ends here, then the counseling would be quite poor. For more person-centered counseling, it is important to *expand the conversation*, based on the answer from the person with dementia. For instance, following the above conversation, if the system could produce one more question like:

VA: I know Hiroshima's specialty is Okonomi-yaki. Do you like it?

then the counseling would be enriched significantly. However, it is not easy for the system to manage all possible prior knowledge necessary to expand the conversation.

To cope with this, the proposed method uses the linked open data (LOD, see Sect. 2.5) to implement on-demand expansion of the conversation. More specifically, when the system detects a characteristic word in user's answer, the system tries to find "linked" words using LOD, and use the new words for the subsequent conversations. In the above example, suppose that the system recognizes the word "Hiroshima" in the answer. Then, the system looks up LOD to obtain information associated with Hiroshima. From "Hiroshima", if "Okonomi-Yaki" is found as a linked word with predicate "specialty", the system says "I know Hiroshima's specialty is Okonomi-Yaki".

The implementation of the method is as follows. First, if a SPARQL endpoint of the LOD is available, the system just queries to the endpoint. For example, a query of DBpedia Japanese that extracts neighboring prefectures of Hiroshima can be written as follows:

```
SELECT DISTINCT *
WHERE{
 <http://ja.dbpedia.org/resource/広島県>
 <http://ja.dbpedia.org/property/隣接都道府県>
 ?o .
}
```

If the LOD is provided via WebAPI, the system executes the API and parses the obtained data. If the LOD is provided as a file, we download the file in advance and import the file to the system database. During run-time, the system looks up the database.

3.4   A3: Generating Personalized Dialogues Using Life History and LOD

In the proposed method, we define an outline of each counseling scenario by a *dialogue template*. A dialogue template is a template of conversation commonly used by all users in a counseling scenario. Each dialogue template has variables to be changed. During run-time, the system updates the variables based on the personal life history and LOD, which generates the person-centered dialogue.

To cover a wide variety of topics, the proposed system has a set of dialogue templates, corresponding to data items in the Life category of the Center

Method. For example, there are birthplace template, hobby template, work template, school template, and so on. When a counseling starts, the system chooses an appropriate dialogue template based on the registered life history information. During the counseling, the system instantiates the template by filling actual values to the variables, using the available life history and LOD.

We illustlate an example of the dialogue template as follows.

```
Where were you born, #{info.name}?
<% var pref = getAnswer(); %>
I know #{pref}'s specialty is #{LOD(pref->{specialty})}.
```

This dialogue template specifies a conversation where a system first asks birthplace of the user and then expands the conversation for a specialty of the birthplace. #{info.name} represents a variable where user's name is assigned. The function getAnswer() in the second line represents an operation that obtains a word from user's answer. The result is assigned to a variable pref, representing a prefecture of birthplace. The last variable in the third line shows an operation that obtains LOD from pref linked with "specialty".

When applying the above dialogue template to user "Seiji", the following personalized dialogue is generated.

```
Where were you born, Seiji?
Seiji: I was born in Hiroshima.
I know Hiroshima's specialty is Okonomi-Yaki.
```

3.5   System Architecture

Figure 4 shows the overall architecture of the proposed counseling system. We call the system that implements the proposed methods A1, A2 and A3 *Virtual Counselor*. To provide a counseling service for many households of people with dementia, the virtual counselor is deployed within a cloud. In each house, a client PC with the virtual agent and the Web browser is deployed. The virtual counselor pushes counseling dialogues via WebAPI of the client PC, and pulls user's response.

We explain how the virtual counselor service is provided. First, a person with dementia and caregiver manually fill the sheets of the Center Method to the extent that they can. The operator registers the information to the system using the feature A1. When a counseling service is executed, the virtual counselor picks up a dialogue template based on the available life history information, and starts a conversation. During the conversation, the virtual counselor dynamically fills variables of the template with feature A3, to generate personalized dialogue. For this, if the feature A3 requires unknown life history data, the virtual counselor asks a question with the VA using feature A1. As the user answers the question via voice or a button, the virtual counselor registers the answer in the database. When expanding the conversation, the virtual counselor queries LOD using feature A2, to retrieve necessary data. All components in

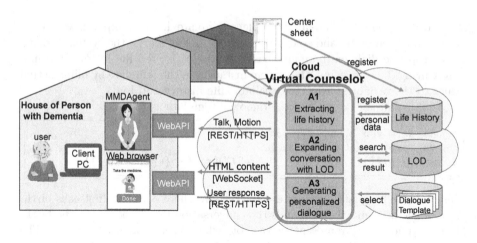

Fig. 4. System architecture of virtual counselor

the cloud and the client PCs are integrated with Web service, considering the principle of service-oriented architecture (SOA) [4]. The architecture facilitates further integration, in the future, with IoT and smart home.

4   Implementation of Prototype

Based on the proposed method, we have implemented a prototype system of virtual counselor. Technologies used in the implementation are as follows:

- System Language: Java 1.8.0_25, Ruby
- Web Server: Apach Tomcat 7.0.69
- Web Service Framework: Jersey 1.19, Apache Axis2 1.6.3
- Virtual Agent: MMDAgent version 1.4
- LOD: DBpedia Japanese [3], LinkData [7]

This prototype implements the personalized dialogue for the user's birthplace. The dialogue template specifies conversations, where the VA first asks a birthplace, and then talks about the specialty of the birthplace.

Figure 5 shows an example conversation generated by the prototype. First, the VA asks the user: "Where were you born, Seiji?" Suppose that the user Seiji answers "I was born in Fukuyama-city." Now, the answered birthplace is not a prefecture, the system looks up DBpedia to find a prefecture where Fukuyama-city exists. The VA confirms that "Do you mean Fukuyama in Hiroshima prefecture?" Then, the user says "Yes." As the prefecture is confirmed to "Hiroshima", the system looks up LinkData to retrieve "Okonomi-Yaki" as a specialty of Hiroshima. Finally, the VA says that "I like Okomomi-Yaki of Hiroshima very much!"

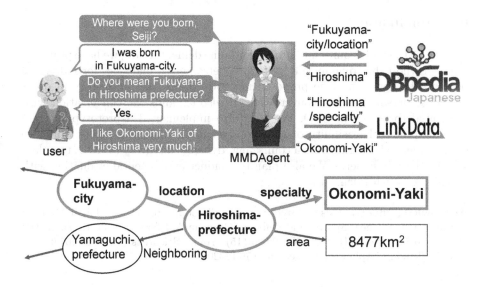

Fig. 5. Personalized dialogue generated by prototype system

5   Discussion

Towards the practical use, we discuss some issues learned through the prototype implementation. First, we have found that only DBpedia and LinkData cannot cover a wide range of topics and individual hobbies and preferences. We may need a method to discover necessary LOD dynamically during the counseling.

Second, the heterogeneous data access methods to LOD, such as SPARQL endpoint, WebAPI or file, make the system difficult to scale. In case that the variety of LOD increases, we need an extra service layer that abstracts the heterogeneous data accesses. With the service layer, the counseling system can acquire data in a uniform format (subject, predicate and object).

Third, in terms of generating effective counseling scenarios, it is important to cooperate with caregivers of people with dementia to know his/her favorite topics. Our current system assumes that an expert service developer creates dialogue templates as system program. In the future, however, we want to develop a method that allows caregivers to generate the templates easily without programming knowledge.

Finally, we have to consider the evaluation method. The evaluation should be conducted quantitatively; how often and how much the counseling system can cure physiologically unstable conditions of people with dementia. We need an empirical analysis of system logs and clinical data. It is also interesting that the system autonomously *learns* the data to find better counseling. The system collects answers of not only multiple-choice questions, but also free-form questions. For this, we need natural language processing to analyze user's utterance.

6   Conclusions

To achieve the daily counseling system for home dementia care, we have proposed a new method that dynamically generates personalized dialogues for individual people with dementia. The proposed method obtains the life history in order to choose person-centered conversation. It also expands the conversation with associated topics using LOD. We have also implemented a prototype system to show practical feasibility of the proposed method. In our future work, we develop methods of triggering a counseling, dynamic discovery of LOD, template creation by non-experts. We also plan to conduct experimental evaluation with actual people with dementia.

Acknowledgements. This research was partially supported by the Japan Ministry of Education, Science, Sports, and Culture [Grant-in-Aid for Scientific Research (B) (No. 16H02908, No. 15H02701, No. 26280115), Young Scientists (B) (No. 26730155), and Challenging Exploratory Research (15K12020)].

References

1. Berners-Lee, T.: Linked data - design issues, June 2009. https://www.w3.org/DesignIssues/LinkedData.html
2. Cabinet Office, G.o.J.: Annual report on the aging society, June 2015. http://www.cao.go.jp/
3. DBpedia Community: Dbpedia japanese, January 2017. http://ja.dbpedia.org
4. Erl, T.: Service-Oriented Architecture: A Field Guide to Integrating XML and Web Services. Prentice Hall PTR, Upper Saddle River (2004)
5. Ministry of Health, Labour and Welfare: The status of new job openings for general employment by key industry and by size, December 2016. http://www.mhlw.go.jp/
6. Kitwood, T.: Dementia Reconsidered: The Person Comes First. Open University, Buckingham (1997)
7. LinkData: Linkdata.org: Opendata utilization support system, January 2017. http://linkdata.org
8. Neal, M., Wright, P.B.: Validation therapy for dementia. Cochrane Database Syst. Rev. **3**(3) (2003)
9. Rokkaku, R.: Care management sheet pack for the elderly with dementia: the center method ver. 03. Nihon Ronen Igakkai zasshi. Jpn. J. Geriatr. **42**(3), 318–319 (2005)
10. Tokunaga, S., Tamamizu, K., Saiki, S., Nakamura, M., Yasuda, K.: VirtualCare-Giver: personalized smart elderly care. Int. J. Softw. Innov. (IJSI) **5**(1), 30–43 (2016). http://www.igi-global.com/journals/abstract-announcement/158780
11. Woods, B., Spector, A.E., Jones, C.A., Orrell, M., Davies, S.P.: Reminiscence therapy for dementia. Cochrane Database Syst. Rev. **2** (2005)

Color Affects the Usability of Smart Phone Icon for the Elderly

Chunfa Sha, Rui Li[(⊠)], and Kai Chang

Jiangsu University, Zhenjiang 212013, Jiangsu, China
li858@purdue.edu

Abstract. With the development of society, the smart phone for the elderly has been developed rapidly. To improve the design of the smart phone icons for the elderly, a set of experiments were made to study the usability differences between multi-colored icons and monochromatic icons. 8 pairs of icons where a pair of icons was composed of a multi-colored icon and a monochromatic icon with the same function were prepared. These 16 icons whose height are 9.81 mm were placed in random order in the Xiaomi MI 4 smart phone installed with the android system. 24 retired teachers aged from 60–70 of the university were called as participants. They were asked to find the right icon as required and click on it with one of their fingers. For every subjects, there were 6 finding tasks followed by satisfaction questionnaire surveys. Eye movement data and satisfaction questionnaire surveys data were acquired and analyzed to get the results: monochromatic flat icons were easier to recognize and operate than the ones that designed with multi-colors for old people, even though they may have monotonous forms; age 60–65 or 66–70 was not the reason one made an operation mistake; some older people liked multi-colored flat icons more than monochromatic flat icons for their colorful vision experience.

Keywords: Multi-colored flat icons · Monochromatic flat icons · Elderly · Usability

1 Introduction

According to China Statistical Yearbook (2016), there are about 144 million people over 65 years old in china by 2015 [1]. Smart phone as a feature of today's society are rapidly becoming a device more and more important for the elderly to keep in touch with the information society. As for the elderly, increasing age means decreasing in memory ability and physical performances, which has required for new needs on smart phone design [2, 3]. Compared to young man, older users experience fear of consequences of using unfamiliar technology and are passive of mobile phones. They prefer products that are easy to deal with [4].

In order to improve the usability of a smart phone for the elderly, many studies have been done towards the design of phone icons which are important part of the mobile phone interface. The word "icon" originates from a Greek word "eikon", which act as an intermediate between the user and the features of the mobile. It is considered to be images, pictures or symbols which display information for users. The icon forms

© Springer International Publishing AG 2017
V.G. Duffy (Ed.): DHM 2017, Part II, LNCS 10287, pp. 173–182, 2017.
DOI: 10.1007/978-3-319-58466-9_17

affect the speed and accuracy that users perceive and interpret these information [5]. For the elderly, metaphor icons help them to recognize faster and easier compared to non-metaphor icon design, and the three elements, familiarity, labeling and resemblance that contribute to the successful recognition [3]. In terms of color, it was found that simplified graphic rendered in warm color attached with text in different colors that is not warm color tone and graphical symbols with extensive rendered with cool color tone help enhance the visibility for the elderly [6]. It was found that among the combinations of dark character/light background, blue and red character on white background is highly recommended; and while that for light character/dark background, white is found to be the best character on blue and green backgrounds [7].

With the development of science, technology and economy, flat design of icons, instead of skeuomorphism design, has already been mainstream for smart phone design [8]. It was proved that user's visual search efficiency is relevant to the icon's size: the search efficiency of skeuomorphism icons is higher at the size of 236px, however the search efficiency of flat icons is higher at the size of 165px and 78px [9].

In summary, there are many factors affect the icon design for smart phone, such as design style, color tone, icon size and so on. The purpose of the study was to investigate how color complexity affect the usability of flat icons of smart phone for the elderly.

2   Researcher Method

2.1   Research Purposes

Monochromatic flat icons and multi-colored flat icons were shown to different older participants for several tasks to find how color number of icons affect the usability, which may be useful for advices on icon design. Monochromatic flat icon is an icon designed with background of only one color and graphical of another color. Multi-colored flat icon is an icon designed with background of only one color and graphical of multi-colors. In this paper, graphical designed with two colors or three colors were took as multi-colored flat icons.

2.2   Participants

24 retired teachers from the university were recruited as participants in this study. They were divided into two groups. There were 7 females and 5 males aged from 60–65 at average of 62.83 in the first group. There were 6 females and 6 males aged from 66–70 at average of 67.33 in the second group. All the subjects had experience of using a smart phone for more than 1 year and still kept one smart phone. None of them had experience in similar study. Gifts as reward for all of the subjects were prepared for the experiment. The mental and physical state of all participants were suitable for the test.

2.3   Experimental Equipment

An experiment platform composed of an eye tracker, a scene camera, a mobile device bracket, an auxiliary handle was built up for collecting experiment data, and the Xiaomi MI 4 smart phone installed with the android system was used to shown the icons, as shown in Fig. 1. The eye tracker Tobii X2 was used to get the eye movement data. The resolution of Xiaomi MI 4 with a 5.0 inches screen is 1920*1080px. All tests were performed in a quiet environment without any interference.

Fig. 1. Experimental platform (left) and Xiaomi MI 4 (right)

2.4   Experimental Materials

The experimental materials were derived from 8 pairs of icons designed in flat style where a pair of icons was composed of a multi-colored icon and a monochromatic icon with the same function, as shown in Fig. 2. According to the former study [9, 10], the size of all the icons were set as 9.81 mm and the shape of them were drawn as square with rounded corners. 8 monochromatic flat icons were made with blue background

Fig. 2. Monochromatic icons (upper row) and multi-colored icon (lower row) (Color figure online)

and white Figures. 8 multi-colored flat icons were made with one color background and multi-colored figures. The figures of all 16 icons had a same height of 7.19 mm.

In order to reduce the bad influence of improper selection of the icons on the experimental results, it avoided to use the icons with high complex form and low color contrast as experimental materials.

2.5 Experimental Procedures

There were two main tasks for all the participants. Firstly, in order to measure the time taken by the elderly people to recognize the icons, an icon was shown to them through Xiaomi MI 4, and the participants had to find it out from the 16 icons placed randomly as soon as quickly by touching the right icon with their fingers, as in Fig. 3. The 6 icons from the pair 3, 4 and 7 were shown randomly one by one for the test. So, there were 6 sub finding tasks for every participant. Secondly, interviews session on participant's subjective satisfaction were made.

Fig. 3. 16 icons placed randomly (left) and 6 icons for the test (right) (Color figure online)

The experiment was carried out one subject by one subject in the testing room to keep out interfere with each other. Before the experiment, several question about mental and physical state was given to make sure that the subject was suitable for the test, or he/she should be replaced by the next one. After age and sex of the participant were gathered and experiment preparatory work, such as eye tracking calibration, was done, the experiment was carried out as follows, as shown in Fig. 4.

- Step 1: The instruction of the experiment was given to the subject to ensure that the subject knew the whole procedure.
- Step 2: The 16 icons placed in a random order were shown for 20000 ms for the participants to get a general view about them, since there were no texts under these icons to explain their means.
- Step 3: An icon from the pairs out of pair 3, 4 and 7 was shown for 2000 ms after the prompt for pre-experiment whose length was 2000 ms.
- Step 4: The 16 icons placed in a random order were shown. It would disappeared if the subject make a choice with touching on any icon.

- Step 5: Another sub finding task was made with another icon from the pairs out of pair 3, 4 and 7 after 2000 ms black screen.
- Step 6: There was a 20 s break after the step 3–5 as the pre-experiment.
- Step 7: The prompt for formal experiment whose length was 2000 ms was shown.
- Step 8: Sub finding tasks made with the 6 icons in a randomly order from pair 3, 4 and 7 were carried out for formal experiment in the way for pre-experiment.
- Step 9: The prompt for the end of the test was shown to finish the experiment.
- Step 10: After the test, interviews were carried out to get participation's satisfactions.

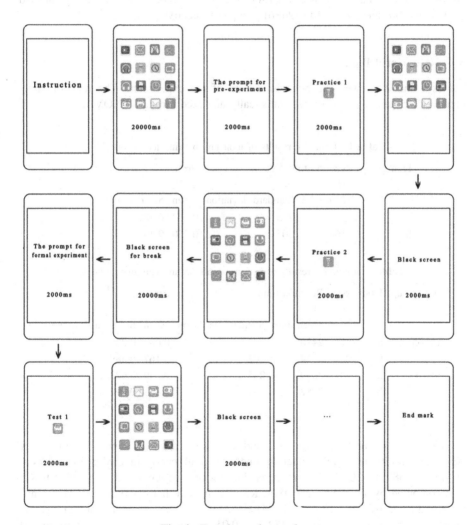

Fig. 4. Experimental procedures

In order to avoid the effect of learning experience of the experiment, it was very important that the positions of the 16 icons were randomly arranged for every sub finding task in the pre-experiment and the formal experiment for every participant. In order to improve sampling rate, subjects were asked to fix their vision on the middle area of the mobile phone screen and keep the correct sitting posture.

3   Results and Discussion

After the first round of the experiment, sampling rate of 2 subjects aged 66–70 were not reaching the standard (lower than 85%). 2 more subjects were randomly selected for the test. So, there were 144 (24*6) groups of effective data.

3.1   Behavioral Data

Tables 1 and 2 showed the behavioral data of the experiment. The reaction time, number of errors of the test were statistically analyzed through ANOVA.

Table 1. Behavior results of icon group a and icon group b

Icon group	Reaction time (ms)		Error	
	Mean time	Standard deviation	Mean	Standard deviation
a	2478	255	0.167	0.482
b	2668	207	0.250	0.442

Table 2. Behavior results of age group 60–65 and age group 66–70

Age group	Icon group	Reaction time (ms)		Error	
		Mean time	Standard deviation	Mean	Standard deviation
60–65	a	2416	209	0.083	0.289
	b	2654	203	0.167	0.389
66–70	a	2539	233	0.250	0.622
	b	2682	291	0.333	0.492

The reaction time for icon group a and icon group b were compared by One-Way ANOVA. Results showed that reaction time were significantly affected by the colors (F $(1, 46) = 8.680$; $p < 0.05$). The reaction time for icon group a and icon group b was also compared by Two-Way ANOVA. Results showed that reaction time was significantly affected by the colors (F $(1, 44) = 9.243$; $p < 0.05$) and was not significantly affected by the age (F $(1, 44) = 1.472$; $p > 0.05$). It was said that the reaction time of monochromatic flat icons was less than that of multi-colored flat icons and the elderly spent similar time to complete these tasks.

The number of errors for icon group a and icon group b were compared by One-Way ANOVA. Results showed that number of errors were not significantly affected by the colors ($F (1, 46) = 0.392$; $p > 0.05$). The reaction time for icon group a and icon group b were also compared by Two-Way ANOVA. Results showed that reaction time were not significantly affected by the colors ($F (1, 44) = 1.543$; $p > 0.05$) and the age ($F (1, 44) = 0.385$; $p > 0.05$). It was said that the number of errors had nothing to do with monochromatic flat icons or multi-colored flat icons, and group aged 60–65 or group aged 66–70.

3.2 Eye Movement Data

Tables 3 and 4 showed the eye movement data of the experiment. The time that a subject spent to fix their vision into target AOI and the fixation counts of the experiment were statistically analyzed through ANOVA.

Table 3. The eye movement data of icon group a and icon group b

Icon group	Time to first fixation in target AOI (ms)		Fixation counts	
	Mean time	Standard deviation	Mean	Standard deviation
a	1472	221	6.541	1.062
b	1671	207	7.500	0.978

Table 4. The eye movement data of age group 60–65 and age group 66–70

Age group	Icon group	Time to first fixation in target AOI (ms)		Fixation counts	
		Mean time	Standard deviation	Mean	Standard deviation
60–65	a	1405	194	6.083	0.996
	b	1655	202	7.167	0.835
66–70	a	1538	234	7.000	0.953
	b	1687	220	7.833	1.030

The time that a subject spent to fix their vision into target AOI for icon group a and icon group b was compared by One-Way ANOVA. Results showed that time was significantly affected by the colors ($F (1, 46) = 9.156$; $p < 0.05$). The time that a subject spent to fix their vision into target AOI for icon group a and icon group b was also compared by Two-Way ANOVA. Results showed that time was significantly affected by the colors ($F (1, 44) = 10.452$; $p < 0.05$) and were not significantly affected by the age ($F (1, 44) = 1.730$; $p > 0.05$). It said that subject spent more time on finding out the multi-colored flat icons than that of monochromatic flat icons.

The fixation counts for icon group a and icon group b were compared by One-Way ANOVA. Results showed that number of fixation were significantly affected by the colors (F (1, 46) = 12.774; p < 0.05). The fixation counts for icon group a and icon group b were compared by Two-Way ANOVA. Results showed that fixation counts were significantly affected by the colors (F (1, 44) = 13.722; p < 0.05) and also the age (F (1, 44) = 6.345; p < 0.05). It was harder for subject to differentiate multi-colored flat icons than monochromatic flat icons. The group aged 67–70 spent more energy to fix their vision on the target icons than the group aged 60–65, although similar time was taken for whole task.

3.3   Satisfaction Data

Interviews were carried out to collect the information of the participant's perceptual evaluation of the design of the 8 multi-colored flat icons and the 8 monochromatic flat icons based on Likert scale [11]. All participants were asked to fill in the questionnaire to show how strongly they agree or disagree with that it was concise, easy to remember, easy to adapt, beautiful of these icons and how the liked them, on a 5 point Likert scale from 1 (= strongly disagree) to 5 (= strongly agree). Participant's subjective satisfactions were analyzed, as shown in Table 5 and Fig. 5.

Table 5. Subjective satisfaction data

	Monochromatic flat icons				Multi-colored flat icons			
	Highest score	Lowest score	Mean	Standard deviation	Highest score	Lowest score	Mean	Standard deviation
Concise	5	3	3.96	1.01	4	1	2.97	1.82
Easy to remember	4	3	3.71	0.69	4	1	3.16	1.69
Easy to adapt	5	1	3.58	1.64	4	1	3.39	1.71
Beautiful	4	2	3.17	1.33	5	3	3.89	0.87
Like	4	3	3.48	0.46	5	3	3.64	0.93

- Monochromatic flat icons were more concise than multi-colored flat icons. This result was also confirmed in the interview.
- For multi-colored flat icons, a variety of colors would also increase the burden on the participant's memory. So it was easier to remember the shape and means of monochromatic flat icons. It was the reason that less time was spent on finding out the target monochromatic flat icon.
- Participants thought there was little difference between monochromatic flat icons and multi-colored flat icons as far as "easy to adapt" was concerned. So, they could complete the experiment successfully. And the error number had nothing to do with the kind of icon.

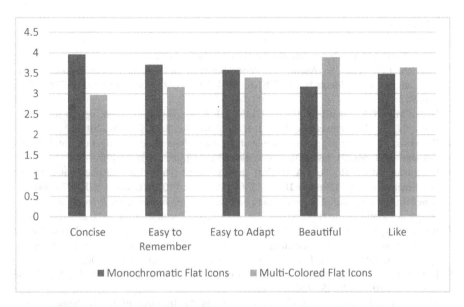

Fig. 5. The bar graph of subjective satisfaction (Color figure online)

- Multi-colors were more beautiful. Because the combination of different colors could bring good visual experience.
- There were little difference as far as "like" was concerned. Although monochromatic flat icons were more concise and easy to remember, many participant thought that the beauty was an important factor for smart phone icons.

4 Conclusion

The study showed that monochromatic flat icons were more concise and easy to remember than multi-colored flat icons for the elderly. Monochromatic flat icons took less time for the elderly to find out them. Aged 60–65 or 67–70 and the kind of the icon were not the reasons that older people made an operation mistake. Some older people liked multi-colored flat icons more than monochromatic flat icons for their colorful vision experience. These results could be used for the smart phone icon design for the elderly.

However, the results indicated in this study did not represent the entire population of the elderly people. The icons designed for experiment did not take color contrast and other factor into concerned. Further work needs to be done to expand the study.

Acknowledgments. We thank the support from the Graduate Student Innovation Project for Common College in Jiangsu Province, China (No. CXLX11-0566).

References

1. China Statistical Yearbook. http://www.stats.gov.cn/tjsj/ndsj/
2. Petersen, J., Thielke, S., Austin, D.: Phone behavior and its relationship to loneliness in older adults. Aging Ment. Health **20**(10), 1084–1091 (2015). doi:10.1080/13607863.2015. 1060947
3. Nadia, M.H.N.A., Nuraihan, M.I.E., Hanis, A.R.F.: Exploring metaphor design for mobile icons: the elderly perspectives. Aust. J. Basic Appl. Sci. **8**(4), 98–106 (2014)
4. Kurniawan, S.: Older people and mobile phones: a multi-method investigation. Int. J. Hum.-Comput. Stud. **66**(12), 889–901 (2008). doi:10.1016/j.ijhcs.2008.03.002
5. Boschman, M.C., Roufs, J.A.J.: Text quality metrics for visual display units: II. An experimental survey. Displays **18**(1), 45–64 (1997). doi:10.1016/S0141-9382(97)00004-8
6. Kingkarn, P., Nopadon, S.: Aging and perception of graphic representation: a case of icon design in mobile phone functionality. Int. J. Comput. Technol. Appl. **5**(2), 293–298 (2014)
7. Bhattacharyya, D., Chowdhury, B., Chatterjee, T.: Selection of character/background color combinations for onscreen searching tasks: an eye movement, subjective and performance approach. Displays **35**(3), 101–109 (2014). doi:10.1016/j.displa.2014.03.002
8. Kim, J.H.: A study on mobile icon design of iPhone7. Cartoon Anim. Stud. **34**, 367–386 (2014). doi:10.7230/KOSCAS.2014.34.367
9. Kai, C.: The Usability Research of Flat Icons in the Interface of Smart Phone. Jiangsu university, Zhenjiang (2016)
10. Im, Y., Kim, T., Jung, E.S.: Investigation of icon design and touchable area for effective smart phone controls. Hum. Factors Ergon. Manuf. Serv. Ind. **25**(2), 251–267 (2015). doi:10.1002/hfm.20593
11. Jamieson, S.: Likert scale: how to (ab) use them. Med. Educ. **38**(12), 1217–1218 (2005). doi:10.1111/j.1365-2929.2004.02012.xSusan

Capturing Activities of Daily Living for Elderly at Home Based on Environment Change and Speech Dialog

Kazunari Tamamizu[1(✉)], Seiji Sakakibara[1], Sachio Saiki[1],
Masahide Nakamura[1], and Kiyoshi Yasuda[2]

[1] Graduate School of System Informatics Kobe University,
1-1 Rokkodai, Nada, Kobe, Japan
tamamizu@ws.cs.kobe-u.ac.jp, masa-n@cs.kobe-u.ac.jp
[2] Chiba Rosai Hospital, 2-16 Tatsumidai-higashi, Ichihara, Japan
fwkk5911@mb.infoweb.ne.jp

Abstract. The ICT-based elderly monitoring systems attract great attention as a promising technology for home elderly care. However, the conventional systems have limitations of deployment cost and invasiveness, the effort of activity labeling, and a lack of communication. To cope with the limitations, we propose a system that captures activities of daily living (ADL) of the elderly, based on speech dialogue triggered by environment changes. Specifically, we deploy Autonomous Sensor Boxes, developed in our previous study, within a house of the elderly. The boxes gather and send house environmental data to the cloud. Then, the Change Finder algorithm is applied to the time-series data, to detect changes in the house online. On detecting a change, the Virtual Agent (VA) in the house asks the elderly what he/she is doing now. The elderly speaks to the VA, by which an ADL is recorded in the system. The proposed system can capture ADL with non-invasive sensing and create an opportunity for communication.

Keywords: Home elderly care · Changing detection · Activity recognition · Virtual Agent

1 Introduction

Nowadays, Japan has been facing a hyper-aging society. In 2025, the total population will decrease to 120 million, while people over the age of 65 will increase to 37 million. Thus, approximately 30% of the population will become the elderly [2]. On the other hands, many facilities of welfare and nursing care suffer from a chronic shortage of workers. As a result, related jobs opening ratio is as high as 2.68 (as of Dec. 2014). The number of nursing home is not sufficient for the number of applicants, who are over 524,000 elderly people. The Japanese government starts to encourage *home care* rather than building new facilities. Needless to say, the elderly care will rely more on home, which poses a burden to the

© Springer International Publishing AG 2017
V.G. Duffy (Ed.): DHM 2017, Part II, LNCS 10287, pp. 183–194, 2017.
DOI: 10.1007/978-3-319-58466-9_18

family as caregivers. Under these circumstances, the system and the technology, which reduces burdens of elderly care at home, attract great attention.

Among many technologies which are being used to realize care at home studied so far, the *elderly monitoring system* based on ICT is a promising system. As examples of the elderly monitoring system, commercialized systems which detect leaving the bed [4] and which safeguard elderly's health and well-being using robots [1] are enumerated. Especially these days, many researchers enthusiastically develop the monitoring system which recognizes *activities of daily living (ADL)* using activity recognition technology, and notifies caregivers of elderly's emergency situations. Under activity recognition technology, a lot of data is collected with sensors such as environment sensors, wearable sensors and cameras, and conditions or activities of a target elderly are estimated and recognized. As examples of activity recognition technology based on sensor data, there are technologies that learn and recognize the presence and ADL [3] using camera images, and learn acceleration data collected with wearable sensors or smartphone and recognize user's actions (e.g. walking, working, at rest) [6], and recognize ADL using many environment sensors which are installed widely in a smart home [10].

However, the conventional monitoring systems have following problems.

Problem P1 (installation cost and invasiveness). When users install the conventional system to general households, they have to do repair work on their house. As a result, this causes a significant cost to increase. For example, users have to upgrade and install sensors in the house to turn into a smart home. Also, the conventional systems using cameras and/or wearable sensors are very invasive for the daily life of elderly.

Problem P2 (burden of labeling data with activity of elderly). Most of conventional systems classify sensor data into each ADL using machine learning. In order to classify the data, the conventional systems need ADL labeled training data. Therefore, on the conventional systems, users must record and input ADL every several minutes. Thus, this is a heavy burden to elderly and caregivers.

Problem P3 (lack of communication with elderly). Almost all of the conventional systems only notify caregivers when an emergency occurs. Most of the conventional systems can not care with communication, which is essentially important in elderly care. Therefore significant burden cutdown of caregivers is not be achieved.

To cope with these problems, in this paper, we propose new sensing system to capture the ADL of elderly based on dialog triggered by environment changes in a home.

First, for P1, we use an autonomous sensor box [7] in a home which our research group has developed in the previous work. The sensor box is an IoT device which consists of seven environment sensors, temperature sensor, humidity sensor, light sensor, atmosphere pressure sensor, sound sensor, vibration sensor, and motion sensor. The sensor box autonomously monitors surrounding environment by only powering up the sensor box and uploads sensor data to a database on the cloud. Also, we can install the sensor box in various places easily. Furthermore, the sensor box is a non-invasive device for elderly because the sensor box monitors the only environment.

Second, for P2, we propose the ADL labeling method based on changing point detection. We use time-series analysis for monitored environment data and we let elderly input ADL only when the environment changes. In this study, we use *Change Finder algorithm* [8] for environment time-series data collected on the cloud and implement the service which detects changing points online.

Finally, for P3, we use speech dialog with a *Virtual Agent (VA)* [5] in order to input ADL by elderly. When Change Finder detects environment changes, the VA in a home asks elderly what he/she is doing now. Then the elderly answering the question with voice, the proposed system records his/her ADL.

Using the proposed system, we can record ADL without too much burden with non-invasive sensing and the proposed system can encourage communication with elderly using dialogue and concern. Thus installing the proposed system is easier than installing conventional systems and the proposed system can provide care, which is more supportive for elderly.

2 Preliminaries

2.1 Home Care for Elderly

Home care workers always perform following three processes.

Observation: This is to monitor the environment and the behavior of elderly. They continuously observe situations in a home such as time, sound, vibration and a place of elderly. And recognizing situations such as what elderly is doing now and if elderly's body is not in any danger, they take precautions for possible danger and care. For example, they observe that "elderly watches TV and laughs" and "elderly almost falls over while walking".

Care: This is to care actually for elderly based on dialogue. Dialogue means that care workers call elderly's name or nickname and talk to elderly slowly, shortly and simply. Based on dialogue, care workers can let elderly talk about their feeling, and check elderly's condition and ease elderly's anxiousness and loneliness. Also, care workers consider and provide appropriate care depending on elderly's activity recognized by dialogue and observation. For example, care workers talk about TV program when elderly watch the TV program and laugh. In the case that elderly almost fall over while walking, care workers support elderly walking and ask his/her condition.

Record: This is to record care provided actually and what happens in the day. Based on records, care workers report to elderly's family on what has happened and what kinds of care they have provided. Also, keeping recording, care workers recognize features of elderly such as interest, and make use of records for better care for elderly. Furthermore, using records, new home workers turn over appropriate care for the elderly easily when home workers switch shifts with new home workers.

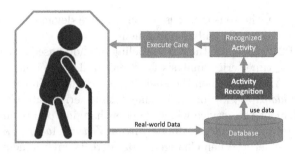

Fig. 1. Common process of monitoring elderly in home based on ICT

2.2   Monitoring Elderly and Recognizing Activities Based on ICT

Figure 1 shows the common process of monitoring elderly in a home based on ICT. In this process, first, systems monitor actual world data and recognize conditions of elderly and the environment around them. Monitored data include biological data (e.g. beat, acceleration of arms, legs, body) and environment data (e.g. temperature, humidity, sound volume, light, motion). Second, on recognition process, systems recognize *activities of daily living (ADL)* of elderly using monitored data. Finally, systems select needed care and provide care actually based on recognized ADL. Supporting parts of observation, care, and record based on ICT, systems ease burdens of home care workers and aim at the improvement of care that the only human provides.

Recently, many researchers enthusiastically study methods estimating ADL of human based on ICT. These methods are expected to be applied to a process of activity recognition, which Fig. 1 shows. These methods try to automatically estimate and recognize activities or postures of users using diverse data monitored by various sensors such as environment sensors, wearable sensors, and cameras. In general, these methods base on machine learning and return labels of concrete ADL based on given row data (time-series data) by *learning without a teacher* or *supervised learning*. In supervised learning, users label data, which are monitored by various sensors, with actual ADL previously to make training data. And picking out feature quantity of training data, systems learn by machine learning methods such as Support Vector Machine (SVM). In learning without a teacher, systems analyze a cluster of given data and perform mapping each cluster to each ADL.

As described in Sect. 1, many methods for activity recognition have been proposed before such as methods using camera images [3], using smartphone [6], and, using indoor positioning with smart home and power consumption [10].

2.3   Problem of Conventional Monitoring Systems

In this paper, we focus on Problem P1, P2, P3 described in Sect. 1 as problems which conventional monitoring systems have.

- *Problem P1 (installation cost and invasiveness)*
- *Problem P2 (burden of labeling data with activity of elderly)*
- *Problem P3 (lack of communication with elderly)*

Problem P1 has roots in that latest activity recognition technologies are still too unreachable for monitoring elderly at general households to use. More non-invasive and lower cost systems are needed to become widely used. Problem P2 means taking a lot of trouble with making training data for machine learning soon after installing systems. Reusing training data collected in other environments is difficult because conditions and living environments of elderly are different for every elderly. Problem P3 has roots in that almost all of conventional systems depend on the care of caregivers. Thoughtful common communication with elderly, who are monitored actually, is needed unless elderly is in an emergency.

2.4   Previous Works

In the previous work [7], we have developed *autonomous sensor boxes* which consist of a small box containing several sensors connected with a single board computer. The sensor box is an IoT device which has seven environment sensors, temperature sensor, humidity sensor, light sensor, atmosphere pressure sensor, sound sensor, vibration sensor and motion sensor. All you have to do is powering up the sensor box and the sensor box monitors autonomously environment. Also, the sensor box uploads monitored data to a database on the cloud. We can access the data collected on the cloud using Web-API. Also, external applications can get arbitrary time-series data using platform-independent Web protocol (REST or SOAP). We can install sensor boxes at anywhere easily and sensor boxes monitor the environment. Thus the sensor box is non-invasive for user's daily living. Therefore the sensor box can be used as the technology supporting to observe and record in home elderly care.

Also, in the previous work [9], we study to use *Virtual Agent (VA)* for supporting communication with elderly. VA is a chat bot program which looks like human and has animation effects and can interact with voice. Elderly can communicate with VA in the display. Therefore VA can be used as voice interface to provide care and dialogue on home care.

3   Proposed ADL Sensing System

To cope with problems P1, P2, P3 described in Sect. 2.3, in this study, we propose new sensing system capturing the ADL of elderly based on dialog triggered by environment change in a home.

3.1   Key Idea

In the proposed system, we install autonomous sensor boxes (refer to Sect. 2.4) in elderly's home and the proposed system monitors environment. This achieves non-invasive and lower cost sensing and we set out to solve Problem P1. Next, the

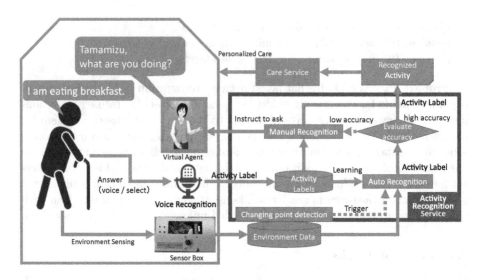

Fig. 2. System architecture of the proposed system

proposed system analyzes data collected by environment sensing and performs *changing point detection* online. Changing point detection identifies changes of data behavior. Using changing point detection, the proposed system estimates environment changing point as activity changing point. And recording elderly's ADL only on the timing of detection, the proposed system eases burdens of labeling described in Problem P2. Furthermore, the proposed system uses communication and dialogue with VA when the proposed system inputs ADL. When environment in the home changes, VA asks elderly what he/she is doing now (we call this *speech dialog*). The elderly answers the question of speech dialog with voice and the system record his/her ADL. This process encourages communication and leads to solving Problem P3.

In the proposed system, it is expected to become less recognition accuracy than conventional activity recognition methods because the proposed system only uses non-invasive environment sensing. However, the proposed system cover all activity recognition by not only sensing but also hearing ADL from elderly directly through communication between elderly and VA. And this creates communication chance and aims to achieve to record ADL with a high degree of accuracy.

3.2   System Architecture

Figure 2 shows the system architecture of the proposed system. The architecture consists of sensing environment, Activity Recognition Service, and Care Service. We present summaries of each part's performance below.

Environment Sensing: We install autonomous sensor boxes in elderly's house and the proposed system monitors the environment. The system gets environment data, temperature, humidity, light, atmosphere pressure, sound volume, vibration, and motion, and these data is uploaded to a database on the cloud with date and time.

Activity Recognition Service: The system periodically detects changing point online each time when the environment data is uploaded. When the system detects changes of environment, this triggers that the system executes *auto activity recognition*. In auto activity recognition, the system outputs estimated activity labels and accuracy. In the case of high accuracy, this service sends the activity label to Care Service. In the case of low accuracy, the system executes *manual activity recognition*. In manual activity recognition, VA greets elderly and asks elderly what he/she is doing now. And elderly answers ADL with voice or touching display. Then the service gets activity label and sends this to Care Service. Also, the proposed service uses this activity label as training data for auto activity recognition.

Care Service: This service selects and executes suitable care based on activity labels received from activity recognition service. This service issues an instruction to VA and lets VA communicate with elderly. Also, in the case of emergency, this service notifies caregivers.

Specifically, in this paper, we focus on changing point detection and manual activity recognition in activity recognition service.

3.3   Changing Point Detection Using Change Finder

Changing point detection is the technology detecting changing point of time-series data. This falls into two categories, *offline detection* and *online detection*. Offline detection uses a batch process for data have been collected and find changing points. On the other hands, online detection judge if the data is changing point in each time when new data is presented. In the proposed system, we use online detection to judge environment changes quickly on monitoring elderly. Specifically, in this paper, we implement *Change Finder* [8], which is one of online changing point detection methods.

Change Finder is characterized by autoregression model (AR model) and two phases learning using smoothing. Change Finder has a mechanism for detecting changes of time-series model and calculates the degree of changes as the changing score. Changing score is high when the degree of changes is high. Also, changing score is low when the degree of changes is low. Change Finder has two AR models. The first model learns original time-series data. The second model learns the degree of changes, which is calculated based on the first model as time-series data. This leads to remove changes raised by small noises. Also, using SDAR (Sequentially Discounting AR model learning) algorithm, Change Finder achieves processing speed as fast as Change Finder can process online. Also, whereas AR model requires stationarity of data, Change Finder can manipulate non-stationary data.

Change Finder in the proposed system processes for time-series data collected by environment sensing as following:

Step 1: Change Finder receives a collected environment data as input and learns the first AR model. In this step, Change Finder updates average, variance, covariance and autoregression coefficients, which AR model has. The equations of the update are given as following.

$$\mu_t = (1 - r)\mu_{t-1} + rx_t \tag{1}$$

$$C_{t,i} = (1 - r)C_{t-1,i} + r(x_t - \mu_t)(x_{t-i} - \mu_t)(i = 0, ..., k) \tag{2}$$

$$C_{t,i} = \sum_{j=1}^{k} a_{t,j}C_{t,i-j}(i = 1, ..., k) \tag{3}$$

$$\hat{x}_t = \sum_{i=1}^{k} a_{t,i}(x_{t-i} - \mu_t) + \mu_t \tag{4}$$

$$\sigma_t = (1 - r)\sigma_{t-1} + r(x_t - \hat{x}_t)(x_t - \hat{x}_t) \tag{5}$$

Here, the step is t, autoregression order is k, input data is x_t, the average is μ_t, autoregression coefficients is $a_{t,i}$, covariance is $C_{t,i}$, the variance is σ_t and forgetting rate is r. Expression (3) is solved by applying the Yule-Walker method and we obtain $a_{t,j}$. In this regard, $C_{t,-i}$ equals $C_{t,i}$.

Step 2: In this step, Change Finder calculates scores using normal probability density distribution based on average and variance that results from Step 1. The equation of calculating score is given as following.

$$y_t = -\log_{10} p_t(x_t) \tag{6}$$

Here, probability density distribution is $p_t(x_t)$ and score is y_t.

Step 3: In this step, Change Finder smoothes scores that result from Step 2 to remove noises. The equation of smoothing is given as following.

$$Score_t = \frac{\sum_{i=0}^{w-1} y_{t-i}}{w} \tag{7}$$

Here, the width of smoothing is w and a result of smoothing is $score_t$.

Step 4: Using $Score_t$ that results from Step 3 as new time-series data, Change Finder performs the second round of learning, calculating score and smoothing just like Step 1–Step 3. And we obtain scores that result from the second round of Step 3 as the changing score. Also, Change Finder judges scores over given threshold as changing points.

3.4   Manual Activity Recognition

In manual activity recognition, using VA, the proposed system asks elderly activities and recognizes ADL from elderly's answer. The system changes the speech into the text using speech recognition. If there were keywords in the answer, that is changed by speech to text, the system would label with ADL. For example, in the case that the answer includes "brekky", the system labels with "breakfast" and inserts to the database. In particular, the system labels with ADL as the following step.

Step 1 (Asking for elderly's ADL): When Change Finder detects changes of environment, VA asks elderly that "Hi, ___. What are you doing now?".

Step 2 (Speech recognition of answer): Elderly answers with a voice for a question from VA. Then the system handles voice recognition for an answer from starting to speak to finishing. And the system changes the voice into the text.

Step 3 (Checking keywords): Users register keywords related to ADL in advance. Next, the system checks if the text, that results from Step 2, includes keywords. When the text includes keywords, the system performs Step 4. On the other hands, when the text does not include keywords, the system performs Step 1 and asks again.

Step 4 (Executing actions): The system executes actions appropriate to a keyword, which is matched in Step 3. The system has functions (e.g. label with ADL, answer using VA and answer using pictures or movies) as actions. In the function labeling with ADL, the system labels with ADL related to keywords and inserts to the database. In the function answering using pictures or movies, the system uses a mechanism which is developed in [9]. Binding keywords and actions is defined in the system as following.

$$[W : w, A : a_1, a_2, a_3, ..., a_n] \tag{8}$$

Here, W is a keyword and A is actions. Also, w is an actual value of a keyword and $a_1, a_2, ..., a_n$ are executed actions. In the case that an answered text matches a keyword in Step 3, the system executes defined actions in sequence, which are $a_1, a_2, ..., a_n$. For example, we use the rule as following to label with "breakfast" and let VA reply that "Do not forget taking medicine".
[W: "brekky", A: registerLabel("breakfast"),
talk("Do not forget taking medicine")]

4 Implementation

4.1 Prototype System

We implemented prototype system that consists of changing point detection, manual activity recognition and labeling with ADL. Technologies used for the implementation are summarized as follows:

- Development language: Java 1.8.0_25, Ruby 2.1.5
- Database: MongoDB
- Web server: Apache Tomcat 7.0.69
- Web service framework: Jersey 1.19, Axis2 1.6.3

Both services are deployed as Web services. Therefore, these services can be consumed with the platform-independent REST protocol. In this prototype system, we implemented changing point detection and labeling with ADL using Java. And changing point detections for seven time-series data, which are collected with sensor boxes, are performed in parallel using thread. Also, we implemented manual activity recognition with Ruby. Changing point detection, labeling with ADL and interaction with VA worked together using call web services with REST protocol.

Furthermore, we implemented GUI to manage changing point detection and labeling with ADL using technologies as follows:

- Development language: HTML, javascript
- javascript library: jQuery 2.1.4
- CSS framework: Twitter Bootstrap 3.1.1

GUI of changing point detection allows users to register a target sensor, a method of changing point detection freely and parameters for detection. Also, GUI visualizes data collected with a target sensor and changing score calculated with changing point detection as a line chart. GUI of labeling with ADL allows users to check, modify and delete actual labeled ADL. Also, this GUI allows users to input ADL label directly without executing manual activity recognition.

4.2   Case Study

As a practical case study, we have set a sensor box in author's room and have conducted the experiment that the system collects environment data. Next, we have used changing point detection for time-series data of light sensor and have visualized actual changing score. Parameters of Change Finder are the first AR model's degree of 50, the first AR model's forgetting rate of 0.05% and the first smoothing width of 5. Also, parameters of Change Finder are the second AR model's degree of 50, the second AR model's forgetting rate of 0.1% and the second smoothing width of 5. Figure 3 shows actual light sensor data and this changing score on Oct. 23, 2016. The left vertical axis shows changing score and right vertical axis shows light sensor value. According to Fig. 3, it can be seen that score becomes high on points where light changes a lot. Therefore, we have confirmed that changing point detection worked as expected.

Also, we have conducted the experiment that the prototype system labels with "breakfast" when elderly answers including a keyword that is "brekky" as the scenario of manual activity recognition. In this experiment, we have set "awake", "sleep", "take a bath", "out of the bath", "go out", "come home" and "brekky" as keywords. Also, we have defined actions for each keyword, which VA answers "You do ___, don't you?" and labels with corresponding ADL. And we have executed manual activity recognition and have confirmed that "breakfast" label is recorded when the subject answers that I am eating brekky.

4.3   Discussion

According to the diary which the subject records ADL during the experiment, the subject slept at 0;52, woke up at 9:50, took a bath at 11:40, went out at 13:17, came home at 13:30, went out at 19:02 and came home at 22:27. As shown in Fig. 3, each change of activities excluding "went out of 13:17" and "came home

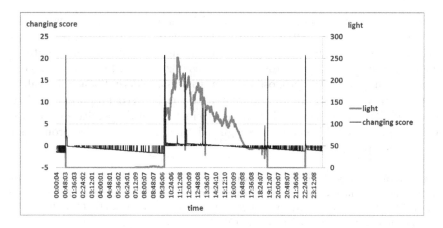

Fig. 3. Light data and changing score on Oct. 23, 2016

at 13:30" are most obvious on changing score. Therefore, the prototype system could estimate parts of timing when ADL changes. As a reason that prototype system can not detect "went out at 13:17" and "came home at 13:30", it is considered that switching light does not contribute illumination intensity of the room because the light sensor is affected by outside light from windows. Also, as a reason that the system can detect other activities, it is considered that opening and closing curtains and switching light of the room contributes illumination intensity and changes of activities are recognized.

On manual activity recognition, we confirmed that the system can record ADL accurately as long as the reply matches keywords prepared in this experiment. However, there are many synonyms such as breakfast and brekky. Thus the system needs to cope with various expressions. We considered that we allow users to register several keywords in the same rule, and to extract keywords which are independent of various expressions and so on to cope with this. Also, in the case of that the system has keywords sounded similar, the probability of false recognition get higher. Therefore we need to adjust rules and try not to register keywords sounded similar one in other rules.

5   Conclusions

In this paper, we proposed new sensing system in order to capture ADL of home elderly. In the proposed system, when the environment around elderly changes, VA talks to elderly. And the proposed system records ADL based on communicating between elderly and VA. This achieves to record ADL with non-invasive environment sensing and promotes communication of elderly. Also, we implemented prototype system. Using the system and changing point detection for light data of author's room, we conducted an experiment in labeling sensor data with ADL. And we preliminarily evaluated the availability of the proposed system.

In our future works, implementing algorithm adjusting threshold which uses to determine changing point, we improve the accuracy of changing point detection. Also, using machine learning (e.g. clustering) for labeled sensor data, we implement the service that automatically recognizes ADL. Furthermore, we let elderly install and use the proposed system to actual elderly home and evaluate the accuracy of changing point detection and activity recognition and evaluate the availability of the system. Finally, we also implement the service which allows users to register suitable cares for recognized ADL and this service promotes to care more supportive for elderly.

Acknowledgements. This research was partially supported by the Japan Ministry of Education, Science, Sports, and Culture [Grant-in-Aid for Scientific Research (B) (No. 16H02908, No. 15H02701, No. 26280115), Young Scientists (B) (No. 26730155), and Challenging Exploratory Research (15K12020)].

References

1. ASUS: Zenbo your smart little companion. https://zenbo.asus.com/, February 2017
2. Cabinet Office, Government of Japan: Annual report on the aging society: 2015. http://www.cao.go.jp/, June 2015
3. Duong, T.V., Bui, H.H., Phung, D.Q., Venkatesh, S.: Activity recognition and abnormality detection with the switching hidden semi-markov model. In: IEEE Computer Society Conference on Computer Vision and Pattern Recognition, CVPR 2005, vol. 1, pp. 838–845. IEEE (2005)
4. Frequency Precision: Bed pressure mats. https://www.frequencyprecision.com/coll ections/bed-pressure-mats, February 2017
5. Horiuchi, H., Saiki, S., Matsumoto, S., Nakamura, M.: Designing and implementing service framework for virtual agents in home network system. In: 2014 15th IEEE/ACIS International Conference on Software Engineering, Artificial Intelligence, Networking and Parallel/Distributed Computing (SNPD 2014), pp. 343–348, Las Vegas, USA, June 2014
6. Kwapisz, J.R., Weiss, G.M., Moore, S.A.: Activity recognition using cell phone accelerometers. ACM SigKDD Explor. Newslett. **12**(2), 74–82 (2011)
7. Sakakibara, S., Saiki, S., Nakamura, M., Matsumoto, S.: Indoor environment sensing service in smart city using autonomous sensor box. In: 15th IEEE/ACIS International Conference on Computer and Information Science (ICIS 2016), pp. 885–890, Okayama, Japan, June 2016
8. Saranya, S., Rajeshkumar, R., Shanthi, S.: A survey on anomaly detection for discovering emerging topics. Int. J. Comput. Sci. Mob. Comput. (IJCSMC) **3**(10), 895–902 (2014)
9. Tokunaga, S., Tamamizu, K., Saiki, S., Nakamura, M., Yasuda, K.: VirtualCare-Giver: personalized smart elderly care. Int. J. Softw. Innov. (IJSI) **5**(1), 30–43 (2016). http://www.igi-global.com/journals/abstract-announcement/158780
10. Ueda, K., Tamai, M., Yasumoto, K.: A method for recognizing living activities in homes using positioning sensor and power meters. In: 2015 IEEE International Conference on Pervasive Computing and Communication Workshops (PerCom Workshops), pp. 354–359, March 2015

F0 Feature Analysis of Communication Between Elderly Individuals for Health Assessment

Yumi Wakita[⊠] and Shunpei Matsumoto

Osaka Institute of Technology, Osaka, Japan
yumi.wakita@oit.ac.com

Abstract. This study explores a system that estimates the health condition of an elderly individual using nonverbal information from daily conversations.

We have already confirmed the effectiveness of using the fundamental frequency (F0) to estimate the atmosphere of a conversation between young individuals. A smooth conversation has a tendency for its average value of F0 (Ave-F0) to increase slightly, and its standard deviation value (SD-F0) to increase significantly compared with a non-smooth conversation. The differences are significant when using a t-test, where the confidence level is 95%. We confirmed that Ave-F0 and SD-F0 are useful in separating laughter utterances from usual speech utterances.

In this paper, we report on the acoustic analysis results of a free conversation between elderly individuals, and compare it with the analysis results of young individuals. We describe the possibility of estimating a health condition using F0 characteristics.

Keywords: Conversation smoothness · Laughter utterance · Fundamental frequency

1 Introduction

Recently, fatal traffic accidents caused by the elderly have increased, as their driving ability declines with age. The key issue here is the lack of awareness in the elderly regarding their compromised driving ability, which appropriately conveyed can make several preventive measures effective. Thus, the role of third parties in perceiving the decline in driving ability in elderly individuals and conveying it to them is becoming important.

We developed a system that provides information about suitable timing by considering the communication atmosphere. The system can understand whether human-to-human communication is proceeding smoothly. When the system senses there has been little progress during the conversation, it attempts to provide a topic that leads to a smoother discussion. We already confirmed that F0 is able to estimate smoothness using a communication database between young individuals. The standard deviation value (SD-F0) for each utterance in a smooth conversation is greater than that of a non-smooth conversation. When the utterance database includes laughter sounds, the

© Springer International Publishing AG 2017
V.G. Duffy (Ed.): DHM 2017, Part II, LNCS 10287, pp. 195–205, 2017.
DOI: 10.1007/978-3-319-58466-9_19

difference between "smoothness" and "non-smoothness" is not significant. Thus, excluding laughter from utterances is necessary for smoothness degree estimation [1]. When determining whether the utterance is laughter or usual speech, the average value of F0 (Ave-F0) and SD-F0 are useful [2]. However, we confirmed the effectiveness of speech by using only the conversations among young individuals.

We would like to use our system to inform the elderly of their decline by estimating their degree of decline from their conversation. For practical use, it is necessary for the system to determine the decline in a person's ability to perform tasks in daily life in addition to determining this situation from an estimation of conversation smoothness. We think the F0 information would also be helpful to estimate the degree of decline.

Several papers illustrated that the acoustic features of the human voice are effective in detecting diseases specific to the elderly. Kato et al. [3]. reported that the prosodic feature is effective in estimating cognitive impairment in the elderly. Taler et al. [4]. reported on the relation between Alzheimer's disease and disorders as found in the prosody. Some characteristics of speech among the elderly were reported. Formant frequency shifts in elderly speech were found by Tanaka et al. [5]. Most analyses did not use free conversations. To notice this impairment in daily life, we should analyze daily conversations.

As an index for evaluating decline, "aging" is an important factor. It is necessary to analyze the relationship between aging and the F0 characteristics. In this paper, we report the F0 characteristics of free dyadic conversations between elderly individuals, and compare these conversations with those of young individuals. Through analysis results, we describe the possibility of using F0 information to detect impairment or a health condition.

2   Structure of the Communication Atmosphere Estimation

Figure 1 shows the structure of our conversation smoothness estimation using F0 information. After extracting F0 from input utterances, we detect whether the utterance is "laughter" or "speech" using F0. Using only the "speech" utterances, the conversation smoothness is estimated.

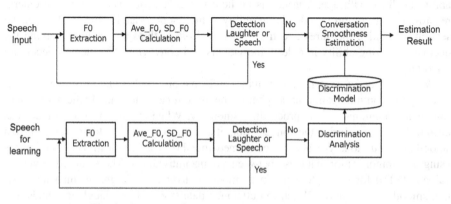

Fig. 1. Structure of conversation atmosphere estimation

3   Conversation Analysis

3.1   Conversation Database

We recorded 12 sets of 3-min free dyadic conversations (between two individuals). Figure 2 shows the conversation recording location. We used two microphones and a video camera for recording. The recording conditions are listed in Table 1. The participating speakers had met each other before, but we made use of pairs of those who have never spoken to one another before.

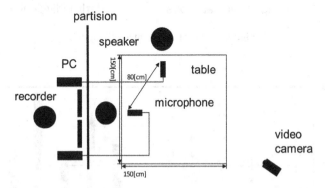

Fig. 2. Conversation recording location

Table 1. Conditions of conversation

Number of speakers	Young (4 males, 2 females) elderly (3 males, 3 females)
Ages	Young individuals: 22 years old Elderly individuals: 67–78 years old
Number of conversations	12 pairs (6 elderly pairs, 6 young-individual pairs)
Conversation periods	3 in/conversation
Conversation condition	Free dyadic conversation

We analyzed 12 conversations by comparing those of the elderly and young individuals. We noted the "silent interval length" and "length of one utterance." Figure 3 shows the "silent interval length" of each conversation, and Fig. 4 shows the "silent interval length" of each conversation.

The results are as follows:

- The differences in "silent interval length" between the elderly and young individuals are not significant, and the lengths are almost the same.
- The "length of one utterance" of the elderly is dependent of speakers. The lengths of some elderly speakers are quite long.

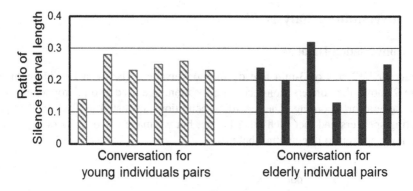

Fig. 3. Ratio of silent interval length

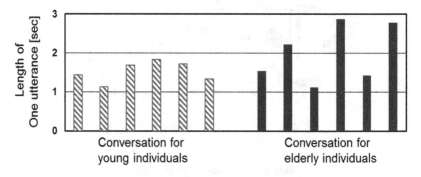

Fig. 4. Length of one utterance

3.2 Laughter Utterance Analysis

Based on our previous analysis using young individuals' conversations, the F0 characteristics are quite different between speech and laughter. We analyzed the conversation speech utterances and non-languagae utterances separately.

3.2.1 Ratio of Non-language Utterance

The conversation database includes speech and several non-language utterances: laughter, cough, clicking tongue, etc. Tables 2 and 3 list the rates of non-language utterances for each conversation.

Table 2. Ratio of each utterance (young person)

Person	A	B	C	D	E	F
Speech	0.89	0.83	0.80	0.70	0.75	0.86
Laughter	0.11	0.17	0.20	0.30	0.23	0.14
Others (breath)	-	-	-	-	0.02	-

Table 3. Ratio of each utterance (elderly person)

Person	G	H	I	J	K	L
Speech	0.72	0.76	0.82	0.84	0.73	0.90
Laughter	0.20	0.24	0.16	0.16	0.22	0.10
Others (cough, clicking tongue etc.)	0.08	-	0.02	-	0.05	-

- In conversation, both the elderly and the young individuals included many non-language utterances. The average ratios are 22% for young individuals and 19% for elderly individuals.
- The t-test results revealed that the ratio of non-language utterances is not independent of age. It is dependent on the speakers.
- Elderly utterances include many types of non-language utterances. In the young individuals, almost non-language utterances are "laughter."

3.2.2 Variable Laughter Utterances

Nishio and Koyama [6] explained that laughter utterances can be classified in general as "pleasantness" or "sociability." We classified laughter into two types: "pleasantness" and "sociability." However, several occurrences of laughter included words. We added two more types: "pleasantness with speech" and "sociability with speech."

We asked two individuals to listen to the conversation database and to classify all laughter utterances in one of four types: "pleasantness," "sociability," "pleasantness with speech," or "sociability with speech." We extracted the laughter utterances that were classified in the same class by them, and compared the ratio of each type between the elderly and the young (Table 4).

Table 4. Ratio of each type for all laughter utterances [%]

	Pleasantness	Pleasantness with speech	Sociability	Sociability with speech
Young (6 pairs)	38.5	10.2	45.4	6.1
Elderly (6 pairs)	27.1	0.0	49.2	23.7

- Both types of conversation (elderly and young) include many laughter utterances, especially the conversations of the elderly include more laughter utterances than the conversations of the young individuals.
- The t-test results revealed that the ratio of non-language utterance is not independent of age. It is dependent on the speakers.

4 Comparison of F0 Between Elderly and Young

4.1 F0 Extracted from Usual Speech Utterances

We extracted the F0 of each utterance using the database of 12 conversations. After removing utterances such as other noises, voices of non-subject individuals, and

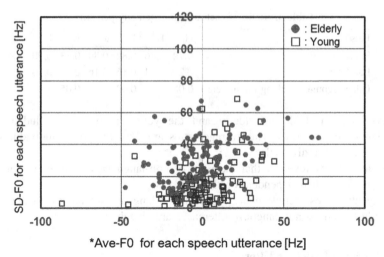

Fig. 5. Distribution of Ave-F0 and SD-F0 of each speech utterance by 12 individuals

non-language utterances, we selected 113 utterances for young individuals and 132 utterances for elderly individuals. We calculated the Ave-F0 and SD-F0 value of each utterance, and compared between these values for young individuals and those for elderly.

Figure 5 shows the distribution of Ave-F0 and SD-F0 values for all speakers. The Ave-F0 values in the distribution are indicated as the differences from the average values of all speech utterances by each speaker. The results show the following:

- The range of Ave-F0 is almost the same between the elderly and the young individuals.
- The SD-F0 values of elderly individuals are higher than those for young individuals. The differences between the elderly and young individuals are significant when using a t-test, where the confidence level is 95%.

4.2   F0 Extracted from Laughter Utterances

As results of the Tables 2 and 3, the utterances of both elderly and young individuals include many laughter utterances. We analyzed the F0 characteristics of laughter utterances.

The comparison of laughter utterances between the elderly and the young indicate that the laughter of the elderly tends to be unvoiced. Table 5 lists the ratios of the laughter utterances where F0 could not be extracted relative to all laughter utterances. The laughter utterances of the elderly tend to become unvoiced utterances in more cases than for young individuals. However, this depends on the person.

We extracted the F0 value of each utterance using the database of 12 conversations. After removing the utterances (including other noises, other voices, and unvoiced

Table 5. Ratio of utterances where could be extracted F0 relative to all laughter utterances

	Young individuals						Elderly individuals					
	A	B	C	D	E	F	G	H	I	J	K	L
Ratio	1.0	0.86	0.90	1.0	0.89	1.0	0.70	0.50	0.62	0.89	0.67	0.89

laughter utterances), we selected 47 laughter utterances for young individuals and 35 laughter utterances for elderly individuals. Figure 6 shows the distribution of the Ave-F0 and SD-F0 values.

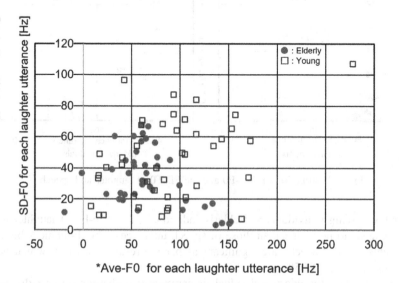

*Ave-F0 : Normalization value by average of speech utterances

Fig. 6. Distribution of Ave-F0 and the SD-F0 of laughter utterance

Figure 6 shows the distribution of the Ave-F0 and SD-F0 values for all speakers. The results show the following:

- The area for the elderly is smaller than that for young individuals. The utterances of the elderly are plotted almost in the young individual's area.
- When both the Ave-F0 and the SD-F0 values of a laughter utterance are large, this indicates that the utterance is from a young individual.

5 Conversation Atmosphere Estimation for the Elderly

To discuss the effectiveness of F0 in estimating health conditions, we analyzed the effectiveness of F0 in estimating the elderly conversation atmosphere. To examine the effectiveness, the following two probabilities, which were already confirmed for young individuals, should be confirmed for elderly individuals.

(1) The laughter utterances can be separated from usual speech utterances.

(2) The differences between smooth utterances and non-smooth utterances are clear.

Figure 7 shows the distributions of the Ave-F0 and the SD-F0 values of utterances. The left-side distribution is for six young individuals, and the right-side figure shows the distribution for six elderly individuals.

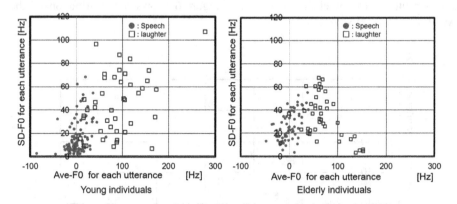

Fig. 7. Distribution of Ave-F0 and the SD-F0 of laughter and speech

- For both young individuals and elderly individuals, the Ave-F0 of laughter utterances tends to be higher than those of speech utterances. The differences between "laughter" and "speech" are significant as per the result of a t-test, which has a confidence level of 95%.
- The distribution for elderly individuals is narrower than that for young individuals. The difference in the elderly SD-F0 values between speech and laughter is smaller than that for young individuals.
- The laughter utterances can be classified to several type of classes. However, the difference of each laughter type is smaller than the difference between "speech" and "laughter."

The results suggest that the Ave-F0 and SD-F0 values for the elderly are more difficult to use for estimating the conversation atmosphere when compared with the values for young individuals. To confirm the ability of the Ave-F0 and SD-F0 values to estimate the conversation atmosphere, we asked three individuals to observe video data and to classify a video scene according to the following two situations:

- Smooth conversation (S): The topic had not been decided yet. Speakers searched for a topic that interested both of them.
- Non-smooth conversation (NS): The topic for both of the speakers was already chosen, and the speakers spoke smoothly or eagerly.

The classifying results from the three individuals were very similar. 88% parts were classified under the same situations by all individuals.

Figure 6 shows the distributions of the Ave-F0 and the SD-F0 values of elderly utterances. The SD-F0 values of the utterances during smooth conversation are higher than those for non-smooth conversation. The t-test, which has a confidence level of 95%, revealed that the differences between smooth and non-smooth conversations for elderly individuals are smaller than those for young individuals; this was confirmed in previous experiments [1]. The difference in the elderly between smooth and non-smooth conversations, however, is significant (Fig. 8).

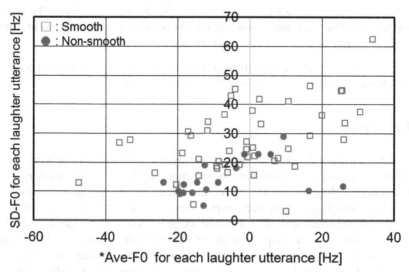

*Ave-F0 : Normalization value by the average of speech utterances

Fig. 8. Distribution between Ave-F0 and SD-F0 of each utterance for six elderly individuals

6 Discussion

We confirmed the differences of the F0 characteristics between elderly and younger individuals through an analysis.

- For elderly speech utterances, SD-F0 tends to be larger than those of younger individuals.
- The length of a silent interval is nearly the same for the elderly and younger individuals, but the length of one utterance of the elderly tends to be longer than that of the young individuals.
- For both the elderly and young individuals, many non-language utterances are included in conversation. Most non-language utterances recorder can be classified as "laughter." However, the elderly utterances tend to include other non-language utterances, coughs, clicking tongues, etc.
- The laughter utterances of the elderly tend to be unvoiced.
- With regard to the distributions of Ave-F0 and SD-F0, the area of the elderly laughter is smaller than that of the younger individuals. When Ave-F0 or SD-F0 is extremely large, the laughter utterances are from the younger individuals.

These results indicate that by calculating the Ave-F0 and SD-F0 values of each utterance, we can estimate whether the speaker is young or elderly. The results also indicate that these values would be useful in assessing impairments in the elderly.

- On the other hand, conversation atmosphere estimation for the elderly is more difficult than for young individuals. However, the t-test results revealed that the difference between speech and laughter is significant, and the difference between smooth and non-smooth conversations is also significant.
- However, several laughter utterances for the elderly were unvoiced. The ratio of unvoiced laughter utterances depends on the person. A total of 32% of elderly laughter utterances were unvoiced utterances.

These results suggest that conversation atmosphere estimation and health condition estimation are limited while using only the F0 information.

7   Conclusion

We reported on the F0 characteristics of free dyadic conversations between elderly individuals and compared them with conversations between young individuals. We confirmed several different points between the elderly and the young individuals. The elderly utterances tend to include several types of non-language utterances and unvoiced laughter utterances. The dynamic range of SD-F0 for elderly individuals tends to be narrower when compared with that of with young individuals. These results show that conversation atmosphere estimation and health condition estimation for elderly individuals using F0 characteristics would be more difficult when compared with estimating for young individuals.

However, the results of confirming the differences between "speech" and "laughter" and between "smooth conversation" and "non-smooth conversation" for elderly individuals indicate that these differences are sufficiently large. The results suggest that F0 information is useful for conversation atmosphere estimation, and would have the ability to estimate health conditions.

In the future, first, we will confirm the reliability of our results using a larger quantity of data. In addition, other factors of nonverbal communication, such as gestures, will be analyzed to obtain a more accurate estimate. Next, we would like to confirm its effectiveness for an assessment of health conditions of the subjects.

Acknowledgments. This work was supported by JSPS KAKENHI Grant Number JP16K01293.

References

1. Wakita, Y., Yoshida, Y., Nakamura, M.: Influence of personal characteristics on nonverbal information for estimating communication smoothness. In: Kurosu, M. (ed.) HCI 2016. LNCS, vol. 9733, pp. 148–157. Springer, Cham (2016). doi:10.1007/978-3-319-39513-5_14

2. Wakita, Y., Matsumoto, S.: Communication' smoothness estimation using F0 information. In: Proceedings of the 4th IIAE International Conference on Intelligent Systems and Image Processing 2016, September 2016
3. Kato, S., et al.: A preliminary study of speech prosody-based relationship with HDS-R scores toward early detection of cognitive impairment in elderly using speech prosody. JSAI **26**(2), 347–352 (2011). SP-H
4. Taler, V., et al.: Comprehensionog grammatical and emotional prosody is impaired in Alzheimers disease. Neuropsychology **22**(2), 188–195 (2008)
5. Tanaka, Y., Igaue, H., Mizumachi, M., Nakatoh, Y.: Study of improvement of intelligibility for the elderly speech based on formant frequency shift. Int. J. Comput. Consum. Control (IJ3C) **3**(3), 57–65 (2014)
6. Nishio, S., Koyama, K.: A criterion for facial expression of laugh based on temporal difference of eye and mouth movement. IEICE **J80-A**(8), 1316–1318 (1997)

A Study of Photographs as Communication Content for Intergenerational Conversation Support System

Xiaochun Zhou(✉), Miyuki Iwamoto, Noriaki Kuwahara,
and Kazunari Morimoto

Kyoto Institute of Technology, Kyoto, Japan
zhou0204@outlook.com

Abstract. With the deepening of aging and low birth rate in China, the single elderly or old couple living alone is more and more, who has a higher risk of senile dementia caused by disuse of cognitive function because of loneliness without communication. We propose an intergenerational conversation support system for Chinese elders for prevention of senile dementia. The most important part of this system is photos as contents, which can provide common topics to make conversation comfortable. This study aims to provide appropriate photos for conversation without burden between the elderly and the young. In order to examine the difference of the mental burden and the quality of communication by using photos as content, we measured the burden of both the young and the elderly depending on photo categories of "Food", "Events", "School" and "Commodity". The methods of measuring burden were stress check, questionnaire and expression analysis. Results suggest that the more photos have in common between the elderly and the young, the less stress they have.

Keywords: Elderly · Photo category · Conversation support · Intergeneration · China

1 Introduction

China, which is in the face of a rapidly aging population and low birth rate as the result of "One Child Policy", and also happens to have very similar demographics to that which existed in Japan two decades prior. First, Japan's dependency ratio in the 1990s – i.e. the ratio of the non-working population, both children (<20 years old) and the elderly (>65 years old), to the working age population – is very similar to China's in 2010 (Fig. 1). Second, the profiles of the number of working age people per dependent is very similar in the two countries (Fig. 2) [1].

As another result, the single elderly or old couple living alone is more and more, who has a higher risk of senile dementia caused by disuse of cognitive function because of loneliness without communication. Whereas specialized dementia care, such as memory/cognitive exercises are still very rare due to inadequate knowledge and few research about it, meanwhile the community-based services are still in the developmental stages in China [2]. For this, the ICT experience in Japan such as e-health etc.

© Springer International Publishing AG 2017
V.G. Duffy (Ed.): DHM 2017, Part II, LNCS 10287, pp. 206–221, 2017.
DOI: 10.1007/978-3-319-58466-9_20

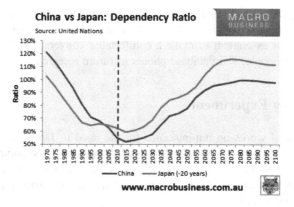

Fig. 1. Dependency ratio of China & Japan

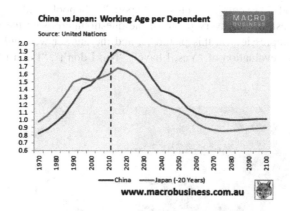

Fig. 2. Working age per dependent in China & Japan

will contribute to China. One of related works in Japan was Conversation Support System between the elderly and the young, which help the elderly and the young volunteer to talk each other without feeling any burden by using photos as common conversation contents [3].

We propose an intergenerational conversation support system for Chinese elders for prevention of senile dementia caused by disuse of cognitive function. The most important part of this system is photos as content, which could provide common topics for the conversation. Due to the large difference between the Chinese elders and Japanese elders in conversation, firstly we conducted the questionnaire survey about photos for Chinese elders in Taizhou and Nanjing city in Jiangsu Province China.

On the basis of the findings of the questionnaire, we used categories of "Food", "Events", "School" and "Commodity" to carry out our experiment of measuring the mental burden of participants in conversation. The experiment place was Suzhou city in Jiangsu Province China. We examined the mental burden of participants depending on photograph categories and photos with methods of stress check, questionnaire and expression analysis. From the results of experiment, we found the photos appropriate for intergenerational conversation in China. Thus it is possible to clarify how to make good use of photos as content to make a comfortable conversation between Chinese elders and young people, and database photos in future research.

2   Preliminary Experiment

Referring to related works on reminiscence for the aged in Japan, there are reminiscence themes of "family", "food", "scenery", "building", "shopping", "school", "sports", "home appliance" and so on [4, 5]. In order to examine if the same themes were appropriate for Chinese elders, according to which we carried out the questionnaire about photos in China.

The preliminary experiment was for 18 elders in Nanjing and Taizhou city in Jiangsu Province China (Fig. 3). The 150 photos were used according to 7 themes, which was "Food", "Events", "Scenery", "Sports", "School", "Money" and "Commodity". The questions for every photo of the questionnaire were the same that "Do you have good impression on this picture?", and the answer was multiple choice by 3-stage subjective evaluation of "Yes, I have", "No, I don't", "I don't know".

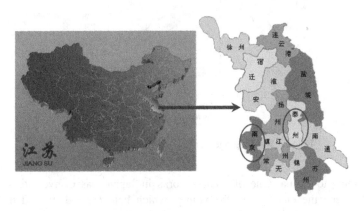

Fig. 3. Map of Jiangsu Province in China

The questionnaire results are shown in Fig. 4. In the photograph categories of "Food", "Events" and "Scenery", there is no photo that may interest elders. Although we know from the related research that Japanese elders are interested in the themes of "Food" and "Events" [5], Chinese elders shows no interest. It may be for economic reasons that Taizhou city is an underdeveloped economy area in Jiangsu Province, where elders suffered from food shortages, low incomes and had work, and had too little money and time to spent on food, holiday and travel when they were young. So they nearly don't have any pleasant impression on "Food", "Events" and "Scenery". For the themes of "Sports", "Money" and "Commodity", more than 60% of elders chose the answer of "Yes, I have (good impression)". Chinese elders shows the most interest in

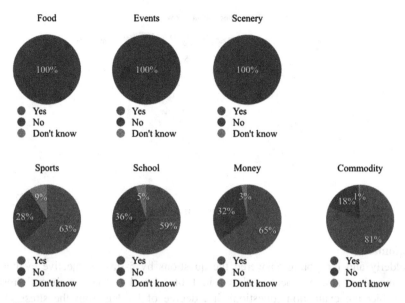

Fig. 4. Questionnaire result (yes = good impression, no = no good impression)

photos of old commodities in 1960s when they were young. It may be for culture reasons that family life is the most important in Chinese traditional concept. Photos of commodities as necessities of family life can recall elders a lot about their family.

3   Experiment

3.1   Summary

In this experiment the young talked with the elderly face-to-face while looking at the photos. We examined the degree of stress for the young, the mental burden of both the elderly and the young, and the feeling of happiness or unhappiness for the elderly depending on each category and photo in conversation.

The purpose of this experiment is for the young and the elderly to feel no burden in any photographic categories in conversation. Thus, when constructing the system, establishing an appropriate content database is considered possible.

3.2   Evaluation Item

Stress Check

The young indicated the degree of mental load on the stress check sheet every minute in conversation. The stress check sheet represented a 1–7-scale. 1 means that there was absence of any stress to continue the conversation, and 7 means that person feels a lot of stress (Fig. 5).

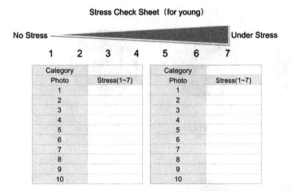

Fig. 5. Stress check sheet

Questionnaire

The elderly and the young answered the questions by 5-stage subjective evaluation each time after the experiment as shown in Tables 1 and 2. The experiment's results show subjective evaluation (questionnaire, degree of burden from the stress check sheet).

Table 1. Post-experiment evaluation (young)

No.	Question
1	Could you communicate naturally?
2	Was the conversation exciting?
3	Could you focus your attention in conversation?
4	Could you carefully listen to your partner in conversation?
5	Did you talk to your partner about your interests or hobbies?
6	Were you interested in what your partner talked about?
7	Was your partner easy to talk to?
8	Did your partner talk to you about her/his interests or hobbies?
9	Did you think the photos can help you find topics for the conversation?
10	Did you feel comfortable in conversation?

Expression Analysis

We analyzed the expressions of the patients from the video recordings. Analysis used the major literature "expression analysis" techniques to understand which photos made the elderly look happy or joyful [6].

In this expression analysis, we defined plus as a state of happiness, and minus as unhappiness. We used degree of happiness or unhappiness as the result for each photo.

Table 2. Post-experiment evaluation (elderly)

No.	Question
1	Could you communicate naturally?
2	Was the conversation exciting?
3	Could you focus your attention in conversation?
4	Could you carefully listen to your partner in conversation?
5	Did you talk to your partner about your interests or hobbies?
6	Were you interested in what your partner talked about?
7	Was your partner easy to talk to?
8	Did your partner talk to you about her/his interests or hobbies?
9	Did you think the photos can help you find topics for the conversation?
10	Did you feel the nostalgia of the topics in conversation?

3.3 Subject

The conversation partners were 7 young female caregivers of Suzhou Social Welfare Home, and the elderly were 4 senior women and 2 senior man without dementia living there. But they don't know each other before.

3.4 Environment of Experiment

Because the function of eyes is often kept better than ears for the elderly, we brought a photograph into close-up and displayed on the screen by projector. The elderly and the young talked to each other face-to-face while looking at the screen to help the person hard to hear or watching.

The layout of the experiment was shown in Figs. 6 and 7 below.

We borrowed a meeting room in the nursing home, in which we placed desks and chairs side by side.

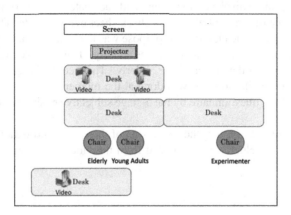

Fig. 6. The layout of the experimental environment

Fig. 7. Experimental environment

We used a MacBook in which photos categorized above were uploaded for a 10-min conversation.

We used a camera to capture the expression of the elderly throughout the sessions.

3.5 Materials and Methods

Materials

According to the results of Preliminary Experiment, this experiment used photograph categories of "School" and "Commodity". Although "Food" and "Events" was shown no interest for the elderly in Taizhou city in Jiangsu Province China in the preliminary experiment, considering the economic reasons that Suzhou city is a richer area than Taizhou in China, this time we still used them. Each category was with 10 photos.

Methods

We prepared photograph categories of "Food", "Events", "School" and "Commodity" with each category of 10 photos by Keynote.

The elderly and the young sit down side by side and faced to the screen. Then we displayed the photos on the screen. They talked to each other while looking at the photos.

Each photo would be displayed for 1 min, and each category for 10 min. The young indicated the degree of stress on the stress check sheet every minute. The stress check sheet was out of sight of the elderly. Our purpose was to check the mental burden of the young, not to check their complaints to the elderly. Thus the young may point it without feeling any burden towards the elderly. They could judge honestly. They continued their talk while pointing was done at the moment.

They answered the questionnaire by the 5-stage subjective evaluation each time after the experiment.

A camera was used to capture the expression of the elderly throughout the sessions. The expression of the elderly was analyzed from the video recording.

3.6   Results

Figure 8 shows the amount of stress of young staffs accumulated for each photo. The horizontal axis shows the photo 1–photo 10 for each category, and the vertical axis represents the accumulation on the numerical stress check sheet. This is a comparison of stress levels for each category and photo, which is a comparison of the burden felt to continue the conversation as the conversation support content. Only the young's stress levels are shown.

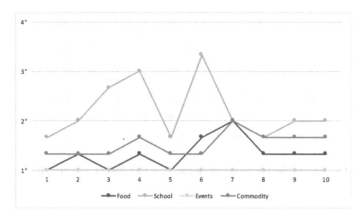

Fig. 8. Stress levels based on photo

The most stress was felt when photos depicting "School" category, in which especially photo 6 shows the most stress and the biggest difference from all other photos (Fig. 9). In the "Events" we found that it got the least stress and there was the same degree of stress for each photo.

Fig. 9. Photo 6 in "School" category

Figure 10 shows the results of the questionnaire for young staffs. The vertical axis represents the numerical value of the 5 rated questionnaire. The horizontal axis shows the questions Q1–Q10 for each category. A more detailed examination of the results of average stress is shown in Fig. 11.

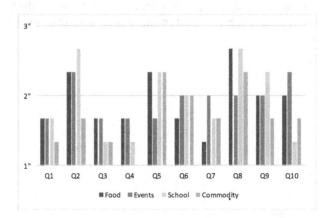

Fig. 10. Results-the young questionnaire (1 = no stress. 5 = extremely stress)

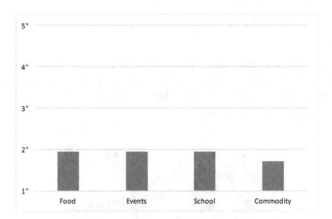

Fig. 11. Question 10 for young -stress levels (1 = no stress. 5 = extremely stress)

Questions for all categories got better results under stage3.

By Q10 of "Did you feel stressful in conversation?", "School" got the least stress, and "Events" got the most stress.

Figure 11 shows the results of average stress levels of young staffs in conversation. In conversation of each category, it was found that the average stress for all categories got less stress under stage 2, "commodity" got the least average stress, and other categories nearly had no difference.

Figure 12 shows the results of the questionnaire for elders. The vertical axis represents the numerical value of the 5 rated questionnaire. The horizontal axis shows the questions Q1–Q10 for each category. A more detailed examination of the results of average stress is shown in Fig. 13.

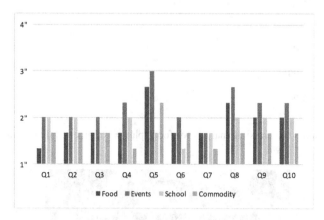

Fig. 12. Results-the elderly Questionnaire (1 = no stress. 5 = extremely stress)

Questions for all categories got better results under stage3.

By Q10 of "Did you feel nostalgia in conversation?", "Commodity" got the least stress, and "Events" got the most stress.

Figure 13 shows the results of average stress levels of the elderly in conversation. "Commodity" got the least stress, and only "Events" got the result over stage 2.

Figure 14 shows the results of expression analysis for "Food" from the content of the video recorded during the experiment. The vertical axis represents the numerical value of elder's happiness or unhappiness. The horizontal axis shows the photo1–10 in

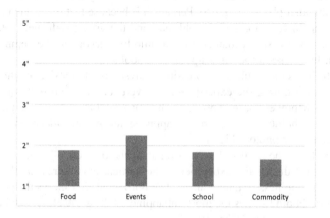

Fig. 13. Question 10 for elderly -stress levels (1 = no stress. 5 = extremely stress)

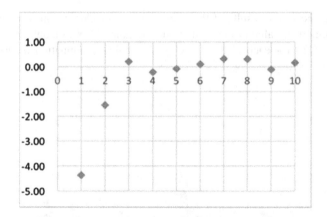

Fig. 14. Results of expression analysis for food (plus = happiness. minus = unhappiness)

Fig. 15. Photo1 in "Food" category

food category. Photo1 shows the most unhappiness felt by the elderly and the biggest difference from other photos (Fig. 15). Perhaps it is because that this is the first photo in first category in conversation and the old man and the young staff met first. From the video recording, the first old man seemed a little bit nervous at the beginning of the conversation, but he soon loosened up talked smoothly.

Figure 16 shows the results of expression analysis for "Events" from the content of the video recorded during the experiment. The vertical axis represents the numerical value of elder's happiness or unhappiness. The horizontal axis shows the photo1–10 in events category. Photo6 shows the most happiness felt by the elderly and the biggest difference from other photos (Fig. 17).

Figure 18 shows the results of expression analysis for "School" from the content of the video recorded during the experiment. The vertical axis represents the numerical value of elder's happiness or unhappiness. The horizontal axis shows the photo1–10 in school category. Photo2 shows the most unhappiness felt by the elderly and the biggest difference from other photos (Fig. 19).

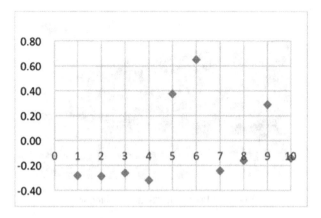

Fig. 16. Results of expression analysis for events (plus = happiness. minus = unhappiness)

Fig. 17. Photo6 in "Events" category

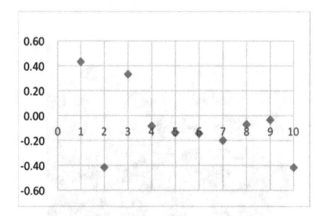

Fig. 18. Results of expression analysis for school (plus = happiness. minus = unhappiness)

Fig. 19. Photo2 in "School" category

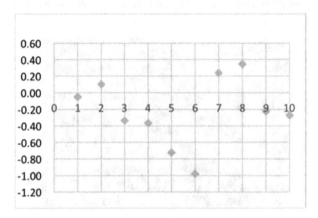

Fig. 20. Results of expression analysis for commodity (plus = happiness. minus = unhappiness)

Fig. 21. Photo6 in "Commodity" Category

Figure 20 shows the results of expression analysis for "Commodity" from the content of the video recorded during the experiment. The vertical axis represents the numerical value of elder's happiness or unhappiness. The horizontal axis shows the photo1–10 in commodity category. Photo6 shows the most unhappiness felt by the elderly and the biggest difference from other photos (Fig. 21).

4 Discussion

From the results we found that there was different stress depending on categories between Japanese elderly and Chinese elderly (Table 3).

Table 3. China vs Japan: stress caused by category

Stress caused by category		China	*Japan
Stress check for the young	The most stress	School (in 1960s)	Lives during the Showa Era (1920s–1980s)
	The least stress	Events	Food events
Questionnaire for the young	The most stress	Events	Lives during the Showa Era (1920s–1980s)
	The least stress	Commodity (in 1960s)	Food events
Questionnaire for the elderly	The most stress	Events	Lives during the Showa Era (1920s–1980s)
	The least stress	Commodity (in 1960s)	Food

Japanese elderly is not interested in "lives during the Showa Era", in opposite, Chinese show great interested in commodity in 1960s, and the same as young people. This result is the same as the preliminary experiment. It may be for culture reason that commodity can recall the Chinese people their family life, which is the most important thing in Chinese tradition.

All four photograph categories of "Food", "Events", "School", and "Commodity" got the less stress results under stage 3. So they were appropriate for both Chinese elders and young people, which can help them to search common topics easily.

Even if the categories are appropriate for both the elderly and the young, different photo can cause different mental burden. The reasons of mental burden caused by photos are:

1. Age reason, such as old schoolbag (Fig. 9) and old schoolhouse (Fig. 19) in "School", old kerosene lamp (Fig. 21) in "Commodity", they are unknown by young people and make them feel stressful in conversation.
2. Regional reasons, such as boiled dumplings (Fig. 15), it is the most famous Chinese food, but in Suzhou city in south China, people doesn't often eat it.
3. Culture reasons: such as photo of "children's day" in "Events" category (Fig. 17), although Chinese elderly are not interested in "Events", but they are very interested in children because in China families take care of disable elderly at home, the

concept of raising children for old age has long been popular, children is hope of Chinese family.

4. Commonality: for example, although the young is the most interested in "Events" (Fig. 8), by contrast, the elderly isn't interested in it (Fig. 12), the young feel stressful when talking about "Events" with elders (Fig. 10).

5   Conclusion

For finding common topics and making an intergenerational conversation comfortable in China, we should make good use of the photos as followings:

- "Food", "Events", "School" and "Commodity" are appropriate categories for both Chinese elderly and young people.
- Photos about family life and children are the best topics for Chinese people.
- A photo with more commonality between two generations make conversation less stress.
- People living in different area of China has different habits and customs, so searching photos should consider the regional characteristics.

Methods of measuring the burden are considered possible to provide contents for comfortable conversation between the elderly and the young. Only a few methods were used in this study, that were stress check for the young, questionnaire for both the young and the elderly, and express analysis for the elderly. In future research we expect more methods of measuring the burden, such as heartbeats check for the young, and measure device easy for the elderly. Further more, it is necessary to make a similar experiment in other categories and more photos to increase appropriate categories for the content of intergenerational conversation support system. The young volunteers of this study are all the caregivers at nursing home, in the future study, we should let the young people without any care experience become the conversation partners.

However, the conversation support system can be considered useful for caregivers with limited psychological knowledge to provide memory/cognitive exercises for elders at nursing house in China.

Acknowledgments. This work was supported by Grant-in-Aid for Scientific Research (15H01698) of JSPS. Thanks are due to staff and the elderly people at Taizhou Zhaoyangyuan Nursing Home, Nanjing Chenguang Hospital Rehabilitation Nursing Center, Nanjing Shuiz-huyuan Community, and Suzhou Social Welfare Home for assistance with the experiments.

References

1. MacroBusiness: China Economy, China Will Grow Old Before It Grows Rich (2013). http://www.macrobusiness.com.au/2013/08/china-will-grow-old-before-it-grows-rich/
2. Chen, Z., Yang, X., Song, Y., Song, B., Zhang, Y., Liu, J., Wang, Q.: Challenges of dementia care in China, Geriatrics (2017)

3. Iwamoto, M., Kuwahara, N., Morimoto, K.: A study of conversation support system between the elderly person and young adults by using facial expression analysis. In: Marcus, A. (ed.) DUXU 2015. LNCS, vol. 9188, pp. 616–627. Springer, Cham (2015). doi:10.1007/978-3-319-20889-3_57
4. Nomura, T.: Reminiscence & Life Review. Chuohoki Publishing Co. Ltd., Tokyo (1998). p. 63
5. Iwamoto, M., Kuwahara, N., Morimoto, K.: Examination of how the presentation of content in conversation support system. Hum. Interface Soc. (2015)
6. Tomomi, O., Mariko, T., Mariko, A., Naoko, K., Yukikazu, S.: Expression Analysis-Comparison of the Characteristics of the Facial Expression, Proposed by Ekman (2010)

Health Data Analytics and Visualization

Measuring Insight into Multi-dimensional Data from a Combination of a Scatterplot Matrix and a HyperSlice Visualization

André Calero Valdez[1]($\boxtimes$), Sascha Gebhardt[2], Torsten W. Kuhlen[2], and Martina Ziefle[1]

[1] Human-Computer Interaction Center, RWTH Aachen University, Campus-Boulevard 57, Aachen, Germany
{calero-valdez,ziefle}@comm.rwth-aachen.de
[2] Virtual Reality Group, RWTH Aachen University, Kopernikusstr. 6, Aachen, Germany
{gebhardt,kuhlen}@vr.rwth-aachen.de

Abstract. Understanding multi-dimensional data and in particular multi-dimensional dependencies is hard. Information visualization can help to understand this type of data. Still, the problem of how users gain insights from such visualizations is not well understood. Both the visualizations and the users play a role in understanding the data. In a case study, using both, a scatterplot matrix and a HyperSlice with six-dimensional data, we asked 16 participants to think aloud and measured insights during the process of analyzing the data. The amount of insights was strongly correlated with spatial abilities. Interestingly, all users were able to complete an optimization task independently of self-reported understanding of the data.

Keywords: Information visualization · Insight · Multi-dimensional visualization · Scatterplot · HyperSlice · Evaluation

1 Introduction

In a heavily technology-assisted work environment, many tasks will shift from manual labor to monitoring, control, and decision-making tasks in the future. To fulfill these tasks process data must be integrated. The underlying data that will be used for these purposes is often intricately interconnected and has multivariate dependencies (e.g., in control-parameters in laser-based welding). Therefore, many of the problems that workers will have to deal with in the future are highly complex. One approach to address this problem is accessing data by visualizations.

An intrinsic attribute of multi-dimensional data is that for visualizing data on a 2D-screen, dimensionality-reduction techniques (e.g., statistical reduction,

© Springer International Publishing AG 2017
V.G. Duffy (Ed.): DHM 2017, Part II, LNCS 10287, pp. 225–236, 2017.
DOI: 10.1007/978-3-319-58466-9_21

projections, higher-order data) are necessary. Here lies a core challenge of multidimensional data visualizations. High-level dependencies are not easily visualized or detected, when the dependencies are embedded in the dimensions that are hidden by the dimension reduction approaches.

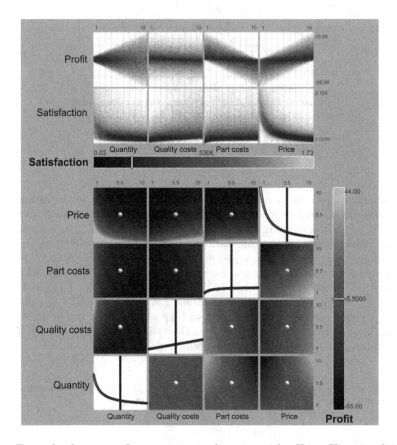

Fig. 1. Example of a scatterplot matrix in combination with a HyperSlice visualization.

One approach to overcome this barrier is HyperSlice [1] (see Fig. 1). This visualization technique displays all pairwise orthogonal, axis-aligned slices through one common point, the focal point, of a multi-dimensional data space. By swiping through the multi-dimensional hyperspace, users can try to reconstruct this space in their mind. While the approach works well in the reconstruction of 3D models from 2D slices, higher dimensions are harder [2] to reconstruct in a mind shaped by evolution in a 3D world. Research even indicates that 5-way interactions can not be processed by the human mind [3].

However, users should be able to analytically think about multi-dimensional dependencies and derive them from visualizations such as HyperSlice. But, all users? Spatial cognitive abilities of users are different. Intelligence differs, experience differs, self-efficacy differs. The question we ask ourselves is: how important are these user differences when using multi-dimensional data visualizations?

In order to get a first understanding of how multi-dimensional data is understood, we conduct a qualitative user study and measure user diversity criteria to understand their influence on visualization insight.

2   Related Work

The question of how to assess the quality of a visualization is hard, because all aspects relevant for a visualization come in a plethora of options [4,5]. The purpose of a visualization can be very different (e.g., reveal new facts of old data, monitor real-time sensor data, visual proofs, etc.), the data can be very different (e.g., static, dynamic, high-dimensional, structured, etc.) and the visual representation can be very different (e.g., HyperSlice, star-coordinates, Cherrnoff-faces, etc.). In this article we address visualizations that are made to be insightful and address multi-dimensional data. We focus on a combination of two visualizations: a scatterplot matrix and a HyperSlice visualization.

2.1   Multi-dimensional Data Visualization

A large body of research exists that is relevant to multi-dimensional data visualization. Each have different benefits and drawbacks [6] depending on their usage. A scatterplot matrix can be used to visualize the probability distributions of multiple variables. Columns and rows indicate two variables, and the cell plot is a scatter plot of these two variables (see Fig. 2 [7]).

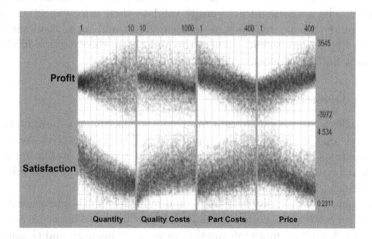

Fig. 2. memoSlice scatterplot matrix. The first row shows the scatterplots for profit and four input variables. The second row shows the scatterplots for customer satisfaction and the same input variables.

A multi-dimensional data visualization that is regularly used is HyperSlice [8]. It represents multiple variables in several plots. In its matrix layout columns and rows represent input variables. Each tile of this layout depicts a slice that maps these inputs to an output variable via color coding (see Fig. 3).

When the task in such a visualization is to find optimal parameters it can be helpful to add gradient trajectories [9,10]. These indicate the steepest ascent and descent in the mutli-dimensional space. Thus, they ultimately lead to the next local extrema and are a useful tool for optimization tasks. By combining both, the scatterplot matrix and the HyperSlice it is possible to re-use the spatial encoding of the columns [7,11] by aligning the plots in the same column. This combination allows users to gain insights on the data on two different levels: first, an overview is granted via projections of randomly sampled points within the data domain through scatterplots. Second, local detail are presented via slices through the focal point in the HyperSlice. Additionally, an overlay of projections of the multi-dimensional gradient trajectories through the focal point enables them to easily identify improved input combinations.

2.2   Visualization Insight

One approach to assess the suitability of a visualization for a given purpose and a given set of data is to measure how many correct facts are derived from data. North [12] proposed measuring insight from a visualization as a key goal for visualization evaluation. Insight in his definition is not just recognition of data but *"complex*, involving all or large amounts of the given data in a synergistic way, not simply individual data values" [12]. Furthermore, insight should be *deep* and built up over time raising new questions in the process. Insight is also *qualitative* in nature – not exact, but uncertain and "can have multiple levels of resolution". A key aspect of insight is that it is unpredictable and *unexpected* for the user. The user should not simply validate their prior expectations. The insights should thus be *relevant*, as in meaningful and more than mere data analytic findings. They should connect the underlying theory of the model with new relevant findings that have domain impact.

2.3   User Diversity

Whether a user is able to gain insight from any visualization is a question that not only depends on the quality of the visualization. Users themselves are different and many effects of user diversity must be considered when evaluating insights from a visualization. Three aspects of user diversity are considered in this paper, with no claim of being complete.

As one aspect of user diversity that could influence multi-dimensional under-standing *fluid intelligence* comes to mind. A higher fluid intelligence is associated with being able to hold more information in working memory and change infor-mation more quickly [13].

The second aspect obviously relevant to this topic, is *spatial visualization abil-ity*. Not all humans are able to manipulate spatial figures in their mind equally

well. Older people typically perform worse than younger ones. Furthermore, men
tend to outperform women [14], but the underlying hormone testosterone seems
to have non-linear effects on spatial cognition. Low testosterone males, and high
testosterone females perform best [14]. Beyond the general effect of spatial abilities on visualization evaluation, domain expertise may also play a role [15].

The last aspect of user diversity that might play a role in using a multi-
dimensional visualization is *self-efficacy*. When using a computer system, the
users' believe in being effective in doing so differs and influences how well they
perform. One scale to measure this influence is the computer self-efficacy scale
by Beier *KUT* [16].

3   Method

The purpose of this study was to investigate how users gain insight from multi-
dimensional visualizations and the effect of user diversity. For this purpose, we
used the visualization application memoSlice [7,11] in a user study with sixteen
(n = 16) participants.

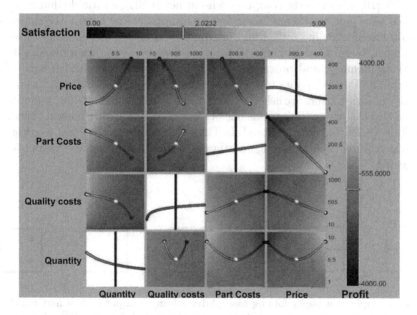

Fig. 3. HyperSlice of a data set with four input variables (columns and rows) and two
output variables (upper and lower part). The graphs on the diagonal map one input
variable to the same output variable as the upper part. By dragging the white focal
point in any tile, all other tiles' slices are shifted in the 4-D hyperspace along the 2 of
from the selected cell.

Our approach is based on a no-benchmark task methodology by North [12].
However, letting participants explore the tool freely is not a fruitful approach, as

memoSlice provides two related views (scatterplot matrix and hyperslice matrix) that each consist of several plots. The amount of visual information is very high, as is the complexity of the underlying data-model (i.e., multi-dimensional dependencies, multiple outcome variables).

In order to get to interesting questions in a limited time-frame a tutorial is necessary. Therefore, we first asked participants to view an introductory video of memoSlice that explained the necessary features to complete six tasks afterwards. Completion of these tasks was not the actual target of the study, but the tasks were a mere guidance to structure the exploration of the tool. Participants were asked to think aloud and explain their insights during their exploration. After the exploration, we conducted a short interview, asking participants about what they liked in this tool and asked them to rate usability of the tool and how well their understanding of the visualizations was on a scale of 1–5 (bad–good).

3.1   Measuring User Diversity

Since multidimensional visualizations might be heavily influenced by spatial thinking capability we asked participants to complete three standardized tests. The *KUT* [16] measures the computer self-efficacy (CSE), a variable that explains how able users perceive themselves in using a computer. The *KAI-N* [17] measures the fluid intelligence in "bit". Fluid intelligence measures the capacity of working memory, by measuring memory span (how long can you retain random items in working memory) and processing speed (how fast can you take in new information). The Paper-Folding test (VZ-2) is used to assess an individuals spatio-cognitive abilities. Users are asked to predict the location of holes after puncturing a folded sheet of paper. This test is one of three tests to measure mental visualization skills [18, 19] and derived from L.L. Thurstone's punched hole test (see Fig. 4). This test requires mental folding and thus also mental rotation and visualization of objects.

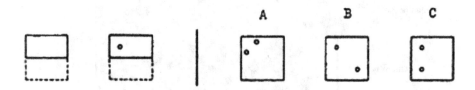

Fig. 4. Example of a paper-folding task. After folding a paper in half and punching a hole into the top left corner, two holes are in the unfolded paper. Participants now have to rate which option (A, B, C) is the layout of the holes in the unfolded paper. C would be correct in this case.

3.2   Measuring Insight

The model task in our study was an optimization task in a production setting. To have full control over the data and the insights that could be gained, we used a forged multi-dimensional function as underlying data model. As the two output variables we chose *profit* and *customer satisfaction*. The four determining input variables were *produced parts, quality costs, part costs,* and *price*. The probabilistic associations of the variables can be seen in the scatterplot matrix of memoSlice (see Fig. 2).

In order to analyze what actual insights users had, we analyzed all think-aloud user studies and recorded insights about both the tool and the underlying data model. We then measured the amount of correctly derived insights about the software and the data.

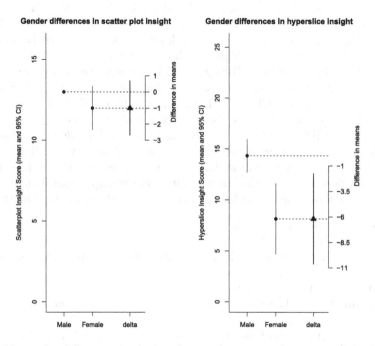

Fig. 5. No gender differences in the insights on the scatter plot matrix (left plot). All males had all 13 insights. Comparison of means of insights found in the hyperslice visualization show gender differences (right plot). Error bars denote CIs.

3.3 Procedure

The sampling method was convenience sampling. We aimed to test a 50% gender ratio and asked only students from an engineering subject, approached directly by us. The tests took between 30 to 90 min. Participants started with the tutorial video, before completing the task-driven think aloud experiment. Next, they completed the questionnaire survey and were then asked to comment on the experiment.

On the counted insights and user diversity criteria we used Pearson correlations (r) and comparison of means. We further report the test statistics with the level of significance (p) or the 95%-confidence intervals for point estimates. Confidence intervals (CIs) were calculated with the assumption of underlying normally distributed data, which can be assumed for the given standardized tests and are reported in square brackets.

4   Results

Our sample consisted of 7 female and 9 male students. Males scored higher in all diversity criteria (see Table 1). Although most differences can not be treated as such for the given sample size. Males showed a higher score in computer self efficacy ($M_{\sigma} = 5.32$, 95% CI [5.06, 5.57], $M_{\female} = 4.59$, 95% CI [3.60, 5.58]). Since the CIs overlap to a large degree no difference in means must be assumed. Similarly males scored slightly higher in the KAI N scale ($M_{\sigma} = 154.2$, 95% CI [126.5, 182.0], $M_{\female} = 120$, 95% CI [95.8, 144.2]), but again because of overlapping CIs no difference in means may be assumed. The difference in the paper folding test ($M_{\sigma} = 15.67$, 95% CI [14.51, 16.82], $M_{\female} = 12.57$, 95% CI [9.60, 15.54]), where males also score higher, is also not statistically relevant.

The best possible score for insights two users received was 30 correct insights. The following insights were derived from the two individual views. The scatterplot matrix had 13 associated insights. The numbers in parentheses refer to the amount of different insights that were counted. For example, four fundamentally different high-dimensional associations were found in the scatterplot matrix (4).

- Rows are output variables (1).
- Columns are input variables (1).
- Identify association of two variables and their direction (positive, negative, or non-linear) (2).
- Interpretation of this association (2).
- Understand higher dimensional associations (e.g., price × profit × satisfaction) (4).
- Identify correct ranges of variables (2) and how to explore them (1).

HyperSlice yielded a maximum of 17 insights:

- Understand meaning of color in both parts of the matrix (2).
- Meaning of focal points and their manipulation (1).
- Meaning of gradient trajectories (3).
- Meaning of diagonal (maximal trajectory) (1).
- Meaning of upper half and lower half (2).
- Understand multi-dimensional associations (e.g., price × profit × part costs) (4).
- Identify correct ranges of variables (2) and how to explore them (1).
- Finding optimal production point (1).

When looking at the amount of insights from both genders, we see no differences in the amount of insights derived from the scatterplot matrix (see Fig. 5). Yet it is interesting to note, that all male participants reported all thirteen

Table 1. Means of computer self-efficacy (CSE), fluid intelligence (KAI N) and spatial capabilities (VZ2) by gender.

	Scale mean ♂	Scale mean ♀
CSE	5.32	4.59
KAI N	154.20	120.00
Paper-folding (VZ2)	15.67	12.57

insights. Differences between genders occurred only when looking at how many insights were derived from the HyperSlice visualization (see Fig. 5). Men on average had 14.3 insights (95% CI [12.46, 16.25]), while women only had 8.14 insights on average (95% CI [3.82, 12.41]).

Men reported a better subjective usability of the software ($M = 4.1$, 95% CI [3.5, 4.7]) than women ($M = 3.2$, 95% CI [2.4, 4.2]). They also report a higher subjective understanding of the underlying data ($M = 4.1$, 95% CI [3.4, 4.8]) than women ($M = 2.8$, 95% CI [1.9, 3.8]). But these differences are statistically not meaningful.

We also looked into how the different variables influence each other when used in correlation analysis (see Fig. 6). We found that both, computer self-efficacy and spatio-cognitive abilities influence scatterplot matrix insights, HyperSlice insights, and subjective understanding of the data model, respectively. HyperSlice insights also correlated strongly with subjective understanding. It is interesting to note, that only hyperslice insights correlate with subjective understanding and therefore no other associations of objective and subjective outcome measures exist in our study. However, this correlation is relatively strong ($r = .58$).

4.1 Qualitative Results

Since all think-aloud studies were audio-recorded and transcribed, more detailed results can be drawn from what participants actually said. For this purpose we categorized all mentions and counted the occurrence of various topics in those mentions. The most frequent topic was the positive mention of *associations*. Eleven participants mentioned that the tool helped them to identify how variables are associated (*"Oh, I can click the points here and they are highlighted in the other scatterplots, too. So I can see the relationship of two variables at the top and three in the bottom."*). The most often mentioned negative topic was the problem of *multi-dimensionality* (8 mentions, e.g.: *"The association of, for example, quality costs and costs per part and satisfaction. How do I set this? I can't. [frustrated] This is because of multi-dimensionality. This is hard to imagine. What does this point, that I see, mean in relation to the other two?"*). A close follow-up in negative mentions were the HyperSlice visualization itself (6 mentions) and the gradient trajectories (4 mentions). Only men commented on the latter and mostly negative (e.g.: *"What do these little worms mean? I have a suspicion [...], the tendency to neighboring points. But what neighbors? Hmm, no idea."*).

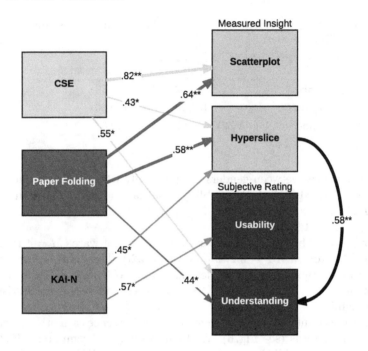

Fig. 6. Correlations of all variables. Numbers denote Pearson's r. Asterisks and line thickness indicate level of significance (thin* $p < .05$; thick** $p < .01$). Gender is dummy-coded, with male coded as 1. CSE is computer self-efficacy, and KAI-N is a standardized test for fluid intelligence.

Most interestingly, all participants were able to complete the optimization task, independently of how well the users reported to understand the underlying data set. Thus, they were able to use the information visualization for one of its intended purposes.

5   Discussion

The data generated from this study focused on measuring insights, is only one part of the story of this case study. We found confirmatory evidence to expected outcomes (e.g. spatial ability predicts understanding of multi-dimensional dependencies). We also found the stereo-typical stronger results for male participants in the HyperSlice insights, based on the assumption of differing spatial abilities. However, one must note that there is no single spatial ability, but a multitude of different abilities. The mental folding of objects, which was used in this study, might be the most relevant for understanding hyperslices, as one has to "fold" dimensions onto each other. Mental rotation, which is important for mental folding, might also be highly relevant. Other Interestingly, almost all users were able to gain insights from the scatterplot matrix, and this also to a large extent. The scatterplot matrix can also be used to find three-dimensional associations by looking at two 2D-associations at the same time in the same row or column. Of course higher order conclusions are present in the data, yet they are not immediately visible to the naked eye.

Only the HyperSlice matrix naturally yields four-dimensional associations by combining two three-dimensional associations. This is were some of the participants struggled, and this is in line with the assumption of Halford et al. who claim no more than four variables can be assessed at the same time [3]. However, even higher order-associations are present in the data. No participant reported any of these. Yet, all were able to find satisfactory input settings in the optimization task.

In order to prevent interviewer effects, we asked a student to conduct the studies, without helping the participants. Interestingly, she reported to have increased insights herself after each trial. But, in the end the gradient trajectories remained a mystery to her.

Lastly, designing a study to quantify insights into complex data is also quite challenging. The sample we selected were a best case scenario of possible users, yet all were new to the visualization application. Domain knowledge effects (i.e. how to set-up quality costs for production) have been neglected in this study.

6 Conclusion

Overall, our case study yielded results that agreed with our hypotheses drawn from theoretical models. The relatively small sample size was caused by the large workload for each individual experiment. However, to our knowledge no research exists that analyzes how user-diversity factors influence insights in multi-dimensional visualizations. Therefore results even with limited statistical relevance are important. It seems to be necessary to develop methods that incorporate user diversity in the measurement process of insights, as without these aspects it will never be fully understood, who is really responsible for understanding multi-dimensional data: Human intelligence, good information visualization, or both? Probably both.

Acknowledgments. The authors thank the German Research Council DFG for the friendly support of the research in the excellence cluster "Integrative Production Technology in High Wage Countries". We also thank Saskia De Luca for conducting the experiments.

References

1. van Wijk, J.J., van Liere, R.: HyperSlice: visualization of scalar functions of many variables. In: Proceedings of 4th Conference on Visualization 1993, VIS 1993, pp. 119–125. IEEE Computer Society, Washington, DC (1993)
2. Murata, M., Hashimoto, S.: Interactive environment for intuitive understanding of 4D object and space. In: Proceedings of International Conference on Multimedia Modeling–MMM, pp. 383–401 (2000)

3. Halford, G.S., Baker, R., McCredden, J.E., Bain, J.D.: How many variables can humans process? Psychol. Sci. **16**(1), 70–76 (2005)
4. Munzner, T.: Visualization Analysis and Design. CRC Press, Boca Raton (2014)
5. Isenberg, T., Isenberg, P., Chen, J., Sedlmair, M., Möller, T.: A systematic review on the practice of evaluating visualization. IEEE Trans. Vis. Comput. Graph. **19**(12), 2818–2827 (2013)
6. Hoffman, P.E., Grinstein, G.G.: A survey of visualizations for high-dimensional data mining. In: Information Visualization in Data Mining and Knowledge Discovery, pp. 47–82 (2002)
7. Gebhardt, S., Pick, S., Voet, H., Utsch, J., Al Khawli, T., Eppelt, U., Reinhard, R., Büscher, C., Hentschel, B., Kuhlen, T.W.: flapAssist: how the integration of VR and visualization tools fosters the factory planning process. In: 2015 IEEE Virtual Reality (VR), pp. 181–182, March 2015
8. Hilda, J.J., Srimathi, C., Bonthu, B.: A review on the development of big data analytics and effective data visualization techniques in the context of massive and multidimensional data. Indian J. Sci. Technol. 9(27) (2016)
9. Dos Santos, S., Brodlie, K.: Gaining understanding of multivariate and multidimensional data through visualization. Comput. Graph. **28**(3), 311–325 (2004)
10. Al Khawli, T., Gebhardt, S., Eppelt, U., Hermanns, T., Kuhlen, T., Schulz, W.: An integrated approach for the knowledge discovery in computer simulation models with a multi-dimensional parameter space. In: International Conference of Numerical Analysis and Mathematics 2015 (ICNAAM 2015), vol. 1738, p. 370003. AIP Publishing (2016)
11. Gebhardt, S., Al Khawli, T., Hentschel, B., Kuhlen, T., Schulz, W.: HyperSlice visualization of metamodels for manufacturing processes. In: IEEE Visualization Conference (VIS), Atlanta, GA, USA, vol. 13 (2013)
12. North, C.: Toward measuring visualization insight. IEEE Comput. Graph. Appl. **26**(3), 6–9 (2006)
13. Lehrl, S., Fischer, B.: A basic information psychological parameter (BIP) for the reconstruction of concepts of intelligence. Eur. J. Pers. **4**(4), 259–286 (1990)
14. Gouchie, C., Kimura, D.: The relationship between testosterone levels and cognitive ability patterns. Psychoneuroendocrinology **16**(4), 323–334 (1991)
15. Downing, R.E., Moore, J.L., Brown, S.W.: The effects and interaction of spatial visualization and domain expertise on information seeking. Comput. Hum. Behav. **21**(2), 195–209 (2005)
16. Beier, G.: Kontrollüberzeugungen im Umgang mit Technik; self-efficacy in the use of technology (engl.). Rep. Psychol. **9**, 684–693 (1999)
17. Lehrl, S., Zipp, A., Schwarzfischer, C., Eissing, G.: Kurztest für allgemeine Intelligenz (KAI) (2016)
18. Carroll, J.B.: Human Cognitive Abilities: A Survey of Factor-Analytic Studies. Cambridge University Press, Cambridge (1993)
19. Eliot, J., Smith, I.: An International Directory of Spatial Tests. NFER-Nelson, Windsor (1983)

Effective Visualization of Long Term Health Data to Support Behavior Change

Corinna A. Christmann[✉], Gregor Zolynski, Alexandra Hoffmann, and Gabriele Bleser

Junior Research Group WearHEALTH, Department of Computer Science, University of Kaiserslautern, Gottlieb-Daimler-Street Building 48, 67663 Kaiserslautern, Germany
christmann@cs.uni-kl.de

Abstract. The reflective stage, which is crucial for behavior change, can be facilitated with suitable visualizations that allow users to answer specific questions with regard to their health data. To date, effective visualizations which combine time series data and the appraisal of this data in one chart are, however, rare. To close this gap in research, twenty participants compared two alternative long-term visualizations of health behavior: an accumulated bar chart and a point chart which both include appraisals of the underlying health data based on current recommendations of leading health organizations, such as the World Health Organization or the European Food Information Council. Participants answered three types of question (progress over time, correlations between different health behaviors, and health consciousness). The sequence of visualization for the underlying data sets was cross balanced over participants. The accumulated bar chart resulted in more trials in which participants were unable to answer. In some cases, this type of visualization also resulted in biased interpretations with regard to progress over time and health consciousness. Summarizing, we recommend the point chart, in which the background is colored according to the recommendation of the respective health behavior. Both types of visualization are, however, not optimal for the identification of correlations.

Keywords: Bar chart · Point chart · Traffic lights feedback · Health app · Mobile Application Rating Scale

1 Introduction

Followers of the quantified self trend assume that collecting biological, physical, behavioral, or environmental information can help to improve one's well-being and performance [1]. In line with this idea, self-monitoring is a frequently used method in behavior change interventions [2]. One risk of this approach is, however, that self-monitoring applications do not help people to reach their personal, actual goals (e.g., reducing subjective stress level), but the collection of data itself becomes the goal [3]. Therefore, the reflective stage [4, 5] is a crucial one before the intended behavior change can occur [6]. To facilitate this stage, it is essential to provide suitable visualizations to allow users to answer health-related questions and to decide whether a certain behavior should be maintained or adapted [7]. Some of these questions about

© Springer International Publishing AG 2017
V.G. Duffy (Ed.): DHM 2017, Part II, LNCS 10287, pp. 237–247, 2017.
DOI: 10.1007/978-3-319-58466-9_22

the user's behavior have already been identified by Li and colleagues [8]. In the context of the visualization of long-term health data we suggest that the following three types of question are of special interest:

1. Progress over time (Has my consumption of e.g. alcohol changed over time?)
2. Correlations between different health behaviors (Is there a correlation between e.g. my subjective stress level and sleep behavior?)
3. Health consciousness (Am I health conscious with regard to e.g. my consumption of coffee?)

2   Data Visualization in Health Apps

Some data visualization heuristics which facilitate the reflection of personal health data are summarized by Cuttone et al. [7]. Aside from avatars [9, 10], notifications [11], and abstract arts [12], charts [5, 13, 14] are the most common form of data visualization in modern health technology.

The common representation for explorations of patterns in time series data is the line plot [7]. The bar chart with time on the x-axis is also often used for long-term visualization (e.g., Sony LifeLog, Fitbit). Superficially, these visualizations seem to be perfect for the first two question types. However, they do not take into consideration how the respective health behavior should be appraised and therefore do not allow making decisions for or against behavior change [15]. Fitbit saves this gap, e.g., by providing additional goal fulfillment charts, which depict in a colored ring to which degree the personal goal of the user is achieved. To date, effective visualizations, which combine time series data and the appraisal of this data in one chart are, however, rare.

3   Methods

3.1   Types of Visualization

To solve this issue, we compared two alternative long-term visualizations of health behavior: an accumulated bar chart and a point chart (see Fig. 1). In the accumulated bar chart, each bar represents the appraisals of data entries for one week (red = not recommendable, yellow = might still be recommendable, green = recommendable). In the point chart, time is displayed on the x-axis and the data values on the y-axis. The background is colored according to current health recommendations by the World Health Organization [16], the European Food Information Council [17], the German Nutrition Society [18], and the National Sleep Foundation [19, 20].

In order to compare these two designs with respect to their suitability to answer the presented question types, four fictional datasets covering the following ten health behaviors and stress-related factors were constructed: sleep [21, 22], exercise [16], portions of unsweetened drinks [23], fruits and vegetables [24], caffeinated drinks [17], alcoholic drinks [25] positive [26] and negative events [27–29], mood [30], and subjective stress level. The data sets covered a period of 8 and 16 weeks.

(a)   (b)

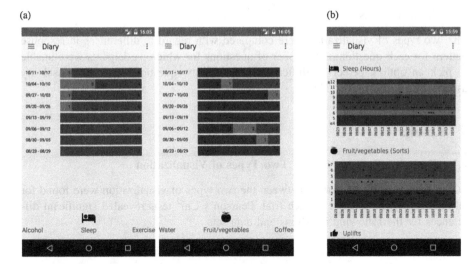

Fig. 1. (a): Accumulated bar chart based on appraisals of data entries for one week for each bar. (b): Point chart with time on x-axis, value on y-axis, the background is colored according to the respective health recommendations (red = not recommendable, yellow = might still be recommendable, green = recommendable) (Color figure online)

3.2   Participants

Twenty young adults participated. All except one (a trainee) were students of the University of Kaiserslautern. The mean age was 23.1 years (age range = 20-27 years, standard deviation = 1.80 years). Participants were randomly assigned to two groups which did not differ with respect to gender distribution (5 males and 5 females per group). The mean age was, however, higher in group A (mean age = 24 years) than in group B (mean age = 22 years), $t(18) = 2.53$, $p = .02$. All participants had former experience with smartphones or tablets.

3.3   Procedure

All participants answered three questions with regard to progress over time, correlations between different health behaviors and stress-related factors as well as health consciousness for all four datasets ($3 \times 3 \times 4 = 36$ questions). The sequence of visualization for the data sets was cross balanced over participants (group A: bar chart for dataset 1 + 2, point chart for dataset 3 + 4; group B: point chart for dataset 1 + 2, bar chart for dataset 3 + 4). After having completed the questions for each type of visualization, participants were asked to rate the usability of each type of diagram based on the following subscales of the Mobile Application Rating Scale (MARS) [31]: performance, ease of use, navigation, layout, visual information, graphics, and visual appeal. The whole procedure was embedded into an interview to allow general comments justifying why the respective answers were chosen. The interview took about 45 min.

3.4   Data Analysis

The two types of visualization were compared with regard to differences in response pattern for each question, the number of questions for which participants were unable to pick an option, perceived difficulty to answer the question, as well as usability aspects based on MARS [31].

4   Results

4.1   Response Patterns for the Two Types of Visualization

Differences in response pattern between the two types of visualization were found for all question types, but not in each trial. Pearson's Chi^2 tests revealed significant differences for the following questions and data sets.

Progress Over Time

- "How has the consumption of fruits and vegetables developed over time?" resulted in the following response patterns: bar chart with 90% "improved" and 10% "stayed the same" answers, point chart with 50% "improved" and 50% "fluctuating" answers, $\chi^2(2) = 7.14$, p = .03 (see Fig. 2).
- "How has the amount of caffeinated drinks developed over time?" resulted in the following response patterns: bar chart with 90% "increased" and 10% "stayed the same" answers, point chart with 10% "increased" and 90% "stayed the same"answers, $\chi^2(1) = 12.80$, p $\leq$ .01 (see Fig. 2).

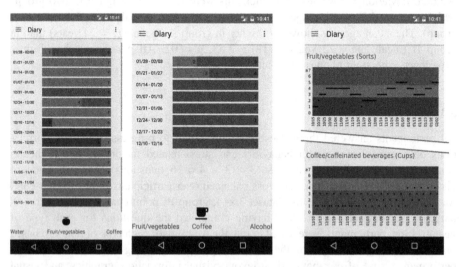

Fig. 2. Both versions of visualization for the consumption of fruits and vegetables in data set 2 (left bar chart and upper point chart) and the consumption of caffeinated drinks in data set 3 (right bar chart and lower point chart).

Correlations

- "Is there a correlation between the amount of exercises and the consumption of water?" resulted in the following response patterns: bar chart with 20% "unable to pick an option" and 80% "no correlation" answers, point chart with 50% "positive correlation" and 50% "no correlation" answers, $\chi^2(2) = 7.69$, p = .02. (actual correlation of scales: r = .51, see Fig. 3).

 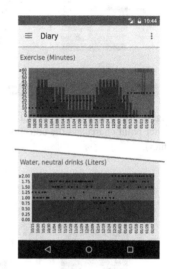

Fig. 3. Both versions of visualization for the amount of exercise in data set 4 (left bar chart and upper point chart) and the consumption of water in data set 4 (right bar chart and lower point chart).

- "Is there a correlation between the amount of sleep and the consumption of alcohol?" resulted in the following response patterns: bar chart with 100% "no correlation" answers, point chart with 10% "positive correlation", 50% "no correlation", and 40% "unable to pick an option" answers, $\chi^2(2) = 6.67$, p $\leq$ .04. p = .02. (actual correlation of scales: r = .09, see Fig. 4).

Health Consciousness

- "Is the person who inserted these data health conscious with regard to the amount of exercises?" resulted in the following response patterns: bar chart with 90% "yes" and 10% "no" answers, point chart with 60% "yes" and 40% "no" answers, $\chi^2(1) = 5.50$, p = .02 (see Fig. 5).
- "Is the person who inserted these data health conscious with regard to his or her consumption of fruits and vegetables?" resulted in the following response patterns: bar chart with 20% "yes" and 80% "no" answers, point chart with 100% "yes" and 0% "no" answers, $\chi^2(2) = 20.00$, p $\leq$ .01 (see Fig. 5).

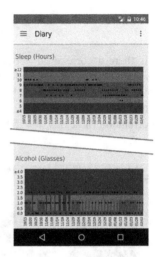

Fig. 4. Both versions of visualization for the amount of sleep in data set 4 (left bar chart and upper point chart) and the consumption of alcohol in data set 4 (right bar chart and lower point chart).

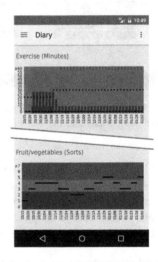

Fig. 5. Both versions of visualization for the amount of exercise in data set 2 (left bar chart and upper point chart) and the consumption of fruits and vegetables in data set 2 (right bar chart and lower point chart).

4.2   Inability to Pick an Option

Concerning the inability to pick an option, an analysis of variance (ANOVA) with sequence of visualization types as between subject factor (group A: bar chart for dataset 1 + 2, point chart for dataset 3 + 4; group B: point chart for dataset 1 + 2, bar chart for dataset 3 + 4) and the within subject factors question type (type 1 = change over time, type 2 = correlations, type 3 = health consciousness) and data sets (data set 1, data set 2, data set 3, data set 4) revealed a main effect of question type, $F(2,36) = 14.28$, $p < .01$, $\eta_p^2 = .44$, that can be explained by the fact that there was no single trial for question type 1 (progress over time) in which participants were unable to choose an option. In contrast, the other two question types (correlations and health consciousness) did not differ from each other, $t(19) = 1.44$, $p = .17$. Moreover, the bar chart (group A data set 1 + 2 and group B data set 3 + 4) resulted in more trials in which participants could not pick an option compared to the point chart (group A data set 1 + 2 and group B data set 3 + 4), $t(19) = 2.46$, $p = .02$, indicated by a significant interaction between sequence of visualization types and data sets, $F(1,18) = 5.76$, $p = .03$, $\eta_p^2 = .24$ (see Fig. 6).

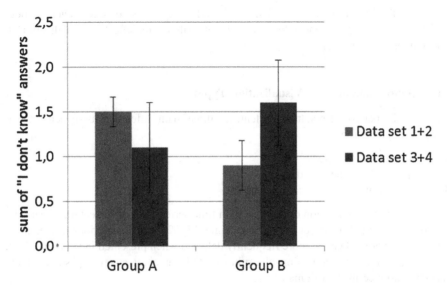

Fig. 6. Mean sum of "I don't know answers" for all three question types, illustrated for the two groups and the different datasets. Trials in which data sets were presented in the bar chart (group A data set 1 + 2 and group B data set 3 + 4) resulted in more "I don't know" answers, as compared to trials in which the data sets were presented in the point chart (group A data set 3 + 4 and group B data set 1 + 2).

4.3   Perceived Difficulty to Answer

The ANOVA for perceived difficulty of answers revealed the following results: There was no systematic difference between the two versions of visualization for perceived difficulty. There was a main effect of question type, $F(2,36) = 23.97$, $p < .01$, $\eta p^2 = .57$, indicating that question type 2 (correlations) is perceived as more difficult compared to question type 1 (change over time), $t(19) = 4.64$, $p < .01$) or question type 3 (health consciousness), $t(19) = 7.45$, $p < .01$, which did not differ from each other, $t(19) = .81$, $p = .43$.

4.4 MARS Ratings

Finally, one ANOVA for each MARS subscale was conducted. The results for the usability aspects were mixed with preference for the point chart with regard to performance, $F(1,18) = 6.79$, $p = .02$, $\eta p^2 = .27$, and preference for the bar chart with regard to graphics, $F(1,18) = 9.97$, $p < .01$, $\eta p^2 = .36$ and visual appeal, $F(1,18) = 7.13$, $p = .02$, $\eta p^2 = .28$. No preferences were found for the remaining scales (ease of use, navigation, layout, and visual information). The overall usability scores were medium to high for both types of visualizations.

5 Discussion

Based on these results, we will discuss the advantages and disadvantages of both versions of visualization and refer to additional tools for the effective visualization of correlations in health apps.

5.1 Comparison of Both Visualization Types

Based on the pattern of results, we identified three main differences be-tween the two types of visualization:

1. Detection of fluctuations
2. Interpretation of the raw data
3. Interpretation of the full color spectrum

Besides the identification of trends within time series data, the detection of periodic patterns has been pointed out to be fundamental [7, 32]. The fluctuations in data set 2 (see Fig. 2) were, however, more frequently detected when presented in the point chart, indicating that the accumulation algorithm of the bar chart covers up some of the periodic variance in the original data.

Moreover, our results support the assumption that participants used the information from the raw data and the y-axis when it was available. Passing the border from green to yellow in data set 3 was interpreted as an increasing trend for coffee intake in the accumulated bar chart, whereas participants who rated the point chart mostly did not observe this trend, as they probably considered the total amount of cups (see Fig. 2). This means that people do not seem to be overloaded by too much information when both the raw data and the corresponding appraisals are provided. This is also supported by the fact that ratings of perceived difficulty to answer did not differ between the two types of visualization and that the point chart resulted in fewer trials in which partic-ipants were unable to pick an option.

Finally, the presentation of the full color spectrum of appraisals also seems to play a role. Persons rated the exercise sheet of data set 2 more frequently as to be health conscious when it was presented in the bar chart (see Fig. 5); probably because in contrast to the point chart, it was not obvious that the full color spectrum also includes green ratings. This bias might be stronger for inexperienced users of such a system, as the traffic light feedback system should be adopted easily over time [33].

Taken together, although both charts resulted in satisfying overall usability scores, our findings are in favor of the point chart, as it allows detecting fluctuations more easily and does not distort the original data. There were no indications of information overload when both raw data and appraisal are presented within one chart.

5.2 Visualization of Correlations

The analysis of the participants' perceived difficulty to answer revealed that the questions regarding correlations were rated with the highest difficulty. This was found for both types of visualization. However, the number of trials in which participants were unable to pick an option was higher for the bar chart. As a result, we recommend using the point chart instead of a cumulated bar chart.

Some participants also suggested using trend lines instead of single points only to facilitate the observation of correlations in the point charts, as this approach reduces unavoidable noise [7]. The most critical factor that complicated the observation of correlations, however, was that the two diagrams were not displayed simultaneously on the screen. Therefore, we recommend using an additional tool in which two point charts or trend lines can be displayed at the same time. Other approaches to visualize correlations have been summarized in Cuttone et al. [7], including scatterplots, scat-terplot matrices, and corrgrams [34].

5.3 Conclusion

The visualization of long-term health data is a challenging task. We suggest that by coupling quantified-self data and appropriate feedback, users can decide more easily, whether they are reaching their goals and if not, how they can adapt their behavior to achieve them. This work provides first insights how appraisals of the respective health data can be integrated by means of a traffic lights feedback system in a bar or point chart.

References

1. Swan, M.: The quantified self: fundamental disruption in big data science and biological discovery. Big Data **1**, 85–99 (2013)
2. Abraham, C., Michie, S.: A taxonomy of behavior change techniques used in interventions. Health Psychol.: Official J. Div. Health Psychol. Am. Psychol. Assoc. **27**, 379–387 (2008)
3. Marengo, A., Rapp, A.: Visualization of human behavior data. In: Huang, M.L., Huang, W. (eds.) Innovative Approaches of Data Visualization and Visual Analytics, pp. 236–265. IGI Global, Hershey (2014)
4. Fleck, R., Fitzpatrick, G.: Reflecting on reflection. In: Viller, S., Kraal, B., Brereton, M. (eds.) OZCHI 2010 [electronic resource]. Conference Proceedings, Brisbane, Australia, 22–26 November 2010, p. 216. ACM Press, New York (2010)

5. Li, I., Dey, A., Forlizzi, J.: A stage-based model of personal informatics systems. In: Mynatt, E., Schoner, D., Fitzpatrick, G., Hudson, S., Edwards, K., Rodden, T. (eds.) CHI 2010 - We Are HCI. Conference Proceedings : The 28th Annual CHI Conference on Human Factors in Computing Systems, p. 557. Association for Computing Machinery, New York (2010)

6. Fogg, B.J.: Persuasive technology. Ubiquity **2002**, 2 (2002)

7. Cuttone, A., Petersen, M.K., Larsen, J.E.: Four data visualization heuristics to facilitate reflection in personal informatics. In: Stephanidis, C., Antona, M. (eds.) UAHCI 2014. LNCS, vol. 8516, pp. 541–552. Springer, Cham (2014). doi:10.1007/978-3-319-07509-9_51

8. Li, I., Dey, A.K., Forlizzi, J.: Understanding my data, myself. In: UbiComp (ed.) Proceedings of the 2011 ACM Conference on Ubiquitous Computing & co-located workshops Large 2011, MLBS 2011, NoMe-IoT 2011, PETMEI 2011, RDURP 2011, SAGAware 2011, SCI 2011, TDMA 2011, UAAII 2011, UbiCrowd 2011, Beijing, China, 17–21 September 2011, p. 405. ACM, New York (2011)

9. Lin, J.J., Mamykina, L., Lindtner, S., Delajoux, G., Strub, H.B.: Fish'n'steps: encouraging physical activity with an interactive computer game. In: Dourish, P., Friday, A. (eds.) UbiComp 2006. LNCS, vol. 4206, pp. 261–278. Springer, Heidelberg (2006). doi:10.1007/11853565_16

10. Froehlich, J., Dillahunt, T., Klasnja, P., Mankoff, J., Consolvo, S., Harrison, B., Landay, J. A.: UbiGreen. In: Greenberg, S, et al. (ed.) The 27th Annual CHI Conference on Human Factors in Computing Systems. CHI 2008 (2008), p. 1043. Association for Computing Machinery, New York (2009)

11. Bentley, F., Tollmar, K.: The power of mobile notifications to increase wellbeing logging behavior. In: Mackay, W.E., Brewster, S., Bødker, S. (eds.) CHI 2013. Changing Perspectives - The 31st Annual CHI Conference on Human Factors in Computing Systems, Conference Proceedings, Paris, France, 27 April–2 May 2013, p. 1095. ACM, New York (2013)

12. Fan, C., Forlizzi, J., Dey, A.K.: A spark of activity. In: Dey, A.K., Chu, H.-H., Hayes, G.R. (eds.) UbiComp 2012. Proceedings of the 2012 ACM Conference on Ubiquitous Computing, Pittsburgh, USA, 5–8 September 2012, p. 81. Association for Computing Machinery, New York (2012)

13. Li, I., Medynskiy, Y., Froehlich, J., Larsen, J.: Personal informatics in practice. In: Konstan, J.A. (ed.) Proceedings of the 2012 Annual Conference Extended Abstracts on Human Factors in Computing Systems, p. 2799. ACM, New York (2012)

14. Cuttone, A., Lehmann, S., Larsen, J.E.: A mobile personal informatics system with interactive visualizations of mobility and social interactions. In: Singh, V.K., Chua, T.-S., Jain, R., Pentland, A.S. (eds.) PDM 2013. Proceedings of the 1st ACM International Workshop on Personal Data Meets Distributed Multimedia, Barcelona, Spain, 22 October 2013, pp. 27–30. Association for Computing Machinery, New York (2013)

15. DiClemente, C.C., Marinilli, A.S., Singh, M., Bellino, L.E.: The role of feedback in the process of health behavior change. Am. J. Health Behav. **25**, 217–227 (2001)

16. World Health Organization: Global recommendations on physical activity for health. http://www.who.int/dietphysicalactivity/leaflet-physical-activity-recommendations.pdf

17. European Food Information Council (EUFIC): Koffein und Gesundheit. http://www.eufic.org/article/de/artid/Koffein-Gesundheit/

18. Deutsche Gesellschaft für Ernährung (German Nutrition Society): 10 guidelines of the German Nutrition Society (DGE) for a wholesome diet. https://www.dge.de/index.php?id=322

19. National Sleep Foundation: National Sleep Foundation Recommends New Sleep Times. http://sleepfoundation.org/how-sleep-works/how-much-sleep-do-we-really-need, bzw. http://sleepfoundation.org/media-center/press-release/national-sleep-foundation-recommends-new-sleep-times

20. Hirshkowitz, M., Whiton, K., Albert, S.M., Alessi, C., Bruni, O., DonCarlos, L., Hazen, N., Herman, J., Katz, E.S., Kheirandish-Gozal, L., et al.: National sleep foundation's sleep time duration recommendations: methodology and results summary. Sleep Health **1**, 40–43 (2015)

21. Alvarez, G.G., Ayas, N.T.: The impact of daily sleep duration on health: a review of the literature. Prog. Cardiovasc. Nurs. **19**, 56–59 (2004)

22. Gallicchio, L., Kalesan, B.: Sleep duration and mortality: a systematic review and meta-analysis. J. Sleep Res. **18**, 148–158 (2009)

23. Popkin, B.M., D'Anci, K.E., Rosenberg, I.H.: Water, hydration, and health. Nutr. Rev. **68**, 439–458 (2010)

24. Oyebode, O., Gordon-Dseagu, V., Walker, A., Mindell, J.S.: Fruit and vegetable consumption and all-cause, cancer and CVD mortality: analysis of Health Survey for England data. J. Epidemiol. Community Health **68**, 856–862 (2014)

25. Deutsche Gesellschaft für Ernährung (German Nutrition Society): Prävention durch moderaten Alkoholkonsum? https://www.dge.de/uploads/media/DGE-Pressemeldung-aktuell-02–2010_Alkohol-Karneval.pdf

26. Cohen, S., Hoberman, H.M.: Positive events and social supports as buffers of life change stress1. J Appl Soc. Pyschol. **13**, 99–125 (1983)

27. DeLongis, A., Coyne, J.C., Dakof, G., Folkman, S., Lazarus, R.S.: Relationship of daily hassles, uplifts, and major life events to health status. Health Psychol. **1**, 119–136 (1982)

28. Kanner, A.D., Coyne, J.C., Schaefer, C., Lazarus, R.S.: Comparison of two modes of stress measurement: daily hassles and uplifts versus major life events. J. Behav. Med. **4**, 1–39 (1981)

29. Lu, L.: Daily hassles and mental health: a longitudinal study. Br. J. Psychol. **82**(4), 441–447 (1991). (London, England: 1953)

30. DeLongis, A., Folkman, S., Lazarus, R.S.: The impact of daily stress on health and mood. Psychological and social resources as mediators. J. Pers. Soc. Psychol. **54**, 486–495 (1988)

31. Stoyanov, S.R., Hides, L., Kavanagh, D.J., Zelenko, O., Tjondronegoro, D., Mani, M.: Mobile app rating scale: a new tool for assessing the quality of health mobile apps. JMIR mHealth and uHealth **3**, e27 (2015)

32. Larsen, J.E., Cuttone, A., Lehmann, S.: QS Spiral: visualizing periodic quantified self data. In: CHI 2013: Changing Perspectives, Conference Proceedings - The 31st Annual CHI Conference on Human Factors in Computing Systems, Paris, France, 27 April–2 May 2013. ACM, New York (2013)

33. Eikey, E., Poole, E., Reddy, M.: Information presentation in health apps and devices: the effect of color, distance to goal, weight perception, and interest on users' self-efficacy for accomplishing goals. In: iConference 2015 Proceedings (2015)

34. Friendly, M.: Corrgrams. Am. Stat. **56**, 316–324 (2002)

That's so Meta! Usability of a Hypergraph-Based Discussion Model

Felix Dietze[1], André Calero Valdez[1]([✉]), Johannes Karoff[1], Christoph Greven[2], Ulrik Schroeder[2], and Martina Ziefle[1]

[1] Human-Computer Interaction Center, RWTH Aachen University,
Campus-Boulevard 57, Aachen, Germany
{dietze,calero-valdez,ziefle}@comm.rwth-aachen.de,
johannes.karoff@rwth-aachen.de
[2] Learning Technologies Group, RWTH Aachen University,
Ahornstr. 55, Aachen, Germany
{greven,schroeder}@cs.rwth-aachen.de

Abstract. Massive online communication systems such as social networks, message boards and comment sections are widely used, yet fail in conveying a diverse public opinion. Limitations of models and protocols do not allow users to precisely express their intention and to maintain a complete overview in large-scale discussions. Data-driven approaches fail as well, as they remove the nuances of human communication and use coarse representations like trends, summaries and abstract visualizations. We argue that a new discussion model and a large-scale communication protocol is needed. We evaluate the comprehensibility of a hyperedge connection in modeling arguments for online discussions. An initial mechanical turk study ($n = 200$) revealed that 30% of the subjects intuitively considered using hyperedges. This was followed by a user study of a prototype ($n = 51$), where 80% actively used hyperedges. Both findings were independent of user diversity factors (age, gender, graph theory knowledge). The prototypical implementation was evaluated positively.

Keywords: Online discussion systems · Argument mapping · Living document · Hypergraph · User study · e-democracy

1 Failure to Communicate

Mass-media, Internet, social media and higher mobility have brought the world closer together by increasing modes and quantity of communication. In particular digitally-mitigated communication has allowed real-time communication across the globe not just between individuals, but also between different and novel versions of public spaces. Traditionally only mass-media like television and newspapers had the opportunity to *broadcast* information. With public spaces such as facebook, twitter and online message boards everyone has—in theory— gained access to broadcasting media (as in twitch, facebook-live, etc.). This new

© Springer International Publishing AG 2017
V.G. Duffy (Ed.): DHM 2017, Part II, LNCS 10287, pp. 248–258, 2017.
DOI: 10.1007/978-3-319-58466-9_23

form of communication, where everyone may communicate with everyone, has the potential to free access to information, publicity and opinions.

Early online mass-communication consisted of forums and chats. Both accumulate a chronologically ordered sequence of text pieces, readable by every participant of a discussion. Participants did not have to be in the same room, and therefore more people could discuss and collaborate online.

Scaling online collaboration to whole societies brings up the concept of e-democracy. In general, there is a trade-off between group size and depth of argument. Many people can collaboratively make a decision only by voting, while small groups can engage in profound discussions. E-Democracy aims at finding solutions for overcoming this trade-off [1].

One approach to deal with the increasing amount of information is to try to extract opinions and summaries via text mining. But the current state only allows for rough summaries, which in the end does not help the individual to participate. However, a structured discussion model could elevate information extraction capabilities.

2   Related Work

Quite a large body of research is relevant to this article. We try to limit the related work to what is relevant for understanding the approach in this paper.

When reading continuous text, the argument structure needs to be inferred linearly through the text. Faridani et al. [2] describe that comment lists do not scale and reinforce extreme opinions. They present a user interface called *Opinion Space* which visualizes comments based on different ratings and compare it to a list and grid interface. They confirm that users like their grid and space interface more than a list interface to navigate.

Studies have shown the benefits of working with *argument maps*, as the critical thinking ability of students increases significantly [3] and also their recall of arguments [4–6]. The idea of structuring argument for analysis and transparency is rather old, e.g., the model of Toulmin [7] for argument analysis or IBIS [8] for tackling wicked problems. The concept of hyperedges is also addressed by Toulmin and SIBYL [9], yet never fully investigated from a users perspective. Also, more modern implementations without hyperedges exist such as Debate-Graph, which was actively used by The Independent newspaper and the White House[1]. Cosley et al. [10] find that oversight increased both the quantity and quality of contributions while reducing antisocial behavior, another benefit of argument maps.

Van Gelder argues, that software like *Rationale* is more useful for argument mapping than word processors, simply, because it was explicitly designed for that task and complements strengths and weaknesses of cognitive capabilities [11]. This strengthens the argument by Davies [5], who argues that argument mapping leads to higher information retention.

---

[1] https://www.whitehouse.gov/blog/2009/06/05/open-government-brainstorm-collaboration-action.

Fu et al. compare the *usability of indented tree and graph visualizations* of ontologies. They find that tree visualization is more approachable and familiar for novice users. Other subjects reported the graph visualization to be more tractable and intuitive, because of less visual redundancy, especially for ontologies with multiple inheritance [12]. Additionally, Fu et al. study the usability with eye-tracking and find that indented lists are more efficient at supporting information searches while graphs are more efficient at supporting information processing [13].

Google Wave was an approach to address the problems that arose with email communication [14]. It models conversations as *living documents*, where users reply inline and can change their written content at any time, similar to the ideas proposed by Sumner & Shum [15].

3   New Requirements

We think that a tool to actually scale online discussions in the number of participants is needed for project teams and democracy. Our idea to create such a tool is twofold.

(1) Create a data model which is able to model human communication in a manner that is as useful as possible. At the same time, this model should reflect the mental model of participants. Users should be able to intuitively express themselves regarding other people's contributions. Content should consist of atomic pieces of information to allow precise referencing.
(2) Create a protocol for participants to develop and improve the current state of discussion as a living document [16]. This includes removing outdated and unnecessary content collaboratively. This is the opposite of traditional discussion protocols, where contributions can only be appended to existing, immutable content.

Our conjecture is that the combination of an expressive data model with a collaborative moderation system allows to break out of the classic model of online communication and therefore scale better in the number of participants. In such a system a new kind of interaction could emerge, where participants collaboratively develop the current state of discussion instead of just lining up pieces of text. This current state could be easily determined by readers as well as new participants to enable immediate contribution.

3.1   Our Contribution

In this work we address the first question of finding a suitable data structure which approximates the expressiveness of human communication as closely as possible, while still being usable for its participants.

We propose an unconstrained hypergraph-based discussion model and a user interface to modify and interact with the discussion. Our proposed model is not completely new, but cherrypicks concepts of both argument mapping models and internet forums (e.g. Toulmin, IBIS, reddit, etc.). In an initial mechanical turk study, we asked participants where they would connect an argument to an existing discussion (see Fig. 2). To verify the results and investigate the impact of our interface, we replicated the study in the lab. Prior user studies were used to fix major usability issues, allowing us to improve our system and focus the evaluation on our model. From the questionnaire based Mechanical turk (mturk) study, we can measure the intuitiveness of the hypergraph model itself. The lab study allows to reason about the acceptance of hyperedges while actively using the prototype implementation. However, this paper does not evaluate scalability, it merely looks into comprehension of a new connection type.

4   Generalizing Discussion Topologies

When a discussion participant cannot explicitly express his intention within a discussion model, the semantics and relation to other contributions can only be described in the unstructured text field. If more text creates higher cognitive load, the barrier to read and contribute will thereby be raised.

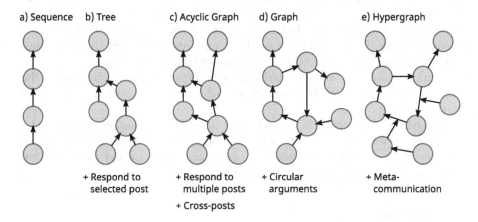

Fig. 1. A sequence (a) of posts corresponds to a protocol of spoken language and has no semantic structure. A tree (b) models a *responds-to*-relation to one parent post, a directed acyclic graph (c) to multiple parents and posts of other threads. A graph with cycles (d) allows to model circular arguments, while a hypergraph (e) allows to model meta-communication.

Typical online conversations are modeled as sequences of posts sorted by creation time (chats, threaded forums, see Fig. 1a). Such a protocol has no semantic structure. Referring to a specific post can only be achieved by quoting, thus inducing redundancy.

Tree based models, such as reddit, make use of a *responds-to*-relation between posts (Fig. 1b), which eliminates the need to repeat content. Still, the tree model forces users to post the argument twice if it applies to two different positions, which creates redundancy.

The tree topology can be generalized as a directed acyclic graph (DAG), allowing redundancy-free posts responding to multiple posts within and across separate discussions (Fig. 1c). E.g., the idea of driving by bike might be an answer to two different questions. Directed graphs with cycles can additionally model *circular arguments* or feedback-loops (Fig. 1d).

Hypergraphs[2] can model a relation between an arbitrary number of posts. This allows to model *meta-communication* by responding to a connection between two posts, which models the act of communication (Fig. 1e). Technically, meta-communication does not require hypergraphs, but using our type of model, which links meta-communication to its referent, simplifies deixis, and thus reduces redundancy from quoting, which is typically used in meta-communication.

4.1   Proposed Discussion Model

To allow users to precisely express their intention and to avoid redundancy in discussions, we propose a hypergraph-based discussion model. Here, posts are the vertices of the graph, which consist of a mandatory title and an optional (more detailed) description. The title is used to visualize many posts in a limited amount of space. This should also motivate participants to split their contribution into separate units with distinct meaning, which increases interactivity [17]. Posts can be connected with directed edges in a *responds-to* semantic. We use the properties of hypergraphs to model cross-posts, circular arguments, and meta-communication.

Depending on context, the correct entry point to a discussion-graph may be ambiguous. Therefore, we use tags to label entry-points. A tag defines a topic and accumulates relevant conversations introducing the concept of abstraction to deal with the complexity of big discussions.

5   Method

In order to understand whether users would use a protocol and model proposed by us, we decided to conduct a two-part study. We first start with a mechanical turk study investigating how users would connect a meta-communication argument to a graph-based visualization ($n = 200$). We then let users use our prototypical implementation and ask the same question about where to connect a meta-communication argument in a graph-based visualization ($n = 51$).

---

[2] A hypergraph consists of a set of vertices and a set of hyperedges. A hyperedge, in contrast to a normal edge, can connect an arbitrary number of vertices. Hypergraphs can be generalized by additionally allowing edges to point at other edges—instead of only nodes. We refer to hypergraphs, even though—in a strict mathematical sense—we are talking about generalized hypergraphs.

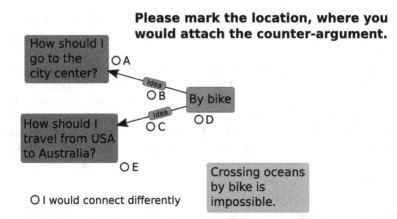

Fig. 2. Task description and six possible answers. By clicking an option the inserted edge was visualized.

5.1 Mechanical Turk Study

The mturk study was designed to capture the opinion of non-informed users. The survey was designed to be as short as possible. We asked for the users' age, gender, graph theory knowledge (GTK) and hypergraph theory knowledge (HGTK). The compensation for the worker was set to 0.06$. The compensation was chosen to ensure an hourly rate of approx. 8.50$. GTK and HGTK were measured by asking the familiarity of graph theory concepts on a six-point Likert Scale (1=very unfamiliar, 6=very familiar).

The main task in the mturk study was for users to attach the (meta-communication) argument "Crossing oceans by bike is impossible" to the argument graph shown in Fig. 2. According to our protocol the correct choice would be option C. Thus the experiment aims to measure how users intuitively attach an argument that does not addresses an idea directly (i.e. a bike is a valuable method of transportation), but its relation to a specific question (i.e. a bike is not a valuable method for crossing an ocean, as suggested in the graph).

5.2 Lab Study

To evaluate the discussion model and the corresponding user interface, we built an interactive website for our prototypical discussion platform. The prototype is based on the concepts described in the previous section. It supports multi-user realtime collaborative editing of discussions in a graph-based visualization.

The prototype was built using Scala [18], the graph database neo4j with renesca [19], AngularJS and D3 [20]. The implementation was iteratively improved in two iterations with nine users to ensure that usability was no major hindrance in the actual experiment.

The goal of the lab study was to see whether using a graph-based discussion system would affect how users would attach a meta-communication argument in a later task.

We recruited 51 users from the authors' social networks and invited them to a lab study. Users were asked the same demographic questions as in the mturk study (age, gender, GTK, HGTK). After completing some tasks in the graph-based discussion system, we asked the users the same meta-communication question: "Where would you attach the following argument?". Furthermore, we assessed usability of the prototype using the System Usability Scale (SUS).

6 Results

We report data as descriptive statistics and 95% confidence intervals when comparing between subjects. We use χ^2-tests to measure effects of categorial variables.

6.1 Mechanical Turk Study

From the mechanical turk study we see that the largest part of the sample wants to map the argument as a hyperedge (C, $n = 59$). The second largest group ($n = 55$) attaches the argument to the question (E). Attaching the argument to the answer and other options were chosen similarly often (see Fig. 3).

When looking at the cats eyes plots of the measured demographic factors (see Fig. 4), we see that no differences in the demographics are evident between any of the chosen connections. Gender showed an effect on choice ($\chi^2(5) = 11.492, p < .05$). Men chose the hyperedge more frequently than women (44% and 20% respectively).

The relative high ratings of GTK and HGTK for the "other" option might be caused by non-serious "click-through" users. We tried removing nonsensical data (e.g. response times too short), but not all could be removed.

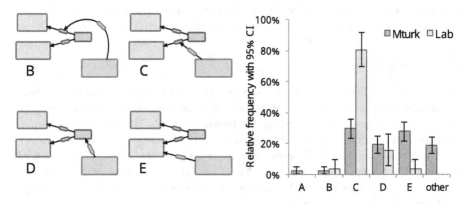

Fig. 3. Relative frequencies of participants that selected a specific connection for the mturk and lab study. Option A was omitted, see Fig. 2.

In order to ensure that the actual visual representation in the main task did not influence the answer (e.g. shortest mouse-paths, etc.) we switched option A and E (and B, C respectively) for 50% of the participants. No significant differences (χ^2-Test) between answers in both groups were found ($p > .05$).

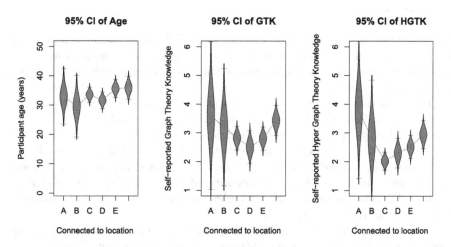

Fig. 4. Demographics for the different connections. 95% CI of means for age, graph theory knowledge and hypergraph theory knowledge. The sixth plot refers to the "other" location.

6.2 Lab Study

Looking at different answer types, we see basically six different representations. Most users attached the response only as a hyperedge (C, $n = 26$), as intended. Some included the idea (C & D, $n = 7$), some the question (C & E, $n = 5$), while two users connected all three positions (C, D, E). Then again, eight who only marked the idea (D) obviously did not use something similar to a hyperedge. Two users marked the wrong hyperedge (B, see also Fig. 3).

From this we can argue that two stances exist. Forty-one users correctly want to address the hyperedge, while eight want to address the node. When comparing user diversity of these two stances, we could not find differences for age ($CI[-8.1; 9.841]$), gender ($p = .181$), system usability ($CI[-8.1; 10.18]$) or graph-theory knowledge (edges $CI[-2.27; 0.48]$ or hyperedges $CI[-1.68; 0.38]$).

The usability of our prototype was rated as above average [21] ($SUS = 76$, $SD = 12$), indicating good usability. Gender was equally distributed in both studies and no gender effect on the SUS scale was found (unequal variances $F = 2.179$, $t(20.294) = .778$, $p = .446$, CI of differences $[-5.96; 13.1]$[3]). Since we

---

[3] Confidence intervals of differences that contain 0, can be seen as non-significant differences, but provide more information then simply reporting significance testing results.

have no further data on gender and other variables, as well as the absence of this effect in the lab study, we assume the effect to be a methodological artifact, for which our data provides no satisfactory explanation. Further research is required.

7   Discussion

Our results show that a large part of users are able to conceptualize and understand meta-communication modeled by hyperedges. Furthermore, when using an argument-mapping system the proportion of people intuitively using a hyperedge increases to 80%.

The main difference between Mturk and the lab study was the prior exposure to our software-prototype. Mturk participants should not use our system, to establish a large sample baseline. The lab study participants could use our system. The difference in percentages is interpreted as caused by the hypergraph-based interface of our system. The Mturk study merely serves as a baseline-measure for using hyperedges without the software-prototype context. No user-diversity factors influenced understanding or the usability evaluation significantly in the lab study.

We conclude from these findings, that using hyperedges in an argument mapping system may indeed be used, without confusing a majority of users.

7.1   Future Work

Large discussions often require a higher level of *abstraction* to express complex arguments besides using tags. This may happen, e.g. when a sub-discussion should be separate but contained in another post. Here, we propose using nested hypergraphs as a possible solution and want to investigate their comprehensibility. A concrete solution could be to merge the concepts of posts and tags to construct overlapping abstraction hierarchies.

As it is hard to investigate the effect of a graph-based argument mapping system on communication without conducting actual arguments, real world tests will need to be carried out next. We want to compare the effect of using our prototype in discussions in the e-learning system of seminars. Two similar seminars will use two different systems (graph-based argument mapping vs. regular message board) and report on usability and expressiveness in their evaluation. This allows to investigate differences between the discussions resulting from the two different protocols.

Before scalability can be evaluated within our approach, challenges are twofold: new methods for visualizing and navigating large graphs must be developed and large discussions must be investigated within our model.

Acknowledgments. The authors thank the German Research Council DFG for the friendly support of the research in the excellence cluster "Integrative Production Technology in High Wage Countries". Thank you to Lena Oden for helping with the mechanical turk setup. Special thanks to all participants.

References

1. Hilbert, M.: The maturing concept of e-democracy: from E-voting and online consultations to democratic value out of jumbled online chatter. J. Inf. Technol. Polit. **6**(2), 87–110 (2009)
2. Faridani, S., Bitton, E., Ryokai, K., Goldberg, K.: Opinion space: a scalable tool for browsing online comments. In: Proceedings of the SIGCHI Conference on Human Factors in Computing Systems, pp. 1175–1184. ACM (2010)
3. Kunsch, D.W., Schnarr, K., van Tyle, R.: The use of argument mapping to enhance critical thinking skills in business education. J. Educ. Bus. **89**(8), 403–410 (2014)
4. Dwyer, C.P., Hogan, M.J., Stewart, I.: The evaluation of argument mapping as a learning tool: comparing the effects of map reading versus text reading on comprehension and recall of arguments. Think. Skills Creat. **5**(1), 16–22 (2010)
5. Davies, M.: Concept mapping, mind mapping and argument mapping: what are the differences and do they matter? High. Educ. **62**(3), 279–301 (2011)
6. Shum, S.B., De Liddo, A., Klein, M.: DCLA meet CIDA: collective intelligence deliberation analytics. In: 2nd International Workshop on Discourse-Centric Learning Analytics, LAK14: 4th International Conference on Learning Analytics & Knowledge (2014)
7. Toulmin, S.E.: The Uses of Argument. Cambridge University Press, Cambridge (1958)
8. Kunz, W., Rittel, H.W.: Issues as Elements of Information Systems, vol. 131. Institute of Urban and Regional Development, University of California Berkeley, California (1970)
9. Lee, J.: SIBYL: a tool for managing group design rationale. In: Proceedings of the 1990 ACM Conference on Computer-Supported Cooperative Work, pp. 79–92. ACM (1990)
10. Cosley, D., Frankowski, D., Terveen, L., Riedl, J.: Using intelligent task routing and contribution review to help communities build artifacts of lasting value. In: Proceedings of the SIGCHI Conference on Human Factors in Computing Systems, pp. 1037–1046. ACM (2006)
11. Van Gelder, T.: The rationale for rationale. Law Probab. Risk **6**(1–4), 23–42 (2007)
12. Fu, B., Noy, N.F., Storey, M.-A.: Indented tree or graph? a usability study of ontology visualization techniques in the context of class mapping evaluation. In: Alani, H., et al. (eds.) ISWC 2013. LNCS, vol. 8218, pp. 117–134. Springer, Heidelberg (2013). doi:10.1007/978-3-642-41335-3_8
13. Fu, B., Noy, N.F., Storey, M.A.: Eye tracking the user experience-an evaluation of ontology visualization techniques. Semantic Web (Preprint), pp. 1–19 (2015)
14. Trapani, G., Pash, A.: The Complete Guide to Google Wave. 3ones Inc., San Diego (2010)
15. Sumner, T., Shum, S.B.: From documents to discourse: shifting conceptions of scholarly publishing. In: Proceedings of the SIGCHI conference on Human factors in computing systems, pp. 95–102. ACM Press/Addison-Wesley Publishing Co. (1998)
16. Garcia-Castro, A., Labarga, A., Garcia, L., Giraldo, O., Montana, C., Bateman, J.A.: Semantic web and social web heading towards living documents in the life sciences. Web Semant.: Sci. Serv. Agents World Wide Web **8**(2), 155–162 (2010)
17. Whittaker, S., Terveen, L., Hill, W., Cherny, L.: The dynamics of mass interaction. In: Lueg, C., Fisher, D. (eds.) From Usenet to CoWebs, pp. 79–91. Springer, London (2003)

18. Odersky, M., Altherr, P., Cremet, V., Emir, B., Maneth, S., Micheloud, S., Mihaylov, N., Schinz, M., Stenman, E., Zenger, M.: An overview of the scala programming language. Technical report (2004)
19. Dietze, F., Karoff, J., Calero Valdez, A., Ziefle, M., Greven, C., Schroeder, U.: An open-source object-graph-mapping framework for Neo4j and scala: renesca. In: Buccafurri, F., Holzinger, A., Kieseberg, P., Tjoa, A.M., Weippl, E. (eds.) CD-ARES 2016. LNCS, vol. 9817, pp. 204–218. Springer, Cham (2016). doi:10. 1007/978-3-319-45507-5_14
20. Bostock, M., Ogievetsky, V., Heer, J.: D^3 data-driven documents. IEEE Trans. Visual. Comput. Graph. **17**(12), 2301–2309 (2011)
21. Sauro, J.: Sustisfied? little-known system usability scale facts. UX Mag. **10**(3), 2011–2013 (2011)

FlowChart Tool for Decision Making
in Interdisciplinary Research Cooperation

Ulrich Jansen[1(✉)] and Wolfgang Schulz[1,2]

[1] Nonlinear Dynamics of Laser Processing,
RWTH Aachen University, Aachen, Germany
ulrich.jansen@nld.rwth-aachen.de
[2] Fraunhofer Institute for Laser Technology, Aachen, Germany

Abstract. A common understanding of the state of a research project is vital for project planning and decision making in interdisciplinary research cooperation. Surveys in a production technology based environment shows, that project planning and decision support tools exist and are known, however they are not used in practice. Interviews indicate that the poor usage of such tools originate from the complexity of the tools and that there is no perceptible added value for the performing researcher in using these tools. A requirements analysis is performed to extract the non-functional and functional requirements of a web-based project planning tool, which is developed and tested in an interdisciplinary research cooperation, called the Cluster of Excellence for production research at the RWTH Aachen University. User interviews show that the acceptance of such tools is strongly related to the presence of all features that are considered vital by the user for project planning and decision support.

Keywords: Project management · Information Systems · Web application

1 Introduction

In larger research collaborations, scientists from many disciplines are involved in research planning and project realization. In the occurrence of decision points during any project phase, it is vital to provide the essential amount of information on the state of the project to all related participants. To visualize the current state of the project, an intuitively understandable representation of research processes in interdisciplinary research cooperation is implemented as a web-based research planning and representation tool. The so called *FlowChart* tool is developed, implemented and tested inside a large research collaboration, the Cluster of Excellence (CoE) for production research at the RWTH Aachen University [1] which consists of more than 150 researchers from various departments and disciplines situated in the broad field of production technology. The *FlowChart* tool displays the initial state, the objectives, the current state and the interlinking of the work packages in one single view. The aim of this tool is to provide a basis for decision making during project meetings and to support the planning process during the whole project. The usability, acceptance and added value to the project is object of current research.

© Springer International Publishing AG 2017
V.G. Duffy (Ed.): DHM 2017, Part II, LNCS 10287, pp. 259–269, 2017.
DOI: 10.1007/978-3-319-58466-9_24

2 Problem Definition

Scientific research projects in interdisciplinary research collaborations bring multiple partners from different scientific disciplines and scientific cultural background together. During project initialization, planning, realization and finalization a clear communication and common understanding about scientific objectives and the allocation of work in the project is vital for project success. Decision points play an important role during the project realization where different options have to be evaluated and the best possible option to realize the project objectives has to be chosen. This usually requires a modification of the project plan by adding or removing work packages. Also the reordering of work packages or adjustment of work package durations might become necessary during the project. This process of modifying the project plan reflects the iterative trial and error approach of scientific research and is typical for collaborative research projects. These readjustments in the project plan usually occur during project meetings, when multiple partners from multiple institutions are present and discuss the progress of the project. Not all partners have the same knowledge about project details and the progress inside the individual work packages, therefor it is necessary to provide an as simple as possible pictorial representation of the project state to offer all project partners the best possible decision support to find the best possible solution to achieve the project objectives.

Project planning tools of different complexity exist, however the acceptance of existing tools in the investigated scientific community suffers from the lack of flexibility. A strong disadvantage of the tools examined is that the added value of the effort to use these tools does not become noticeable to the research assistants that carry out the work inside the project. The essential character of scientific working, fast iterations, systematic trial and error and rapid adjustments, is not represented by tools currently on the market.

3 State of the Art

Tools to generate project plans and extend all elements of a project by additional information exist. The effectiveness of such tools on project or even multi-project management is analyzed by Jaafri and Manivong [2], who introduces the term Smart Project Management Information Systems (smart PMIS). As essential requirements of SPMISs Jaafri invokes (1) management and real time adjustment of all important data belonging to an individual project (2) integration of all information along the project life cycle to provide decision support at any phase of the project (3) processing, reporting, alerts and measurement of the impact of decisions (4) proactivity facilitation by objective functions like total life cycle cost and (5) inter-operability and compatibility to existing systems and to provide all partners of the project team with the necessary amount of information. Jaafari's paper includes 25 functions of an idealized PMIS. Raymond and Bergeron [3] studies the influence of PMISs on project leaders and project success according to a success model including five components: (1) quality of the system (2) quality of the results provided by the system (3) usability and acceptance (4) impact on individual success and (5) impact on project success.

Raymond carries out a quantitative analysis by questionnaires and draws the conclusion, that PMISs contribute significantly to project success.

Ngai and Chan [4] posts five essential requirements for Knowledge Management Systems (KMS): (1) web-based system to provide easy access via a web browser (2) scalability to manage thousands of users (3) access control and security of the system (4) customizability of the user interface (5) integration into the current working environment. Ngai also provides guidelines for the evaluation of KMSs using the Analytic Hierarchy Process method, which is based on pairwise comparisons between distinct tools.

Marques et al. [5] provides a metric for fine grained performance measurement based on (1) key performance indicators (2) effectiveness, efficiency and relevance and (3) tasks. The resulting performance cube is intended to provide dedicated decision support for project managers. Caniëls and Bakens [6] detects a spillover effect in multi-project PMISs, if the system offers poor information quality. Project managers tend to assume poor information quality by the whole system, if poor information quality was provided for single projects. Therefor it is of major importance that PMISs offer good quality information to become an accepted tool for decision support. Tromp [7] analyzed the implementation phase of a PMIS using the complex responsive process approach and concluded that the success and acceptance of a PMIS highly depends on the quality of information that can be retrieved from the system.

4 Methodology

Interview studies show, that the principal reasons for missing acceptance of the existing tools refer to poor usability for untrained users and the missing ability of these tools to adapt and track changes within the project. To provide a proper project planning and decision making tool for research projects and to analyze the essential objectives usability, acceptance and added value, a completely new tool is implemented and tested in the Cluster of Excellence. A requirements analysis carried out by expert interviews revealed three essential needs of such a tool: view of the current project state on a single screen, an easy and intuitively usable interface and the ability to rapidly change the planning of a project and keep track of these changes. Focusing on the usability and the acceptance aspect, additional requirements include seamless integration into existing work flows and compatibility to commonly used tools, little or even zero learning effort and easy access to the tool itself.

4.1 Requirements Analysis

During a scientific colloquium of the Cluster of Excellence a World Café survey [8] was performed to collect keywords about knowledge management tools in scientific environments. Around 80 active researchers took part in this colloquium and during coffee breaks, they were asked to write down small notes regarding three questions: (1) Which tools and methods are being used at your institution for your internal knowledge management? (2) Which tools and concepts you can imagine to enhance the knowledge management inside the Cluster of Excellence? (3) Which requirements a web-based scientific cooperation platform should meet? The answers for question 1 are grouped into four classes:

- Software solutions: Wiki, Jammar, Citavi, internal web pages, version control systems
- Documentation: QM-documents, handbooks, publication collections
- Social: Conversations, regular know-how transfer meetings, regulars' table, after work beer
- Other: Work instructions, international conference visits

The following concepts for knowledge-management inside the cluster were written down: Know-how transfer meetings, chat programs, journal-club, regular knowledge exchange meetings, StackExchange (as example).

As requirements for a web-based scientific cooperation portal these notes were indicated: single-sign on, "that it makes me smarter", RSS-feeds, email notifications, easy to use, modification of files online without downloading them, WebDAV file space.

Using these keywords as a starting point for a requirements analysis on knowledge management and knowledge transfer systems, expert interviews were planned and conducted in the institution of the author.

4.2 Expert Interviews

The interview session was divided into three parts: (1) Which type of project planning do you perform today? (2) Which demands do you have for an ideal project planning tool? (3) What are the reasons, that project planning tools are not well established in scientific environments?

The interviewed subjects were research assistants, senior scientists and the leading professor of the modeling and simulation group at Fraunhofer institute for laser technology. The first question block also included a description of typical research projects. Three typical scenarios were identified:

1. Individual project performed by one individual scientist. Typically these type project is publicly funded and proposed, planned, performed and reported by one single scientist with supervision of his/her professor. These type of project usually requires little planning effort during project realization since only one person is involved and a clear research plan has been formulated in the proposal.
2. Bilateral projects including two project partners from two different institutions. This type of project is either publicly funded or university/industry co-operation, funded by the industrial partner. Especially for the latter case there is a strong need for proper project planning as industry partners often demand clear project planning and monitoring during the realization as these partners have to justify the use of funds to their administration. Bilateral projects including industry partners often have short project durations in the order of several months. In an ideal case there are multiple consecutive projects between two research partners, which depict the rapid development cycles in industrial environments.

3. Multi-lateral projects in larger research collaborations, usually publicly funded including partners from university and sometimes also from industry. These projects are usually split into multiple sub-projects, so that the number of partners involved in a specific research project is comparable to a bilateral project. A major difference to industry funded projects is the project duration which is often split into multiple phases, typically in the order of several years.

As tools known for project management there were only three different types: Microsoft Project, Excel (GANTT-charts) and the written project plan in the corresponding research proposal. Another pictorial representation of a research plan was performed in Microsoft PowerPoint and is depicted in Fig. 1. The latter representation was the most used one in the inspected research group and provided the base for the developed *FlowChart* tool.

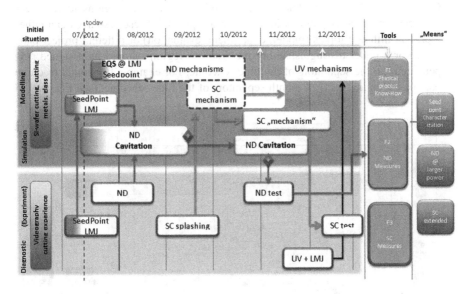

Fig. 1. Example of an initial version of a research plan used in the analyzed research group. The plan is generated using Microsoft PowerPoint.

As demands for an ideal project planning tool in scientific research environments the following non-functional requirements were summarized from the interviews: decentralized and easy access including per project permissions, no additional software requirements, intuitive and easy to learn user interface, easy updateable project plans "modifications in less than a minute, including access to the tool itself", agile project planning during project meetings, tracking of changes during project realization and compatibility to tools currently used. These non-functional requirements were translated into functional requirements in the form of Volere SnowCards [9]. The essential requirements are:

1. Client/server architecture using a web-frontend: to meet the easy and decentralized access and the use of available software requirement, the only remaining option is to create the tool as a web application.
2. Single project view: the tool should provide a view of the project state on a single screen without the need to scroll, zoom or hide elements from the project plan.
3. Initial situation: the project view should provide a dedicated areal to depict the starting point of a project. This is important to demonstrate project partners the state and value of preliminary works before the project starts.
4. Objectives: the project view should provide a dedicated region for project objectives. The representation of project objectives should ensure that all steps during project planning are focused to the project objectives.
5. Time schedule: initial situation and project objectives should be connected by a time schedule on which work package boxes can be allocated.
6. Grouping: The time schedule should include one or more regions to represent different resources or partners involved in the project. These resources can either represent different topics (model, experiment, evaluation) or different project partners. For a better distinguishability the resource regions should be assigned perpendicular to the separators of the time schedule. For example horizontal resource bars placed below vertical month separators of the time schedule. (see Fig. 2)

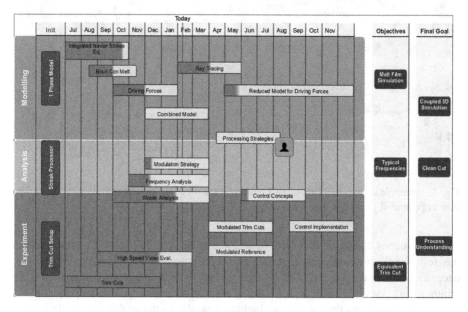

Fig. 2. View of the new developed *FlowChart* tool

7. Work packages: individual work packages should be placed on the time schedule. The left and right edges of a work package indicate start and end date, the vertical position in the time-schedule displays the association to an individual resource. Using gradient filling, the fulfillment level of a work package can be represented.

8. Dependencies: relationships between work packages should be indicated by arrows. The direction of the arrow expresses a dependency between the work packages and the system should be aware of this dependency, so alerts can be implemented if there is a risk detected, that certain dependencies cannot be met.
9. Resource allocation: resources like researchers or machines should be assignable to individual work packages. If resources are multiply assigned in different projects, the system should post an alert.
10. Points of interest: important events inside the project like milestone meetings or decision points have to be clearly indicated in the project plan.
11. Change tracking: all changes undertaken in the project plan should be tracked and browsable for the user. An element-wise undo function should exist and a snapshot-functionality to create revisions should exist.
12. Comments: all elements should include optional comments fields, where every user can post comments for this element.

Taking these requirements into account a class and database design of the *Flow-Chart* tool has been carried out and the tool was implemented as web application.

4.3   Implementation Cycles

As the *FlowChart* tool should depict the agile character of project planning in a research project, an agile implementation approach was chosen. After the realization of essential features, the tools was rolled out for beta-testing and small usage studies aimed at the latest implemented feature were conducted. The results of these studies were directly used for bug fixing and enhancement of the tool. As soon as the results were satisfying, the next feature was implemented, chosen by the result of the question which feature is missed the most. One important finding from these implementation cycles is, that an already working tool is not used by the researchers as long as they do not experience a clear advantage of the planning tool for their daily work.

4.4   Usability Studies

The usability studied of the tool are carried out as expert interviews at the end of the implementation cycles qualitatively. As the tool has not reached its full functionality today, the acceptance of the tool is not that high, that an elaborated usage study incorporating a larger test group can be performed. As the participation on the test phase of the tool is on a voluntary base, the user has to experience a direct advantage on the use of the tool. The expectation is, that as soon as the tool provides good planning capabilities for research projects, the users will accept it and are willing to take part in a survey. Therefor the acceptance and usability of the tool is analyzed by short interviews with a small number of subjects to gain direct feedback on the capabilities of the tool. These interviews are split into three parts: (1) Solution of specific tasks like create a new flow-chart or create new work packages (2) questions about the performance of the task (3) general questions about the tool and its ability to provide support in project planning and decision making. The last part also includes a question about the feature that should be implemented next.

5   Results

The substantial result of the initial survey is, that tools for project planning exist and are known to the users. However they are not used in scientific environments because they do not offer a perceptible added value for the researcher. To cope with the agile character of iterative trial and error cycles in scientific projects a new tool has been implemented to support project planning and decision making.

5.1   The *FlowChart* Tool

To meet the requirements gathered by the requirements analysis, the *FlowChart* tool is implemented as a web based application which is integrated into the scientific corporation portal [10] of the Cluster of Excellence. Its client-server approach allows the decentralized view and modification of research plans interactively. To track user actions and update all connected clients, modern web techniques like Asynchronous Javascript and XML (AJAX) and web sockets are used to ensure that all users share the same view. All user actions are recorded in a central database as individual changelets and sent to all connected clients. Due to this changelet approach, the change history of every *FlowChart* item can be tracked and inspected by every user who has access to the corresponding project.

Details of Implementation. Ruby on Rails version 5 [11] is used as web application development framework. It is designed for agile web development using a strict model-view-control pattern to separate back-end and front-end parts of the implementation. The front-end view makes heavy use of bootstrap [11] design elements for menus and dialogs. The *FlowChart* view itself is utilized as a scalable vector graphics (SVG) which is modified via JavaScript. To manage the interactions between the SVG flow-chart elements, the Data Driven Documents JavaScript library D3js is used. The d3 library provides an easy to use interface to create callback functions for almost any user interaction on any of the SVG elements visible for the user. User actions that need to be transferred to the server are sent with the Asynchronous JavaScript and XML technique. These browser built-in objects provide callback functions that can handle the answer of the server, so that error or success messages can be generated. Since the *FlowChart* tool is a web based application, a concurrent access of one single flow-chart may occur, if two users open the same project at a time and modify the content of one of the elements inside. To prevent outdated information in the view of one of the users, changes performed by any user connected to a specific flow-chart have to be transmitted to all users, who have an active view of this flow-chart. Therefor a return-channel from the server to the browser is required. Basically there exist four different approaches to provide such a return-channel: short polling, long polling, server-sent events and web-sockets. For reasons of performance and complexity of the implementation, the polling approaches have been dismissed. An early implementation using server-sent events (SSE) worked as intended. However modern virus scanning software including a download protection feature interpret the SSE channel as a never-ending download and therefor do not hand over retrieved data packages directly to the front-end. This fact makes SSEs unsuitable for real-time updates of changes performed by a single user, if such a download protection is activated. Because of this, the only remaining technique for the return channel is web-sockets. Thankfully the latest version of the Ruby on Rails frame-work provides an easy to use mechanism for web-sockets, called action cables. These incorporate easy-to-use real-time features into the corresponding application and are supported by all modern browsers, virus scanners, proxy servers and web servers.

Change Tracking. An essential feature of an agile project management system is the ability to perform changes on project tasks in an easy manner and track these changes along the whole project duration. The *FlowChart* tool allows the modification of project tasks or other elements by direct user interaction. Each element inside the flow-chart view carries various properties (e.g. start date, end date, fulfillment level, y-position) which are initialized upon creation of the object. By modifying the object, for example drag the right edge of a project task box to another end date, specific properties of the object are changed. The collection of changed properties by one individual change action is called *ChangeLet* and is assigned to the corresponding flow-chart element. As an example the motion of a project task inside the flow-chart view will change up to three properties: start-date, end-date and y-position. The new values of these properties are stored along with the user-id of the logged-in user, the date and time of the change action and a boolean flag if this ChangeLet is applied or not. This allows an element-wise undo action and also an element-wise history of changes. By storing the ids of not applied ChangeLets and the id of the latest ChangeLet a revision feature for flow-charts can be easily implemented. These revisions allow users to save and restore states of flow-charts.

5.2   Missing Features

According to the initial requirements analysis, there are still features that are missing for a complete version of the tool. Interviews indicate that the acceptance of the tool would rise instantly, if these features were implemented. Users even accept unintuitive work flows or a handling of the tool that is considered complicated, as long as all required features are supported. Any missing feature that is considered vital by the user eliminates the acceptance of the tool and the willingness of the user to use this tool in practice. For the current version of the FlowChart tool the missing features which are considered vital are:

- Arrows: users which are familiar with Microsoft PowerPoint expect an arrow-tool feature, which connects boxes by placing the arrow start and end nodes on the frame of the boxes.
- Free-form boxes and texts: beyond the strict set of elements provided by the *FlowChart* tool, users expect the capability of the tool to provide free elements like boxes and texts that can be placed anywhere inside the flow-chart view to add customized highlights.
- PowerPoint export: as the flow-chart view itself is provided as SVG graphics, an export as SVG or PDF is available. An export as PNG picture is also possible, however users expect a PowerPoint export which allows modification of the individual elements inside the flow-chart in PowerPoint slides.

Especially the last expectation posed by the users is critical. The intention of the user is to include the current state of the project into slides for a project report or a project meeting. This expectation is understandable, however it breaks the idea of a centralized project planning and decision tool to cut off the capability of direct user interaction and agile project planning during project meetings. As the tool relies on the acceptance of the user to be used in practice, this feature will be added in future versions of the *FlowChart* tool, however there will be no import feature for project plans changed in PowerPoint slides.

Other features that were collected in the requirements analysis are considered as important by the users, but not vital for the acceptance of the tool and indicated as "nice-to-haves". These include resource allocation to work packages and conflict detection mechanisms inside one project and across multiple projects, to check if resources are over-allocated.

6   Conclusion and Outlook

The tool supports communication behavior between project partners and tightens cooperation activities identifying the fast and frugal research path towards the objectives or even adapting the objectives itself. In particular, the planning process be-comes flexible enough to follow the propositions during repetitive project meetings.

A first working version of the implemented *FlowChart* tool is installed as web-app on the collaboration portal of the Cluster of Excellence and tested by users of the portal. In the initial state, usability and acceptance aspects are key issue in current research. The much harder measureable aspect of added value to the project is investigated qualitatively by expert interviews. Generating quantitative measures for this aspect will be part of future research. The main finding in rolling out a tool for project planning and decision making in scientific environments is, that as long as any feature that is considered vital by the user, the acceptance of the tool is nonexistent.

7   Limitations

The findings presented in this paper were obtained by qualitative expert interviews in a production technology based environment. The tool developed here is tailored for close university/university or university/industry collaboration depicting short project cycles with the demand for agile project planning. To gain quantitative results, elaborated usability studies including questionnaires have to be performed on a larger test group. This type of study will be performed, when qualitative interviews indicate a final state of the software and the missing features declared in this paper are implemented.

Acknowledgement. The authors would like to thank the German Research Foundation (DFG) for its support within the Cluster of Excellence "Integrative Production Technology for High-Wage Countries" at RWTH Aachen University.

References

1. Brecher, C., et al.: Integrative Production Technology for High-Wage Countries. Springer, Heidelberg (2012)
2. Jaafari, A., Manivong, K.: Towards a smart project management information system. Int. J. Project Manag. **16**(4), 249–265 (1998)
3. Raymond, L., Bergeron, F.: Project management information systems: an emperical study of their impact on project managers and project success. Int. J. Project Manag. **26**, 213–220 (2008)
4. Ngai, E.W.T., Chan, E.W.C.: Evaluation of knowledge management tools using AHP. Expert Syst. Appl. **29**, 889–899 (2005)
5. Marques, G., Gourc, D., Lauras, M.: Multi-criteria performance analysis for decision making in project management. Int. J. Project Manag. **29**, 1057–1069 (2010)
6. Caniëls, M.C.J., Bakens, R.J.J.M.: The effects of Project Information Systems in decision making in a multi project environment. Int. J. Project Manag. **30**, 162–175 (2012)
7. Tromp, J.W., Homan, T.: How unplanned changes emerge while implementing a Project Management Information System (PMIS) in a complex multi project R&D environment. Procedia – Soc. Behav. Sci. **194**, 211–220 (2015)
8. Brown, J., Isaacs, D.: The World Café. Shaping Our Futures Through Conversations That Matter. McGraw-Hill Professional, New York (2005). ISBN 978-1-57675-258-6
9. Robertson, J., Volere, S.: Requirements Specification Template, 15th edn. Atlantic Systems Guild, London (2010)
10. Vaegs, T. et al.: Enhancing scientific cooperation of an interdisciplinary cluster of excellence via a scientific cooperation portal. In: The International Conference on E-Learning in the Workplace ICELW 2014. June 11–13. New York (2014)
11. Ruby, S., Thomas, D., Hansson, D.H.: Agile Web Development with Rails 4. Pragmatic Bookshelf, Dallas (2013). ISBN: 1937785564, 9781937785567
12. Bootstrap framework. https://getbootstrap.com

Using EEG Data Analytics to Measure Meditation

Hong Lin[1](✉) and Yuezhe Li[2]

[1] Department of Computer Science and Engineering Technology,
University of Houston-Downtown, Houston, TX, USA
linh@uhd.edu
[2] Department of Mathematics, Illinois State University, Normal, IL, USA
yli3@ilstu.edu

Abstract. This paper presents the study we have done to detect "meditation" brain state by analyzing electroencephalographic (EEG) data. We firstly discuss what is "meditation" state and some prior studies on meditation. We then discuss how meditation state can be reflected in the subject's brain waves; and what features of the brain waves data can be used in machine learning algorithms to classify meditation state from other states. We studied the suitability of 3 types of entropy: Shannon entropy, approximate entropy, and sample entropy in different circumstances. We found that overall Sample entropy is a good tool to extract information from EEG data. Discretization of EEG data enhances the classification rates by using both the approximate entropy and Shannon entropy.

Keywords: Meditation · Machine learning · Electroencephalogram (EEG) · Entropy · Classification

1 Introduction

Chan, or Dhyāna in Sanskrit, is a school of Mahāyāna Buddhism, which means "meditation". The literal meaning of Chinese character Chan (禅) is transfer of the sovereign power. In Chan Buddhism, Chan means the transfer of Dharma eye, or prajna, which can be roughly interpreted as insightful wisdom. Chan has played an important role in the history of Eastern countries. In modern societies, Chan has also shown direct effects on people's physical and psychological conditions.

Meditation is an essential part of Chan practice, and the primary way to achieve Chan state. Chan requires that the practitioners watch their thoughts at every moment, allowing them to arise and pass away without interference. This methodology, which is termed mindful meditation, is the most effective way to regulate one's mind.

The four Dhyanas (catvari-dhyanani) theory clearly depicts the procedure of meditation in four stages, viz., the first Dhyana through the fourth Dhyana, named below.

1. First Dhyana: Bliss Born of Separation: One's pulse stops, but this doesn't mean one is dead. This brings a particular happiness which is unknown to those in the world.

V.G. Duffy (Ed.): DHM 2017, Part II, LNCS 10287, pp. 270–280, 2017.
DOI: 10.1007/978-3-319-58466-9_25

2. Second Dhyana: Bliss Born of Samadhi (proper concentration and proper reception): One's breathe stops. There is no detectible breathing in and out, but at that time an inner breathing takes over.
3. Third Dhyana: Wonderful Happiness of Being Apart from Bliss: One renounces the *dhyana*-bliss as food and the happiness of the Dharma that occurs in initial samadhi. One goes beyond that kind of happiness and reaches a sense of wonderful joy. It is something that one has never known before, that is inexpressible in its subtlety, and that is inconceivable.
4. Fourth Dhyana: Clear Purity of Casting Away Thought: In the Third Dhyana thoughts were stopped–held at bay–but they still had not been renounced altogether. In the heavens of the Fourth Dhyana, not only are thoughts stopped, they are done away with completely. There basically are no more cognitive considerations. This state is extremely pure, subtly wonderful, and particularly blissful.

(http://www.bhaisajyaguru.com/buddhist-ayurveda-encyclopedia/four_dhyanas_sz-chan_sz-jing-chu_catvari-dhyanani_jhana.htm)

Patriarch Zhi Kai (智凱, AC 523-597), the first patriarch of the Tiantai School, gave the detailed methods of Dharma practice for each Dhyana stage with specific state of mind, the realm of sensory perspectives, possible interaction with spiritual beings, and methods to avoid deviations from the right path.in each stage [1]. His book has been used as guidance for meditation ever since.

While each Dhyana has specific bodily manifestations, four Dhyanas is actually very high achievement level in meditation practice and not so many meditators can achieve the four Dhyana levels. Therefore, in order to develop a physiological model of "meditation" state of common people, we have to use data analytics methods to test one's proficiency level of meditation.

As accomplishments in Chan entail good behaviors and self-control, the effects of meditation may be reflected by mental health indicators, e.g., lust, anger, fear, cautiousness, balance in personality, etc., and these health indicators may be measurable by using psychological indicators, e.g., Functional Assessment of Cancer Therapy—General (FACT-G) [2], which consists of four subscales assessing physical well-being, social well-being, emotional well-being, and functional well-being. Another metric is Profile of Mood State, which measures mood [3]. Mruk & Hartzell, analyzed the therapeutic value of meditation and proposed six Zen (Japanese term of meditation) principles of psychotherapeutic value: acceptance (suffering), fearlessness (courage), truth (enlightenment), compassion (toward self and others), attachment (desire), impermanence (letting go) [4]. In addition, Zen is analyzed against the phenomenology of traditional psychotherapy in the biological approach, the learning theories, the cognitive approach, the psychodynamic perspective, and the humanistic approach.

The presentation of this paper will be as follows. In the second section, we will review how electroencephalogram (EEG) can be used to measure brain states. We will also discuss the feasibility of measuring meditation using EEG data by examining some sample data. In the third section, we will present the experimental results we have obtained. We will give concluding remarks in the end.

2 Brain State Detection Using EEG Data

Since the renowned scientist Galvani discovered electrical activity in living organism in the 18th century [5], EEG has been becoming a popular non-invasive technique to record brain activity in clinical and research settings. Hans Berger is the first electro physiologist who successfully recorded electrical activity from the human brain by measuring voltage oscillations due to ions flow in the neurons of the brain. Nowadays, EEG data have been widely used in various areas including human computer inter-action, neurological sciences, and psychology. Recent development in data analytics aroused interests in brain state detecting by applying machine learning algorithms to EEG data. Using mathematical models and computing technology, scientists tried to decipher the complex relationship between brain activities and brain waves generated during those brain activities.

Brain waves are classified into five major waves, each linked to certain brain activities (Table 1). For example, Beta waves are associated with consciousness, while alpha waves are indicators of disengagement [6]. Theta waves are often shown in motionless but alert state [7], and finally, Delta waves are related to sleeping.

Table 1. Brainwave frequencies

Brainwave type	Frequency range	Mental states and conditions
Delta	0.1 Hz to 3 Hz	Deep, dreamless sleep, non-REM sleep, unconscious
Theta	4 Hz to 7 Hz	Intuitive, creative, recall, fantasy, imaginary, dream
Alpha	8 Hz to 12 Hz	Relaxed, but not drowsy, tranquil, conscious
Low beta	12 Hz to 15 Hz	Formerly SMR, relaxed yet focused, integrated
Midrange beta	16 Hz to 20 Hz	Thinking, aware of self and surroundings
High beta	21 Hz to 30 Hz	Alertness, agitation

In the study of brain-computer interaction (BCI), Yang et al. have proposed some novel feature extraction method to classify left and right hand motor imagery [8]. They have achieved 90% recognition accuracy in the separation of the classes extracted by proposed method. In a different study, Zhuang et al. analyzed the spectrum brain waves using specific music stimulus and various statistical models [9]. This study showed the positive correlation between upper alpha wave generation and memory formation in the brain.

EEG is also used in healthcare and biomedical research. Studies have been done to discover links between emotional states and brain activities using machine learning algorithms [10]. By analyzing EEG data collected during various emotional states from 40 Parkinson disease patients and healthy subjects using bispectrum feature, Yuvaraj et al. concluded that the higher frequency bands such as alpha, beta and gamma played important role in determining emotional states compared to lower frequency bands, delta and theta. In a different study, Direito et al. designed a model to identify the different states of the epileptic brain using topographic mapping relative to delta, theta, alpha, beta and gamma frequency [11]. The method achieved 89% accuracy in pre-dicting abnormal vs normal brain states. These studies have revealed the variability in analysis due to two factors, viz., the feature extraction methods and the number of variables used in modeling. It is found that the model is directly proportional with the increase in the constant variables associated with the modeling equation.

Research pertaining to meditation generally can be classified into two major types. The first types involves using statistical tools to analyze the feedback, either objective or subjective, from the subjects, and find effects of meditation. The second type tries to find physiological indicators during the meditation practice [12]. One example of the first type is to study finite differences within the minds of those practicing meditation, and those who do not. Loizzo et al. performed a 20-week contemplative self-healing program study, which showed that a contemplative self-healing program can be effective in significantly reducing distress and disability among the testers [13]. Lengacher et al. performed a 6-week mindfulness-based stress reduction program, in which subjects demonstrated significant improvements in psychological status and quality of life compared with usual care [14]. In another study using EEG technologies, a group of Qigong practitioners were compared to a control group. Positive impact on the quality of life of cancer patients were observed [15].

Our research presented in this paper falls into the second type of the approaches. We focus on the statistical classification methods to analyze EEG collected from different brain states to build a model, and then use the model to test EEG data to find out the subject's brain state. We consider using feature extractions from raw EEG data to improve the correct classification rates. Given that different areas of human's brain exhibit different features while the brain stays in the same state [16], and sometimes EEG record also changes spontaneously [17], multiple statistical classification methods are used in analyzing EEG data. Supervised machine learning models include tree bagging, boost [18], random forest [19], and support vector machine [20]. We also used unsupervised machine learning algorithms, such as hierarchy clustering. Moreover, entropy was used as features of EEG data to improve the classification rates. For example, sample entropy measures the uncertainty inside a sequence of data [21]. We explored the effects of different types of entropy.

We measured an experienced meditator's brainwaves while meditating and compared them to several other states including idle and talking. We found prominent differences between the experienced meditator's brainwaves and those of other states. The experienced meditator's brainwaves clearly displayed a stable state most of the time, as shown in Fig. 1(a), except for some certain times after the initial meditation stage, when extraordinary high waves were observed, as shown in Fig. 1(b).

Figure 2 shows the brainwaves of idle, talking, and meditating from an inexperienced meditator. We can clearly see that the irregularities of these states are higher than the experienced meditator's state, especially the idle and the talking states. The inexperienced meditator showed some similarity to the state shown in Fig. 1(a) but it didn't show the features in Fig. 2(b). This initial study indicates that trained meditators can demonstrate regularity during meditation practice.

In the following section, we demonstrate the results of the state classification using machine learning algorithms and feature extractions.

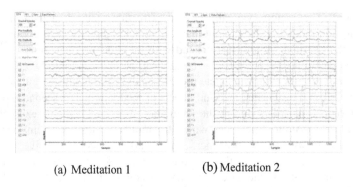

(a) Meditation 1   (b) Meditation 2

Fig. 1. Experienced meditation

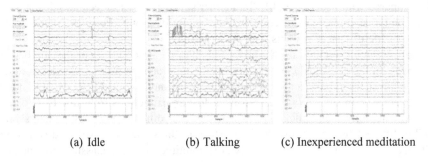

(a) Idle   (b) Talking   (c) Inexperienced meditation

Fig. 2. Other states

3   Identifying Meditation State

The regularity observed in the brain waves of meditation state suggests that entropy might be a right feature to use in the classification of brain states including meditation state. Entropy was introduced to calculate complexity or regularity of the real world in 1991 [22]. Shannon entropy is the basis of various types of entropy calculations. Approximate entropy (ApEn) was introduced as an approximation of entropy estimation for the imperfect biological data, while sample entropy (SampEn) is intended to measure the order in a time series [23].

The machine learning algorithms we use to classify EEG data are tree bagging, support vector machine (SVM), and Gaussian Mixture Model (GMM).

Tree bagging, or decision tree bootstrap aggregation, is an algorithm based on decision tree. It was proposed by Leo Breiman in 1994 to improve the classification by combining classifications of randomly generated training sets [24].

A Support vector machine (SVM) is a discriminative classifier formally defined by a separating hyperplane. Its kernel function projects data from a lower dimensional space to a higher dimensional space, thus gives the algorithm more flexibility comparing to other linear classification algorithms. This algorithm creates the boundary that achieves the least misclassified training data. The data located near the boundary are referred to as support vectors, as they are crucial for boundary determination [25].

A Gaussian mixture model (GMM) is a parametric probability density function represented as a weighted sum of Gaussian component densities [26].

We collected EEG data from subjects in three brain states, viz., idle, meditating, and talking, using Emotiv EPOC headsets. We used the well-contacted channels (AF3, F7, T7, O2, T8, F8, AF4, shown in Fig. 3, to ensure the quality of the EEG data. Based on our previous work, when we use tree bagging, we set number of trees equal to 2500, and we use linear kernel in support vector machine [27].

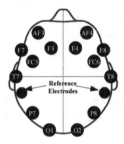

Fig. 3. Emotiv EPOC headset nodes

We firstly used approximate entropy as a feature in the machine learning procedure. We have misclassification rate of the three above methods in Table 2. Parameters are chosen by finding the largest mean of Hurst exponents of data. For GMM, we used EEE model type, which gave the least misclassification rate. This is also because approximate entropy from different channels had similar variances.

Table 2. Misclassification rates using approximate entropy

Paremeter	Misclassificaton rate		
	Tree bagging	GMM	SVM
time = 1 s, lag = 1	0.322	0.312	0.290
time = 1 s, lag = 4	0.247	0.301	0.301
time = 10 s, lag = 4	0.042	0.208	0.042
time = 20 s, lag = 4	0.292	0.375	0.333
time = 30 s, lag = 1	0.143	0.190	0.190

We can see that when time length is 10 s and embedding lag is 4, we have the smallest misclassification rate, which is around 4% given by either tree bagging or support vector machine. Compared to some of our previous misclassification results without using entropy (30% in [27]), this is significant improvement. Table 2 also shows that when using approximate entropy, the misclassification rate does not necessarily decrease when the time length increases. It is also observed that tree bagging has a higher likelihood to give the smallest misclassification rate.

We further test similar parameters and classification models using sample entropy. Unlike approximate entropy, which is an estimation of the true entropy, sample entropy tends to measure the level of chaotic complexity of a time series data. Our misclassification results can be seen in Table 3. It can be observed that for sample entropy the misclassification rates decrease when the time length increases. This makes sense according to the nature of sample entropy.

We exhibit the plots of sample entropy with different time lengths and embedding lags in Fig. 4. In the plots, the sample entropy in talking is represented by triangles.

Table 3. Misclassification rates using sample entropy

Paremeter	Misclassificaton rate		
	Tree bagging	GMM	SVM
time = 1 s, lag = 1	0.065	0.065	0.075
time = 1 s, lag = 4	0.140	0.161	0.108
time = 10 s, lag = 4	0.042	0.042	0.042
time = 30 s, lag = 4	0	0	0
time = 60 s, lag = 4	0	0	0
time = 60 s, lag = 6	0	0	0
time = 60 s, lag = 12	0	0	0

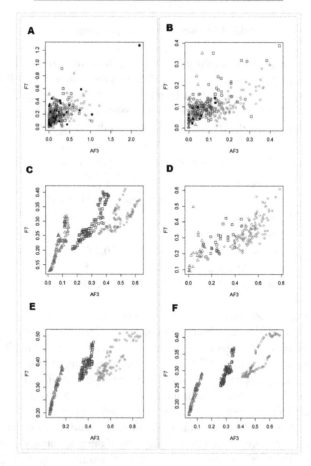

Fig. 4. Sample entropy with different parameters. A. time = 1 s lag = 4 B. time = 1 s lag = 1 C. time = 30 s lag = 4 D. time = 10 s lag = 4 E. time = 60 s lag = 4 F. time = 60 s lag = 6

Circles stand for the sample entropy in mediation, and rectangles are sample entropy in the idle state. Black filled shapes mark the misclassified data. We can see that with the increasing time length, sample entropy from different brain states tend to be more separated. We also notice that embedding lag becomes less influential when time length increases. Tree bagging, again, gives the smallest misclassification rates in most cases. Comparing our results from approximate entropy with those from sample entropy, we can see that sample entropy provide a more solid base to classify different brain states when using original EEG data.

We further explored the use of discretized EEG data. A discretization method divides an attribute with continuous value into several intervals on amplitude axis, each interval is labeled with a different value, and all the data within an interval are assigned to the value of the interval's label. We split the data into K intervals of the same range and label each range with a level, from 0 to K − 1. Therefore, continuous data are transformed into discrete data. We then calculate approximate entropy based on discretized data, and use the same techniques to classify different brain states. Based on our aforementioned results, we choose to use lag = 4 when we calculate approximate entropy. Figure 5 shows the comparison between the approximate entropy calculated

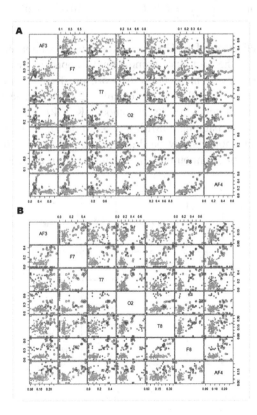

Fig. 5. Approximate Entropy with continuous (A) and discrete (B) EEG data. Blue circles – idle; green triangles – meditation; red rectangles - talk (Color figure online)

from original (continuous) EEG data (Fig. 5(A)) and that calculated from discrete EEG data (Fig. 5(B)). Here we use time = 10 s, lag = 4; for B, K = 40. We can see that after discretization, approximate entropy calculated from EEG data exhibits less overlapping. We expect decreased misclassification rates using discretized data.

The misclassification rates are in Table 4, which confirms our prediction.

We can also see that with the increase of time length, misclassification rates decrease. It also appears that increasing discretization level does not necessarily decrease misclassification rates, suggesting that information redundancy could lead to confusion. Overall, tree bagging is the best performed algorithm, which is consistent with our previous observation.

Table 4. Misclassification rates using approximate entropy with discretization

Paremeter	Misclassificaton rate		
	Tree bagging	GMM	SVM
time = 10 s, K = 10	0.042	0.083	0.042
time = 10 s, K = 40	0.021	0.043	0.043
time = 30 s, K = 40	0	0	0
time = 30 s, K = 100	0	0.011	0.011

Moreover, discretization of EEG data makes using Shannon entropy for classification possible, given the fact that, comparing to approximate entropy or sample entropy, Shannon entropy is more likely to work on discrete cases. Calculation of Shannon entropy is also faster than either calculating approximate entropy or sample entropy. Based on our previous results, we choose K = 40, time = 30 s. Misclassification rates given by tree bagging, GMM, and SVM are 0, 0.043, and 0.022, respectively. We present Shannon entropy on different channels in Fig. 6. We can see that there is a clear pattern of Shannon entropy calculated from different brain states.

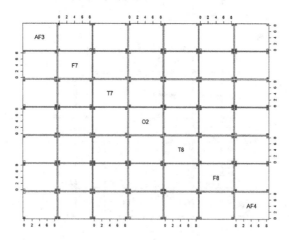

Fig. 6. Shannon entropy with discrete EEG data. Blue circles – idle; green triangles – meditation; red rectangles - talk (Color figure online)

4 Conclusion

Meditation is a well-defined method for psychological and physical wellness training through the histories of multiple cultures. However, given the difficulty of reaching deep meditating state, how to define meditation state using physiological data, especially within practitioners below the master level, remains a research topic. In this paper, we present an experiment of using EEG data to classify meditation from other states. Our result shows that entropy is a great tool for this purpose, given the fact that the brain waves during meditation state tend to show greater regularity. The use of entropy decreases the misclassification rates strikingly. Discretizing EEG data can also improve the classification results. Approximate entropy based on discretized EEG data enhances classification results. Classification based on Shannon entropy gives slightly higher misclassification rates but with significant less computational complexity. Overall, tree bagging gives the least misclassification rates in all the cases. Our experimental results suggest that measuring meditation state using EEG data is feasible.

References

1. Kai, Z., Ma, R.: Translation and Annotations of <<Essentials of Meditation≫. In: Wang, M. (ed.) Series of Chinese Secret Archives of Life Caring. Beijing Science and Technology Press, Beijing (1995)
2. Cella, D.F., Tulsky, D.S., Gray, G., et al.: The functional assessment of cancer therapy scale: development and validation of the general measure. J. Clin. Oncol. **11**, 570–579 (1993)
3. McNair, D., Loor, M., Droppleman, L.: Profile of mood status (revised). EdITS/Educational and Industrial Testing Services, San Diego (1992)
4. Mruk, C.J., Hartzell, J.: Zen & Psychotherapy: Integrating Traditional and Nontraditional Approaches. Springer Publishing Company, New York (2003)
5. Kropotov, J.: Quantitative EEG, Event-Related Potentials and Neurotherapy, p. 2009. Elsevier Inc., Amsterdam (2009). 525 B Street, Suite 1900, San Diego, CA 92101-4495, USA
6. Larsen, E.: Classification of EEG Signals in a Brain-Computer Interface System. Norwegian University of Science and Technology, Norway, PhD thesis (2011)
7. Sławińska, U., Kasicki, S.: The frequency of rat's hippocampal theta rhythm is related to the speed of locomotion. Brain Res. **796**(1), 327–331 (1998)
8. Yang, R., Song, A., Xu, B.: Feature extraction of motor imagery EEG based on wavelet transform and higher-order statistics. Int. J. Wavelets Multiresolut. Inf. Process. **8**(3), 373–384 (2010)
9. Zhuang, T., Zhao, H., Tang, Z.: A study of brainwave entrainment based on EEG brain dynamics. Comput. Inf. Sci. **2**(2), 81–86 (2009)
10. Yuvaraj, R., Murugappan, M., Ibrahim, N., Sundaraj, K., Omar, M., Mohamad, K., Palaniappan, R.: Optimal set of EEG features for emotional state classification and trajectory visualization in Parkinson's disease. Int. J. Psychophysiol. **94**(3), 482–495 (2014)
11. Direito, B., Teixeira, C., Ribeiro, B., Branco, M., Sales, F., Dourado, A.: Modeling epileptic brain states using EEG spectral analysis and topographic mapping. J. Neurosci. Methods **210**(2), 220–229 (2012)

12. Lin, H.: Measurable meditation. In: Proceedings of the International Symposium on Science 2.0 and Expansion of Science (S2ES 2010), The 14th World Multiconference on Systemics, Cybernetics and Informatics (WMSCI 2010), Orlando, Florida, 29 June–2 July 2010, pp. 56–61 (2010)

13. Loizzo, J.J., Peterson, J.C., Charlson, M.E., Wolf, E.J., Altemus, M., Briggs, W.M., Vahdat, L.T., Caputo, T.A.: The effect of a contemplative self-healing program on quality of life in women with breast and gynecologic cancers. Altern. Ther. Health Med. **16**(3), 30–37 (2010)

14. Lengacher, C.A., Johnson-Mallard, V., Post-White, J., Moscoso, M.S., Jacobsen, P.B., Klein, T.W., Widen, R.H., Fitzgerald, S.G., Shelton, M.M., Barta, M., Goodman, M., Cox, C.E., Kip, K.E.: Randomized controlled trial of mindfulness-based stress reduction (MBSR) for survivors of breast cancer. Psychology **18**(12), 1261–1272 (2009)

15. Oh, B., Butow, P., Mullan, B., Clarke, S.: Medical Qigong for cancer patients: pilot study of impact on quality of life, side effects of treatment and inflammation. Am. J. Chin. Med. **36** (3), 459–472 (2008)

16. Hölzel, B.K., Ott, U., Hempel, H., Hackl, A., Wolf, K., Stark, R., Vaitl, D.: Differential engagement of anterior cingulate and adjacent medial frontal cortex in adept meditators and nonmeditators. Neurosci. Lett. **421**(1), 16–21 (2007)

17. Fox, M.D., Raichle, M.E.: Spontaneous fluctuations in brain activity observed with functional magnetic resonance imaging. Nature Rev. Neurosci. **8**(9), 700–711 (2007)

18. Sun, S., Zhang, C., Zhang, D.: An experimental evaluation of ensemble methods for EEG signal classification. Pattern Recogn. Lett. **28**(15), 2157–2163 (2007)

19. Fraiwan, L., Lweesy, K., Khasawneh, N., Wenz, H., Dickhaus, H.: Automated sleep stage identification system based on time–frequency analysis of a single EEG channel and random forest classifier. Comput. Methods Programs Biomed. **108**(1), 10–19 (2012)

20. Guler, L., Beyli, E.D.U.: Multiclass support vector machines for eeg-signals classification. IEEE Trans. Inf Technol. Biomed. **11**(2), 117–126 (2007)

21. Song, Y., Lio, P., et al.: A new approach for epileptic seizure detection: sample entropy based feature extraction and extreme learning machine. J. Biomed. Sci. Eng. **3**(06), 556 (2010)

22. Lebowitz, J., Lewis, M.S., Schuck, P.: Modern analytical ultracentrifugation in protein science: a tutorial review. Protein Sci. **11**(9), 2067–2079 (2002)

23. Johnson, M.L., Brand, L.: Numerical Computer Methods, Part E, vol. 384. Academic Press, Cambridge (2004)

24. Prasad, A.M., Iverson, L.R., Liaw, A.: Newer classification and regression tree techniques: bagging and random forests for ecological prediction. Ecosystems **9**(2), 181–199 (2006)

25. Suykens, J.A., Vandewalle, J.: Least squares support vector machine classifiers. Neural Process. Lett. **9**(3), 293–300 (1999)

26. Xuan, G., Zhang, W., Chai, P.: EM algorithms of Gaussian mixture model and hidden Markov model. In: 2001 Proceedings of the International Conference on Image Processing, vol. 1, pp. 145–148. IEEE (2001)

27. Li, Y., Chang, Y., Lin, H.: Statistical machine learning in brain state classification using EEG data. Open J. Big Data (OJBD) **1**(2), 19–33 (2015). RonPub UG (haftungsbeschränkt), Lübeck, Germany

Enhance the Use of Medical Wearables Through Meaningful Data Analytics

Kurt Reifferscheid and Xiaokun Zhang$^{(\boxtimes)}$

School of Computing and Information Systems, Athabasca University,
Athabasca, Canada
kreiffer@gmail.com, xiaokunz@athabascau.ca

Abstract. Increasing wearable usage in healthcare faces the challenge in low long-term adoption partially due to a redundancy of devices and lack of meaningful uses of wearable technology. This paper aims at the reality needs to present a holistic view of data analytics and medical wearables; and clarify how to apply analytics techniques to a wearable problem or opportunity. The paper addresses the challenges related to undergoing data analytics with medical wearables, details how certain data mining and analytical techniques impact on processing wearable data, and outlines a framework developed for using data analytics with medical wearables data.

Keywords: Medical wearables · Ubiquitous computing · Data analytics

1 Introduction

As the use of wearable technology increases nowadays, healthcare research is exploring ways to use these devices to simplify, transform and accelerate patient care. Wearables can play a significant part in furthering the application of ubiquitous computing. Currently, one in six people in the U.S. make use of consumer wearable technology [14]. At the same time, industry data shows that a significant number, over 30%, of people are abandoning their wearable device after just six months [8]. The paradox of increasing wearable market growth and low long-term adoption is partially due to a redundancy of devices and lack of meaningful uses of wearable technology [17].

The research of the paper is motivated by (i) a lack of studies that present a holistic view of data analytics and medical wearables; and (ii) a lack of clarity on how to apply analytics techniques to a wearable problem or opportunity. In this paper, we intend to answer the following research questions:

RQ1 – What are the challenges related to undergoing data analytics with medical wearables?
RQ2 – How can challenges be addressed in an open and holistic framework?

This paper provides an analysis of existing literature to examine current methods and techniques used to capture and analyze medical data from wearables. We examine wearables that uniquely position themselves away from smartphones (i.e. on-body sensors) and leverage data for predictive analytics and epidemiology uses. Moreover, the paper details how certain data mining and analytical techniques facilitate processing

© Springer International Publishing AG 2017
V.G. Duffy (Ed.): DHM 2017, Part II, LNCS 10287, pp. 281–296, 2017.
DOI: 10.1007/978-3-319-58466-9_26

wearable data. Finally, based on this meta-analysis, some challenges are identified with a framework developed for using data analytics with health wearables.

The paper addresses RQ1 for the challenges to data analytics and medical wearables, including privacy and security, legal compliance and ethical concerns, data standards, reliability and a clinical acceptance of the data and knowledge provided by the wearable analytics system, and analytical complexity. RQ2 is addressed by presenting an open framework (or model) for which analytical processing can be applied to medical wearables data. The framework makes provisions for each of the challenges discovered in the paper. The medical wearables analytic framework is to provide a guideline to facilitate data analytics by injecting medical wearable data from large masses of people. Further to this, the objective of the framework is to indicate the types of interfaces required, visually represent the numerous challenges that exist in mining wearable data, clearly indicate the analytical techniques that can provide deeper meaning to data, and provide a holistic all-inclusive model that could be implemented in an open community (Wiki-like) fashion.

Finally, data analytics scenarios are illustrated to address the medical wearable/analytical issues and how the framework can be applied.

2   Related Work

The precursor literature review by Reifferscheid (i.e. TMA2 -Human Challenges and Barriers Preventing the Adoption of Wearable Technology) found that long-term wearable adoption may be negatively impacted by a lack of meaningful use and a redundancy of devices [17]. Increasing meaningful use requires an examination of where wearables are uniquely positioned to add value. One area where wearables can provide unique value is in capturing data via sensors that monitor biological vital signs such as electrocardiogram, respiratory rate, oxygen saturation, heartrate, or blood glucose levels. Exploiting biometric wearable data with analytics is perhaps the most significant method for enhancing meaningful use in wearables with the possibility of enhancing patient care and increasing quality of life.

Medical wearables that rely on simple metrics and reporting (i.e. lack analytical processing) produce results that have limited utility. For example, wearable devices that capture and report on trivial daily activity such as sleep and step counting do not provide much in the way of predicting future health events or disease diagnosis. A study by Banaee, Ahmed and Loutfi shows that medical information that undergoes analytical processing can produce results that provide deeper meaning and increase end user value [4]. That is, medical wearable data that involves analytical processing provides more value that simple activity reporting.

In the previous study, Reifferscheid shows meaningful use with respect to other adoption variables; trust and comfort [17]. Apart from motivation, it is felt that meaningful use has the greatest potential to increase both scale (number of users) and time (long-term retention of a device) of wearables. Furthering the precursor study, we focus our attention exclusively on expanding meaningful use through use medical wearables and analytics (Fig. 1).

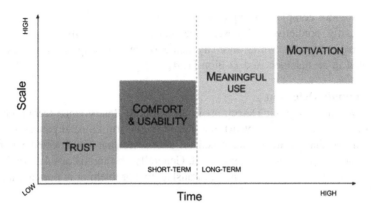

Fig. 1. Adoption framework [17]

2.1 Analytical Terminology

Existing studies show that data collected from medical wearable sensors can be analyzed to extract deeper meaning and useful knowledge, but it seems that the literature falls short of describing how various analytical techniques can be applied and what outcome they produce. Additionally, current literature shows an inconsistency in the usage of terms and definitions around analytical areas and techniques. This section describes four analytical areas that are relevant to medical wearable data. Lastly, we also attempt to highlight the format and structure of wearable medical data and sensors.

Dozens of analytical techniques exist for analyzing medical wearable data [12]. It is important to note that popular medical wearable data today can be considered as structured data (see Sect. 2.2). This is import as analytical techniques vary depending on the structure of the source data. Analytics techniques are used for different purposes such as describing, diagnosing, discovering data as well as predicting or treating an event [1, 10, 15, 19]. With respect to medical wearables, a study by Banaee, Ahmed and Loutficarried carried out a literature review on over eighty papers and extracted the core data mining techniques directly related to medical wearables [4]. Our study builds upon their classifications and includes a new area from Simpao et al. called 'Prescriptive Analytics' [19]. The four areas below are meant to give an indication of the variations in how wearable data can be processed to provide deeper meaning.

1. Anomaly Detection – simple outlier detection, the most basic form of data analysis.
2. Descriptive Analytics – examining why an event happened or describing what happened in an event.
3. Predictive Analytics – predicting what is likely to happen.
4. Prescriptive Analytics – provides decision support in what should or can be (i.e. treatment) done about health event.

An item to note here is that knowledge and insight increases as we move from area 1 to area 4 (4 = highly insightful). Also, the more insightful areas, such as predictive analytics, can make use of and leverage outcomes from the lower areas (1 and 2). As capabilities increase so does the complexity of implementation. For example, it is significantly more complex to implement prescriptive analytics over simple anomaly detection. Lastly, predictive and prescriptive analytics are generally supervised (run by a subject matter expert), while anomaly detection and descriptive analytics can be implemented in an unsupervised fashion [1, 4].

2.1.1   Anomaly Detection

Anomaly Detection (Outlier Detection) is the simplest data science technique that is used to recognize an item (or event) that does not conform to usual pattern [4, 21]. In practice, simple alarms are issued based on anomalies that are detected when comparing sensor data points to a larger dataset. Generally, the anomalous data (a deviation or outlier) that differs from the norm will translate to a problem or in our case a medical event [4].

2.1.2   Descriptive Analytics

Descriptive Analytics is a division of data science that is exploratory and attempts to describe what is happening or why something happened. In the context of medical wearables, this area can assist in diagnosing a medical condition. This branch of analytics makes use of numerous techniques and algorithms. The following examples provide the most commonly used:

– Clustering - grouping a set of data based on similarities. A common technique for statistical data analysis, used in bioinformatics. A cluster (or group) is considered as building block for other analysis. However, it can be useful in detecting disease distribution (geographically or temporally) [21].
– Regression - a statistical modeling technique that estimates the strength of relationships among variables. Regression can be used to determine relationships between the independent and dependent variables [1, 4, 20].
– Social Network Analysis (SNA) – the analysis and discovery of levels and types interaction amongst groups of people (i.e. not to be confused with analysis of Facebook, and other commercial Social Networks) [14].
– Rule-based Relations - enables the discovery of relations (i.e. dependencies) of two variables in large databases. Rule-based relations can also make use of the association rule learning technique and 'if-then' or 'what-if' scenarios [10].

2.1.3   Predictive Analytics

Predictive Analytics is a division of data science that attempts to provide foresight and make predictions about the likelihood of a future event (with a high degree of success). Predictive analytics expands upon descriptive analytics by considering regression/cluster analysis statistical modeling [10, 12, 22]. By using a collection of techniques, wearable data can be used to predict, with a high likelihood, the occurrence of a future medical event such as an impending heart attack. Predictive analytics can also utilize components of machine learning (and neural networks) and artificial intelligence (AI). To put it simply, machine learning is a type of artificial intelligence (AI) that allows computer systems to learn from data without being manually programmed [1]. Neural networks are an advanced type of AI that creates a mathematical model of the human brain and its neurons [10]. These techniques are meant to discover insights from the data in an unsupervised fashion.

Beyond AI, predictive analytics can also make use of supervised Decision Tree and Bayesian Classification [1, 22]. This model is an iterative inquiry based approach that uses an inverted tree for visualizing and population by splitting into smaller segments.

2.1.4   Prescriptive Analytics

Prescriptive is the most complex and evolving branch of data science and is meant to provide support for making decisions on patient care, or some cases independent form its own decisions [19]. Prescriptive analytics involves advanced machine learning and AI. This study focuses on prediction rather than AI related treatment of health events/management. For that reason, we consider Prescriptive Analytics to be out of the scope of this study and is included here for completeness.

2.2   Data Structure, Scope and Sources

A common theme throughout the four identified areas is that as a dataset gains users, the analytical value of the dataset increases. A larger dataset results in a larger sample size and is thus more representative of the population. Additionally, large datasets allow for the power of statistics to be more accurate at prediction and anomaly detection [10]. Thus, a community approach (put forth in Sect. 5) to sharing medical data could result in benefits for all users.

It is important to have a basic understanding of the structure and type of data that is capture by medical wearables. The literature on wearable sensors and the data they capture is vast and includes hundreds of possible attributes and datatypes. Most studies operate on the following three premises; (1) wearable medical data is of the structured (rather than unstructured) nature; (2) data is captured in a simple two-dimensional (2D) format (X, Y) with X being time and Y being the measure; (3) many 'commodity' sensors exist that can capture common vital signs data such as: Electrocardiogram (ECG), Electroencephalogram (EEG), Oxygen Saturation (OS), Heartrate (HR), Blood glucose (BG), Respiratory Rate (RR), Blood pressure (BP) [1, 4, 12] (Table 1).

Table 1. Example data set – EGC

Date/Time	Amplitude
2016.08.12:12:01:00	800
2016.08.12:12:01:01	801
…	
Adapted from [20]	

The three data-type premises (structured, two-dimensions, commodity) purposely exclude multivariate and complex data types. Complex data type capture is an emerging trend and is beyound the scope of this paper. However, the data analysis phase (rather than capture phase) may include transforming simple data types to complex ones.

Captured data can be stored in many systems. Health monitoring systems can be classified into the three categories below:

1. Remote health monitoring systems (RHMS) – systems which can send data to/or from a remote location. These types of systems are well positioned for heavy analytical processing as they usually reside in a datacenter [1, 2].
2. Mobile health monitoring systems (MHMS) refer to mobile devices (i.e. smartphone or tablets) which are used as the main processing unit [2].
3. Wearable health monitoring systems (WHMS) refer to wearable devices or biosensors that can be worn by patients consisting [2].

WHMS generally work in conjunction with MHMS and RHMS to provide a wide array of analytical capabilities. While the model proposed in Sect. 5 considers capabilities of each of the three systems. As quite common in practice, most analytical processing is carried out offline in the RHMS, while the WHMS is focused on data capture. Offline processing at a RHMS allows for data aggregation from multiple sources as well as scaling processing power [12]. The Open Medical Wearables Framework (OMWF) presented in Sect. 5 (Fig. 2) follows this approach.

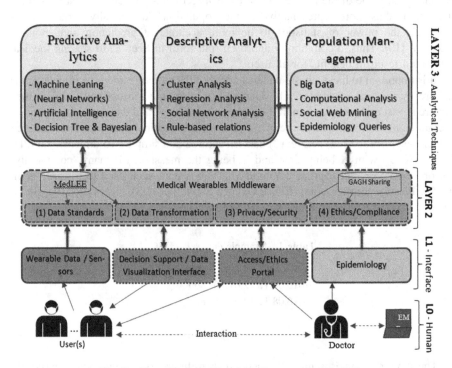

Fig. 2. Open Medical Wearables Framework (OMWF)

3 Methodology

3.1 Research Approach

This study completed a meta-analysis of existing literature (see Table 2). Material selection was completed by searching for relevant works in leading peer-reviewed journals (IEEE, ACM). Additionally, as this study is intended to review the state of the art in this field, we focused our attention on material between 2010 and 2016. The materials were filtered using search terms such as "medical wearables", "wearables analytics, and "epidemiology". Of the resultant papers, study cases were selected if they satisfied the criteria of assisting in building a case to answer the research questions of this study. This study is intended to present a real-world usable framework and as such a preliminary review was performed within a short-list to ensure the existence material relevant to this framework. Certain purely theoretical models were not included. Finally, we are left with several publications that provide the building blocks for a working model or framework that could be implemented today. In the subsequent sections, we analyze the selected papers which represent the state-of-the-art in medical wearables using analytics over medical data.

Table 2. Survey and classification of literature

Classification	Description	Related Studies
Wearables/Remote Health Monitoring	(11) Studies that explore the uses of remote health monitoring and medical wearables	[1, 2, 4–6, 10, 12–14, 17, 25]
Data Science (Analytical) Techniques	(9) Studies, health and non-health related that explore analytics techniques and data science	[4, 7–10, 12, 19, 21, 22]
Ethics, Legal Compliance, Governance	(2) Studies that examine compliance, ethics and legalities of storing/sharing medical data	[3, 7]
Epidemiology	(10) Studies that examine traditional epidemiology practices	[8, 11, 15, 16, 18–20, 22–24]

This study examined and analyzed 25 key works. The surveyed literature can be classified into the four key areas below. Note that certain studies touched upon two or more areas.

3.2 Limitations

There are two primary limitations to this study. The first is that this study does not address governance issues with respect to decentralized hosting, mining and managing of wearable data in the OWMF model. This is by no means an indication of its importance (or lack of), due to the limit scope of the papers. A future study could potentially explore governance models for managing, resourcing this OWMF.

The second limitation of this study is the decision to simplify data capture to unsophisticated 2D data types rather than complex multivariate data types. Thus, wearables such as brain computer interfaces and mind-machine direct interfaces are not covered. This approach was justified by the fact data standards and data complexity is a challenge in this area (Sect. 4.2).

4 Challenges to Data Analytics and Medical Wearables

4.1 Privacy and Security

The precursor study by Reifferscheid noted that privacy and security (i.e. trust) are concerns with systems that track personal health information (PHI) [17]. The importance of this issue is also reflected and reinforced in existing medical wearable literature. Of the eleven studies related to medical wearables or remote monitoring systems, six [1, 4, 10, 13–15] indicate privacy as an important issue.

In addition to privacy, security of medical wearable data can be problematic [14]. This is especially true in a community model where wearable data from a group of users is used for data mining and analytical purposes [15]. Encryption, unauthorized access and hacking are all concerns cited by existing research [14]. Additionally, consumer wearables often have a clause that provides ownership of the data the manufacturer. The manufacturer will often sell anonymized or aggregated data to interested parties [14]. The privacy and security findings may seem obvious; however, solutions meant to further meaningful use through medical wearables must include a model for protecting privacy and ensuring security of users.

4.2 Legal Compliance and Ethical Concerns

In addition to privacy and security, the health industry must meet and comply with legal and government legislation such as the U.S.'s Health Insurance Portability and Accountability Act (HIPAA) and Alberta Canada's Health Information Act (HIA) [3, 4]. This compliance can also relate to how healthcare providers integrate medical wearable data/knowledge with other systems they operate such as Electronic Medical Record (EMR) systems. Perhaps the larger issue is data stewardship and responsibly for ownership of alerts or treatment actions. While EMR systems can be improved with new medical wearables data, ownership of potentially complex and unreliable data creates issues with respect to the meaningful use of data.

Ethical concerns and informed consent are key components to sharing medical data and discussed in five studies [1, 3, 7, 15, 16]. Patients (or medical wearable users in our case) must have an adequate amount of information before they provide their PHI.

Patients may have a limited understanding of health care or wearable data, so confirming that a patient has been adequately informed and has granted consent can be challenging [3]. In adherence to the doctrine of informed consent, the health care provider is required to fully disclose information about potential risks and benefits of the proposed solution. In the context of this study, the medical wearable user needs to be sufficiently informed to participate in a model where PHI is shared. Furthering this issue is that data mining and transforming simple data to complex data (and sharing in an online community) makes informed consent and ethics a big concern.

4.3   Data Standards, Reliability and Acceptance

For healthcare providers to take ownership and act upon wearables data there must be a clinical acceptance of the data and knowledge provided by the wearable analytics system. Additionally, as more and more wearable and non-wearable (i.e. EMR and hospital systems) data is collected the process of accepting clinical outcomes becomes more challenging [14]. Acceptability and ultimately interpretation of the wearable and analytical data is a constantly changing. New models for wearable data collection and interpretation should be flexible and consider new unforeseen data sources, such as brainwave or neuro-sensing.

Data sensors must provide the proper type and amount of data to allow for data mining. Also, the time sensitivity of data is important for emergency predictive events. Today's wearable sensors can provide data for a wide range of health concerns such as cardiovascular disease, respiratory diseases, stress, and neurological conditions. However, the means in which wearables collect this information is ad-hoc and non-standardized [15]. This presents problems with data mining and the data provided by the wearable can vary in quality, validity and precision [15]. Clinical acceptability ultimately comes down to three core issues; (1) data classification and standards; (2) clinical rigor around process around data interpretation; (3) interoperability with existing systems [4, 14–16, 23].

1. Data Standards – a lack of standards on both capturing and interpreting data creates confusion and inefficiencies within the healthcare provider community [16]. A study on clinic data standards by Richesson and Krischer shows that variations of data standards and duplicate terms can complicate clinical diagnosis efforts [16]. Thus, a high degree of training is required to comprehend the standard.
2. Analytical Process – existing research shows that healthcare providers feel that the data analysis process (specifically on wearable data) lacks 'clinical grade' rigor. Thus, healthcare providers feel they are unable to disseminate information to patients [4].
3. Interoperability – 90% of U.S. physicians make use of electronic medical record (EMR) [23]. Interoperability of EMR's with external systems, such as a data analytics model, can be problematic [4]. Additionally, interoperability issues increase as the number of medical wearables, wearables data, and hospital systems continue to proliferate. EMR integration and interoperability is a complex problem that involves governance issues (governments, private sector and physicians) in addition to legal compliance.

4.4   Analytical Complexity

Many medical wearables provide simple visual interfaces for predetermined biometric vital signs such as the ECG, heart rate and oxygen saturation [12]. However, current research lacks an all-inclusive platform meant to support large-scale data interpretation and analysis for web-scale user's bases and high volume medical wearable data streams. Without this platform, analytical processing capability is extremely compromised and limited.

Matching an analytical technique to a problem domain is far from easy and intuitive [4]. This can result in situations where researchers or practitioners are unaware of how deeper meaning can be extracted by making use of well-established analytical techniques. For example, in scenarios where analytics are applied, a lack of understanding can result in subject specific or hard-coded analytical model being developed. This can result in limited flexibility or missed opportunities [24]. As discussed in Sect. 2.1, analytical techniques often build upon one another in a complementary fashion. This adds to the complexity by creating a scenario where techniques are highly coupled.

5   Medical Wearables Framework

The previous section addresses RQ1 by highlighting the challenges of using medical wearables with data analytics. This section intends to address RQ2 by presenting an open framework (or model) for which analytical processing can be applied to medical wearables data. OMWF (Fig. 2) makes provisions for each of the challenges discovered in Sect. 4.

By introducing the medical wearables analytic framework, it is important to recall its purpose and intent. The overarching purpose of the framework is to provide a guideline or recipe that, if implemented, can facilitate data analytics by injecting medical wearable data from large masses of people. Further to this, the objective of the framework is the following:

1. To indicate the types of interfaces required (Layer 1).
2. To visually represent the numerous challenges that exist in mining wearable data (Layer 2).
3. To clearly indicate the analytical techniques that can provide deeper meaning to data (Layer 3).
4. Provide a holistic all-inclusive model that could be implemented in an open community (Wiki-like) fashion.

Note that, in Fig. 2, solid lines represent areas that have existing solutions (techniques, systems or processes). Dotted lines represent areas specific to this study that require further research and development.

5.1   Privacy, Security, Ethics and Compliance

Sections 4.1 and 4.2 discuss challenges with respect to privacy, security, ethics and compliance (PSEC). In the precursor study by Reifferscheid, privacy and security (and trust) were noted as being concerns and therefore impacting general wearable adoption. It was suggested that social acceptance will evolve as meaningful use increases. Additionally, open and transparent frameworks, such as Apple's 'Research Kit' attempt to address these concerns.

Ethical concerns follow the same principles and user privacy. Essentially, the user needs to explicitly provide informed consent to the use of their information and understand who has access and for what purpose. Existing studies postulate that open models can increase compliance with regulatory bodies [7]. OWMF deals with PSEC concerns by borrowing from the Global Alliance for Genomics and Health (GAGH) approach to data sharing. This multidiscipline alliance developed a model for responsible sharing of genomic health data [15]. The framework considers identity management, access control, privacy protection, audit logs, data integrity and cryptography/non-repudiation. This is represented in OWMG at the end-user interface layer titled 'Access/Ethics Interface' in layer 1. Additionally, layer 2 in meant to show the data sharing approach suggested by GAGH.

This study expands GAGH with respect to access levels. Two (or more) levels of security granularity should be introduced to allow an adjustment of anonymizations rates of the data that flows up to layer 3, analytical techniques. That is, a least amount of access principle could allow a user to share their data to with layer 3 (analytics), but only include simple demographical information such as gender, race, weight, height in addition to selecting specific vital signs. Lastly, users would interact with health provider offline to ensure they understand all the potential risks and benefits.

5.2   Data Standards and Transformation

Medical terminology can be complex and ambiguous with multiple phrases for similar terms. This can result in the need for the guidance on how the terminology fits into an information model [16]. From a data science perspective, this is not ideal as a lack of data understanding impacts the ability to analytically process this data. To partially deal with complexity, the OMWF makes use of simple data types provided by most wearables.

Even simple data types should incorporate a data standardization process. There are two ways that data standardization can be accomplished. One is to enforce strict standards on data capture at input. The second is to allow for non-standardized data to inputted into the model with weak (or no) standards. The former requires extensive up-front effort to formulate and communication of standards and potentially creates a barrier for wearable data providers. The second requires more work in the layer 2 as data needs to be cleanse or transformed into a standard format that can be further analyzed by layer 3.

It is felt that the OMWF could be a hybrid of those two, in that it could provide data guidelines in additional to data transformation. Research into data guidelines for medical information shows that, at a bare minimum, the following should be considered [5, 15]:

- Measurement validity from wearable sensors should be scored on data validity relative to existing or similar metrics.
- Data quality can vary by individual participants and their level of engagement. Precision should not be considered equal across all participants.
- Selection bias from the participants who opt in to participate and have sufficient technological knowledge and access.

With respect to transformation of data, OMWF could be implemented to take advanced of Friedman's medical terminology database called MedLEE (developed at

Columbia University and Queens College of CUNY). MedLEE's goal is to extract transform and encode medical information in a structured format that can then be used for further medical analytical processes [11].

5.3 Clinical Acceptance

Clinical acceptance is a complex issue that cannot be tackled by one specific approach. Recall that clinical acceptance must consider concerns with data standards, analytical processing/complexity and clinical system interoperability. An epidemiological study by Ramachandran shows that clinical acceptance amongst health providers must begin with awareness around data type expectations. That is, healthcare providers must be made aware of the following conditions [4, 12, 15]:

- Continuous monitoring and health data (i.e. wearables) may not directly match the tests done in the clinic.
- Clinical grade precision may need to be sacrificed for more frequent and volumi- nous data (from wearables). Large datasets and the power of statistics can mitigate precision.

For OWMF to become a clinically accepted model, further research studies are required, specifically with respect to analytical processing. Future studies should seek to experimentally test various medical scenarios. By way of example, three clinical case studies are provided in Sect. 5.5. It would be expected that as clinical scenarios are tested and proven valid and reliable, clinical acceptance would be incrementally increased over time. However, until clinical validity and data analytics matures, healthcare providers could use OWMF as assistance tool. A study by Taneja carries out a clinical experiment using analytics with ECG data to edict patient heart disease. The authors suggest that physicians should use their techniques in a complementary fashion to traditional care [22].

OMWF interoperability with EMR/clinical system integration is a problem that is not meant to be solved by an analytics framework. Moreover, it was felt that this should purposely be an offline task for caregivers. This is represented in 'layer 0 – the human layer' where the physician willfully chooses to include or exclude patient records in an EMR.

5.4 Data Analytics

The framework in Fig. 2 provides an overview of existing analytical techniques and illustrates which methods are most applicable to medical wearable data. Section 2.1 classifies data analytics from the dimension of outcomes or results (e.g. descriptive, predictive, and prescriptive). Analytical techniques can also be viewed from the per- spective of supervised or unsupervised [1, 4]. That is classifying whether the analytical technique runs under the guidance of a user, or just run unsupervised. Figure 2 suggests using both kinds of methods; unsupervised for descriptive and supervised for predictive.

The analytical process itself following goes through various states collection (layer 1-interface for data capture from wearables), data preprocessing/transformation (layer 2), analysis (layer 3) and evaluation (layer 0 - human layer) [4]. Acampora et al. found the data mining algorithms for wearables begin with descriptive and unsupervised learning (i.e., clustering, association, summarization) and following with predictive and supervised learning (i.e. machine learning, AI) [1]. OWMF is meant to indicate this analytical flow and coupling of techniques.

5.5   Data Analytics Scenarios

By this point of the study, you should have a good understanding of the medical wearable/analytical issues and how the OMWF can be applied. However, it may not be clear how data mining and analytics can help in a real-world scenario. We provide three examples that attempt to illustrate how analytical techniques, such as regression and cluster analysis can add patient value. This section is mean to explicitly answer RQ2 and illustrate how the OMWF can be applied to a real-world scenario.

5.5.1   Scenario 1: Detecting Disease and Epilepsy

A study by Acampora et al. demonstrates real-world analytical examples that make use simple wearable sensors such as ECG, EEG, RR and ambient noise [1]. Their first example demonstrates real-time anomaly detection and prediction of cardiovascular disease and emergency events. Their approach makes use of neural networks and machine learning. The authors provide a second example where similar sensors (and analytical processing) predict the onset of epilepsy seizure. A third example shows the use anomaly detection (data deviations) to surmise a fall in an elderly patient. This was accomplished through of ambient noise sensors (raw data) in conjunction statistics and regression [1].

5.5.2   Scenario 2: Using Mobile ECG Sensors and Analytics for Acute Stress Detection

Mobile (i.e. wearable) ECG and ECG sensors capture the heart's electrical voltage. That data is then statistically analyzed and used, in-real time, to assess patient acute stress. Salahuddin and Desok show that variability (i.e. regression) and anomaly detection of the QRS complex (ventricular contraction) can differentiate normal from abnormal [18]. In epidemiology, specific abnormal QRS readings are known to be indicators of acute stress. The complete ECG cycle (and QRS component) is shown in Fig. 3. The combination of wearables, analytics and epidemiology makes realtime detection possible.

5.5.3   Scenario 3: CVD Prediction with Analytics

A study by Taneja provides a working example of predicting heart disease [22]. Cardiovascular disease (CVD) is a leading cause of death in modern society with twelve million yearly deaths worldwide [22]. Heart attacks often happen rapidly with little warning. Timely and accurate diagnosis of patients presents a challenge to healthcare providers. Proactive, diagnosis and proactive treatment of the CVD can be highly effective; however, costs in some regions are prohibitive (e.g. India). Taneja hypothesizes that analytical diagnosis can by effective and cost efficient by using common techniques.

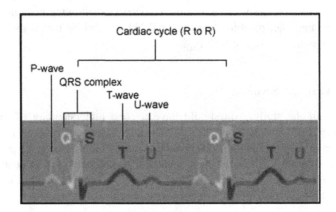

Fig. 3. Electrocardiogram (ECG) data streams [18]

Their study completes four experiments with three supervised analytical techniques (two descriptive and one predictive), namely Decision Tree, Bayesian, and Machine Learning/Neural Networks. The study makes use of clinical echocardiography (EGC) datasets that were pre-captured. However, ECG sensors are common today and could have been used to produce similar datasets. Datasets were analyzed with the best models receiving a classification accuracy of 95.56% [22]. The authors prove their original hypothesis with outcomes showing analytical techniques effectively and efficiently predicting heart disease cases. In practice, the authors feel that outcomes such as these could be used as clinical assistant tool by cardiologists.

6   Trends and Future Challenges

There are several emerging trends in medical wearables and health analytics. This includes IT buzzwords such as Internet of Things (IoT) and Big Data. Large central repositories and millions of data collectors can add environmental context and may drive a fundamental shift in health analytics. IoT and Big Data leverage to discover patterns in behavior and Social Network Analysis. Smart cities with a wide range of sensors can capture environmental data such as air pollution/quality, humidity, pollen count, ambient temperature, etc. Environment and behavior data, when analyzed together with wearable vitals, can generate valuable information for healthcare providers/epidemiologist [12]. While our study focused on prediction rather than AI related treatment of health events/management. Prescriptive Analytics is an area that will continue to see development and perhaps the most significant meaningful uses. Soon, AI and computers may be better positioned than physicians to treat certain health conditions.

Lastly, this field will see continued development of wearable sensor technology. Wearable medical sensors, such as ECG's, are seeing applications where they are woven into clothing textiles or placed directly on skin [13, 14]. As this technology develops, data capture capabilities will advance thus furthering potential novel analytics uses in areas that are unimaginable today.

7 Conclusion

With the assistance of analytical techniques, medical wearable data can be transformed to provide deeper meaning. The original driver from the precursor study related to the paradox of massive market growth and low long-term wearable adoption rates. This study furthered the precursor study by presenting meaningful uses linked to use cases where wearables are uniquely positioned (on body medical biometrics). Section 4 explicitly answers RQ1 by evaluating current HCI literature and synthesizing results into an adoption framework. Section 5 addresses RQ2 by providing a framework that incorporates the many challenge areas. Potential future research in this area may incorporate a study on governance and framework implementation. Additionally, integrating data from smart cities sensors with medical wearables can provide a contextual dimension that is currently lacking. Finally, moving health analytics from predictive to machine learning and AI-based prescriptive analytics could be a catalyst for change in healthcare diagnosis, treatment and prognosis.

References

1. Acampora, G., Cook, D.J., Rashidi, P., Vasilakos, A.V.: Data analytics in pervasive health. In: Healthcare Data Analytics, pp. 533–576 (2015)
2. Baig, M., Gholamhosseini, H.: Smart health monitoring systems: an overview of design and modeling. J. Med. Syst. 37(2), 1–14 (2013)
3. Bailey, J.: Informed consent: what must a physician disclose? Ethics 12(7), 197–201 (2010)
4. Banaee, H., Ahmed, M.U., Loutfi, A.: Data mining for wearable sensors in health monitoring systems: a review of recent trends and challenges. Sensors (Basel) 13(12), 17472–17500 (2013)
5. Bonato, P.: Wearable sensors/systems and their impact on biomedical engineering. IEEE Eng. Med. Biol. Mag. 22(3), 18–20 (2003)
6. Chaudhary, K., Sharma, D.: Body area networks: a survey. In: 2016 3rd International Conference on Computing for Sustainable Global Development (INDIACom), pp. 3319–3323 (2016)
7. Deloitte Analytics in power and utilities – driving performance through power insight (2013)
8. Gamble, M.: Wearables, Big Data, and Analytics in Healthcare (2015)
9. Huffman, W.E., Evenson, R.E.: Science for agriculture: a long-term perspective (2008)
10. Kaur, H., Wasan, S.K.: Empirical study on applications of data mining techniques in healthcare. J. Comput. Sci. 2(2), 194–200 (2006)
11. Lai, A., Freidman, C.: MedLEE, a Natural Language Processing Service, on the Public Health Research Grid, Department of Biomedical Informatics, Columbia University (2008)

12. Mukherjee, A., Pal, A., Misra, P.: Data analytics in ubiquitous sensor-based health information systems. In: Proceedings of 6th International Conference on Next Generation Mobile Applications, Services and Technologies, NGMAST 2012, pp. 193–198 (2012)

13. Pantelopoulos, A., Bourbakis, N.G.: Prognosis-a wearable health-monitoring system for people at risk: methodology and modeling. IEEE Trans. Inf Technol. Biomed. **14**(3), 613–621 (2010)

14. Piwek, L., Ellis, D.A., Andrews, S., Joinson, A.: The rise of consumer health wearables: promises and barriers. PLoS Med. **13**(2), 1–9 (2016)

15. Ramachandran, V.S.: Keynote Address: The Future of Cardiovascular Epidemiology: Current Trends? (2016)

16. Richesson, R.L., Krischer, J.: Data standards in clinical research: gaps, overlaps, challenges and future directions. J. Am. Med. Inform. Assoc. **14**(6), 687–696 (2007)

17. Reifferscheid, K.: Human Challenges and Barriers Preventing the Adoption of Wearable Technology, Athabasca University, COMP648 TMA2 (2016)

18. Salahuddin, L., Desok, K.: Detection of acute stress by heart rate variability using a prototype mobile ECG sensor. In: Proceedings of International Conference on Hybrid Information Technology, ICHIT, pp. 1–25, November 2006

19. Simpao, A.F., Ahumada, L.M., Gálvez, J.A., Rehman, M.A.: A review of analytics and clinical informatics in health care. J. Med. Syst. **38**(4), 1–7 (2014)

20. Suh, M., Chen, C.-A., Woodbridge, J., Tu, M.K., Kim, J.I., Evangelista, S., Sarrafzadeh, M.: A remote patient monitoring system for congestive heart failure. J. Med. Syst. **35**(5), 1165–1179 (2011)

21. Tan, P., Steinbach, M., Kumar, V.: Cluster analysis: basic concepts and algorithms (Chap. 8). In: Introduction to Data Mining (2005)

22. Taneja, A.: Heart disease prediction system using data mining techniques. Orient. J. Comput. Sci. Technol. **6**, 457–466 (2013)

23. Technology Office of the National Coordinator for Health Information. Percent of REC Enrolled Primary Care Providers by Credentials Live on an EHR and Demonstrating Meaningful Use (2016)

24. Yang, G., Atallah, L., Lo, B.: Can pervasive sensing address current challenges in global healthcare? J. Epidemiol. Glob. Health **2**, 1–13 (2012)

25. Youm, S., Lee, G., Park, S., Zhu, W.: Development of remote healthcare system for measuring and promoting healthy lifestyle. Expert Syst. Appl. **38**(3), 2828–2834 (2011)

User-Driven Semantic Classification for the Analysis of Abstract Health and Visualization Tasks

Sabine Theis[✉], Peter Rasche, Christina Bröhl, Matthias Wille,
and Alexander Mertens

Institute of Industrial Engineering and Ergonomics,
RWTH Aachen University, Aachen, Germany
{s.theis,p.rasche,c.broehl,m.wille,
a.mertens}@iaw.rwth-aachen.de

Abstract. Present article outlines characteristics of a general task analysis in terms of digital health visualization evaluation and design. Furthermore, a number of methodological approaches are discussed. One example, in which a hierarchical structure was empirically built with semantic classification by 98 users, will be discussed together with the expected benefits of its successful implementation with respect to system development and human factors research on health data visualizations. It is concluded that experimental approaches to taxonomy construction offer considerable promise in capturing tasks which are relevant but that further investigation is needed validating and iteratively extending the abstract task structures. We thus recommend based on our experiences to conduct a combination of semantic classification with users and hierarchical task analysis to capture all needed task abstraction levels.

Keywords: Task analysis · Methods · Task abstraction · Generalizability

1 Introduction

The volume of data circulating throughout the world is growing rapidly every year. Also in the healthcare sector, more and more researchers, companies and physicians are working with huge amounts of data. Health data are no longer collected only in practice and in studies, but are also captured by patients themselves – be it via mobile phones and body-worn sensor devices, via mobile apps or with social networks. Large amounts of health data open up promising new perspectives for the research, prevention, diagnosis and treatment of diseases.

In this article we consider interconnected information and communication technology aiding healthcare professionals and patients to manage illnesses and health risks, as well as promoting health and wellbeing as digital health systems. Digital health applications support the user in a various amount of tasks. Most consumer applications serve personal monitoring tasks like monitoring of medication intake [1, 2]

V.G. Duffy (Ed.): DHM 2017, Part II, LNCS 10287, pp. 297–305, 2017.
DOI: 10.1007/978-3-319-58466-9_27

or monitoring of health specific vital parameters and health-related behavior in which visualizations are applied to influence users behavior [3–8].

On the professional side of digital health systems the major part of the applications focusses on communicating medical test results and personal health records [9–12]. Digital health systems for example aggregate medical data from different sources so that data appreciates in value if related to events, or correlated with vital sensor or behavioral data. Automation may support the analysis to some extent, but given the dynamics, flexibility and the creativity of the human brain it can hardly be substituted by machines. To integrate users into data driven health processes data visualization are an effective layer between abstract mathematical concepts and human cognition. Finding the right information, understanding and making sense of in large amounts of structured and unstructured health data is strongly influenced by human capabilities, but deriving generalizable results from ergonomic visualization evaluation requires a set of tasks which are relevant to all or as much digital health applications as possible.

For general research purposes, there is a need for some generalizable knowledge about human activities across applications and over time. But not only research generalizability, also the design of efficient and effective digital health systems requires an analysis of relevant tasks. Thereby it needs to be investigated to which extent a task can be supported by a certain technology when performed by patients and professionals. Together with patients and professionals goals they build the reference against which system functionalities then can be tested. Here, besides a behavioral description of the activity, considerable effort is oriented to the specific case serving development oriented purposes. A combination of the research approach and the development approach is where factors will be measured during a task conducted with a system. When data of a human conducting a task with a certain system is collected, this can also have an emphasis either on research or on development objectives.

We consider the research perspective here as aiming at generalizable output of a controlled laboratory experiment. There are thus different objectives for the tasks resulting from a task analysis.

We differentiate following objectives for the tasks resulting from a task analysis and assign them with different degrees of abstraction, a degree of specificity in terms of users and tasks or domain (Table 1):

Table 1. Task objectives in terms of task abstraction and domain/user specificitie as very high (++), high (+), low (−) or medium (o)

Objectives	Domain specificity	Task abstraction	User specificity
Measure factors depending on a task (performance, human error, strain e.g.)	++	−	+
Design a system that supports a task (user-centered/participatory design)	+	−	++
Measure factors depending on a task supported by a system (usability test, system evaluation, visualization evaluation)	+	+/−	+

A challenge regarding controlled visualization evaluation is the choice of task, which needs to be relevant to real world use of the visualization. Particularly in controlled studies, it can be easy finding a task that is modestly measurable by disregarding its relevance for the application context. This article looks at methods to find tasks which can be used during controlled experiments to measure human factors depending on the task supported by visualization.

2 Abstraction in Visualization Tasks

Abstraction levels of tasks have been discussed within the visualization community. Rind and his colleagues [13] for example describe tasks as different in terms of abstraction, composition and perspective. In order to disambiguate the use of task terminology they also construct a three-dimensional conceptual space of visualization tasks. According to this three-dimensional conceptual space a task has a certain level of abstraction ranging from concrete to abstract. Furthermore, a task disposes of a granularity level when broken down in several sub-tasks. The authors describe on the one hand why a task is done by the objective and on the other hand how it is done by different actions.

Munzner [14] provided a model of nested layers for the design and evaluation of visualizations. At the outer level the domain and problem of interest are defined while during the following step the data and task abstractions for that problem are identified. At the third layer visual encodings and interaction methods for data and task abstractions are developed so that at the innermost level according algorithms will be developed. This model invokes domain problem descriptions or objectives followed by an identification of according data and task abstractions as preparation for generalizable human factors evaluation results.

A task framework with different abstraction levels covering objectives on the why-dimension and actions on the how-dimension was developed by Brehmer and Munzner [15]. Subsequently, Brehmer et al. [16] characterize task sequences related to visualizing dimensionally-reduced data. This time, information from interviews with 24 analysis experts was classed with the multilevel typology of abstract visualization task framework. Even if interview questions and the translation of interview transcriptions into abstract visualization tasks is not described in detail, it becomes clear, that their task analysis considers concrete analytical procedures applied by analysts in different domains. This task analysis focusses on objectives and actions during the handling of a specific data type (Fig. 1).

In addition, Miksch and Aigner [17] described an abstract framework to guide visualization designers in constructing time-based visualizations with the data-user-task design triangle. The authors describe tasks as manifold and depending on the type of data that has to be analyzed. Following the authors, tasks are defined by the questions users want to answer with the help of visual representations. Two task types are described as twofold [18]: elementary tasks address individual data elements like groups of data or individual values. To look up a blood-pressure value at one point in time for example. Then the user has a target and just wants to find it within the data.

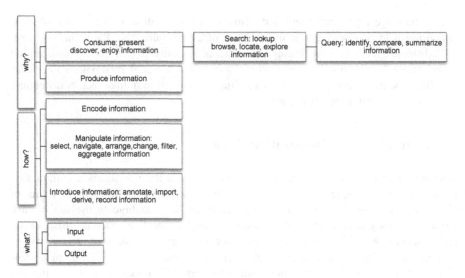

Fig. 1. The multi-level typology of abstract visualization tasks represents the 'why', 'how' and 'what' dimensions of visualization tasks [15]. Task abstraction is made explicit.

3   Task Abstraction of Digital Health Tasks

While researchers in the field of data visualization are aware of the importance of abstract tasks for evaluation and while there is a large number of work on how to construct hierarchical structures, the analysis of abstract tasks in the medical field is, if at all, only implicit. Furthermore, classifications are applied to make concepts and their relation clear in order to differentiate ambiguous terms representing the concept of IT supported medical processes [19, 20]. Using them as basis for ergonomic evaluation bears the risk of findings with minor practical relevance. On the other hand, domain specific tasks only serve a differentiation of ambiguous terms representing the concept of IT supported medical processes. Bashshur et al. [20] constructed the taxonomy of telemedicine necessary to that end. They differentiated among other dimensions, user tasks when describing the functionality dimensions *consultation*, *diagnosis*, *monitoring* and *mentoring*. Unfortunately, his research remains vague when it comes to the origin of his classification. So current study takes them as starting point for a user oriented perspective on digital health task and data analysis by having it verified from a domain expert's perspective and extend it if needed (Fig. 2).

4   Task Analysis Methods

As illustrated different abstraction levels, user and domain specificity of tasks are relevant when targeting generalizable results of data visualization evaluation. At the same time, methods to analyze tasks produce results differing in these dimensions. Different methods for analyzing tasks exist. Subsequently common human factors

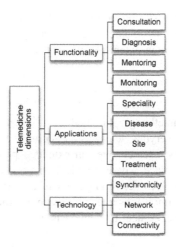

Fig. 2. Taxonomy of telemedicine considers abstract tasks of digital health systems within the functionality dimension. Task abstraction remains implicit here.

methods for task analysis are described: hierarchical task analysis (HTA), cognitive task analysis (CTA) and observation. In addition, a method is described which is less common: semantic classification by users.

4.1 Hierarchical Task Analysis

The idea behind the *Hierarchical Task Analysis* (HTA) is to subdivide tasks performed by humans into sub-tasks in order to create an abstract hierarchical model by clustering. Tasks that bear close resemblance to each other are assigned to one group and must be part of at least one group but may be part of several groups. Groups are then labeled in terms of the work domain or the work functions and can be iteratively refined or regrouped. So an observation of a very specific task with a specific user or user group has to be made resulting of unstructured lists of words describing actions which to organize using notation or diagrams. The task analysis involves users only as observation object, not as integrated into the task analysis process.

4.2 Cognitive Task Analysis

Cognitive Task Analysis (CTA) aims at understanding tasks that require a lot of cognitive activity from the user, such as decision-making, problem-solving, memory, attention and judgement. The CTA methods analyze and represent the cognitive activities users utilize to perform certain tasks. Some of the steps of a cognitive task analysis are: the mapping of the task, identifying the critical decision points, clustering, linking, and prioritizing them, and characterizing the strategies used. For the purpose of CTA various interview and observation procedures are applied in order to capture a description of the knowledge that experts use to perform complex tasks. Complex tasks are defined as those where performance requires the integrated use of both controlled (conscious, conceptual) and automated (unconscious, procedural or strategic) knowledge to perform tasks that often extend over many hours or days.

4.3 Observation

Participant *observation* is an ethnographic method in which a researcher participates in, observes, and records the everyday activities and cultural aspects of a particular social group. It typically includes research over an extended period of time (rather than a single session) and takes place where people live or work (rather than in a lab). Participant observation involves active engagement in activities in contrast to observation where researchers simply observe without interacting with people. Often this method can be part of a hierarchical task analysis.

4.4 Semantic Classification

During *semantic classification* for analysis of work tasks, each task of the worker is described verbally. Characteristics of words and frequencies found with the sematic differential then lead to the development of a task taxonomy. Consensus judgements of tasks lead to a relevance ranking and structure of the tasks. Semantic classifications are able to support task descriptions and hence the measurement during an evaluation. They perfectly provide conceptual clarity and categorize information for an increased theoretical understanding and predictive accuracy in empirical research. In order to understand the differences to previously mentioned methods we provide following example:

4.5 Example

Given example illustrates how general tasks are identified by digital health systems users with the help of semantic classification. Via online questionnaire professionals in the domain of health and digital health as well as patients

1. rated relevance of given abstract medical tasks [20],
2. rated relevance of given abstract visualization tasks [15, 21]
3. rated abstract visualization tasks relevance for digital health tasks.

The sample of 98 participants consisted of a group of 47 digital health experts and a group of 51 older adults with a mean age of 55.76 representing the patient perspective. Group differences were computed in order to illustrate the extent to which general health and visualization tasks are relevant. The study was able to verify and extend existing abstract visualization and digital health systems. Abstract tasks from the visualization and health domain could be mapped to domain tasks. A chi-square test of independence was performed to examine the relation between relevance frequency counts and user group (older adults, tele medical experts). The relation between these variables was highly significant for mentoring, X^2 (4, N = 67) = 14.14, p = .002** and monitoring, X^2 (4, N = 70) = 22.13, p = .00**. User rankings and group differences were synthetized in taxonomy. Group differences could be found most often for the abstract visualization tasks. Root node of resulting taxonomy was "digital health systems task". Ranked domain tasks from closed question (1) monitoring, (2) consultation, (3) diagnosis and (4) mentoring built the next level. On the same level tasks resulting from open questions were added according to their code count frequency as siblings to previously mentioned tasks (4) therapy, (5) communication, (6) cooperation, (7) documentation and (8) quality management. Each of these eight main tasks were complemented by (1) data types from open questions, which provide a qualitative description of the data from the user perspective, (2) data types from closed questions and (3) top-ranked on total sample abstract visualization tasks.

5 Discussion

This paper emphasizes abstraction levels of tasks with regard to objectives when using tasks resulting from a detailed task analysis. It was stated that intended generalizability of research results relates to the required abstraction level of an experimental task together with the data types/application domain and user. Based on our experiences from a user study on the classification of abstract visualization and health tasks we can state that relevance of tasks for digital health systems can be easily judged by users. Semantic classification by users provides thus a feasible method to build and rank abstract tasks and to join tasks from different domains (health and visualization). A precise task definition should be given to the participant but it should be avoided to give specific examples as this would prime the user and the level of abstraction from resulting tasks would decrease. While task abstraction is one parameter the user and domain specificity has to be controlled, too. That means a result list of tasks is more generalizable if all important user groups of an application domain agree on the importance of a task. User type variability and sample size increase validity of the results from user driven semantic classifications. The initial goal of deriving tasks which would produce as generalizable visualization evaluation results as possible instead requires further investigation of semantic classifications connecting tasks through different levels of abstraction. In comparison, HTA and CTA are too specific to investigate abstract tasks, but their procedures might be of interest for bridging abstract to specific tasks. One could for example let users subdivide the abstract tasks until they have the granularity required for described evaluation purpose. Further type of presented research type also might utilize a more extensive set of given tasks. One major definitional problem for task analysis and semantic classification is that it is difficult to agree on what a task is. Any set of behavior represented by a textual label can be considered as a task here. A possible solution could be to concentrate on describing tasks just in verbs instead of nouns in order to disconnect them from the application context and user specificities.

Acknowledgements. This publication is part of the research project "TECH4AGE", which is funded by the German Federal Ministry of Education and Research (BMBF, Grant No. 16SV7111) supervised by the VDI/VDE Innovation + Technik GmbH.

References

1. Browne, S.H., Behzadi, Y., Littlewort, G.: Let visuals tell the story: medication adherence in patients with type II diabetes captured by a novel ingestion sensor platform. JMIR Mhealth Uhealth **3**(4), e108 (2015)
2. Theng, Y.-L.: Socially-mediated mobile system for tuberculosis public health alert, care and education (MobiTB-ACE). In: Medicine 2.0 Conference (2012)
3. Jones, A.P.: Indoor air quality and health. Atmos. Environ. **33**(28), 4535–4564 (1999)
4. Subramonyam, H.: SIGCHI: magic mirror - embodied interactions for the quantified self. In: Proceedings of the 33rd Annual ACM Conference Extended Abstracts on Human Factors in Computing Systems, pp. 1699–1704. ACM (2015)
5. Brown, B., Chetty, M., Grimes, A., Harmon, E.: Reflecting on health: a system for students to monitor diet and exercise. In: CHI 2006 Extended Abstracts on Human Factors in Computing Systems, pp. 1807–1812. ACM, New York (2006)
6. Ali-Hasan, N., Gavales, D., Peterson, A., Raw, M.: Fitster: social fitness information visualizer. In: CHI 2006 Extended Abstracts on Human Factors in Computing Systems, pp. 1795–1800. ACM, New York (2006)
7. Swan, M.: Sensor mania! The internet of things, wearable computing, objective metrics, and the quantified self 2.0. J. Sens. Actuator Netw. **1**(3), 217–253 (2012)
8. Frost, J., Smith, B.: Visualizing health practice to treat diabetes. In: CHI 2002 Extended Abstracts on Human Factors in Computing Systems, pp. 606–607. ACM (2002)
9. Milash, B., Rose, A., Widoff, S., Shneiderman, B., Plaisant, C.: LifeLines: visualizing personal histories. In: Proceedings of the SIGCHI Conference on Human Factors in Computing Systems, pp. 221–227 (1996)
10. Kim, M.I., Johnson, K.B.: Personal health records: evaluation of functionality and utility. J. Am. Med. Inform. Assoc. **9**(2), 171–180 (2002)
11. Archer, N., Fevrier-Thomas, U., Lokker, C., McKibbon, K.A., Straus, S.E.: Personal health records: a scoping review. J. Am. Med. Inform. Assoc.: JAMIA **18**(4), 515–522 (2011)
12. Frost, J., Massagli, M.: Social uses of personal health information within PatientsLikeMe, an online patient community: what can happen when patients have access to one another's data. J. Med. Internet Res. **10**(3), e15 (2008)
13. Rind, A., Aigner, W., Wagner, M., Miksch, S., Lammarsch, T.: User tasks for evaluation: untangling the terminology throughout visualization design and development. In: Proceedings of the Fifth Workshop on Beyond Time and Errors: Novel Evaluation Methods for Visualization, pp. 9–15. ACM, New York (2014)
14. Munzner, T.: A nested model for visualization design and validation. IEEE Trans. Vis. Comput. Graph. **15**(6), 921–928 (2009)
15. Brehmer, M., Munzner, T.: A multi-level typology of abstract visualization tasks. IEEE Trans. Vis. Comput. Graph. **19**(12), 2376–2385 (2013)
16. Brehmer, M., Sedlmair, M., Ingram, S., Munzner, T.: Visualizing dimensionally-reduced data: interviews with analysts and a characterization of task sequences. Submitted to ACM BELIV Workshop, pp. 1–8 (2014)
17. Miksch, S., Aigner, W.: A matter of time: applying a data–users–tasks design triangle to visual analytics of time-oriented data. Comput. Graph. **38**, 286–290 (2014)
18. Andrienko, N., Andrienko, G.: Exploratory Analysis of Spatial and Temporal Data: A Systematic Approach. Springer Science & Business Media, Berlin (2006)
19. Ingenerf, J.: Telemedicine and terminology: different needs of context information. IEEE Trans. Inf. Technol. Biomed. **3**(2), 92–100 (1999)

20. Bashshur, R., Shannon, G., Krupinski, E., Grigsby, J.: The taxonomy of telemedicine. Telemed. J. e-Health: Off. J. Am. Telemed. Assoc. **17**(6), 484–494 (2011)
21. Shneiderman, B.: The eyes have it: a task by data type taxonomy for information visualizations. In: Proceedings/IEEE Symposium on Visual Languages, September 3–6, 1996, Boulder, Colorado, pp. 336–343. IEEE Computer Society Press, Los Alamitos (1996)

EEG Features Extraction and Classification of Rifle Shooters in the Aiming Period

Liwei Zhang, Qianxiang Zhou(✉), Zhongqi Liu, and Yu Wang

Key Laboratory for Biomechanics and Mechanobiology of the Ministry of
Education, School of Biological Science and Medical Engineering,
Beihang University, Beijing 100191, China
zqxg@buaa.edu.cn

Abstract. A basic problem in the design of EEG signal based devices, which
could help the upper limb disabled soldiers carrying on their shooting tasks, is
presented by the extraction and classification of EEG features. Such system can
extract EEG signals features during soldiers act their shooting tasks and transform the features into binary control signals for operation. This paper is about
analyzing the EEG signals of health soldiers during their rifle practice during the
aiming period, which is the most vital step for shooting and extracting EEG
features. We put the special features into a support vector machine to classify
two classes signals and compare the signals of the holding period with an aiming
period. Results show that the power of alpha and beta in occipital and parietal
regions have significant changed, so does the power of theta rhythm in frontal
area. Thus, we put the combine of alpha and beta power which as EEG features
into our support vector machine's classification device, then get the accurate
classification rates compare with the one that comes from theta power. The alpha
and beta power join as the characters get higher classification accuracy than the
theta.

Keywords: Shooting · Aiming period · EEG · Features extraction and
classification

1 Introduction

The purpose of studying the characteristics of electroencephalographic (EEG) signals
in the rifle shooting process is to develop an assistive tool that can assist the upper-limb
disabled soldier to continue the firing task and provide a new direction for the man-
ufacture of weapons. The key point of the tool is to analyze and extract the feature of
the EEG signal that can regulate control system. Aiming is a very important part [1] in
the process of shooting; the aiming performance determines the accuracy of shooting.
Accordingly, the content of the data was of interest for the purpose of gaining a better
understanding of the psychophysiological characteristics of an expert shooter during
the aiming period and adopting signal processing approach to verify the feasibility of
the assistive tool solution.

EEG recordings have been employed in studies of the aiming period in the
shooting. Bouchard and Tetreault studied the visual impairment effects on the body

© Springer International Publishing AG 2017
V.G. Duffy (Ed.): DHM 2017, Part II, LNCS 10287, pp. 306–317, 2017.
DOI: 10.1007/978-3-319-58466-9_28

stability at the time of aiming [2–4]. Joy Myint's researched using auditory to aid defective shooter (vision impairment) to aim [5]. Combining the technologies of EEG and eye tracking has been advocated by Janelle et al. as a means of gaining a better understanding of the underlying mechanisms that regulate human visual attention [6]. Hatfield exposed the cortex activity of shooting experts and novices while aiming [7–9]. To better analyze cortical functioning in the shooting or archery and the "neural efficiency hypothesis", Event Related Desynchronization/Synchronization (ERD/ERS) analysis has been used by researchers [10–13]. Vijn et al. [14, 15] proposed the concept of occipital EEG alpha power during the aiming period, and M. Doppelmayr studied the time course of frontal midline theta (Fmθ) during the aiming period in rifle shooting [16]. But few people extracted the feature of EEG signal when aiming.

In this paper, we analyzed the characteristics of the EEG from the rifle shooting experts during the aiming period to get the EEG feature which is the mark of the cerebral cortical activity and the brain region where the feature located. We used the wavelet transform to denoise and feature enhancement. Then the power of alpha, beta and theta were calculated. Support vector machines were used to classify the two classes of signals (the holding signal and the aiming signal), after extracting the EEG features.

2   Method

2.1   Participants

Ten excellent soldiers from the army volunteered to take part in the study. The shooters, who were aged 25–40 years, had a minimum of 4 years of shooting experience. All shooters were healthy men, had visual acuity or corrected visual acuity of 4.8 or more, held the rifle in their right hand and used their right eye for aim. Each participant had signed consent before taking part in the experiment.

2.2   Procedure

The participants were initially informed about the procedures and provided verbal and written instructions regarding the shooting task. After a warm-up period in a shooting range, the shooter was asked to perform three 50-shot runs to the target, using a standard 56-type semi-automatic rifle. The distance between the shooter and the target was 70 m. Each shot involved three periods: preparatory period, aiming period, the shot release period. Voice cures played at the beginning of each period with which the subject was instructed to perform the task. Figure 1 shows a 2-min for break time between the two runs, and the two trials interleaved with 1 s.

2.3   Data Collection

EEG data was recorded from 32 electrodes arranged according to the 10–20 system [17] in a BP cap (ElectroCap Inc, Florida, USA), and was made using BP ActiCHamp

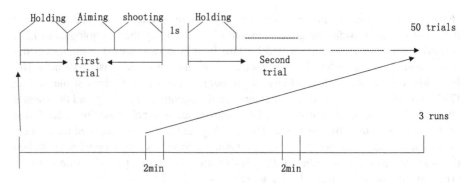

Fig. 1. Shooting experiment

amplifiers. EEG data continuously recorded with 1000 Hz sampling frequency. The ground electrode and common reference were positioned at Cz to ensure low impedance values (generally below 5 KΩ). Eye-movement (EOG) artifact monitored with two electrodes attached superior to and on the external canthus of the right eye. An eye patch was worn over the left eye to minimizing muscle artifact in the EEG record due to squinting while aiming.

2.4   Data Analysis

EEG data were band-pass filtered between 0.1 to 45 Hz. After wavelet decomposing and reconstructing, the data were quantified in the Theta (4–8 Hz), low Alpha (8–12 Hz), and Beta (16–24 Hz) bands. We have used four parameters (the alpha bands power, the beta bands power, the theta bands power, the beta bands power and theta power (β/θ)) to compare the differences between the data of the holding period and the aiming period. Then the features were extracted and the two classes of the signals were classified by SVM.

2.4.1   Methods

Wavelet Transform. The essence of the wavelet transform (WT) [18] is to decompose the signal into a series of wavelet functions, and they perform multiscale refinement analysis by stretching and translation. WT has the characteristics of multi-resolution analysis. It based on this characteristic that wavelet transforms better for those non-stationary signals, especially those with rapidly changing signals. In practice, the wavelet transform is effective in signal de-noising, weak signal extraction and signal singularity analysis.

Let $x(t) \in L^2(R)$ ($L^2(R)$ is the square integrable function space on R), then the formula of wavelet transform of x (t) as follows [19]:

$$WT_x(a, \tau) = \frac{1}{\sqrt{a}} \int x(t) \phi^* \left(\frac{t - \tau}{a} \right) dt = \langle x(t), \phi_{a\tau}(t) \rangle \tag{1}$$

Where $\phi(t)$ is a function called elementary wavelet or mother wavelet, a > 0 is the scale factor, τ reflects the displacement, the value can be positive or negative.

The equivalent frequency domain expressed as

$$WT_x(a, \tau) = \frac{\sqrt{a}}{2\pi} \int x(w) \psi^*(aw) e^{jw\pi} dw \tag{2}$$

The discrete wavelet transform written as

$$WT_f\left(\frac{1}{2^j}, \frac{k}{2^j} \right) = \langle f, \psi_{j,k} \rangle \tag{3}$$

Then,

$$\psi_{j,k}(t) = \psi_{\frac{1}{2^j}, \frac{k}{2^j}}(t) = 2^{j/2} \psi(2^j t - k) \tag{4}$$

$\{ \psi_{j,k} \}_{j,k \in Z}$ is the Riesz basis of L2 (R).

Let the sampling rate of the discrete signal is fs, the original signal and the sub-band signal distribution relationship as follows:

$$\left[0, \frac{f_s}{2} \right] = \left[0, \frac{f_s}{2^{L+1}} \right] \cup \left[\frac{f_s}{2^{L+1}}, \frac{f_s}{2^L} \right] \cup \ldots \cup \left[\frac{f_s}{2^2}, \frac{f_s}{2} \right] \tag{5}$$

The sub-frequency band signals corresponding to these sub-bands are: $x_L^a(n), x_L^d(n), \ldots, x_2^d(n), x_1^d(n)$, then

$$x(n) = x_L^a(n) + \sum_{j=1}^{L} x_j^d(n) \tag{6}$$

Where L is the number of decomposition steps and $x_L^a(n)$ is the low-pass approximation component, $x_j^d(n)$ is the detail component under different scales.

Support Vector Machine. Support Vector Machines (SVM) has a unique advantage in dealing with small sample learning problems [20]. It has many advantages, such as strict theory, strong adaptability, global optimization, high training efficiency and good generalization performance. The SVM derived from the optimal classification surface. The optimal classification surface is that the classification surface can not only divide the two types of samples correctly but also make the classification gap maximum. Let train sample set $\{(x_i, y_i), i = 1,2, \ldots, n\}$, then, $x_i \in RN$ belong to class 1, denote y_i as 1, otherwise denote y_i as -1. The goal of learning is to construct a discriminant function that classifies the two types of test data as accurately as possible.

In the case of linear separability, there exists a hyperplane such that the training samples are completely separated, and the classification hyperplane is

$$w * x + b = 0 \tag{7}$$

Where w is an n-dimensional vector and b is an offset. (x_i, y_i) in the training set D is satisfied:

$$\left. \begin{array}{l} w * x + b \geq 1, y_i = 1 \\ w * x + b \leq -1, y_i = -1, i = 1, 2, \ldots n \end{array} \right\} \tag{8}$$

Where $w * x$ is inner product. The above formula can abbreviated as:

$$y_i(w * x_i + b) \geq 1, i = 1, 2, \ldots, n \tag{9}$$

If all the vectors in the training sample set are correctly partitioned by a hyperplane and the distance between the sample data closest to the hyperplane and the hyperplane is the largest, then the hyperplane is the optimal hyperplane, like Fig. 2.

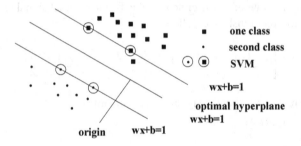

Fig. 2. Optimal classification hyperplane

The optimization of the hyperplane can transformed into the quadratic programming problem, and the training data satisfy the following formula:

$$\left. \begin{array}{l} \min_{w,b} \frac{1}{2} ||w||^2 \\ y_i(w * x_i + b) \geq 1, i = 1, 2, \ldots, n \end{array} \right\} \tag{10}$$

In this paper, two firing states are separated by SVM. The appropriate kernel function of SVM can make the accuracy of classification optimal. We use the Soft Spaced Support Vector Machine (SVM) whose kernel function is radial basis function (RBF).

2.4.2 Data Preprocessing

To weaken noise and enhance feature in the signals of aiming electroencephalogram data, the independent component analysis (ICA) were applied to identify and remove any remaining artifacts (e.g., eye blinks). The data acquired had a total amplitude of less than 100 uV. They were band-pass filtered between 0.01 to 45 Hz, segmented into single epochs of 2 s duration, with each epoch starting at -2 s with respect to t = 0 (i.e. the instant when the shot was released). The holding data were also 2 s of each epoch. During the aiming period, the blink of right eye leads to a larger signal artifact in the forehead region, so the signal of FP2 channel had a strong noise. Finally, we dropped the channels in the brain's frontal region (F3, Fz, F4), frontal-center region (FC5, FC6), central region (C3, Cz, C4), parietal region (P3, Pz, P4) and occipital region (O1, Oz, O2). After Preprocessing, we got two data sets XA and XB who stored in the form of 'trials × time × channels'. Their size both were 1500 × 2000 × 14.

2.4.3 Data Analysis Process

The collection process of the signal shows the number of observed signals is less than the independent signals. For this reason, the sub-signals of alpha, beta and theta obtained by multi-resolution analysis of the wavelet transform. The data of holding period and aiming period were decomposed and reconstructed using db6 wavelet function as wavelet basis. Since the 'Daubechies' wavelet has smoothing property and the total entropy value obtained by using db6 was the smallest. The power of the sub-signals of alpha bands, beta bands, theta bands and beta/theta calculated separately, and the data format saved as 14 × 1500 × 4. Figure 3 shows the signals of alpha, beta and theta of the F3 channel in the holding period and the aiming period.

Alpha, beta, theta spectral power and beta/theta in the five regions of the brain were subjected to separate 2 × 14 × 1500 × 4 (shooting period × channels × time × parameters) Paired T-test with repeated measures on channels. The parameters with significant changes used as input vector of SVM and the classification results of two classes at channel O1 and O2 obtained. In this paper, the kernel function of SVM was Gaussian radial basis function, and the marginal factor were 25, 35, 45 respectively.

3 Results

During the aiming period and the holding period, the results obtained by pairwise T-test of the four parameters (α, β, θ, β/θ) in the 14 channels (F3, Fz, F4, FC5, FC6, C3, Cz, C4, C3, Cz, C4, O1, Oz) are shown in Table 1. We inferred statistical significance levels ($p < 0.05$ and $p < 0.01$) from the 95th and 99th percentiles of the distribution.

From the summary of group mean EEG power in Table 1, we can see that statistical analysis revealed several significant differences in power for the frontal region. In detail, during the holding period and the aiming period, the power of α existed obvious differences ($p < 0.01$) in frontal, frontal- central, central (C3, Cz), parietal, occipital region. Similarly, there was a main effect ($p < 0.01$) for the β power in the region of frontal, central, parietal, occipital, with significant changes ($p < 0.05$) in the frontal and parietal region for θ power. Meanwhile, the θ/β was significant differences ($p < 0.05$) in frontal, frontal- central, occipital region.

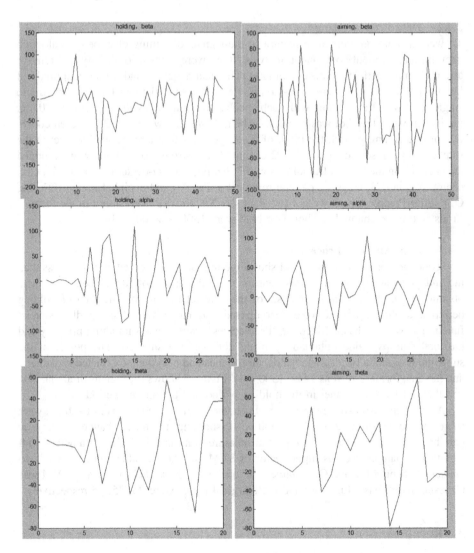

Fig. 3. The holding period and aiming period, the signal of alpha, beta and theta at the F3 channel

The results of power analysis in the alpha band and beta band shown in Fig. 4, during the aiming period, the power increased significantly in both the left and right hemispheres of the brain, especially in the occipital and apical regions. Figure 5 shows power in the left hemisphere of the brain to increase more than the right. It can be seen from Fig. 6 that there was a significantly reduced at the F3 site for the theta power, with obviously increased at the F4 and Cz site.

The combined of alpha power and beta power as the input of SVM and SVM was used to calculate the classification accuracy of the two classes signals (the holding signals and the aiming signals) at O1, O2, Oz site. Similarly, theta was used as input to

Table 1. The results of the paired T-test

Channel	α	β	θ	β/θ
F3	0.002	0.001	0.002	0.001
F4	0.001	0.001	0.002	0.05
Fz	0.002	0.001	0.007	0.001
FC5	0.001	0.001	0.660	0.001
FC6	0.001	0.001	0.893	0.001
C3	0.001	0.001	0.705	0.001
C4	0.056	0.001	0.020	0.539
Cz	0.001	0.001	0.001	0.669
P3	0.001	0.001	0.927	0.001
P4	0.001	0.001	0.008	0.013
Pz	0.001	0.001	0.026	0.036
O1	0.001	0.001	0.624	0.002
O2	0.001	0.001	0.296	0.001
Oz	0.001	0.001	0.675	0.001

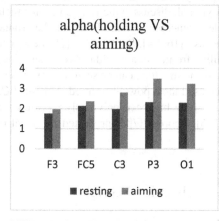 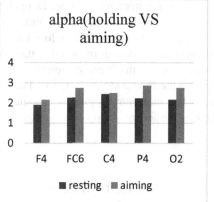

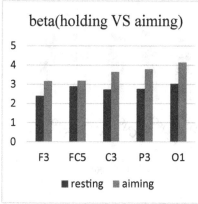 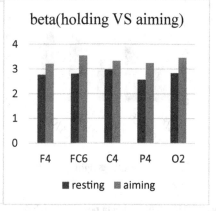

Fig. 4. Alpha and beta power in the holding period and aiming period

the SVM to compute the classification accuracy (shown in Table 2) of the two classes signals at Fz site. In the data set, 1200 trials data as training data, and other 300 trials as the test data.

4 Discussion

The comparison of the cortical activity patterns obtained from the marksmen during the holding period and the aiming period of the target shooting task revealed that the differences observed in each of the frequency bands assessed. Based on the activation patterns it seems plausible to conclude that the eye, especially the right eye, plays a dominant role during the aiming period. This deduction based on the finding of increased alpha power and beta power in the parietal and occipital regions of the experts during the aiming period of the target shooting task and the power on the left hemisphere of the brain was greater than the right hemisphere which can be seen in Fig. 5. This result was similar to that reported previously [21–23]. Additional insights regarding the psychological processes of the expert performers were enabled by examination of spectral content beyond that typically reported in the sports psychophysiology literature. Such as, Doppelmayr et al. discussed the frontal midline theta (Fmθ) could be observed in the human electroencephalogram (EEG) at the frontal midline electrode location Fz before shot release [16, 24]. Smith et al. [25] described this spectral component recorded at the midline frontal area as indicative of sustained attention. Such a finding also showed in Fig. 6 and in which can be seen increased theta power in the frontal region (F3, F4). The increased theta power observed at channel Cz means that the central region is activated, but little has been previously reported and requires further validation. Lutsyuk et al. [26] reported θ/β represented the level of

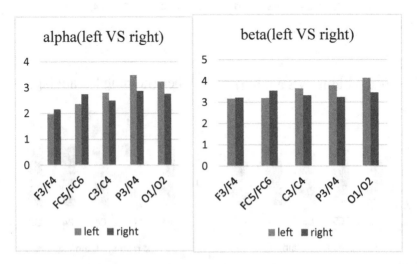

Fig. 5. The alpha and beta power in the left and right hemispheres of the brain during the aiming period

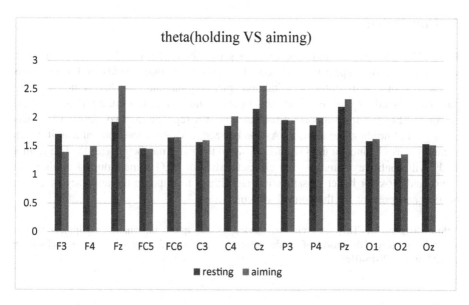

Fig. 6. Theta rhythm in holding and aiming state of the power value

attention. From Table 1, we can see that the value of θ/β in the frontal, apical and occipital regions were significantly changed, indicating that the marksmen possess a higher degree of attentional focus.

During the aiming period, the main cognitive task of the shooter was to stare at the target and the attention intensification. One could deduce that the alpha power and beta power in the occipital region (O1, O2, Oz) were the feature vectors of the EEG during the gazing period and theta power in the frontal region (Fz) was the EEG feature vector during focused concentration. It can be seen from Table 2 that the SVM can separate the two classes of signals (the holding signal and the aiming signal) in above the four cases. The optimal classification results were obtained by combining alpha power and beta power as EEG feature at the channel of O1. In the three cases (marginal factor was 25 or 35 or 45), when the marginal factor was 25, the optimal classification accuracy was obtained.

Table 2. The accuracy at Fz, O1, O2 and Oz channel with different marginal factor

Channel	25	35	45
Fz	70%	74.29%	75.71%
Oz	68.57%	68.57%	68.57%
O1	77.5%	75%	75%
O2	65.7%	65.7%	65.7%

316 L. Zhang et al.

5 Conclusion

The EEG signal of excellent shooters during the aiming period of rifle shooting were analyzed by power spectrum method. The power of alpha bands and beta bands increased significantly in the occipital and apical region, and theta bands increased the power at F3 and F4 channel. Both alpha-power and beta power combination, or theta power as EEG feature, support vector machine can separate the two classes of signals (the signal of holding and aiming). As can be seen in Table 2, the optimal classification accuracy was obtained at the O1 channel when the marginal factor was 25. The further study will continue to analyze the characteristics of EEG signals during aiming and firing, and look for better classification algorithms to improve the accuracy of classification and prepare for the control system.

Acknowledgement. This research was funded by Electronic information equipment system research of Key laboratory of basic research projects of national defense technology (DXZT-JC-ZZ-2015-016).

References

1. Goodman, S., Haufler, A., Jae, K.S., et al.: Regular and random components in aiming-point trajectory during rifle aiming and shooting. J. Mot. Behav. **41**(4), 367–382 (2009)
2. Bouchard, D., Tetreault, S.: The motor development of sighted children and children with moderate low vision aged 8–13. J. Vis. Impair. Blind. **94**, 564–573 (2000)
3. Portfors-Yeomans, C.V., Riach, C.L.: Frequency characteristics of postural control of children with and without visual impairment. Dev. Med. Child Neurol. **37**, 456–463 (1995)
4. Willis, J.R., Vitale, S.E., Agrawal, Y., et al.: Visual impairment, uncorrected refractive error, and objectively measured balance in the United States. JAMA Ophthalmol. **131**, 1049–1056 (2013)
5. Myint, J., Latham, K.: The relationship between visual function and performance in rifle shooting for athletes with vision impairment. BMJ Open Sport Exerc. Med. **2**, 1–7 (2016)
6. Janelle, C.M., Hillman, C.H., Hatfield, B.D.: Concurrent measurement of electroencephalographic and ocular indices of attention during rifle shooting: an exploratory case study. Int. J. Sports Vis. **6**(1), 21–29 (2000)
7. Hatfield, B.D., Haufler, A.J., Hung, T.M., Spalding, T.W.: Electroencephalographic studies of skilled psychomotor performance. J. Clin. Neurophysiol. **21**, 144–156 (2004)
8. Babiloni, C., Del Percio, C., et al.: Golf putt outcomes are predicted by sensorimotor cerebral EEG rhythms. J. Physiol. **586**, 131–139 (2008)
9. Del Percio, C., Babiloni, C., et al.: Visuo-attentional and sensorimotor alpha rhythms are related to visuo-motor performance in athletes. Hum. Brain Mapp. **30**, 3527–3540 (2009)
10. Hatfield, B.D., Kerick, S.E.: The psychology of superior sport performance: a cognitive and affective neuroscience perspective. In: Tenenbaum, G., Eklund, R.C. (eds.) Handbook of Sport Psychology, 3rd edn, pp. 84–109. Wiley, Hoboken (2007)

11. Haufler, A.J., Spalding, T.W., Santa Maria, D.L., Hatfield, B.D.: Neuro-cognitive activity during a self-paced visuospatial task: comparative EEG profiles in marksmen and novice shooters. Biol. Psychol. **53**, 131–160 (2000)

12. Janelle, C.M., Hillman, C.H., Apparies, R.J., et al.: Expertise differences in cortical activation and gaze behaviour during rifle shooting. J. Sport Exerc. Psychol. **22**, 167–182 (2000)

13. di Fronso, S., Robazza, C.: Neural markers of performance states in an Olympic Athlete: an EEG case study in air-pistol shooting. J. Sports Sci. Med. **15**, 214–222 (2016)

14. Vijn, P.C.M., Van Dijk, B.W., Spekreijse, H.: Visual stimulation reduces EEG activity in man. Brain Res. **550**, 49–53 (1991)

15. Kononen, M., Partanen, J.V.: Blocking of EEG alpha activity during visual performance in healthy adults. A quantitative study. Electroencephalogr. Clin. Neurophysiol. **87**, 164–170 (1993)

16. Doppelmayr, M., Finkenzeller, T., Sauseng, P.: Frontal midline theta in the pre-shot phase of rifle shooting: differences between experts and novices. Neuropsychologia **46**, 1463–1467 (2008)

17. Jasper, H.: The ten-twenty electrode system of the international federation. Electroencephalogr. Clin. Neurophysiol. **10**, 371–375 (1958)

18. Li, S.: Wavelet Transform and Application. Higher Education Press, Beijing (1997)

19. Guan, J.A., Ling, J., Zhao, J.: Direct neural interface and control technology. Foreign Med. Biomed. Eng. **27**(6), 337–341 (2004)

20. Blanchard, G., Blankertz, B.: BCI competition 2003-data set IIa: spatial patterns of self-controlled brain rhythm modulations. IEEE Trans. Biomed. Eng. **51**(6), 1062–1066 (2004)

21. Hatfield, B.D., Landers, D.M., Ray, W.J.: Cognitive processes during self-paced motor performance: an electroencephalographic profile of skilled marksmen. J. Sport Psychol. **6**, 42–59 (1984)

22. Landers, D.M., Han, M., Salazar, W., Petruzzello, S.J., Kubitz, K.A., Gannon, T.L.: Effect of learning on electroencephalographic and electrocardiographic patterns on novice archers. Int. J. Sport Psychol. **25**, 313–330 (1994)

23. Loze, G.M., Collins, D., Holmes, P.S.: Pre-shot EEG alpha-power reactivity during expert air-pistol shooting: a comparison of best and worst shots. J. Sports Sci. **19**, 727–733 (2001)

24. Ishihara, T., Yoshii, N.: Activation of abnormal EEG by mental work. Rinsho Nohha Clin. Electroencephalogr. **8**, 26–34 (1966)

25. Smith, M.E., McEvoy, L.K., Gevins, A.: Neurophysiological indices of strategy development and skill acquisition. Cogn. Brain Res. **7**, 389–404 (1999)

26. Lutsyuk, N.V., Ismont, E.V., Pavlenko, V.B.: Modulation of attention in healthy children using a course of EG-feedback sessions. Neurophysiology **38**(5/6), 389–395 (2006)

Design for Safety

Safety Does Not Happen by Accident, Can Gaming Help Improve Occupational Health and Safety in Organizations?

Cameron Chodan, Pejman Mirza-Babaei(✉),
and Karthik Sankaranarayanan

University of Ontario Institute of Technology (UOIT),
2000 Simcoe Street North, Oshawa, ON, Canada
Cameron.Chodan@gmail.com, {Pejman,Karthik}@uoit.ca

Abstract. In 2015, the Association of Workers' Compensation Boards of Canada recorded around quarter-million workplace injuries, a staggering figure which does not include incidents that go undocumented. A lack of health and safety training and/or lack of safety awareness can lead to workplace injuries and in the worst cases a workplace death. It is imperative that organizations make Occupational Health and Safety (OHS) one of their top priorities.

In this paper, we explore the implementation of an adaptive personalized learning support system within a game that is centered on health and safety training. The design of the game incorporates a feedback loop that constantly evaluates the player's performance while they complete learning challenges. As the players proceed within the game's environment their profile is constantly updated thus providing an insight into their strengths and weaknesses. The game is evolutionary i.e. it is designed to adjust the challenges given to the player in order to focus on improving the player's underperforming skills. This game is a step towards overcoming a lack of health and safety training observed in small and medium enterprises. Through this game we try to create a fun and motivating environment where workers are being exposed to the health and safety mindset and learning through relevant challenges.

The game is made in collaboration with the public services health and safety association (PSHSA) based in Toronto. The learning challenges aim to better the player's health and safety performance in the organizational performance metric (OPM) and hone their underlying health and safety skills.

Keywords: User-centered design · Game development · Serious games · Adaptive learning · Case study

1 Introduction

Employees are an integral part of an organization and their skills can be considered a competitive advantage. In most scenarios, organizations train their employees in order to equip them with a skillset(s). Health and Safety forms an important cornerstone in such trainings. In spite of this training and attention, employees are still prone to injuries. According to the Association of Workers' Compensation Boards of Canada,

© Springer International Publishing AG 2017
V.G. Duffy (Ed.): DHM 2017, Part II, LNCS 10287, pp. 321–332, 2017.
DOI: 10.1007/978-3-319-58466-9_29

there were around a quarter million recorded workplace injuries in 2015[1]. One needs to keep in mind that many workplace injuries also go unrecorded.

Health and safety prevention is a very broad field, covering a wide range of organizational sectors. Preventing health and safety issues is not a new concept and is often done through training, but new techniques, resources and tools are being researched. There is a plethora of resources available for organizations and employees to educate themselves. These resources include textbooks, and training courses.

With the current development in digital media many organizations are exploring the potential of digital resources (such as e-learning and serious games) for training. E-learning could be generalized as interactive educational tools in a digital format. Closely tied to e-learning are serious games, which are often defined as games with the main objective being teaching or training players how to react to certain situations [8]. Various research studies showed that both e-learning and serious games are effective at teaching players [8, 14]. Previous efforts in e-learning and serious games in health and safety focused to tackle a small portion of the overall sectors.

Our current research focuses on building a serious game that adapts its content based on users' industry sector as well as what they need to learn with respect to health and safety.

A way to achieve such a goal is to implement a system that adapts and personalizes based on user's needs. Adaptive systems are a departure from the 'one-size-fits-all" approach and aims to tailor the environment around the user. Adaptive systems are focused on increasing learner satisfaction, effectiveness and engagement [10].

Studies showed that adapting to the user's feedback could make a major impact on user's satisfaction and motivation [17]. Video games can be considered as powerful medium to explore adaptive learning systems. Zualkeman et al. [19] constructed an adaptive game that changes the content and delivery of the content based on the player's abilities [19]. Such a design may provide a more motivating approach to learning for the audience.

In the following sections, we elucidate and explore the above-mentioned topics in detail. We describe game design efforts with the focus on adaptive learning followed by our case study in collaboration with Public Safety and Health Service Association (PSHSA). PSHSA is located in Toronto, Canada and dedicated to providing easily accessible client-focused solutions for eliminating workplace injuries, illness and fatalities. Through their regional offices scattered around Ontario, PSHSA serves more than 10,000 organizations that employ more than 1.6 million workers[2].

2 Adaptive Games for Learning

According to Entertainment Software Association (ESA), fifty-four percent of Canadians are gamers with the average age of the Canadian gamer being thirty-three [5]. Not only are there a large number of gamers in Canada there is also a growing

---

[1] http://awcbc.org/?page_id=14.

[2] http://www.pshsa.ca/about-us/.

interesting in game companies. From 2013 to 2015, Canada saw 143 new companies raising the overall number to 472 [5]. With the growing number of games and gaming companies, there is also growing academic interest in the potential applications of games. Games serve a wide gamut of objectives ranging from, entertainment, education, and aiding physical rehabilitation [12, 16].

In education, games are suitable medium for entertaining and motivating students. With a game providing enough intrinsic motivation for continued play, studies have shown that people are more receptive to learning when motivated thus making games a powerful tool [13, 16]. Educators and game developers are looking into utilizing this strength and applying it to learning in games.

Many games create a desire to play through the self-determination theory (SDT) [15]. The self-determination theory posits that three basic psychological needs should be satisfied to trigger human motivation. The first is competence i.e. the need to overcome problems and seek mastery. The second is relatedness, the want to interact with others. The last is autonomy, the need to control one's own actions. Keeping this theory in mind when designing a game helps capture player's motivation.

Flow theory is another design principle many game researchers have discussed to keep players immersed in the game [1]. The goal of flow theory is to keep the player in situations where they have enough skill to overcome the challenge encountered in the game. This situation often referred to as the flow channel as show in Fig. 1. If there is too much challenge and not enough skill, the player will have anxiety. In contrast if there is too little challenge and ample skill, the player will get bored. This is just one point on how commercial games try to motivate players. Many game-based learning applications are aiming to borrow similar design elements from commercial games.

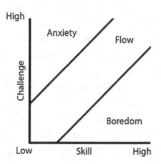

Fig. 1. Flow theory

Gamification is the application of game design elements in non-game context [3]. Thus gamification is designed to be a supportive and motivating factor that engage players to participate in performing non-game activities. Gamification's primary objective is to correct behaviour or creating desired behaviours [2]. Gamification helps the players to develop skills and behaviours through motivating and facilitating continuous play [7].

Gamification is designed to enhance an individual's intrinsic motivation [4]. For gamification to work there needs to be a drive to accomplish/achieve the desired outcome [6]. Gamification is very powerful when designed and applied intelligently. One of the more common designs for gamification is to award a player with meaningful rewards when the player performs the desired behaviour [11]. When the rewards have meaning to the players this will motivate them to want to complete the task the next time [9].

We followed user-centered design (UCD) process to focus our design on the user's needs and goals [11, 18]. PSHSA conducted various internal interviews and focus groups to determine user needs. We do not delve into the interviews and focus groups results as it is beyond the scope and focus of this paper. This paper focuses on our involvement in establishing the requirements for the game and prototyping different possible approaches. The next section explains the game prototypes as well as provides the current game flow framework and how we designed the adaptive system based on the data provided by users.

2.1   Case Study: PSHSA Game Prototypes

Although PSHSA has a wealth of resources and training materials for organizations, they realized a lack of utilization by small and medium enterprises (SME's). Through internal studies, PSHSA has identified a need for an engaging application to motivate SME's to learn about health and safety prevention. We are collaborating with PSHSA and its partnering associations to create a digital application for motivating SME's to learn and continue learning about health and safety prevention through the use of game design.

The digital application is based on the Institute for Work and Health Organizational Performance Metrics (IWH-OPM). IWH-OPM is an eight-question survey designed to assess an organization's occupational health and safety performance[3]. IWH-OPM uses a Likert scale questionnaire where each one of eight questions is targeted to determine the performance of an organization in a specific area. IWH-OPM provides a benchmark for organizations within the same sector to compare their performance.

As mentioned before, we followed UCD process in this project. In order to better understand the user needs, PSHSA had conducted interviews and focus groups. The focus groups and interviews highlighted features that needed to be covered in the game and how the application would perform. Based on these initial studies PSHSA identified three key requirements for this work: (a) the main focus of the application would be to motivate users to perform better in the IWH-OPM questionnaire; (b) Focus on motivation and retention of users for continued learning and (c) The game must also be applicable to 16 public sectors[4] (in terms of learning objectives).

---

[3] http://www.iwh.on.ca/opm.

[4] Sectors: Pulp and Paper, Forestry, Mining, Construction, Transportation, Electrical and Utilities, Agriculture, Tourism and Hospitality, Retail and Wholesale, Office and Related Services, Vehicle Sales and Service, Industrial and Manufacturing, Health and Community Care, Education and Culture, Emergency Services (Fire, Police and Medical), and Government and Municipal.

In order to create a digital application for promoting and motivating users to assimilate health and safety knowledge, the first step was to discuss the skills that the application needed to teach. We held brainstorming sessions to determine and discuss the skills related to each of the eight IWH-OPM questions. This included asking the collaborator's series of questions such as: "if the output of the task is 'x' what skill is needed to carry out the task". These sessions were effective in generating a finite list of the underlying skills for each IWH-OPM question. For example, the first IWH-OPM question "Formal safety audits at regular intervals are a normal part of business" the resulting key skills identified were: Time management, Assessment of validity and fit with organization, Organization Skills and Attention to detail.

First Prototype

Our first design iteration of the project was to focus on retaining the player through the use of mini-games each covering a few skills needed to perform well in the IWH-OPM. The project was designed to be a small collection of mini-games that motivate the player for continued play while intrinsically or inherently teaching the user both health and safety skills and concepts. The mini-games were designed to be abstracted from the sectors in an attempt to make them apply to all the sectors. In order to excel at the mini-games the users would need to be demonstrating their skills. Health and safety concepts would be interjected as the contents of each mini-games in an attempt to keep the play relevant.

We prototyped one of the small games, this game aimed to teach users time management, assessment of validity and attention to detail skills (aforementioned first IWH-OPM question). This game borrowed game design elements from the game 'Cook, Serve, Delicious!'[5]. Cook, Serve, Delicious is a restaurant simulator that tasks the player to take, prepare and serve orders from non-player character (NPC) entering the player's restaurant. The game has an emphasis on time management, as the player needs to quickly complete orders. In addition, assessment of validity and attention to detail are present, as the player needs to correctly prepare orders as the NPCs wishes.

The prototype created tasked the user to play as a project manager assigning priorities and completing task. Similarly, to how 'Cook, Serve Delicious' tasks the player to fill out orders and make sure they are completed in the specified way, in the prototype the player has to finish a task. A task is an item that the player needs to complete. Completing the task requires the player to read a description about the task and assign specifics requirements mentioned in the description to the task.

Extending from 'Cook, Serve, Delicious' the player starts the day by reading the agenda for the day, noting down the in game company's priorities and assigning time frames for major tasks to be completed. After the day setup is completed, the player would have to prioritize, prepare, and hand in tasks. The player needed to recognize the prioritized task put forth by the agenda and make sure those tasks were completed first. Completing a task, made the player check if all the elements of the challenge were completed correctly before submitting the task to who assigned the task. An example task for the player could be, 'Select the proper audit for warehouse safety and conduct

---

[5] http://www.vertigogaming.net/blog/.

it'. The prototype got its relevance to health and safety from the tasks it assigned the player while the game design was more focused on fun gameplay.

Reviewing the design and prototype with PSHSA found that the prototype would not work for the intended goal. Ultimately, the failure of the first design came down to the abstraction and the struggle of the design to be relevant enough to health and safety. While the design would have made a motivating game and taught the players the identified skills, having these taught intrinsically left little to be relevant to health and safety. The lack of relevance to the player, make the game hard for the player so see the point of playing. This failure prohibits the player from finding intrinsic motivation to continue to play the game. Another major problem with the first prototype was that it could not be adapted well enough to player needs from different sectors. Therefore, we decided to try a different design with a large focus on relevance and adaptability to different sectors.

Second Prototype

The second iteration of the prototype shifted the game design to focus on directly teaching health and safety to the player by implementing a large database of health and safety challenges. Each of these challenges would be tagged to identify their relevance towards a certain need. Challenges have the ability to be tagged to show their relevance towards an IWH-OPM question, an identified skill, and/or other relevant identifiers. The shift from mini-games to challenges also meant a shift from intrinsic style of learning to an extrinsic style. The challenges are much more direct in their teaching. Each challenge can be setup to be played in a standard way of multiple choice, etc.; but some can also be played in a more gamified way.

Another addition that came with the second prototype of that game is inclusion of an adaptive personalized system. The goal of the system is to learn from the user's performance and change what challenges are presented to the player. In order to get this system to work from the start each player is now required to fill out a short profile to give the system some context of the user's skills before presenting any challenges. The system also learns from the user performance while they play the game.

A large focus is still on motivation and retention. Motivation is kept high through the use of gamification. Giving meaningful rewards to user when desirable actions are completed such as the successful completion of a challenge or by meeting goals set up by the game. Retention is captured from the use of quests. Quests are used to give more reason to come back and play the game. A quest tasks the player with playing a number of challenges in a row, complete a number of challenges in a day, or in a week, or month. Each quest is designed to increase retention and motivation in the time period it is needed most.

The second iteration fits better with PSHSA's needs. Through the use of gamification with meaningful rewards the requirement for motivation will be satisfied. The use of adaptive personalized system user retention can be obtained by the use of quests. The system captures relevance to the user's learning needs by keeping the challenges to health and safety while also only presenting the challenges that will most help the user learn.

2.2   Game Flow

Figure 2 shows the flow of the game and how the game design functions. The entry point of the game is the user profile. To reiterate, the user profile is a set of basic information the user enters before starting the game. The entered data includes the following: user's information about their organization's IWH-OPM score in each of the eight questions, the sector that the organization is grouped in, and some generic information. The user profile is crucial to the start of the personalization of the game. As the user plays the game their profile is constantly updated with the score from the challenges. The user can get a glimpse of how well they are performing from graphs and statistics displayed in their home page.

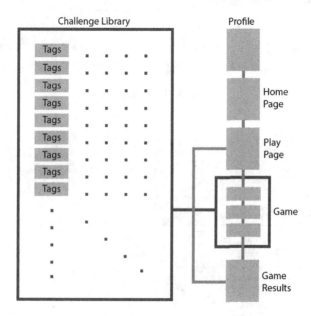

Fig. 2. Game flow

The home page (Fig. 3) is the screen from which the user can see graphs showing their performance multitude of different metrics. The metrics are to showcase the user's stats in a wide array of areas from the amount of points awarded in a week compared to the last week, to the amount of correctness achieved in a week compared to the last week. The home page is targeted to be a motivator for the user wherein it shows improvement as well as quests completed. Challenges as mentioned briefly before are tasks that the user can complete for extra points. The main focus of the challenges is to increase the retention of the user by the promise of potential large rewards if the task is correctly completed. From the home page the user can enter the play page.

On the play page (Fig. 4) the user is provided with a list of challenges picked by the adaptive game engine. The game picks relevant challenges and presents only a handful for the user to play. Alongside the challenges presented will be potential score for each

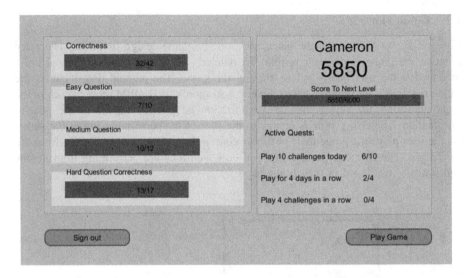

Fig. 3. Home page

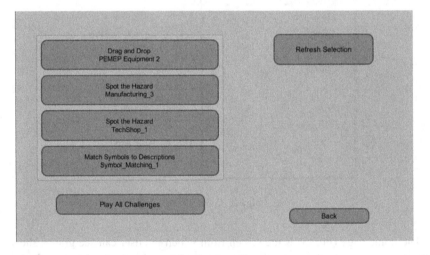

Fig. 4. Play page

challenge if completed correctly. In order to discourage demotivation a 'Refresh Selection' button is present to refresh unwanted challenges. When the user selects a challenge they are now tasked to play that challenge.

Play All Challenge is when the user plays a short game. These games last from 20 s to a minute. The reason for the short playtime is to keep users engaged. Another benefit of the short playtime is that the user can play without having to allocate a large portion of time to ensure they can play the game in its entirety. As mentioned before, these challenges are played through a variety of ways. From classical multiple choice, true or

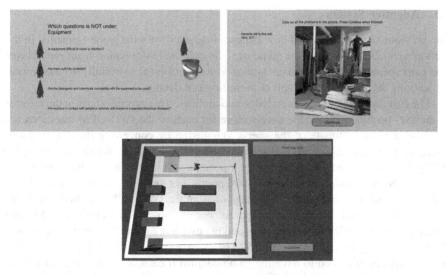

Fig. 5. Multiple choice (top left), find the problems (top right), find the safe path (bottom)

false; to games like finding problems, finding safe paths (Fig. 5). After the user has completed the game they are moved to the game result page.

The game result page (Fig. 6) is where the users are awarded points for their performance in the game. In addition, if users had completed any of their quests they would be awarded the points. In summary, this page is where the user is given their rewards or incentives for playing the challenge. Once the user has had time to review their score and performance in the challenge they can move to the play page to continue the game loop and their game session.

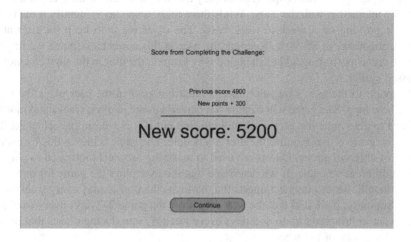

Fig. 6. Game result page

2.3   Adaptive System

The previous section explained how the user interacted with the game elements. In this section we elaborate on how the game uses the collected information from each player. The game personalizes three main aspects at its control: (a) user skill; (b) motivation; (c) learning style. Below we look at these in more details.

The first one is the user's knowledge and abilities. This process starts at the creation of the user profile. We take the user's score for each of the IWH-OPM questions and construct a rough estimate of the user's knowledge by converting their score into a points system. The scores from IWH-OPM range from 0 to 4. When converting the IWH-OPM score to the points system the process is as follows: change the range to 0–1, then multiply the resulting number by 1000 points. For getting a rough estimate of their ability to perform skills we take an average of all of the IWH-OPM question scores that relate to the skill and convert it into a points. For example, if an identified skill is only present in 2 of the IWH-OPM questions and the user got 2.4 and 3.6 for those questions the user would get a point score of 750 i.e. $(((2.4 + 3.6) / 2) / 4 * 1000)$. The initial profile statistics will need to have the game confirm if each of the rough estimates are true. Testing an estimate is done through getting a user to play a challenge that requires the specific skill to complete. Over a liberal amount of iterations, we will be able to get a real sense of the user's knowledge and abilities. The advantage of initial profile statistics is that we can start to test the user's knowledge and abilities in the areas that have the lowest estimate making the game personalized right out of the gate.

The game attempts to personalize and adapt to the user by tracking and promoting the user's ability and the user's motivation. In addition, the game also personalizes, when it can, the type of challenges presented to the user, more on this later. The key factors we are looking for is if the user has the ability to correctly complete challenges related to the IWH-OPM questions and the identified skills. Through focusing on the IWH-OPM and identified skills the user is under performing in we hope to increase his skills in the areas. The correctness of the user is calculated in an overall scope and a weekly scope. The overall scope helps display any improvements during the entirety of the user's interaction with the game. While the weekly scope helps identify if the user's skill is improving on a week-to-week basis. The objective is to keep the user at an overall correctness of 80–90%. Keeping the user in this correctness range we hope to keep the game motivating and challenging why keeping the user in the flow channel we discussed earlier.

Adapting to the user's retention means identifying when the user plays the game and for how long. The game will capture the player's usage in days, weeks and months. We need to determine the user's schedule to find out if it is a desirable schedule. The goal of the game is to normalize the user's schedule. The game achieves this by using a number of different quests. Quests are used to make the user feel motivated to play the game at different schedule. If we determine that the user plays the game for one week out of a month, we can interject quests that motivate the user to play every week in the month. Similarly, if we find that the user only plays the game 2–3 days every week, we would want to bring that up to 4–5 days every week by introducing quests that reward playing every day of the week.

The last adaptive trait of the game is based on the user's ability to complete a specific type of challenges. As discussed before, the type of challenge refers to the way a challenge is played. If we store how the user scores for each challenge type, we can determine if the user is having problems with a specific challenge type. If difficulties are detected, the game can shy away from the identified challenge type and give the user challenge types they can comfortably perform.

3 Conclusion and Future Work

In this paper we have shown how through the use of personalization and adaptive learning principles a serious game can be made relevant, motivating, and captivating (help retain users better). We also show with the help of a case study how by using a user centered design (UCD) one can create a serious game centered on health and safety training. In the case study we show how the requirements for the game was established from which a prototype was designed. The first prototype had its strengths but ultimately from the stakeholder's feedback, it was clear that it lacked relevance to the user. The feedback prompted the second design, which showed us that for PSHSA, an adaptive system can focus the gameplay around what is most relevant for the user and aids in learning. Moreover, we have shown how such a system can benefit from adapting rewards to increase both motivation and user retention.

Finally, as a part of future work we will conduct an evaluation of the game design. Evaluation involves experimentation i.e. conducting pilot runs to see if the new design holds up to its expectations. We intend to collect user data after the pilots to see what part of the game design kept them motivated and what did not. Both qualitative and quantitative data will be collected from the pilot study to infer the effectiveness of our design. We envision multiple changes to the game design, which might include changes in the user interface as well as in the game flow.

Acknowledgements. We would like to thank UOIT, PSHSA and IWH for their research support. We would also like to thank Brandon Hope, Derek Chong, Jeff Lyons, Michael Van Vaals, and Nelly Hamid their contributions to this project.

References

1. Cowley, B., Charles, D., Black, M., Hickey, R.: Toward an understanding of flow in video games. Comput. Entertain. **6**(2), 1 (2008). http://doi.org/10.1145/1371216.1371223
2. Deterding, S.: Gamification: designing for motivation. Interactions **19**, 14–17 (2012). http://doi.org/10.1145/2212877.2212883
3. Deterding, S., Dixon, D.: From game design elements to gamefulness: defining "gamification". In: MinTrek 2011, pp. 9–15 (2011). http://doi.org/10.1145/2181037.2181040
4. Domínguez, A., Saenz-De-Navarrete, J., De-Marcos, L., Fernández-Sanz, L., Pagés, C., Martínez-Herráiz, J.J.: Gamifying learning experiences: practical implications and outcomes. Comput. Educ. **63**, 380–392 (2013). http://doi.org/10.1016/j.compedu.2012.12.020

5. Entertainment Software Association of Canada (ESAC): 2015 Essential Facts about The Canadian Video Game Industry (2015). http://theesa.ca/wp-content/uploads/2015/11/ESAC_2015_Booklet_Version02_14_Digital.pdf
6. Francisco, A., Luis, F., González, J.L., Isla, J.L.: Analysis and application of gamification. In: INTERACCION 2012, pp. 17:1–17:2 (2012). http://doi.acm.org/10.1145/2379636.2379653
7. Glover, I.: Play as you learn: gamification as a technique for motivating learners play as you learn. In: Proceedings of World Conference on Educational Multimedia, Hypermedia and Telecommunications 2013, pp. 1998–2008 (2013). http://shura.shu.ac.uk/7172/
8. Guillén-Nieto, V., Aleson-Carbonell, M.: Serious games and learning effectiveness: the case of It's a Deal! Comput. Educ. **58**(1), 435–448 (2012). http://doi.org/10.1016/j.compedu.2011.07.015
9. Mekler, E.D., Brühlmann, F., Opwis, K., Tuch, A.N.: Disassembling gamification: the effects of points and meaning on user motivation and performance. In: CHI 2013 Extended Abstracts on Human Factors in Computing Systems on - CHI EA 2013, p. 1137 (2013). http://doi.org/10.1145/2468356.2468559
10. Mulwa, C., Lawless, S., Sharp, M., Arnedillo-Sanchez, I., Wade, V.: Adaptive educational hypermedia systems in technology enhanced learning: a literature review. In: ACM Conference on Information Technology Education, pp. 73–84 (2010). http://doi.org/10.1145/1867651.1867672
11. Nicholson, S.: A user-centered theoretical framework for meaningful gamification a brief introduction to gamification organismic integration theory situational relevance and situated motivational affordance. In: Games+Learning+Society 8.0 (2012)
12. Rego, P., Moreira, P.M., Reis, L.P.: Serious games for rehabilitation: a survey and a classification towards a taxonomy. In: 2010 5th Iberian Conference on Information Systems and Technologies (CISTI), pp. 1–6 (2010)
13. Ritterfeld, U., Weber, R.: Video Games for Entertainment. Playing Video Games-Motives, Responses, and Consequences, pp. 399–413 (2006)
14. Ruiz, J.G., Mintzer, M.J., Leipzig, R.M.: The impact of e-learning in medical education. Acad. Med. **81**(3), 207–212 (2006). http://doi.org/10.1097/00001888-200603000-00002
15. Ryan, R.M., Rigby, C.S., Przybylski, A.: The motivational pull of video games: a self-determination theory approach. Motiv. Emot. **30**(4), 344–360 (2006). http://doi.org/10.1007/s11031-006-9051-8
16. Shute, V.J., Rieber, L., Van Eck, R.: Games … and … learning. Trends Issues Instr. Des. Technol. **3**, 1–31 (2012). http://myweb.fsu.edu/vshute/pdf/shutepres_i.pdf, http://www.pearsonhighered.com/pearsonhigheredus/educator/product/products_detail.page?isbn=0132563584&forced_logout=forced_logged_out
17. Tsai, T.-W., Lo, H.Y., Chen, K.-S.: An affective computing approach to develop the game-based adaptive learning material for the elementary students. In: Proceedings of 2012 Joint International Conference on Human-Centered Computer Environments - HCCE 2012, vol. 8 (2012). http://doi.org/10.1145/2160749.2160752
18. Zammitto, V., Mirza-Babaei, P., Livingston, I., Kobayashi, M., Nacke, L.: Player experience: mixed methods and reporting results. In: CHI EA 2014, pp. 147–150. ACM, New York (2014). https://doi.org/10.1145/2559206.2559239
19. Zualkeman, I., Pasquier, M., Jibreel, M.M., Zakaria, R.S., Tayem, R.M.: An adaptive learning RPG game-engine based on knowledge spaces. In: ICETC 2010-2010 2nd International Conference on Education Technology and Computer, vol. 2, no. 5, pp. 223–227 (2010). http://doi.org/10.1109/ICETC.2010.5529397

Autonomous Robotic System for Pipeline Integrity Inspection

John Costa, Gavin DeAngelis, Daniel Lane, Chris Snyder,
Abdelmagid Hammuda, Khalifa Al-Khalifa, Elsayed Elsayed,
and Kang Li$^{(\boxtimes)}$

Rutgers University, Piscataway, NJ 08854, USA
kl419@rci.rutgers.edu

Abstract. In this paper, we present an external pipeline inspection robotic system capable of detecting the surface defects on above-ground pipelines and modeling their degradation. This system consists of two subsystems, the main base and the sensing system. The main base is a self-driving autonomous ground vehicle (AGV) equipped with Lidar, acoustic sensors and motor encoders, which can track the pipeline on uneven terrains. The sensing system includes two cameras attached to a C-arm, which rotates around the pipe. The two cameras are placed 180° from each other and can take pictures at 90° intervals, allowing the system to analyze the full 360° of the pipe with only half of the rotation as compared to a single camera system. When the C-arm encounters a flange or support, it retracts off the pipe, moves past the obstacle, and extends back to continue taking images. These images are used for defect detection. The detected defect data is then used for modeling the defect degradation and predicting when the defects become critical and require maintenance.

Keywords: External pipeline inspection · Defect detection · Self-driving · Autonomous ground vehicle · Degradation modeling

1 Introduction

There are around half a million miles of high-volume pipeline transporting natural gas, oil, and other hazardous liquids across the United States [1]. The nation's pipeline networks are also widespread, running alternately through remote and densely populated regions, some above ground and some below. These systems are vulnerable to accidents and terrorist attack. Due to the extended network of pipelines, the number of incidents has increased with the increase in pipeline mileage. In the last three years, there has been an annual average of 353 reported pipeline accidents [1]. This amounted to a loss of over 87,000 barrels of oil and over $460,000,000 in property and environmental damage [1].

Stress corrosion and defects accounted for the majority of accidents on transmission pipelines from 1991–2005 as shown by the Lithuanian Energy Institute (LEI) [2]. The stress cracks form from the combined influence of pipeline stress due to its pressurized contents and a corrosive medium. Interlinking crack clusters form over time and

© Springer International Publishing AG 2017
V.G. Duffy (Ed.): DHM 2017, Part II, LNCS 10287, pp. 333–342, 2017.
DOI: 10.1007/978-3-319-58466-9_30

eventually lead to pipeline failure. It was found that external defects are eight percent more common than internal defects.

Using advanced imaging techniques supported by an autonomous robotic system may present a practical solution for detecting defects on pipelines before failure. In the present work, we aim to develop a robotic system to identify pipeline defects and flag them for operator review as well as predict the degradation of the defects. We have designed and built an autonomous ground vehicle (AGV) (Fig. 1) with the capability to identify the relative position of a pipeline and adjust itself to the proper range and angle to scan the pipe for defects. We have also incorporated a model commonly used, as well as industry standards for the threshold of when a crack is considered critical and will require maintenance, to forecast defect growth to make an accurate prediction of expected degradation of the defects over time after successful identification of cracks and defects. A variety of sensors were used in this robotic system, including ultrasonic proximity sensors, an RPLIDAR system, a thermal camera, and two optical cameras.

Fig. 1. Rutgers autonomous pipeline inspection system

2 System Design

2.1 Physical Design

The main base of the robotic system consists of a suspension system comprised of 70 custom individual aluminum parts. The basis of this design is a double wishbone suspension system, shown in Fig. 2, which enables the mobile platform to move upon multiple terrains. Additionally, the system utilizes two 24 V motors to power the

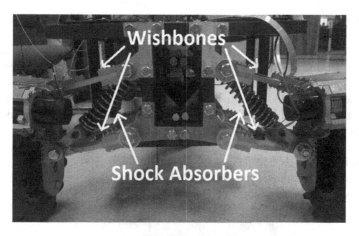

Fig. 2. Suspension system

driving subsystem. They are capable of producing approximately 6 N-m of torque which provides the ability for the system to negotiate more rugged terrains.

The second subsystem consists of the sensing unit, housed in a structure that is referred to as the C-clamp (seen in Fig. 3). The C-clamp is driven by a linear actuator and uses ultrasonic sensors to detect obstacles along the pipeline. When the system moves too close to a flange or support, this sensor will trigger the machine to stop, retract the arm off the pipe, move forward past the pipe and extend back out to resume the scanning process. If there is no support detected, the system moves in three inch increments and a Raspberry Pi sends signals to the other controllers to take pictures or to rotate the C-clamp.

Two Raspberry Pis are used on the system, and both are programmed using Python. The first Raspberry Pi controls a digital camera which receives a serial communication when it is necessary for the cameras to take pictures. The captured images are

Fig. 3. C-arm (left) and C-clamp (right)

processed in MATLAB using specific User-Defined Functions, and the results are stored in an Excel file. This file will be used later for analysis of the pipeline, and a user can access the file by utilizing the GUI accordingly. The second Raspberry Pi controls a second digital camera as well as the RPLIDAR. It continuously communicates with the Arduino responsible for driving to share obstruction information and the correction factor, which is explained in further detail in the following paragraph. The Arduino connected to the second Raspberry Pi is responsible for controlling both drive motors as well as the linear actuator used to extend and contract the C-arm. It is also responsible for obtaining the readings from the ultrasonic sensors which are used to detect pipeline supports and flanges. A second Arduino receives this signal through serial for timing the movement of the C-clamp using a stepper motor driver. The overall flow of the systems software can be seen in Fig. 4.

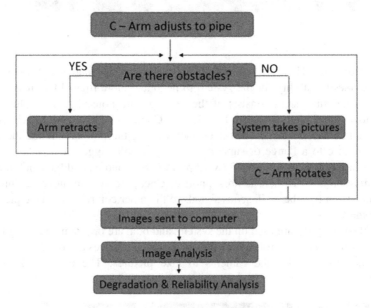

Fig. 4. Software flow chart

2.2 Automation

The RPLIDAR A2 is a Lidar system which has a laser rangefinder that spins, enabling it to map distances in a single plane, as shown in Fig. 5. It has a refresh rate of 4000 samples per second. Connected to the raspberry pi using a serial adapter, it is integrated using python. The RPLIDAR is used for two purposes: obstacle detection and pipe distance and parallelism. If the Lidar detects that a point falls within a predetermined distance threshold, regardless of whether it's in front, behind, or to the side of the system, it will send a signal to stop driving. The Lidar will also send a correction factor to the Arduino that controls the driving motors. This correction factor is defined as the ratio of the distance at a given angle to the correct hypotenuse at that angle for the system to be parallel. The equation is given as follows,

$$f_n = a\left(\frac{d\cos(\theta)}{d_p}\right)^s + (1-a)f_{n-1}, \ n \in \mathbb{N}, \ a \in [0,1] \tag{1}$$

Where f_n is the nth correction factor, d is the distance at angle θ taken by the lidar for $\theta \in [30°, 50°]$, d_p is the distance perpendicularly to the pipe (d for $\theta = 0° \pm 5°$), and s is the scale factor. Note that for $\theta \in [330°, 350°]$, the first term is inversed (s is negative). This means that if the system is travelling parallel to the pipe, the correction factor is equal to 1.00. If it is headed towards the pipe, the correction factor is greater than one, and vice versa. The correction factor is smoothed to prevent rapid overcorrection or system instability from faulty measurements. Empirically, $\alpha = 0.75$ was chosen. As soon as the correction factor is calculated by the Raspberry Pi, it is sent to the Arduino which multiplies it with the inner drive wheel's PWM value, and its inverse with the outer wheel's PWM value. This ensures feedback to the motors so that the system can maintain its parallelism with the pipe. If this difference needs to be exaggerated or diminished, s can be increased or decreased, but it was found that $s = 1$ is a good solution. Note that for all values, $f \in [0.50, 2.00]$, otherwise the motors would receive values from the Arduino that are greater than 255 (the max value at their resolution).

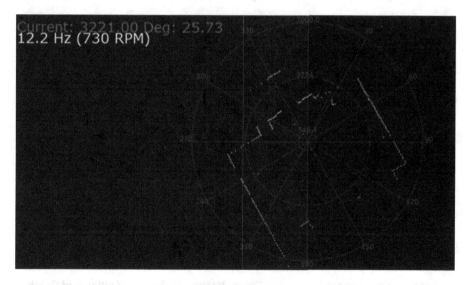

Fig. 5. Lidar mapping application

2.3 Crack Identification

After the images are taken from the digital cameras, both the section of pipe scanned and the angle at which the images was taken (Fig. 6) are recorded.

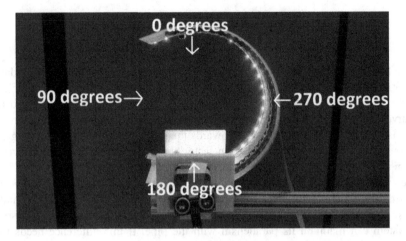

Fig. 6. C-clamp region notation

Each image is processed in three phases including crack detection, degradation modeling and reliability analysis. During the first phase, the digital pictures are first analyzed using several image processing techniques which are shown in Fig. 7.

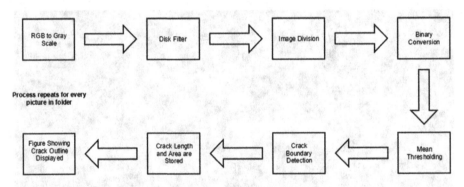

Fig. 7. Image processing flow chart

After data processing, the cracks (Fig. 8) are identified and the measurements of the crack such as the length and area are extracted.

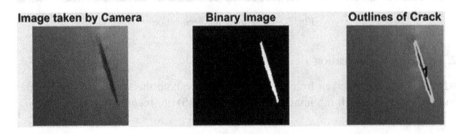

Fig. 8. Crack detection

In order for these results to be accurate, it is critical that the pictures be taken at consistently bright lighting, supplied by an attached LED strip (Fig. 6), as well as consistent spacing between the pipe and all three cameras. This ensures that the sizes of all three images stay the same which is a necessity for the dimensions of the crack to be accurate and repeatable.

2.4   Degradation Modeling

If the path for which the crack length propagates is considered to be random with normal distribution, it may be considered a form of Brownian motion. At any point in the future, the crack has a probability of reaching the threshold given by the CDF of the normal distribution, ϕ. This yields the reliability of the pipeline at time t as,

$$R(t) = \phi\left(\frac{D^* - D(0) - \mu t}{\sigma_D \sqrt{t}}\right) - \exp\left(\frac{2\mu(D^* - D(0))}{\sigma_D^2}\right)\phi\left(\frac{D^* - D(0) - \mu t}{\sigma_D \sqrt{t}}\right) \quad (2)$$

Where D(0) is the initial value, μ is the drift parameter, σ_D is the diffusion parameter, and D* is the failure threshold level [3].

Using the initial crack lengths stored, predictions can be made for the crack growth over time, an example of which can be seen in Fig. 9. Additionally, a threshold can be designated within the code to indicate when the pipe will require maintenance or when it is in danger of failure.

Due to the fact that this process is random, different iterations using the same data will result in different conclusions. To account for this, the calculations are performed

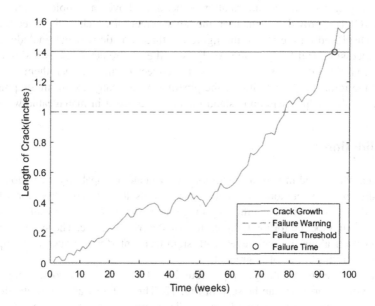

Fig. 9. Crack length growth over time

1000 times and are grouped together for a more accurate representation, seen in Fig. 10. The time at which a crack growth crosses the threshold is known to follow the inverse Gaussian distribution, as the histogram suggests. The remaining useful life of the pipeline is calculated by taking the average of the failure times generated in the histogram.

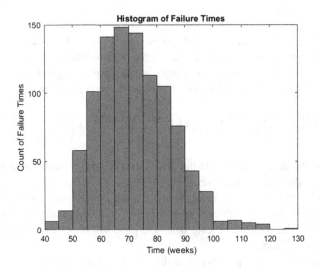

Fig. 10. Reliability analysis

For easy access to the information generated above, a simple graphical user interface (GUI) is provided to the user, the home screen of which is displayed below in Fig. 11. Displayed on the left of the figure are three functions which include Cracks, Image Processing, and Degradation Analysis, and each are activated by a simple push button. From this GUI, a user can analyze the collected images, track them over time, and find the remaining useful life of the pipeline. With many useful infographics and instructions, this helps users understand the data and use it in manageable ways.

3   Validation

The system was tested in various conditions to evaluate its capability for various tasks. It was driven in an outdoor environment to test its terrain capability, for which it performed very well. Since significantly long pipe was not obtained, a wall was used to simulate a long pipeline for the Lidar correction described before. The system was able to correct itself along the wall, even with significant interference such as an operator intentional moving it out of alignment.

To test the cameras along a pipe, four inch PVC was used composing of two sections with supports as can be seen in Fig. 12. The system was able to iterate scans along the pipeline as well as avoid the middle support. Cracks were simulated in the

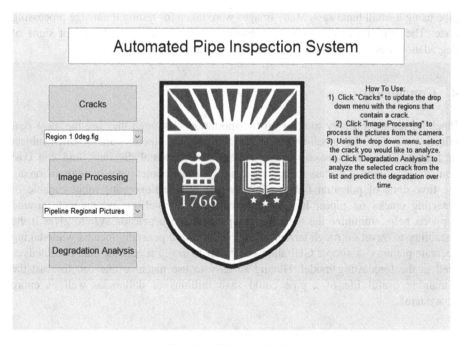

Fig. 11. GUI home display

Fig. 12. Inspection demonstration

pipe using a small hand saw. Many images were taken for testing the image processing code. The artificial cracks were all identified and those pictures devoid of signs of degradation were successfully dismissed and separated.

4 Conclusion

Pipelines are the primary tool for oil transportation. Although they are the most cost effective way for oil companies to transfer their product, pipelines are too often subject to failure. These failures can cause deaths, environmental disasters, and can cost companies billions of dollars in the long run. Cracks and other types of degradation are the first signs of potential failure. This system is an autonomous robot capable of detecting cracks on pipes. Its ability to maintain parallelism and navigate around supports helps minimize the need for an operator. Its suspension system gives it the capability to travel on rough terrain where pipelines are generally located while taking accurate pictures. A simple GUI allows any user to easily access the data collected, as well as the forecasting model. Having an easy to use machine that can forecast the remaining useful life of a pipe could save millions of dollars as well as entire ecosystems.

References

1. Parfomak, P.W.: Keeping America's Pipelines Safe and Secure: Key Issues for Congress. DIANE Publishing (2012)
2. Dundulis, G., Grybanas, A., Janulionis, R., Kriakiena, R., Rimkevicius, S.: Degradation mechanisms and evaluation of failure of gas pipelines. Mechanics 21(5), 352–360 (2015)
3. Elsayed, E.A.: Reliability Engineering, 2nd edn. Wiley, New York (2012)
4. Huang, X.P., Moan, T., Cui, W.: Fatigue crack growth under variable-amplitude loading. In: Schijve, J. (ed.) Fatigue of Structures and Materials, pp. 329–369. Springer, Heidelberg (2009)

Interactive Design of Digital Car Dashboard Interfaces

Rui Li, Qing-Xing Qu, and Zhangping Lu$^{(\boxtimes)}$

Jiangsu University, Zhenjiang, China
li858@Purdue.edu

Abstract. The effects of digital car dashboard interface factors on driving experience were studied. Specifically, representative car dashboard interface design elements were analyzed and five representative samples were selected. Four aspects were explored, including dashboard design style, interface layout, information framework, and hierarchical table. The color proportions and shape division of dashboards were analyzed both longitudinally and transversally. By studying and analyzing the five samples, we find to design digital car dashboards, designers have to obey the rules of simple layout, color precision and experience richness. This study has high practical significance and values.

Keywords: Digitization · Automobile instrument panel · Interface · Experience design

1 Research Background

The car dashboard is a bridge for information exchange between the driver and the vehicle. Owing to the high contrast and glaring colors of the thin-film transistor (TFT) liquid crystal display (LCD), the digital dashboard will become the information and control center of future vehicles. Thus, studying the effects of digital dashboard interface design factors on safety driving is of high significance and contributes to improving the driving experience. So far, the dashboard of a passenger car mainly consists of the main dashboard facing the driver and the auxiliary dashboard beside the driver. In particular, the main dashboard contains all instruments on the car that monitor the rotating speed, speed per hour, oil mass and water temperature. Great achievements have been made in research on car dashboard interfaces.

Many efforts have been devoted to combatant instrument layout, lens hood, vision blind field, light reflection, glare, pointer, colors, characters and sound, and to the proposal of optimized design. For instance, a dashboard surface designed as a large semicircle satisfies the requirements of most dashboards. Designing the same characteristics of dashboard interface elements can save driver much time in information processing, but otherwise, it would prolong the driver's exploration. As for old drivers, females depend more on information acquisition than males, so a suitable reduction of interface contrast can improve the driving behaviors of old drivers. Meanwhile, along with the development of new energy, the design of car dashboards will be targeted at interaction, automation, synthesization and diversification. As reported, a digital dashboard with identifying ability is capable of on-line information collection,

© Springer International Publishing AG 2017
V.G. Duffy (Ed.): DHM 2017, Part II, LNCS 10287, pp. 343–353, 2017.
DOI: 10.1007/978-3-319-58466-9_31

targeting at resource management and share. However, in China, relevant research is focused on electronic instruments, which fail to meet the increasingly intensified requirements for driving. In this regard, we selected five representative dashboards from the 2014 World Automobile Safety Ranking, which was jointly worked out by US Insurance Institute for Highway Safety (IIHS) and US National Highway Traffic Safety Administration (NHTSA). We analyzed and studied the interface designs of these five dashboards.

2   Longitudinal Analysis of Car Dashboard Interfaces

With the Volvo S60 dashboard as example, the longitudinal analysis covered four aspects (dashboard pattern, overall layout, information framework, basic information list) as well as the color ratios. The results are listed in Table 1.

Table 1. The vertical analysis of the instrument panel interface of the Volvo S60

Time	Dashboard style	Layout	Information architecture
First Generation 2013			
Second Generation 2013-2014			
Third Generation 2014-Now			

2.1   Structural Simplification

Information During the transition from G1 to G2, the dashboard has changed largely from a dual-dial shape to a mono-dial shape, but it reserved the traditional dial pointer pattern (Table 1). From G2 to G3, the shape has changed very little, but the TFT-supported G3 S60 dashboard adopts full-animation and its dials have changed along with the driving speed, which contributes to safe driving. Due to the decrement of dial, the overall layouts of both G2 and G3 have been simplified, as the central display screen mainly exhibits the speed per hour and range, but other information including rotating speed, oil mass and temperature is concentrated on the bilateral histograms, which save the occupied space and highlight the important information, thus contributing to the driver's cognition.

2.2 Framework Hierarchy

The information framework is the carrier of visual information expression, including contents, layout and hierarchy. It focuses on the expression and transfer of information. The vehicles have brand-related information framework patterns and obvious family characteristics. The information framework of a Volvo S60 dashboard is showed in Fig. 1. The basic contents displayed include vehicle speed, rotating speed, time, temperature, driving range, gears, oil mass and indicator lamps. These contents are not largely different among the three generations, except for layout and hierarchy. The G1 dashboards adopted two-dial layout and two-level hierarchy. The speed per hour and rotating speed were at the parallel layer, or the first level, and the contents displayed on the controlled zone also belonged to this level. Other information displayed on the dashboard belonged to the second level. In particular, the first level contains rich information about driving, which is hard to be differentiated and thus prolongs the driver's time in information processing.

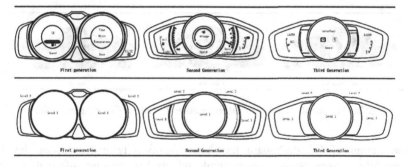

Fig. 1. The family dashboard information architecture

The major difference of G2 from G1 is the single-dial layout, which directly affects the design style of dashboard interfaces and contains three levels of information. The central dial mainly displays vehicle speed and continuous range, which belong to the first level. Information including rotating speed and oil mass is mainly displayed on the bilateral histograms of the large dial and belongs to the second level. Secondary information including gears and indicator lamps is mainly displayed on the bilateral dashboards of the histograms and belongs to the third level. Such three-level information management is divided into obviously primary and secondary parts and saves the driver's time in information processing. The information hierarchy of a Volvo S60 dashboard is showed in Fig. 1. G3 dial inherits from G2, and neither their overall layouts nor hierarchies are largely different, except that the ratio design is more humanistic. The ratios of first level to second level are largely different, which helps the driver with information identification.

Generally, the evolution of the information framework of Volvo S60 dashboards shows that the overall dashboard design becomes increasingly simplified and the driving information management becomes more humanistic, which provide more values for reference.

2.3 Color Diversification

G1 dashboards met the basic driving requirements and their traditional pattern of red pointers and yellow caution icons attracted the driver's attention within short time. In comparison, G2 dashboards had more colors. The newly-added green danger zone indicates the colors are worth of reference, but this half-animatic display has some limitations, as it is unable to display the complete information. Moreover, the exposed dials tend to cause visual fatigue. The patterns of G1 and G2 Volvo S60 dashboards are showed in Fig. 2.

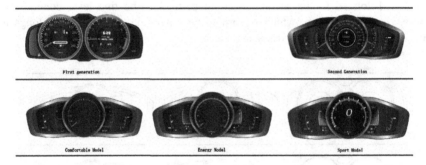

Fig. 2. The family dashboard information architecture (Color figure online)

The design of G3 dashboard has been significantly improved, as the TFT high-resolution screen is fine and textural and displays concise information. Such design is fully human-oriented and has inherited the conventional Scandinavian style. The three patterns of elegance, ecology and optimization have enriched the driver's driving experience. Meanwhile, the proportion of colors is obviously increased, which improves the human-machine affection and reflects the principle of personal experience. With the dazzling pattern as example, the single-circular main dashboard displays both speed per hour and rotating speed, and the large-area red color is regarded as generality and naturalness, which brings the driver with infinite dynamic experience. The pattern of a Volvo S60 G3 dashboard is showed in Fig. 2.

By studying the characteristics of Volvo S60 G3 dashboards, we find the general design has been gradually improved with innovations. The dashboard shape and information framework become increasingly simplified and the colors are gradually enriched. The use of TFT increases the storage of dashboard information and largely improves the driver's driving experience. Clearly, an appropriate layout directly affects the information framework, promotes the hierarchical management of driving information and plays an unignorably role in safe driving.

3   Transversal Analysis of Car Dashboard Interfaces

Here the top five dashboards from 2014 world vehicle safety ranking were selected and used into transversal analysis, which covered six aspects: dashboard pattern, overall layout, information framework, basic information list, color collocation ratio, and styles. The results are listed in Table 2.

Table 2.   The horizontal analysis table of five sample instrument panel

Dashboard style	Layout	Information architecture	Information list
			Speed Revs Time Temperature Miles Oil Light
			Revs Time Temperature Miles Oil Light
			Speed Revs Time Temperature Miles Oil Light
			Speed Revs Time Temperature
			Speed Revs Time Temperature

3.1   Obvious Brand-Related Characteristics

The five dashboards have different patterns and obvious brand-related characteristics. The Volvo S60 single-dial dashboard has a simple layout and inherits the previous Scandinavian style. Subaru Legacy has a circular or semi-circular collocation dial, and the overall layout is significantly different. Meanwhile, the double "cannon-typed" dial is matched with a red pointer, which improves the attention and indicates a sense of activity and vitality. Mazda 3 Axela barrel-shaped single-dial has a layout with a red remarkable zone, which conveys an "active" style of both passion and strength. Lincoln MKZ adopts a circle and large-semicircle combined pattern for information display, which is unique and brightly-colored. This layout inherits the Ford style with obvious American elements and a strong sense of scientificness. The Infiniti Q50 dashboard, known for its sensibility, obeys the traditional overall layout, but the "double-wave" strength aesthetic design integrates both functionality and visual aesthetics from the field ergonomics. The seemingly traditional layout embodies a detailed design, and the wave-shaped frillings with remarkable and fresh blue color express the flexibility and softness of sea elements.

3.2   Information Framework Personalization

By analyzing the information frameworks of Volvo S60 dashboards, we find the information framework would directly promote the hierarchical management of driving information and save the driver's time in information processing. The information frameworks of the five tested dashboards are showed in Fig. 3, including the frameworks and contents in Table 2. These five dashboards basically have the same contents, including vehicle speed, rotating speed, time, temperature, gears, driving range, oil mass, water temperature and indicator lamps, but they are different in layouts. The information management is divided into three levels of "large, small, large", indicating a trend of individuation, except Infiniti Q50, whose layout is very traditional (two-level). These four dashboards all place the first-level information into the central part with a large area in the dial. The second-level information is only after the first level and accounts for a smaller area, while the third level occupies the remaining area, which is very large. The second-level information attracts the driver's attention through

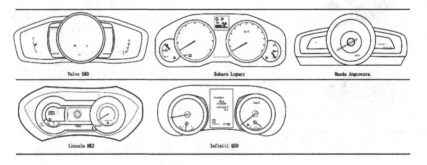

Fig. 3. The information architecture of five sample instrument panel

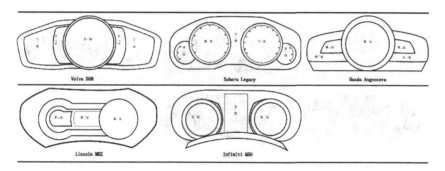

Fig. 4. The layout and information level of five sample instrument panel

a very special shape. For instance, the Volvo S60 is cylinder-shaped; the Subaru Legacy is a 3/4 circle; Mazda 3 Axela is wing-shaped; Lincoln MKZ has a very special shape in both the second and third level information, which deserves further analysis. On this basis, the personalized hierarchical information management is mainly manifested as the shape and ratio of the second level information. The layouts and information hierarchy of the five samples are showed in Fig. 4.

3.3   Rich Interface Vision Elements

The final trait is the effects of frills on the dashboard. Frills play a highlighting role in dashboard shapes, but may be easily ignored. Of the five dashboards, frills were only done by Infiniti Q50. Specifically, it inherited the sea elements, as the wave-shaped design strengthened the style of strength esthetics and showed a strong feeling of perceptual design.

By analyzing these five dashboards, we find the dashboards have obvious brand-related characteristics and their information frameworks indicate a trend of individuation. Specifically, hierarchical information management is accompanied by special shape elements, which contribute to the driver's height identification. Moreover, as for design of interface vision elements, the number of dials also affects the trend of dashboard shapes. Frills, as a part of detailed design, frills play a highlighting role and contribute to the driver's driving experiences. Among the five dashboards, the biggest breakthrough is from the digital hidden design of Volvo S60, which improves the driver's perception accuracy and largely contributes to safe driving.

The interface visual elements of a car dashboard include size, shape and color of graphs, and in particular, the elements that should be displayed on media, including texts, graphs, insets, pics, tables, frills and color blocks. During interface design, the use of visual elements affects the direction of interface styles.

First, we selected five dashboards and adopted the display pattern of TFT animation. The five dashboards are illustrated in Fig. 5. The difference is that the Volvo S60 adopts a TFT intellectual multi-pattern digital dashboard that is fully created by liquid crystal screen, while the other four dashboards only use local liquid crystal effect and reserve the characteristics of physical dial meters. Based on the advantages of TFT, the Volvo

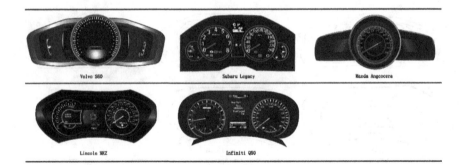

Fig. 5. The style of five sample instrument panel (Color figure online)

S60 dashboard has an outstanding trait – digital hidden design. The data vary along with the change of speed, and the match of striking colors could improve the precision.

The second trait is the effects of shape and colors on the whole dashboard. Of the five dashboards, the dial has a significant effect on the shape of the whole dashboard. The single-dial dashboards represented by Volvo S60 and Mazda 3 Axela have significantly different shapes from the other three double-dial dashboards. The single-dial shape is narrower and longer and shows a feeling of flexibility, while the double-dial shape is thicker and expresses a feeling of heaviness. Color is a key influence factor on the pattern of the whole dashboard, and the design of large-area color blocks interferes with user experience. With the middle display zone of Lincoln MKZ as example, based on its entertainment function, this zone has rich colors and enhances the feeling of driving experience.

The final trait is the effects of frills on the dashboard. Frills play a highlighting role in dashboard shapes, but may be easily ignored. Of the five dashboards, frills were only done by Infiniti Q50. Specifically, it inherited the sea elements, as the wave-shaped design strengthened the style of strength esthetics and showed a strong feeling of perceptual design.

By analyzing these five dashboards, we find the dashboards have obvious brand-related characteristics and their information frameworks indicate a trend of individuation. Specifically, hierarchical information management is accompanied by special shape elements, which contribute to the driver's height identification. Moreover, as for design of interface vision elements, the number of dials also affects the trend of dashboard shapes. Frills, as a part of detailed design, frills play a highlighting role and contribute to the driver's driving experiences. Among the five dashboards, the biggest breakthrough is from the digital hidden design of Volvo S60, which improves the driver's perception accuracy and largely contributes to safe driving.

4   Rules in Digital Car Dashboard Interface Design

4.1   Concise Layout

During dashboard interface design, the key information is displayed on the first level and should be conveyed to the driver as soon as possible, while the supplementary information is exhibited at the second and third levels or the interactive sub-interface. An efficient way is to provide such marking information on the start-up screen of the program, so that such information could be designed in a very attractive way and inform the driver they are entering the corresponding program [10]. Otherwise, the large amount of information puzzles a new user and reduces the speed of a mature user, as well as increases the possibility of wrong operation. Thus, the layout information hierarchical management should be conducted at an appropriate way. Another way is the rule of "less is more". The Volvo S60 dashboard interface offers a good reference.

4.2   Color Appropriateness

Color is a key step during the user-dashboard interfacial interaction and should be used carefully. Jakob Nielsen proposed three rules for color use during interface design. First, do not use too many colors, and appropriately 5–7 colors. Also light-gray or soft colors are more suitable than bright colors for being used as background colors. Second, ensure the interface can be used in different colors, so that the user can use the interface if he/she is unable to differentiate colors, such as the blind people. Third, use colors only for differentiation and emphasization, rather than for provision of information, especially quantitative information. These three color use rules can be well validated by the five samples. As for selection of bottom color, we suggest black or gray, and the sample has 5–7 colors. Some important information colors, such as pointer, scale, character colors, and indicator light, can also be well redundantly indicated, ensuring it is accessible to special populations.

4.3   Color Appropriateness

Perception and experience are needed in cognizing higher-efficiency higher-level design. Research on perceptual experience is generally divided into two patterns. First, the Western emotional design or experience design is able to acquire user-related information about emotion or experience, through user participation in research or activities, and use into design. The other is the Japanese perceptual design, which focuses on the mapping between perceptual elements and design elements as well as algorithms, and its research method is more quantitative. From the perspective of experience design, the tested five dashboards all reserve the respective brand characteristics in style and type, and have brought users with different driving experiences. The most representative is still Volvo S60, which provides three patterns of ecology, elegance and optimization that promote the human-machine interaction and bring good news to the boring drive. This modern esthetics with strong human kindness has catered to the public.

The above design rules suggest that the dashboard interface should be designed to be concise and efficient (Fig. 6).

Fig. 6. Interface design of automobile instrument panel

5 Conclusion

Research on car dashboard interface design under the background of digitalization is a novel topic, which deserves systemic development from the perspectives of design contents, methods and flowchart as well as abundant experimental validation. With the popularization of the Internet+ technology, the car dashboards will bring new experiences in design contents and interactive technology, but are also faced with challenges. In this study, we selected only five dashboards for systematic research and proposed some design rules, which should be further explored. Nevertheless, with the technical progression, the human-dashboard interaction will become increasingly efficient under the premise of safe driving. Personalized driving experience is a key trend in the field of dashboard design.

References

1. Zhu, L.: Based on the KE of Auto Dashboard Interface Design. Wuhan Textile University, Wuhan (2011)
2. Wu, Z.-x., Wang, Y.-s., Jia, C.-q.: Design and analysis of typical cab human-machine engineering car. Internal Combust. Engine Parts **2014**(6), 11–14 (2014)
3. Cui, K.: The analysis of the cockpit display interface's color effects on novice drivers' visual pre-attentive progress. Chin. J. Ergon. **20**(2), 35–40 (2014)
4. Owsley, C., Mcgwin, G., Seder, T.: Older drivers' attitudes about instrument cluster designs in vehicles. Accid. Anal. Prev. **43**(6), 2024–2029 (2011)
5. Huang, Z.-f., Li, X.: On the Image Perception and Promotion Pattern of Tourist Destination. Tourism Tribune, Beijing (2002). (in Chinese)
6. Tang, Y.-y.: Research on the evolution of instrument panel under the background of new energy resource. Art Des. **2014**(11), 96–98 (2014)
7. Iandoli, L., Quinto, I., Liddo, A.D., et al.: A debate dashboard to enhance online knowledge sharing. Vine **42**(1), 67–93 (2012)
8. Ki, J., Han, K.: Dashboard design factors on emotional change: how separation between center-fascia and center-console, button orientation and button arrangement influence emotion. Commun. Comput. Inf. Sci. **434**(1), 95–100 (2014)

9. Tan, H., Tan, Z.-y., Jing, C.-h.: Automative Human Machine Interface Design. Publishing House of Electronics Industry, Beijing (2015)
10. Nielsen, J.: Usability Engineering. China Machine Press, Beijing (2004). (Translated by, Z.-J. Liu)
11. Qiu, Q.: 2016 China Mobile Consumer Analysis. China Business and Market, Beijing (2017). (in Chinese)

Emergency Usability Lab - Concept to Evaluate the Usability of Healthcare Systems in Emergencies

Peter Rasche$^{(\boxtimes)}$, Alexander Mertens, and Christopher M. Schlick

Chair and Institute of Industrial Engineering and Ergonomics of RWTH Aachen University, Bergdriesch 27, Aachen, Germany
p.rasche@iaw.rwth-aachen.de

Abstract. In the healthcare sector the number of patients rises while the staffs cover is decreasing. Due to cost pressure hospital stays are shortened. Thereby more and more clinical activities are migrated into the home environment, especially if these activities have a nursing character. Examples for these activities are infusion therapies or the need of a respiratory device. Due to this trend and the increasing cost pressure in healthcare more and more patients are incorporated as agents in their own care. Thereby more and more clinical products are used by patients and their nursing relatives. This raises the question whether the used medical devices have a proper usability for the use in home healthcare. For such investigations we introduce the "Emergency Usability Lab". Focus of this lab is to evaluate and ensure usability of a medical product for the homecare environment in critical situations and emergencies.

Keywords: Healthcare · Home environment · Emergency · Usability

1 Introduction

Healthcare is experiencing a major system redesign as well as paradigm shift [1]. Cost pressure and an increasing number of patients cause the system to find new ways of delivering efficient healthcare services. Thereby an increasing number of health services are migrated from clinical setting to the patient's household. In this home healthcare settings the patient self is in charge of providing the necessary operations [2, 3]. Therefore some researches even speak of 'do it yourself healthcare' [4]. In most cases these transferred activities have a nursing character like for example home based dialysis or infusion therapy [5]. Due to the rapid speed of this ongoing process most patients use devices which were developed for a clinical context. Thereby more and more complex medical devices from clinical practice migrate into home healthcare [6]. Besides this trend also counter movement exists. More and more consumer products like smartphones or other smart devices get integrated into classical healthcare services [7]. Thereby healthcare is changing and classical domains like clinical context and home healthcare get mixed up [1].

Due to this process classical methods and paradigms regarding the design and usability of medical devices needs to be reconsidered and maybe changed. Devices

© Springer International Publishing AG 2017
V.G. Duffy (Ed.): DHM 2017, Part II, LNCS 10287, pp. 354–364, 2017.
DOI: 10.1007/978-3-319-58466-9_32

used in home healthcare needs to fit different requirements then devices for clinical practice. Not every household is designed and equipped the same way. Furthermore patients and their nursing relatives have a different level of experience in performing health activities then experienced and educated health professionals (see Fig. 1).

Fig. 1. Example of a possible critical situation in future of personal home healthcare.

Especially if we think about the operation of medical devices like a dialysis machine or an infusion pump by a patient or a nursing relative, topics like prior experience, training and knowledge are different than in a clinical context [8]. Additionally topics like fear or daily form become important for this setting. Therefore the ergonomic considerations and usability guidelines of medical products as well as smart devices need to be reconsidered.

In case of an emergency existing guidelines and best practices for clinical setting applied to home healthcare needs to be reconsidered. In clinical practice unsuitable usability could be addressed by training but in the described home healthcare setting this seems unrealistic due to time and cost factors [8]. Therefore a new approach is needed to ensure suitable usability of medical devices in home healthcare even in case of an emergency.

In medical terms emergencies are defined as time pressures decision making in a situation related to life threatening harm of a patient [9]. Taking the approach of work under extreme conditions proposed by Luczak (1991) it is possible to transfer the definition of an emergency into the field of human factors and ergonomics [10]. Luzcak introduced this concept to link environmental conditions like heat or noise with the performance of an individual. He explains that stressors like heat or noise reduce the individual's abilities and performance based on the stress and strain concept [10, 11]. Based on the stress and strain concept extreme conditions could be seen as mismatch between the individuals' abilities and the necessary demand due to the stressor to cope the job. Taking the idea of work under extreme conditions and linking it to the stress and strain concept we are able to access emergency situations in home healthcare in terms of human factors and ergonomics.

As defined above in an emergency the clinical professional has to work under time pressure and the knowledge of life threatening harm to a patient. Thereby he or she works under at least two different stressors. The effect of these two stressors might be decreased by experience and training of the professional regarding performance in emergency situations. Now we exchange the clinical professional by a patient who operates the medical device solving the emergency situation him- or herself. Also in this case we have the two already defined stressors but now we could extend this list of stressors for example by fear or pain. On the other side according the stress and strain concept abilities like training or experience might be missing. Due to this usability becomes much more important as a bad one additionally reduces the patient's performance. In home healthcare more situations are problematic than just mentioned emergencies. Also daily form and mood of a patient could influence his or her ability to operate a medical device. Again in clinical setting these stressors can be compensated by training, but due to the missing training in home healthcare also these stressors needs to be considered as a critical factor. The mentioned combination of stress and strain concept and work under extreme conditions allow us to model situations in home healthcare as described. By differentiating the severity of stressors we are able to differentiate between several levels of severity of an emergency.

Thereby it is possible to link the methods of the field of Human Factors and Ergonomics with the medical context of diseases and their critical and life-threatening situations.

2   Method

Based on the stress and strain concept and the idea of work under extreme conditions we will introduce in this chapter the 'Emergency Usability Lab' and how it is developed. The idea behind this lab is to incorporate well known stressors from clinical stress research into lab based usability studies to simulate extreme conditions. Following three studies are presented which give more insight into the 'Emergency Usability Lab'. Figure 2 gives an overview how these studies are connected.

2.1   Study ET1: Physiology Under Simulated Extreme Condition

Research Questions. This exploratory laboratory experiment investigates different stressors independently due to their physiological impact on an individual. Investigated stressors are traffic noise [12], white noise [13], cold pressor [14] and the PASAT-C test [15]. The objective of this experiment is to determine the physiological impact of different stressors on the human operator respective intra- and interindividual differences measured by the Empatica E4 [16].

Method. In total 60 participants separated in two age groups (AG1: 20–40 yrs; AG2: 60–80 yrs) take part in this study. All participants will experience each stressor in random order. Between each exposure the participants will be given a break to recover. The participants' tasks during each stressor exposure are employed to investigate the physiological change in performance. Therefore the Purdue Pegboard [17] and TAP 2.3 [18] will be incorporated. To investigate the intraindividual influences in more detail, the participants will take part in this experiment twice at two different days. The experiment will only take part in the morning due to natural change in performance during the day [13]. Dependent variables in this experiment are participants' performance, electrodermal activity and heart-rate-variability. Both will be measured by the Empatica E4 [16]. Furthermore the subjective mental workload during the stressor exposure will be assessed by the Rating scale of mental effort [19]. Control variables in

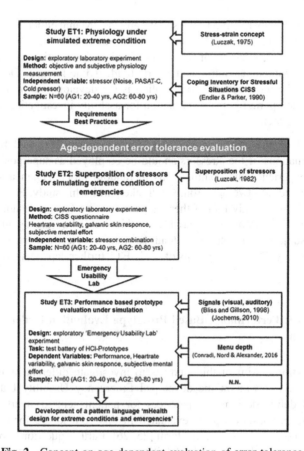

Fig. 2. Concept on age-dependent evaluation of error tolerance.

this experiment are stress in personal life measured by the perceived stress scale [20] and coping strategies for stressful situations accessed by the Coping inventory for Stressful Situations [21].

2.2 Study ET2: Superposition of Stressors for Simulating Extreme Conditions of Emergencies

Research Questions. In critical and emergency situations in most cases individuals do not experience just one stressor individually but several ones in combination. A common combination is time pressure and pain [9]. In the field of Human Factors and Ergonomics such combinations of stressors are referred as superposition [22].

In the context of clinical stress tests superposition of several stressors is a common concept to increase the effect of the physiological stress reaction of the individual [23].

Examples for such superposition stress tests are the 'Mannheimer Multicomponent-Stress-Test' [13] as well as the 'Maastricht Acute Stress Test' [25].

Therefore the basic question of this study is which combination of stressors is best to induce stress without an intra- and interindividual interference. Objective of the identification of the most suitable combination is the development of an 'Emergency Usability Lab' incorporating this combination for usability investigations of healthcare systems for emergencies.

Method. Based on the best practices and requirements investigated by study ET1 different combinations of the stressors should be employed as superposition. All participants will experience the combinations in random order. Again a sample of 60 participants divided into two age groups will take part in this study. Participants' tasks will be the same as in study ET1 if there is no indication for a redesign based on the results of study ET1. Dependent variables within this study are again participants' performance, subjective mental workload as well as electro dermal activity and heart-rate-variability. Due to the results of study ET1 further dependent variables might be defined.

2.3 Study ET3: Performance Based Prototype Evaluation Under Simulation

Research Questions. Aim of this study is to investigate different human computer interaction prototypes with in the developed Emergency Usability Lab to evaluate guidelines and define design best practices for patient centred smart device based healthcare systems. Design aspects evaluated in this context are for example alarm signaling in visual as well as auditory form [25, 26]. Further questions investigated are suitable font sizes or colorization. In Addition appropriate menu depth will be investigated [27]. The object of this study is to develop basic software design guidelines for use under extreme conditions.

Method. In total a number of 60 Participants separated in two age groups will take part in this study. All participants will operate the prototypes via a self-developed test battery app. By representing the participants several prototypes differentiated by levels of font size, colorization and menu depth, suitable combinations for use under extreme conditions should be determined. Dependent variables in this study will be chosen based on the results of the studies ET1 and ET2. Considered variables are participants' performance, electro dermal activity and heart-rate-variability.

3   Initial Results of the Emergency Usability Lab

Initial tests showed that it would be best to use a quiet and clean room. Therefore with in our laboratory a white colored and soundproof room was set up (see Fig. 3). Thereby participants are not distracted by their surrounding and can focus on the product and tasks. Stressor exposure is done via headphones. We decided to use the 't.bone

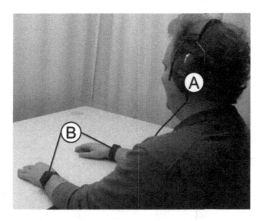

Fig. 3. Experimental setting of the Emergency Usability Lab (A = Headphones, B = E4 Wristbands).

HD990D' which has full size earcups reducing outside sounds up to 22 dB. Furthermore these headphones are able to produce sounds up to 105 dB which is a lot higher than the usually used 80 dB in clinical stress tests [12, 13, 24]. Recording of physiological reaction is done by the 'Empatica E4' [16]. For the pre-test we incorporate two Empatica wristbands, one for the dominant and one for the non-dominant hand wrist, to get as accurate data as possible.

Within an initial approach six participants (1 female, 5 male) in the age of between 24 years and 34 years took part in the pre-test of study ET1. For all participants electro dermal skin conductance and heartrate were recorded meanwhile they were exposed to three different stressors (white noise [12], traffic noise [13] and PASAT-C test [15]). The experiment was time triggered. After start all participants completed the experiment guided by an audio file, they were ordered to listen to. Further tasks were not defined. Thereby interference with this experiment by the investigator as well as a certain task was avoided. The experimental timeline is shown in Fig. 4.

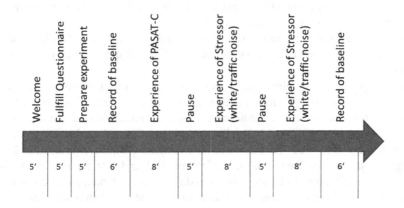

Fig. 4. Procedure of the experiment with time in minutes for each step.

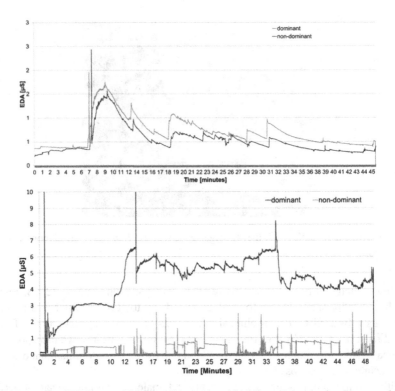

Fig. 5. Example of EDA record for a good (upper) and bad (lower) connection between skin and E4 wristband.

Figure 5 shows the recorded EDA signal over duration of the experiment. The upper part of Fig. 5 shows the EDA signal in case the E4 wristbands are adjusted in a suitable way. The lower part of Fig. 5 shows recorded data for the case the E4 wristband is not adjusted the right way. In this special case the signal for the non-dominant hand got lost during the experiment (see Fig. 5). This problem indicates the usefulness of measuring EDA signal at both hands to have backup data in case the E4 losses proper connection to the participant's skin.

Due to incomplete data the recorded EDA signal of participants ID2, ID3 and ID6 were excluded. Figures 6 and 7 show the recorded EDA signal over the duration of the experiment.

The comparison of the Figs. 6 and 7 shows that EDA signal measured at the wrist of each participant just differs in its amplitude. The signal is weaker for the dominant hand than for the non-dominant one. Furthermore shows this initial data a difference between the first stressor (PASAT-C) and all following stressors. Based on this data PASAT-C was objectively measured the most stressful stressor. Subjective evaluation by the participants showed different results. Participants ID1 and ID4 reported white noise followed by traffic noise to be the most stressful stressors. Participant ID5 named the PASAT-C test followed by white noise to be the most stressful stressors. These initial results indicate that it is useful to measure objective stress level as well as subjective one.

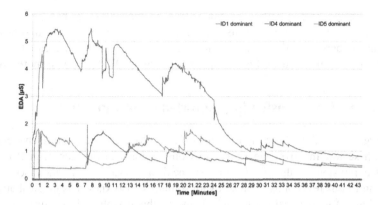

Fig. 6. Results of the experiment for dominant hand of participants.

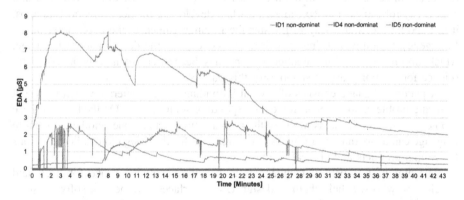

Fig. 7. Results of the experiment for non-dominant hand of participants.

Figure 8 shows the heartrate signal recorded for all six participants. The heartrate was measured for each hand wrist. For this figure the mean heartrate per participant was calculated.

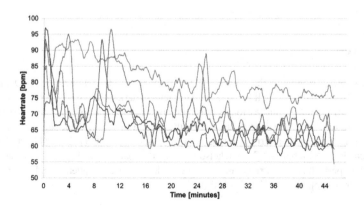

Fig. 8. Heartrate per participant during experiment

Recorded heartrate signals are interesting as they show a habituation to the experiment. In the beginning of this experiment all participants had a high heartrate, during the experience of the three different stressors heartrate decreased. A more detailed analysis of this data, for example with Kubios HRV will give more insights.

4 Concept for Transferring Knowledge into Practice

An Emergency Usability Lab alone is not sufficient to address the future challenges in the health sector. In 2016, the European Commission and the European Parliament adopted a revision of the regulations on medical devices within their scope [28]. According to this revision, simple software solutions, also known as medical apps, are classified as active medical products. This means that established manufacturers, such as start-ups, are obliged to submit software and applications to a conformity assessment procedure in accordance with the Medical Devices Act. In order to take the error and emergency robustness into consideration when developing medical software and apps, it is important to find a way to transfer the findings gained in the application of the Emergency Usability Lab into practice. The concept of the design pattern language, which originates from the architecture and has been used intensively in computer science for several years, is suitable for this purpose.

A pattern language consists of several individual design patterns, which represent recurring problems together with the corresponding solution [29]. On the basis of these problems and solutions, as well as their connection among one another, an entire language can arise, ranging from basic requirements for the design to detailed solutions for certain products and clinical pictures.

The aim of this pattern language is to provide a solution space for users and developers, who will help them to design User interfaces and medical software solutions for home healthcare, being the error and emergency robust design the top priority.

Acknowledgments. This publication is part of the research project "TECH4AGE", which is funded by the German Federal Ministry of Education and Research (BMBF, Grant No. 16SV7111) supervised by the VDI/VDE Innovation + Technik GmbH. For more details and information, please see www.tech4age.de.

References

1. Holden, R.J., Carayon, P., Gurses, A.P., Hoonakker, P., Hundt, A.S., Ozok, A.A., Rivera-Rodriguez, A.J.: SEIPS 2.0: a human factors framework for studying and improving the work of healthcare professionals and patients. Ergonomics 56(11), 1669–1686 (2013)
2. Unruh, K.T., Pratt, W.: Patients as actors: the patient's role in detecting, preventing, and recovering from medical errors. Int. J. Med. Inform. 76(Suppl. 1), 236–244 (2007)
3. Holden, R.J., Schubert, C.C., Mickelson, R.S.: The patient work system: an analysis of self-care performance barriers among elderly heart failure patients and their informal caregivers. Appl. Ergon. 47, 133–150 (2015)

4. Greene, J.A.: Do-it-yourself medical devices–technology and empowerment in American health care. New Engl. J. Med. **374**(4), 305–308 (2016)
5. Ewers, M.: Häusliche Infusionstherapie (HIT): Herausforderung für Pflege und public health in Wissenschaft und Praxis. Pflege und Gesellschaft **5**, 37–41 (2000)
6. Klasnja, P., Pratt, W.: Healthcare in the pocket: mapping the space of mobile-phone health interventions. J. Biomed. Inform. **45**(1), 184–198 (2012)
7. Devine, M., Hasler, R., Kaye, R., Rogers, W., Turieo, M.: Human factors considerations in the migration of medical devices from clinical to homecare settings. Proc. Hum. Factors Ergon. Soc. Annu. Meet. **48**(15), 1685–1689 (2004). doi:10.1177/154193120404801512
8. Kirchberg, D.: Keine Anwendung ohne Einweisung. Medizinprodukte sicher anwenden und betreiben. Schlütersche (Pflege Kolleg), Hannover (2014)
9. St. Pierre, M., Hofinger, G., Buerschaper, C.: Notfallmanagement Human Factors und Patientensicherheit in der Akutmedizin. Springer, Berlin (2011). 2. aktualisierte und erw. Aufl.
10. Luczak, H.: Work under extreme conditions. Ergonomics **34**(6), 687–720 (1991)
11. Rohmert, W.: Ergonomics: concept of work, stress and strain. Appl. Psychol. **35**(2), 159–180 (1986)
12. Wagner, J., Cik, M., Marth, E., Santner, B.I., Gallasch, E., Lackner, A., Raggam, R.B.: Feasibility of testing three salivary stress biomarkers in relation to naturalistic traffic noise exposure. Int. J. Hyg. Environ. Health **213**(2), 153–155 (2010)
13. Kolotylova, T., Koschke, M., Bär, K.-J., Ebner-Priemer, U., Kleindienst, N., Bohus, M., Schmahl, C.: Entwicklung des "Mannheimer Multikomponenten-Stress-Test" (MMST). Psychother. Psychosom. Med. Psychol. **60**(2), 64–72 (2010)
14. Van Orden, K.F., Benoit, S.L., Osga, G.A.: Effects of cold air stress on the performance of a command and control task. Hum. Factors: J. Hum. Factors Ergon. Soc. **38**(1), 130–141 (1996)
15. Lejuez, C.W., Kahler, C.W., Brown, R.A.: A modified computer version of the paced auditory serial addition task (PASAT) as a laboratory-based stressor. Behav. Therapist **26**(4), 290–293 (2003)
16. Garbarino, M., Lai, M., Bender, D., Picard, R.W., Tognetti, S.: Empatica E3 - a wearable wireless multi-sensor device for real-time computerized biofeedback and data acquisition. In: 2014 EAI 4th International Conference on Wireless Mobile Communication and Healthcare (Mobihealth), pp. 39–42 (2014)
17. Tiffin, J., Asher, E.J.: The Purdue Pegboard: norms and studies of reliability and validity. J. Appl. Psychol. **32**(3), 234 (1948)
18. Zimmermann, P., Fimm, B.: Testbatterie zur Aufmerksamkeitsprüfung-Version 2.2: (TAP); [Handbuch]. Psytest, Austin (2009)
19. Zijlstra, F.: Efficiency in work behaviour: a design approach for modern tools. Ph.D. thesis, TU Delft, Delft University of Technology, Soesterberg (1993)
20. Cohen, S., Kamarck, T., Mermelstein, R.: A global measure of perceived stress. J. Health soc. Behav. **24**(4), 385–396 (1983)
21. Endler, N.S., Parker, J.D.: Coping Inventory for Stressful Situations (CISS): Manual (Revised Edition). Multi-Health Systems Inc., Toronto, October 1999. edited by Furedi, F. (2009)
22. Luczak, H., Brüggmann, M.: Mehrfachbelastungen. In: Landau, K., Pressel, G. (eds.) Medizinisches Lexikon der beruflichen Belastungen und Gefährdungen. Definitionen - Vorkommen – Arbeitsschutz, 2. 2., vollständig neubearbeitete Auflage, pp. 662–664. Gentner Verlag, Stuttgart (2009)
23. Bali, A., Jaggi, A.S.: Clinical experimental stress studies: methods and assessment. Rev. Neurosci. **26**(5), 555–579 (2015)

24. Smeets, T., Cornelisse, S., Quaedflieg, C.W., Meyer, T., Jelicic, M., Merckelbach, H.: Introducing the maastricht acute stress test (MAST): a quick and non-invasive approach to elicit robust autonomic and glucocorticoid stress responses. Psychoneuroendocrinology **37** (12), 1998–2008 (2012)
25. Bliss, J.P., Gilson, R.D.: Emergency signal failure: implications and recommendations. Ergonomics **41**(1), 57–72 (1998)
26. Jochems, N.: Altersdifferenzierte gestaltung der mensch-rechner-interaktion am beispiel von projektmanagementaufgaben. Ph.D. RWTH Aachen (2010)
27. Conradi, J., Nord, B., Alexander, T.: Gestaltung von Menühierarchien für mobile IT-Geräte beim Gehen. In: Gesellschaft für Arbeitswissenschaft (Hg.): Arbeit in komplexen Systemen. Digital, vernetzt, human?! Dortmund, pp. 1–6 (2016)
28. Council of the European Union Regulation of the European Parliament and of the council on medical devices, and amending Directive 2001/83/EC, Regulation (EC) No. 178/2002 and Regulation (EC) No. 1223/2009 (9364/3/16 REV 3) (2016)
29. Rasche, P., Theis, S., Bröhl, C., Wille, M., Schlick, C.M., Mertens, A.: Building and exchanging competence interdisciplinarily design patterns as domain mediator. In: Proceedings of the International Symposium on Human Factors and Ergonomics in Health Care, pp. 19–24 (2016)

Watch Out!

User-Centered Feedback Design for a V2X-Smartphone App

Teresa Schmidt[1]([⊠]), Ralf Philipsen[1], Dzenan Dzafic[2], and Martina Ziefle[1]

[1] Human-Computer Interaction Center, RWTH Aachen University, Aachen, Germany
{schmidt,philipsen,ziefle}@comm.rwth-aachen.de
[2] Embedded Software, RWTH Aachen University, Aachen, Germany
dzafic@embedded.rwth-aachen.de

Abstract. Mobility is a fast developing, technological and simultaneously human field of research. V2X-technology is one major contributor that will influence the behavior, efficiency and safety of traffic participants. To include all participating members of traffic, we developed a V2X-smartphone application to empower vulnerable road user to be part of the technological integration. With a two-tiered research approach, we focused on both, the iconography and the feedback design of that application. One key finding of the presented work is a clear recommendation of combined features (color, size and geometrical form) for rear-end collision scenarios. The article concludes with practical recommendations that facilitate visualization-varieties from a users' perspective.

Keywords: V2X-technology · Smartphone application · Feedback design · Usability · Mobility

1 Research Perspective and State of the Art

Mobility is a key issue in today's society. People use and depend on different types of transport vehicles and want clean, safe and efficient ways to reach their destination comfortably. With a steadily growing number of road users, the number of drawbacks like congestion and high CO^2 emissions, which need to be taken care of, is getting more serious. One of the biggest challenges, however, is still the high number of (fatal) accidents in road traffic [1].

Although, the overall number of accidents in road traffic decreased in the last ten years, 390.000 fatalities are still tremendous and not bearable (2014 in Germany: [2]). From January to September 2016, the number of traffic accidents increased by 6.4% (2428 fatalities in total in Germany) compared to the same period in 2015 [3]. Therefore, road safety remains a key issue for society and politics.

© Springer International Publishing AG 2017
V.G. Duffy (Ed.): DHM 2017, Part II, LNCS 10287, pp. 365–383, 2017.
DOI: 10.1007/978-3-319-58466-9_33

In order to increase safety, the federal government published he program *Strategy for automated and connected driving* and announced the goal to diminish the traffic incidents by 40% until 2020 [2, 4]. In addition to a growing enforcement of road traffic regulations and a better training of the road users, the program also provides for the promotion of intelligent technologies. The continuous implementation and development of connected technology based driver assistance systems can be detected, while the most important and frequently used way to travel is still the personal car. Aiming at improved traffic safety, new driving support systems were implemented and reportedly decreased the number of crashes since integrating them into vehicles [5, 6]. Taking a closer look on this proceeding, several system features and boundaries, which are not sufficiently researched out of a social science perspective, can be detected.

The multi-level effects of connected and (semi-) automated vehicles on the driver is a focused topic today, but integrating also the vulnerable road users (e.g. wheelchair users, pedestrians or bicyclists) into intelligent transportation systems is a future challenge.

To address this challenge, an exchange of information between different road users and technical elements in the infrastructure will be necessary. The communication of vehicles among themselves and with elements of the infrastructure is summarized as V2X ("Vehicle-to-Everything"). Modern vehicles are already equipped with numerous technologies such as radar, ultra-sonic and sensor cameras designed to reduce the risk of accidents. Via this way of connected communication, the reduction of rear-end collisions and a more energy-efficient driving mode is intended, e.g. by an optimization of the traffic flow [7]. Although, recent studies focus cooperative interactions with road users [8] or the usability of reminder applications [9], there seems to be a gap in how to integrate vulnerable road users into the intelligent networking of V2X-technology. Following the approach of including the e.g. pedestrians into V2X-communication, GPS and WLAN based prototypes have been tested in recent years [10, 11].

One approach to connect vulnerable road user to V2X-communication is the integration via smartphone applications. The proliferation of mobile devices has grown strongly in recent years: in 2016, 66% of the German population owned a smart device (95% of the 14- to 29-year-old age group in Germany), promising an effective way of connection [12]. Today's devices are also equipped with numerous sensors, which allow to track the position and speed of a user, which promises a technical way of integration as well [13].

Assuming that pedestrians, cyclists and wheelchair users need special protection in road traffic, their inclusion into vehicle communication could further increase road safety. Taking into account that the detection of vulnerable traffic participants without the solution of a smartphone application is only possible to a limited extent, because the sensor technology of vehicles, such as lasers, radars or video-based solutions, must be in the field of view of the sensor system, a smartphone solution seems effective and efficient. If, for example, a pedestrian is concealed by a parking car, it is difficult to detect by the sensor system of an approaching vehicle [14]. With a V2X-smartphone application however, this challenge could be directly addressed.

2 V2X-Application: Watch Out!

System Architecture. The V2X-smartphone application presents the current traffic situation to the user and alerts him in case of a critical situation with a warning instruction. Aiming the interconnection of different (smart) traffic technologies, an overview of the own position and all traffic participants of the current situation will be displayed.

The entire system consists of a control server, which is connected to all components (see Fig. 1). These components include traffic lights, smartphones, Cohda boxes and some laser and HD cameras. The Fig. 1 shows only the components that are relevant to this work.

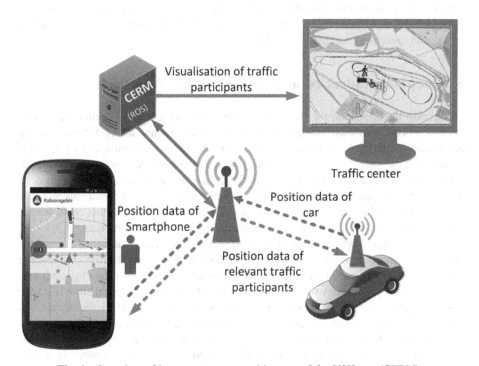

Fig. 1. Overview of important system architecture of the V2X-app (CERM)

The control server is connected directly to the traffic center. This traffic center observes the traffic so that an administrator can step in the event at any time. Furthermore, the control server connects with the Cohda box in the car via a WLAN router and also with the V2X-app on the smartphone. On the one hand, the V2X-app sends all position and motion data to the control server and on the other hand, the app receives the position of all relevant traffic users. This means that when a car passes by on the smartphone and it is no longer a threat, the control system automatically stops to send information to the smartphone. The same happens with the car, concretely meaning, the Cohda box sends all information to the control server and receives all the data from the relevant users.

The data, shared by the V2X-app to the server, are the GPS positions, GPS accuracy, linear acceleration and traffic type. The traffic type defines whether the traveler is by foot, with an E-wheelchair or with a bicycle. In case the type of traffic is set to E-wheelchair, there is the possibility that the control system connects to the control of the E-wheelchair via the smartphone (Bluetooth). In case the E-wheelchair user does not react in time due to his disability, it is possible to brake the wheelchair through the control system until the danger is over. Furthermore, the entire data transfer of the components will be stored and can be used to analyze, to anticipate and finally to avoid critical situations using the neural networks.

Although the previous investigations highlight the technical feasibility, the visualization of the application on the smartphone has so far largely been neglected – out of a social science perspective. However, designing a user interface is crucial to whether or not users are using an application [15].

3 Questions Addressed and Methodological Approach

To develop the application's user-interface and feedback-system a multi-stage development process was used, integrating the users' requirements and preferences during every iteration loop. At first, the theoretical foundations have been acquired by identifying both the state-of-the-art and existing knowledge gaps. As can be seen in Fig. 2, the literature research resulted in two parallel development strands. One of them dealt with the graphic representation of traffic situations, including the map display, the illustration of road users and the visualization of hazardous situations that could lead to collisions between motorized traffic participants and the smartphone user.

The other strand broached the issue of developing the ideal, multi-modal feedback and warning to grab the vulnerable road user's attention in order to trigger a reaction (usually to stop movement) that could avoid a potential collision. Thereby, both efficiency and user preferences were taken into account. Both development strands started with interview- and questionnaire based studies and used low-level prototypes, i.e. animations and wizard-of-oz based systems, in laboratory settings.

After that, both the resulting user interface and the warning system will be implemented into the Android-based application to carry out user studies in a controlled environment on test track in order to iteratively optimize the system before testing under real traffic conditions.

3.1 User Interface Development

Aiming and focusing the development and feedback of the applications' user interface, we conducted a two-tiered approach using both qualitative and quantitative empirical methods.

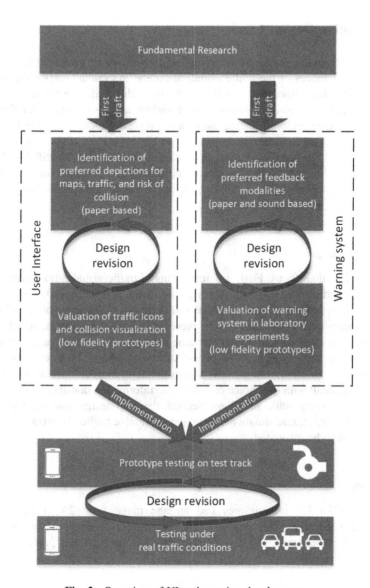

Fig. 2. Overview of UI and warning development

First, recognizable and lean road-user icons for the applications' interface were designed and evaluated via an interview-based preliminary user study. Second, the revised user interface was evaluated with a large-scale questionnaire study combining paper-based and animated prototype elements.

4   Qualitative Design Circle

The first questionnaire-supported interview study was set to gain insights of users' application preferences of the traffic visualization and to evaluate early prototypes for the visualized traffic participants. To display the individual traffic on the map, icons are used: they serve as a visual representation of various aspects of a user interface [16]. According to the definition of Pierce, an icon is a representation of an object, which is represented only by the distinctive features it exhibits [17]. Here, different aspects need to be considered: the used icons must first be easily and quickly identifiable. Further, different locomotion-roles of vulnerable traffic participants were focused to integrate possible user-centered feedback. Here, perspectives from pedestrians, bicyclists and wheelchair users were interrogated.

4.1   Study Design

The study had a dual focus: First, different forms of traffic visualization were studied. Thereby, the participants had to perform identification and rating tasks. The identification tasks took place as follows: Various visualizations of traffic situations adapted to common smartphone screen sizes were presented to the participants, which had to identify the illustrated road users to determine the average detection rate. The icon set consisted of top view depictions of pedestrians, wheelchairs, bicycles, motorcycles, cars, busses, trucks, trams and the user's own position. In addition, rating tasks were conducted that dealt with the choice of colors, the information density and the potential help during assessing traffic situations. Second, the map design was evaluated distinguished by different traffic situations. Here, the alternative traffic visualization of a heat map view had to be evaluated.

4.2   Sample

The twelve (N = 12) interviewees had an age range from 24 to 62 years old (Mean = 35.5, Standard Deviation = 13.9). The gender distribution was quiet symmetrical with seven men and five women, further, two of the participants were wheelchair users.

4.3   Results: Icon Design

The participants were invited to identify several items on displayed pictures (in smartphone display size) with icons of traffic participants. According to the International Organization for Standardization (ISO), icons with a recognition rate of 67% are still considered acceptable [18]. This mark was reached for the icons displaying Bicycle, Car, Pedestrian, Position and Bus (as can be seen in Tables 1 and 2).

Table 1. Absolute frequency of correctly identified traffic icons (N = 12).

Item	Bicycle	Car	Pedestrian	Wheelchair	Position
Icon					
Correctly identified N (%)	11 (91.7)	12 (100)	9 (75.0)	3 (25.0)	10 (83.3)

Table 2. Absolute frequency of correctly identified traffic icons (N = 12).

Item	Motorcycle	Bus	Truck	Tram
Icon				
Correclty identified N (%)	4 (33.3)	12 (100)	7 (58.3)	7 (58.3)

The icons *Wheelchair*, *Motorcycle*, *Truck* and *Tram* were not identified correctly according to the ISO mark. The icon *Wheelchair* was e.g. taken for a pedestrian, whereas the icon *Motorcycle* was misinterpreted for e.g. a bicycle and the *Tram* icon as long truck.

Due to the low identification rate of the mentioned traffic icons above, a quantitative re-evaluation was conducted, also validating the beforehand positive results of the correctly identified traffic icons.

4.4   Results: Map Design

To evaluate, whether a street map view with the given icons is the right design, the participants were invited to assess a different design: the heat map (see Fig. 3).

Here, the lack of important information was criticized, e.g. the specific color meaning ("vehicles on the street" vs. "critical situation"). One participant concluded, that this type of view might be considerable for a driver of a vehicle, but not for vulnerable road users like pedestrians. Due to the lack of positive feedback and many misunderstandings in the meaning of the visualization, the heat map view was no part in the further study design.

Fig. 3. V2X-application heat map-view ("Berlin Stadtmitte U2", Data source: © 2017 Geobasis-DE/BKG (©2009), Google)

5   Quantitative Design Circle

Taking the results from the qualitative study into account, the user interface was further improved and evaluated by conducting an online survey. A special focus was placed on the presentation format for the current traffic situation and the design of the warning instructions.

5.1   Study Design

The first part of the study dealt with the iconography. Participants had to both identify visualized road users and evaluate the different icons for a road user type in direct comparison. Therefore, three revised icons for each type that showed insufficient detection rates during the preliminary study were presented to identify the optimal representation with regard to identifiability on a smartphone screen. There was also a focus on the distinguishability of road user pairs that had often been confused: pedestrians vs. wheelchairs and bicycles vs. motorcycles.

The second part of the study broached the issue of preferred illustration for safety critical situations. Five different animated sequences were laid out to the participants, all in common mobile device size.

The first sequence shows a colored (red) geometrical figure (circle) with a growing opacity level within the collision warning phase (see a section of it in Fig. 4):

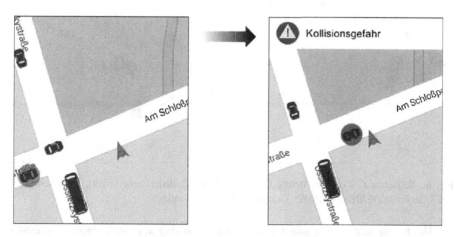

Fig. 4. Sequence A geometrical figure before (left) and during collision time (right). Data source: © 2017 Geobasis-DE/BKG (©2009), Google (Color figure online)

The second sequence shows also a colored geometrical figure (red circle) with a growing opacity level within the collision phase, but the size of the circle form increases as well (see a section of it Fig. 5):

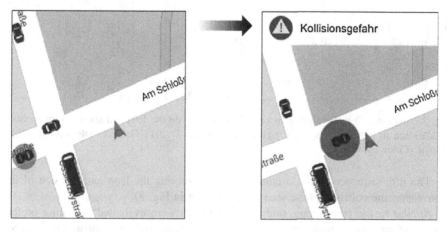

Fig. 5. Sequence B geometrical figure and size before (left) and during collision time (right). Data source: © 2017 Geobasis-DE/BKG (©2009), Google (Color figure online)

The third sequence displays an increasing of the icons' size within the collision phase, without any coloring (see a section of it in Fig. 6):

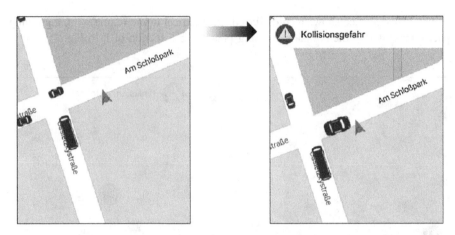

Fig. 6. Sequence C icon size before (left) and during collision time (right). Data source: ©
2017 Geobasis-DE/BKG (©2009), Google (Color figure online)

The fourth sequence displays a three-tiered coloring approach (green – yellow –
red), in a safe phase, short before a critical situation and during collision time (see
sections of it in Fig. 7).

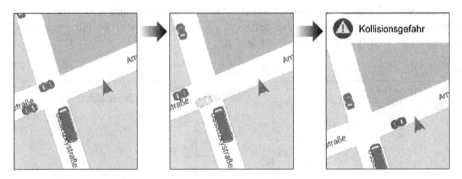

Fig. 7. Sequence D icon coloring in safe phase (green: on the left) and short before (yellow:
middle) and in collision time (red: right). Data source: © 2017 Geobasis-DE/BKG (©2009),
Google (Color figure online)

The fifth sequence shows a combination of coloring the icon and the size of the
icon within the collision phase (see a section of it in Fig. 8).

Similar to the preliminary study, all sequences were evaluated regarding preferences, information completeness, deflection, and situation assessment. Last, demographic data, mobility behavior and technical self-efficacy [19] as user characteristics
were surveyed.

6-point Likert-scales were used for all rating tasks (min = 0 "no agreement at all",
max = 5 "full agreement"). The level of significance was set to $\alpha = .05$. Parametric
statistical methods were used to analyze the data and crosschecked by their

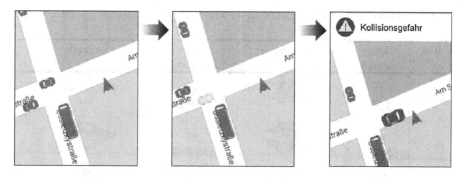

Fig. 8. Sequence E icon coloring and size before (green: on the left) and short before (yellow: middle) and in collision time (red: right). Data source: © 2017 Geobasis-DE/BKG (©2009), Google (Color figure online)

non-parametric counterparts if there were slight violations of requirements. However, for clarity and legibility reasons only the results from parametric procedures will be reported.

5.2   Sample

186 (N) participants replied to the questionnaire. Altogether, 53.2% were male and 46.8% female. The mean age was 37.7 years (SD = 15.6), ranging from 16 to 86 years. The educational level of the sample was rather high: 66.1% of participants had a university degree, 19.9% graduated from high school and 8.6% completed vocational trainings. Furthermore, the sample showed a high average technical self-efficacy with M = 3.54 (scale maximum = 5, SD = 1.08).

The vast majority of participants owned a smartphone (92.5%, n = 171). Map and navigation applications were used frequently by 28.1% and occasional by 46.8% of those. Of all participants, 93.5% owned a driving license. However, 86.2% mentioned that they often cover journeys on foot and 9.9% still from time to time. To better differentiate between preferred modes of transport, groups for pedestrians, bicyclists and wheelchair user were classified depending on usage frequencies:

All participants stating a rare use of bicycles (never to max. one time a month), but a high frequency of walking were defined as pedestrians (44.5%, N = 82). Further, participants stating a rather regular use of bicycles (several times a month to daily) were defined as bicyclists (50.0%, N = 93). The third group was identified due to their use of a wheelchair (4.8%, N = 9).

5.3   Results: Icon Design

Taking the icons Wheelchair, Motorcycle, Truck and Tram into account (not identified correctly according to the ISO mark in the preliminary study), two to three revised icons were presented and in comparison to another evaluated (see Tables 3 and 4).

Table 3. Frequency of chosen traffic icon for wheelchair user and motorcycle (N = 186).

Item	Chosen Icon (in %)	Wheelchair	Chosen Icon (in %)	Motorcycle
Icon 1	13 (7.0%)		15 (8.1%)	
Icon 2	46 (24.7%)		93 (50.0%)	
Icon 3	127 (68.3%)		78 (41.9%)	

Table 4. Frequency of chosen traffic icon for truck and tram (N = 186).

Item	Chosen Icon (in %)	Truck	Chosen Icon (in %)	Tram
Icon 1	45 (24.2%)		5 (2.7%)	
Icon 2	141 (75.8%)		75 (40.3%)	
Icon 3		-	106 (57.0%)	

The most selected traffic icon for *Wheelchair* is Icon 3 with a total of 68.3% (N = 186, see Table 3). The icon shows detached individual parts of a wheelchair user from a top view. Still, some participants expressed their wish to visualize the *Wheelchair* like the "common 2D symbol from side view".

An expected confusion with other traffic participants (e.g. pedestrians) could be avoided in all three visual representations: In several identification tasks, in which the participants had to decide whether the presented icon is a pedestrian or a wheelchair user, the traffic icon was successfully identified from at least a total of 87.6% (N = 186).

Further, the most selected traffic icon for *Motorcycle* is Icon 2 with 50.0%, (N = 186), followed by Icon 3 with 41.9% (see Table 3). Here, a closer look to the identification task, in which the participants had to decide whether the presented icon is a motorcycle or a bicycle shows, that both icons were identified successfully (Icon 2: 80.1% and Icon 3: 82.3%). Here, Icon 1 was not identified correctly: 46.8% believed it to be a bicycle and 44.1% identified it as a motorcycle. The icons vary from one another with different helmet sizes of the motorcycle driver and thickness of wheels.

Regarding the traffic icon for *Truck*, 75.8% selected Icon 2 as preferred representation (see Table 4). The Icon 2 shows a vehicle from top view with a detached driver cabin. With 57.0%, the representation most selected for *Tram* was Icon 3, followed by Icon 2 with 40.3% (see Table 4). The preferred icon shows a clear distinction between two railway wagons and a pantograph on one of the wagons. Also the connection to further wagons is portrait, again from top view.

5.4   Results: Feedback Design

The presentation of the results of the feedback design will be structured as follows: First, the comparisons between the possible sequences will be presented. Second, user group specific differences will be analyzed.

Overall Comparison of Sequences. As can be seen from both Figs. 9 and 10 several differences in the evaluation of the different possible visualizations were found.

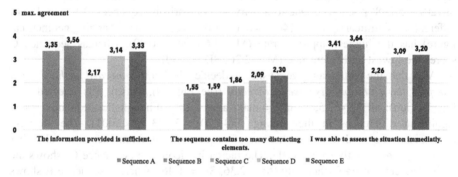

Fig. 9. Arithmetic means of statement agreement differentiated by sequences A to E (5 = max. agreement).

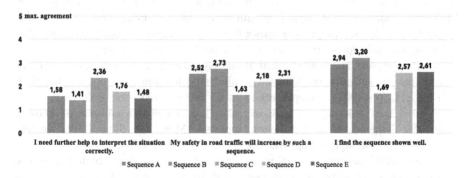

Fig. 10. Arithmetic means of statement agreement differentiated by sequences A to E (5 = max. agreement).

First, the participants were invited to evaluate, whether *the information provided was sufficient*. Overall, the sequences evaluation differentiated significantly from each other $F(4,732) = 66.76$, $p < .001$). A pairwise comparison shows that only sequence A and E did not differentiate significantly ($p \geq .05$).

A closer look shows that sequence B has highest approval rate (M = 3.56, SD = 0.97), followed by sequence A. The evaluation of sequence C reveals a slight disapproval to the given information (M = 2.17, SD = 1.36).

Next, the participants were questioned whether the sequence *contained too many distracting elements*, which was rejected (see Fig. 9 (middle): all M < 2.5, whereas 5 = max. agreement). Overall, the sequences evaluation differentiate significantly from each other ($F(4,736) = 20.95$, $p < .001$). A pairwise comparison shows that only sequence A and B did not differentiate significantly ($p \geq .05$). The lowest approval rate scored sequence A, the colored geometrical figure with a growing opacity level (M = 1.55, SD = 1.01).

Third, *the assessment of the situation* was evaluated. Here, four out of five sequences were agreed upon an immediate assessment of the situation (see Fig. 9). Again, almost all sequences are evaluated with a significant difference (F $(4,720) = 56.98$, $p < .001$). Due to a pairwise comparison sequences D and E do not differentiate significantly ($p = .146$). Sequence B (color and size changing geometrical figure) has the highest approval rate (M = 3.64, SD = 0.99), whereas sequence C scores the lowest agreement rate (M = 2.26, SD = 1.30).

After that, the participants were asked to decide whether they *needed further help to interpret the situation displayed correctly* (see Fig. 10), which was rejected (see Fig. 10 (left): all M < 2.5, with 5 = max. agreement) although the sequences show significant differences in their rating ($F(4,720) = 30.93$, $p < .001$). The pairwise comparison shows that the evaluation of sequence C differentiates from all other sequences significantly ($p \leq .001$). The increasing icon size (sequence C) shows the highest agreement on further help (M = 2.36, SD = 1.46), whereas sequence B shows the lowest approval (M = 1.41, SD = 1.15).

An *increasing road safety by using the application* was evaluated next. Here, the overall approval was rather low (see Fig. 10). Only the sequences A (M = 2.52, SD = 1.51) and B (M = 2.73, SD = 1.56) could score an average approval over 2.5. Again, all sequences show significant differences in their rating ($F(4,732) = 43.64$, $p < .001$). A pairwise comparison shows that only sequence D and E did not differentiate significantly ($p \geq .05$). Sequence C scored the lowest approval.

Finally, the participants were asked, if *the sequence shown was perceived well*. To sum up, the sequences were evaluated significantly different from one another (F(4, 724) = 57.18, $p < .001$), except sequences D (three-tiered icon coloring) and E (three-tiered icon coloring and size increasing) as a pairwise comparison showed ($p \geq .05$). Sequence C scored lowest approval (M = 1.69, SD = 1.30), whereas sequence B had the highest approval rate (M = 3.20, SD = 1.29).

Summarizing the iterative evaluation, sequence B showed the highest approval rates considering all statement agreements and given qualitative feedback. A closer look at the sequence reveals a warning icon sign combined with a text at the top of the screen (see a section of it in Fig. 11), faded in, when the situation is becoming increasingly serious. All sequences share this information.

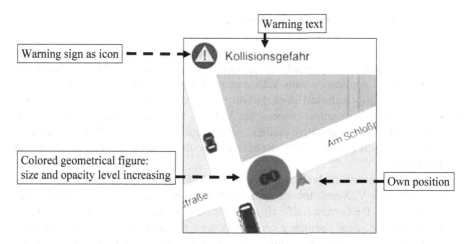

Fig. 11. Section of "best choice" sequence B (colored geometrical figure with growing size and opacity level before collision phase) portrait with all given information. (Color figure online)

Further, a red colored geometrical figure overlaid on the traffic icon of the upcoming vehicle is shown. The geometrical figure, a circle, increases in size and opacity level by coming closer to the own position, here, displayed as purple arrow. The combination of figure size, opacity level and warning reference is the recommended visualization for a collision warning in our smartphone application.

User Diverse Comparison of Sequences. To gain a first insight of possible user diverse evaluation patterns, further statistical analyses were performed, addressing different mobility groups, gender and age.

First, a comparison of the sequence evaluation by the *mobility groups* (bicyclist, pedestrian and wheelchair user) was conducted. No significant differences of the mean agreement ratings could be identified, revealing a joint result of the sequence evaluation.

Further, *gender* was focused as possible influencing user factor. Again, no significant difference in the evaluation could be found.

Nevertheless, concerning *age* several indications could be identified. Whereas no significant difference could be found regarding sequence A, sequence B showed a negative, significant correlation ($r = -.166$, $p = .023$, $N = 186$). Younger participants agreed significantly stronger to the statement, that the sequence provided sufficient information. Another finding indicates, that older participants agreed significantly stronger to the statement regarding help to interpret the situation correctly ($r = .192$, $p = .009$, $N = 186$).

Sequence C as well as sequence E showed no significant differences according to age. The only further finding regards sequence D: here, older participants agreed significantly stronger to the statement that the road safety will increase, if they use the application ($r = .184$, $p = .012$, $N = 185$).

6 User-Centered Feedback Design

Aiming a first step towards enhancing safety in road traffic, we addressed vulnerable road users like pedestrians, wheelchair user or bicyclists in order to integrate them via V2X-smartphone application into V2X-communication systems. We worked with a well educated, highly technical affine, but diverse sample in terms of mobility behavior. The multi-stages development process was laid out, followed by presenting results in both qualitative and quantitative studies, which addressed the icon design of all participating road users as well as the user centered feedback design in a rear-end collision traffic scenario.

Due to the results of both studies, a suitable feedback design interface recommendation for the V2X-smartphone application could be developed. Here, an adequate representation of the current traffic situation by using distinctive icons could be identified. In addition, new upcoming challenges with the user interface were detected. Thus, a further development of this application is essential, bearing an enormous potential for future research.

Addressing the first research approach (icon design), recognizable and lean road-user icons for the interface were evaluated (in both the preliminary interview-based study and the online survey). At first, most of the presented icons (like car or bicycle) could be easily identified – meeting the definition of Pierce [17] and the ISO mark. However, four icons had been misinterpreted (e.g. wheelchair user for pedestrian) and showed challenges, probably due to the smartphone display size. After re-designing the icons and re-evaluation, new recommendations with promising identification marks could be developed. Most of the re-designed icons have now detached parts, making it easier to be spotted. Another reason for the better identification success may be attributed to the research procedure: the first study was a qualitative procedure with paper-prototypes, whereas the following study was an online survey, making it possible for the participants to see the icons on-screen in much higher quality. Nevertheless, it was possible to clarify the misinterpretations with the new icons. Here, a clear recommendation of traffic user icons can be given. Understanding the participants wish to rely on already established icons, like the 2D side view wheelchair icon, a definite recommendation for a top view icon can also be given.

Further addressing the second research approach (map design), a preferred layout can be recommended. After testing a different map layout in the qualitative study, namely the heat map design, we decided to work with a classic top view of a street map design. According to Bojko [20], "[h]eat-maps help us quickly see 'the big picture' including any patterns or trends that may exist in the data", but the layout made it difficult for the participants to identify individual traffic participants or understand the colors intuitively.

Aiming a recommendation for a user centered display visualization for safety critical situations in traffic, we therefore evaluated five different animated sequences in a street map view. Here, the participants evaluated the information completeness, deflection and the situation assessment. All sequences varied in size of the used traffic icon, use of geometrical figures, coloring or combinations of all features.

Regarding the sufficiency of information, all sequences were evaluated positively. However, the given information handled a rather low information density, which need to be taken into account. Therefore, it is only logical, that the question whether one of the sequences contained too many distracting elements was fully rejected. Here, a closer look to different traffic scenarios, such as traffic jam, rush hour or emergency drive-thru may reveal, if the given details are still transparent enough to assess the situation immediately.

Only two sequences, namely A and B (both using a geometrical, colored figure to alert the application user about a possible collision), were evaluated positively regarding the question, whether the road safety will increase by using the application with the introduced feedback design. This leads to the conclusion, that a combination of features for feedback design of a V2X-smartphone app is the right direction. Both sequences seem to convey a perception of enhanced safety for its user, providing a manageable overview of information and enabling an independent use of that information.

Stepping ahead, sequence B showed additionally the highest (arithmetic mean) approval rates for an overall positive impression, which corroborates the recommendation of the combined features of that particular sequence for feedback design. In comparison, sequence C (change of icon size) was evaluated "worst choice". As only sequence without influence of color in comparison to the other sequences, a key factor for feedback design could be identified. Coloring obviously helped the participants to successfully assess a situation without further help, validating the statement of Baldassi and Burr [21], which claim that changes in size as the only distinguishing feature are less pronounced.

A final look on user diverse evaluation patterns showed only a few interesting results. Whereas the preferred form of mobility and gender had no significant effect at all on the evaluation, the consequence arises that the forms of mobility were probably to similar to one another. Only distinguishing by speed, all of the analyzed forms were vulnerable road user – and, even more important – the evaluation was an on-screen testing. A hands-on evaluation in a test environment (e.g. on a stationary bicycle) could reveal differences in a next evaluation loop of the application.

The only influencing user factor so far was age, only affecting single statements in different sequences. Here, younger participants agreed significantly stronger to the statement, that the information level (in sequence B) was sufficient – but, overall – the information level was also agreed on being sufficient. This result could hint to personal adjustments in terms of information density on-screen.

7   Outlook and Limitations

The findings revealed interesting insights into iconography and feedback design as well as small user diverse effects of a first V2X-smartphone application prototype. Although, the results identified further needed development and evaluation loops on both topics, first clear and lean recommendations could be made. The general perception of a safety increase via V2X-app could be determined. Due to the small participating wheelchair users in the the study, the sample is not representative for all vulnerable road users. A closer analysis of the icon and feedback design with cooperative feedback from actual wheelchair users will be necessary. Low-level prototyping and animations are just the first step in our methodological approach and will be taken further with hands-on outdoor tests in real environments. User studies in controlled environments like a test track and further, testing under real conditions, are future steps in the development of the application and our goal of integrating vulnerable road user into the traffic infrastructure: Watch out!

Acknowledgements. We would like to thank the research group on mobility at RWTH Aachen University, which works in the Center for European Research on Mobility (CERM) supported by the Excellence Initiative of German State and Federal Government. Many thanks go also to Florian Groh, Pierre Schoonbrood and Christian Klein for their valuable research input.

References

1. Timotheou, S., Panayiotou, C.G., Polycarpou, M.M.: Transportation systems: monitoring, control, and security. In: Kyriakides, E., Polycarpou, M. (eds.) Intelligent Monitoring, Control, and Security of Critical Infrastructure Systems. SCI, vol. 565, pp. 125–166. Springer, Heidelberg (2015). doi:10.1007/978-3-662-44160-2_5
2. Federal Ministry of Transport and Digital Infrastructure (2015). http://www.bmvi.de/SharedDocs/DE/Publikationen/StB/broschuere-strategie-automatisiertes-vernetztes-fahren.html
3. Statistisches Bundesamt: Verkehrsunfälle [traffic accidents], vol. 8, no. 7 (2016). https://www.destatis.de/DE/Publikationen/Thematisch/TransportVerkehr/Verkehrsunfaelle/VerkehrsunfaelleM.html
4. European Commission: White Paper – Roadmap to a Single European Transport Area (2011). http://ec.europa.eu/transport/themes/strategies/2011_white_paper_en
5. Farmer, C.M.: Effect of electronic stability control on automobile crash risk. Traffic Inj. Prev. **5**(4), 317–325 (2004)
6. Breuer, J.J., Faulhaber, A., Frank, P., Gleissner, S.: Real world safety benefits of brake assistance systems. In: 20th International Technical Conference on the Enhanced Safety of Vehicles (ESV). BMVI (2007)
7. Themann, P., Zlocki, A., Eckstein, L.: Energieeffiziente Fahrzeuglängsführung durch V2X-Kommunikation. In: Siebenpfeiffer, W. (ed.) Fahrerassistenzsysteme und Effiziente Antriebe. ATZ/MTZ-Fachbuch, pp. 27–33. Springer, Wiesbaden (2015). doi:10.1007/978-3-658-08161-4_4
8. Pech, T., Gabriel, M., Jähn, B., Kühnert, D., Reisdorf, P., Wanielik, G.: Prototyping framework for cooperative interaction of automated vehicles and vulnerable road users. In: Schulze, T., Müller, B., Meyer, G. (eds.) Advanced Microsystems for Automotive Applications 2016. LNM, pp. 43–53. Springer, Cham (2016). doi:10.1007/978-3-319-44766-7_4
9. Abusaber, W.: Remembering future tasks: a usability study of reminder apps (Doctoral dissertation). Auckland University of Technology Auckland (2015)
10. Sugimoto, C., Nakamura, Y., Hashimoto, T.: Prototype of pedestrian-to-vehicle communication system for the prevention of pedestrian accidents using both 3G wireless and WLAN communication. In: 3rd International Symposium on Wireless Pervasive Computing, pp. 764–767. IEEE (2008)

11. Engel, S., Kratzsch, C., David, K.: Car2Pedestrian-communication: protection of vulnerable road users using smartphones. In: Fischer-Wolfarth, J., Meyer, G. (eds.) Advanced Microsystems for Automotive Applications 2013. LNM, pp. 31–41. Springer, Heidelberg (2013). doi:10.1007/978-3-319-00476-1_4

12. ARD/ZDF Media Commission: Online survey 2016 [Onlinestudie] (2016). http://www.ard-zdf-onlinestudie.de/

13. Caplan, E.M.: MapMyFitness: tracking your training and routes. Br. J. Sports Med. (2016). doi:10.1136/bjsports-2016-096361

14. Flach, A., David, K.: A physical analysis of an accident scenario between cars and pedestrians. In: 70th IEEE Vehicular Technology Conference Fall (2009)

15. Nielsen, J.: Usability 101: Introduction to Usability (2012). https://www.nngroup.com/articles/usability-101-introduction-to-usability/

16. Rogers, Y.: Icons at the interface: their usefulness. Interact. Comput. 1(1), 105–117 (1989)

17. Gatsou, C., Politis, A., Zevgolis, D.: The importance of mobile interface icons on user interaction. Int. J. Comput. Sci. Appl. (IJCSA) 9(3), 92–107 (2012)

18. Dewar, R.: Design and evaluation of public information symbols. In: Zwaga, H.J.G., Boersema, T., Hoonhout, H.C.M. (eds.) Visual Information for Everyday Use: Design and Research Perspectives, pp. 285–303. Taylor & Francis Ltd, London (1999)

19. Beier, G.: Locus of control when interacting with technology [Kontrollüberzeugungen im Umgang mit Technik]. Rep. Psychol. 24, 684–693 (1999)

20. Bojko, A.A.: Informative or misleading? Heatmaps deconstructed. In: Jacko, J.A. (ed.) HCI 2009. LNCS, vol. 5610, pp. 30–39. Springer, Heidelberg (2009). doi:10.1007/978-3-642-02574-7_4

21. Baldassi, S., Burr, D.C.: "Pop-out" of targets modulated in luminance or colour: the effect of intrinsic and extrinsic uncertainty. Vis. Res. 44, 1227–1233 (2004)

Safety Performance Evaluation Model
for Airline Flying Fleets

Yijie Sun[1(✉)], Min Luo[1], Yanqiu Chen[1], and Changhua Sun[2]

[1] China Academy of Civil Aviation Science and Technology, Beijing, China
{sunyj,luomin,chenyq}@mail.castc.org.cn
[2] Civil Aviation Administration of China, Beijing, China
ch_sun@caac.gov.cn

Abstract. The idea of Reason's model is applied to the establishment of civil aviation safety performance index system. The index types and the multiple lines of defense of the unsafe events are placed in one-to-one correspondence to set five dimensions of the index types, including safety result, operation quality, risk management, safety assurance and safety foundation. Taking into account the management complexity and operating characteristics of different flight fleets, the concept of management difficulty coefficient is introduced to improve efficacy coefficient method, and the safety performance evaluation model is established based on the improved efficacy coefficient method. The data of 5 flying fleets in an airline is used as an example of application to verify the feasibility and applicability of the evaluation model. The evaluation results show that the evaluation model can compare fleet safety performance from five dimensions quantitatively, as well as obtain the results of comprehensive evaluation of safety performance for each fleet.

Keywords: Civil aviation · Safety performance · Performance index · Efficacy coefficient method

1   Introduction

Safety performance is one of the important components of airline safety management system, and it is an important index which can reflect the safety management level of airlines. According to Safety Management Manual (ICAO DOC 9859) [1], safety performance is a State's or service provider's safety achievement as defined by its safety performance targets and indexes. Therefore, the evaluation of the safety performance of an airline flying fleet is a proactive and prior safety management approach, and is an important step to test the safety performance of the entire company and the effectiveness of the implementation of the safety management system.

Safety performance evaluation for airline flying fleets has great practical significance. First of all, airlines can understand the current overall safety level and find the existing problems of different flying fleets, and do vertical comparison of different time on entire company's or different flying fleets' safety level. Second, the results of performance evaluation can be used as the basis of incentive system. Based on the safety performance, the airline can encourage employees to become more engaged, and

V.G. Duffy (Ed.): DHM 2017, Part II, LNCS 10287, pp. 384–396, 2017.
DOI: 10.1007/978-3-319-58466-9_34

help to promote performance-oriented safety culture. Thus, it can improve the safety level of the whole company. Third, the results of safety performance evaluation can be used as an important basis for the development and effectiveness test of safety measures.

In recent years, there are many researches on safety performance of civil aviation. Zhang applied fuzzy comprehensive evaluation method to evaluate the safety performance of airlines by using ANP method to determine the index weight [2]. Wang utilized the evidence theory to determine the index weight for the airline safety risk assessment model [3]. Shyur used the data of unsafe events caused by human errors to establish a quantitative model to assess the safety risk [4]. But in these studies, there is no theoretical support for the safety performance index system of airlines, and the index system is not comprehensive, since the safety status are only measured by the high consequence indicators such as accidents and incidents, but not paid enough attention to the low consequence indicators such as management indicators and process indicators. In addition, the existing safety performance evaluation methods do not take into account the complexity of the operation of different flying fleets and the difficulty of management, which lead to the mismatch between evaluation results and subjective perception.

In view of the above problems, based on Reason's model, the index system of airlines safety performance is established. And the concept of management difficulty coefficient is introduced and the efficacy coefficient method is improved to establish the safety performance evaluation model.

2 Safety Performance Index System Based on Reason's Model

A systematic and scientific index system is required to assess an organization's safety status comprehensively and accurately, which can reflect the safety results and expose operational and management issues at the same time. Therefore, the index system should not only contain high-consequence indicators which are the safety results indexes, but also contain low-consequence indicators which are process indexes and management indexes.

2.1 Principle of Setting Safety Performance Indexes

Reason's model [5] is proposed by Professor James Reason. It's a classical theoretical model used in aviation accident investigation and analysis. In this paper, the Reason's model is applied to the establishment of the safety performance index system. Multi-level performance indicators are built from the active failure defense and the latent failure defense to fully reflect the safety level of the airline fleets.

According to Reason's model, besides the happened occurrence has a response chain for itself, there is also a set of penetrated failure defenses. The contributed factors of unsafe events and the shortcomings (or safety risks) of the organization on each layer are long-standing, but do not cause significant disasters necessarily. Once multiple levels of defenses have been broken by some contributed factors sequentially or at the same time, the unsafe event will be occur. Therefore, in addition to the analysis of unsafe acts, it needs to pay more attention to analyze the preconditions of unsafe acts, unsafe supervision and organization factors. By this way, these defects could be recognized comprehensively. In order to set scientific and comprehensive indicators of safety performance, it can follow the principle of Reason's model. If the safety performance indicators are corresponding to the multiple layers of defense which lead to the unsafe events, the index types can be divided into five categories, as shown in Fig. 1.

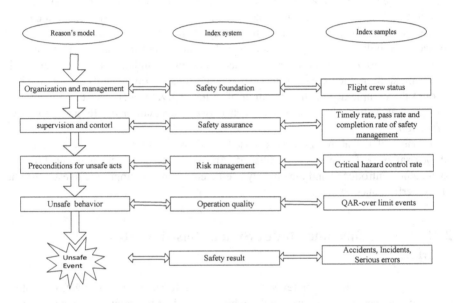

Fig. 1. Principle of setting safety performance index

The first one is safety result. These indicators are corresponding to the occurrences themselves, which are high-consequence indicators used to assess the risk of unsafe events such as accidents, incidents, and serious errors in flight fleets.

The second one is operation quality. In accordance with the unsafe acts, these indicators are low consequence process indicators that can evaluate operational technical conditions and the risk of operational bias of the flight fleets.

The third one is risk management. Corresponding to the preconditions of unsafe acts, these indicators can assess the effectiveness of the fleet's control of all types of risks, especially the critical risks.

The fourth one is safety assurance. These indicators are corresponding to the first-line supervision, which can evaluate the development level of safety supervision.

The fifth one is the safety foundation. These indicators are corresponding to the organizational factors, which are used to reflect the appropriate degree of flight crew composition and the state of crew fatigue.

Following the classification method above, there are 430 safety performance indicators have been set up for a comprehensive evaluation of the airline fleet safety level.

2.2   Methods for Setting Various Types of Safety Performance Indexes

Setting of Safety Result Indexes. According to China Civil Aviation "civil aircraft incident standard" and "event sample", combined with airline's serious errors, the general errors and other unsafe events criteria, safety result indicators can be established. Usually, the safety results indicators are described as the rate of occurrence such as accident, serious incident, general incident, serious error, general error and other unsafe event. Some indicator samples are shown in Table 1. After recognizing the indicators, it needs to establish risk value calculation model for different types of indicators based on Heinrich's Law to build a safety performance evaluation model.

Table 1. Safety result indexes samples

Occurrence rank	Indicators sample
Accident	Aircraft in operation resulted in 10 or more serious injuries
Serious incident	Landing on wrong runway
General incident	Gravely deviates from the scheduled course
Serious error	Flight turns back or lands at an alternate airport caused by human error
General error	Wrong parking caused by human error
Other unsafe event	Aircraft fly with foreign objects

Setting of Operation Quality Indexes. According to the airline's safety management objectives and historical data on occurrences, 11 critical risks of the airline are reviewed, including loss of control, runway overrun/excursion, tail wiping and so on. Then, the possible direct or indirect causes can be derived from the critical risks by applying the method of qualitative fault tree analysis (FTA). In the cause analysis, SHEL model and Reason's model can be used synthetically to analyze the unsafe behavior or status of the critical risks, as shown in Fig. 2. In order to obtain quantifiable indicators, it's helpful to make the unsafe behavior or status corresponding to QAR monitoring items, and set them as operation quality indicators. Table 2 is an example of partial indicators.

Setting of Other Types of Indexes. Indexes of risk management, safety assurance and safety foundation are used to evaluate the progress and effectiveness of operation management and safety management. They can be collectively referred to as management indicators. These three types of indicators can be set up by using the brainstorming method combined with the safety management system elements method. In other words, it needs to organize aviation management experts to discuss weaknesses in the actual

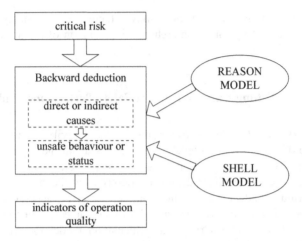

Fig. 2. Approach of operation quality index setting

Table 2. Operation quality indexes samples

Critical risks	Indicators sample
Tail wiping	Speed low at rotation
	Pitch high at liftoff
	Pitch rate high at rotation
	Touch and go
	Pitch high at landing
Hard landing	Drop rate high
	Pitch low at landing
	Touch down with throttle lever

Table 3. Risk management, safety assurance and safety foundation indexes samples

Category of other indicators	Indicators sample
Risk management	Effectiveness of critical risk control
	Timely rate of risk management work
Safety assurance	Execution rate of occurrence investigation
	Proportion of internal audit issues
	Proportion of repeat issues
Safety foundation	Crew fatigue status
	Proportion of safety management staffs

work under 12 elements of safety management system (SMS), and design the management category indicators for assessing the implementation and effectiveness of these SMS' elements. Table 3 shows the examples of these management category indicators.

3 Safety Performance Evaluation Model Based on Improved Efficacy Coefficient Method

According to the safety performance index system established in Sect. 2, we can see that the airline safety performance evaluation system is a multi-index and multi-level system. To evaluate safety performance of the airline flying fleet, it is required that the computation cost of the evaluation model should not be too big, and should not rely too much on expert experience. The evaluation model should be able to carry out multi-dimensional quantitative comparison, and the evaluation results should be consistent with the subjective cognition of the management.

The existing comprehensive evaluation methods for safety performance include analytic hierarchy process (AHP), fuzzy comprehensive evaluation, principal component analysis (PCA), etc. These algorithms have their own application scope and limitations. AHP can't solve the problem of decision making with high quantitative requirements alone, and requires decision-makers to have a deep and comprehensive understanding of the problems faced. The fuzzy comprehensive evaluation method is more complex and has a large amount of calculation. PCA has a high requirement on the quantity and quality of samples, and the meaning of the principal component is fuzzy. In addition, the existing comprehensive evaluation models of safety performance don't take into account the operation complexity and the management difficulty of different flying fleets. For airlines, it often leads to the deviation between the final evaluation results and the management's subjective cognition.

In view of the above problems and the actual needs of airlines, the concept of management difficulty coefficient is introduced in this paper, and the safety performance evaluation model is established based on the improved efficacy coefficient method.

3.1 Safety Performance Evaluation Model Establishment Scheme

Five types of safety performance indexes are established in this paper, the data sources and characteristics of the indexes are different, so the evaluation models for different types of indexes are not the same. The safety performance evaluation model establishment scheme is shown in Fig. 3. For the indexes of safety result and operation quality, risk value model is established based on the principle of risk evaluation and Heinrich's Law. For the indexes of risk management, safety assurance and safety foundation, the index value is calculated according to the airline's internal assessment methods and AHP. In order to make different types of index values obtained by different calculation models comparable, the improved efficiency coefficient method with management difficulty coefficient is introduced to standardize the various indexes. The results of the evaluation model can not only show the different dimensions of the evaluation objects by radar chart, but also evaluate the comprehensive evaluation results of different evaluation objects.

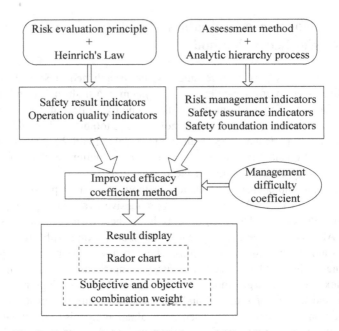

Fig. 3. Safety performance evaluation model establishment scheme

3.2   Procedures and Methods of the Evaluation Model

3.2.1   Risk Value Model for the Indexes of Safety Result and Operation Quality

Risk is the combination of the likelihood and consequences of a particular hazardous situation, which characterizes the probability and severity of a hazardous event. According to the principal of risk assessment, the risk value calculation model needs to be integrated with the probability and severity of risk events. For the indexes of safety result and operation quality in this paper, probability is the frequency of the occurrence of unsafe events, while the severity needs to develop uniform quantitative standards. The severity of different levels of unsafe events is assessed according to Heinrich's Law.

Heinrich's Law is the rules about aviation safety. According to Heinrich's Law, behind every serious accident, there are bound to be 29 minor accidents, 300 accident precursors and 1000 potential hazards. The occurrence of explicit high consequence unsafe events is the result of the accumulation of hidden low consequence events, and the explicit events and the hidden events are regularly proportional. When the severity of different levels of unsafe events is assigned, the severity coefficient can be defined as reciprocal of occurrence frequency according to Heinrich's Law. For different airlines, the proportion of explicit and hidden events is not exactly the same. Based on the historical data related to unsafe events of the airlines, the proportion of different levels of unsafe events in Heinrich's law needs to be adjusted to establish the severity coefficient in line with the actual operation of the airline.

Through collecting and sorting out the historical data of the airline in the past three years, the frequency of occurrence of unsafe events at each level is calculated, and the reciprocal is taken to get the severity of different levels of safety result indexes, as listed in Table 4.

Table 4. Severity of safety result indexes

The level of unsafe events	Severity
Accident/serious incident	3000
Incident	1500
Serious error	300
General error	150
Other unsafe event	20

On the basis of the calculation method of the possibility and severity of each index, the risk value R of safety result indexes of a flying fleet in a given evaluation period is as follows.

$$R = \frac{\sum(\text{severity of each index corrending to unsafe event happened})}{\text{flight movements}} \quad (1)$$

The calculation methods of the severity and risk value for operation quality indexes are similar to safety result indexes.

3.2.2 Calculation for the Indexes of Risk Management, Safety Assurance and Safety Foundation

These three types of indexes are management related process control indexes. The scores of each management related index is defined in airline's internal assessment methods. Take safety assurance indexes as an example, the weight of different indexes can be calculated by AHP, and the index value of safety assurance index can be obtained using the method of weighted arithmetic average.

3.2.3 Data Standardization Based on the Improved Efficacy Coefficient Method

The calculation methods and the units of measurement for different types of indexes are different, and data range is too large for comparison. In order to make the various types of indexes have uniform measurement, and reflect the operation complexity of different flying fleets in the evaluation of safety performance, the management difficulty coefficient is introduced to improve the efficacy coefficient method.

For the flying fleets in airlines, the factors that affect the operation complexity and management difficulty include models, machine age, route structure, professional system and fly missions, etc. The importance of the factors is sorted by the method of expert investigation, and the historical data of the fleet is combined with to determine the management complexity coefficient α of each flying fleet, as listed in Table 5.

Table 5. Management complexity coefficient of each fleet

	Flying fleet 1	Flying fleet 2	Flying fleet 3	Flying fleet 4	Flying fleet 5
α	1.02	1.02	1.01	1.01	1.00

The management complexity coefficient α is introduced to efficacy coefficient method for data standardization.

$$x'_{ij} = c + \frac{x_{ij} - m'_j}{M'_j - m'_j} \times (100 \times \alpha - c) \qquad (2)$$

In Eq. (2), α is the management difficulty coefficient, c is minimum value of desired data range, M'_j is the satisfaction value and m'_j is the not-allowed value.

3.2.4 Safety Performance Comprehensive Evaluation Results

After the data standardization, there are two ways to show the results of comprehensive evaluation.

1. Five dimensions of the flying fleet safety performance evaluation results can be displayed in the form of radar chart.
2. Comprehensive evaluation of each fleet can be calculated by using of subjective and objective combined weights method [6]. Subjective weighs can be calculated by analytic hierarchy process, objective weighs can be calculated by entropy value method, and combined weights can be calculated based on optimality theory. The comprehensive evaluation results of the fleet safety performance can be obtained through the weighted arithmetic mean method.

4 Application Examples

The airline's operational data of 2015 are used to verify the safety performance evaluation model established. And the safety performances of five flying fleets are evaluated.

4.1 Calculation of Safety Result Indexes

According to the risk value model for safety result indexes in Sect. 3.2.1, the number of unsafe events occurred in each fleet is collected, and the severity is calculated based on the event level. Risk value R of safety result indexes of each flying fleet at every month is calculated according to Eq. (1). And part data of the risk value of safety result indexes in 2015 are shown in Table 6.

According to Eq. (2), the data in Table 6 are standardized. Management difficulty coefficient of each fleet is set according to Table 5, c is set to 50, and M'_j and m'_j are the maximum value and minimum value of the risk value of safety result indexes respectively. The data standardization results are listed in Table 7.

Table 6. Risk value of safety result indexes

	Flying fleet 1	Flying fleet 2	Flying fleet 3	Flying fleet 4	Flying fleet 5
Jan	0.95	170.30	0.00	0.00	0.00
Feb	0.00	0.00	0.00	0.00	338.75
Mar	0.90	1.43	0.00	0.00	0.00
...	...	...	...	...	...
Dec	20.82	324.09	0.00	0.00	0.00
2015	3.29	25.94	13.27	3.83	23.00

Table 7. Data standardization results of safety result indexes

	Flying fleet 1	Flying fleet 2	Flying fleet 3	Flying fleet 4	Flying fleet 5
Jan	101.85	75.86	101.00	101.00	100.00
Feb	102.00	102.00	101.00	101.00	50.00
Mar	101.86	101.78	101.00	101.00	100.00
...	...	...	...	...	...
Dec	98.80	52.25	101.00	101.00	100.00
2015	101.49	98.02	99.00	100.42	96.61

4.2 Calculation of Operation Quality Indexes

The calculation methods of risk value and data standardization for operation quality indexes are similar to safety result indexes. And the results are listed in Table 8.

Table 8. Data standardization results of operation quality indexes

	Flying fleet 1	Flying fleet 2	Flying fleet 3	Flying fleet 4	Flying fleet 5
Jan	87.71	92.62	93.00	94.86	100.00
Feb	87.11	92.09	89.48	91.85	99.90
Mar	85.04	92.27	92.46	90.71	98.31
...	...	...	...	...	...
Dec	85.36	96.61	95.85	94.13	96.97
2015	83.60	93.99	93.39	92.37	97.04

4.3 Calculation of the Indexes of Risk Management, Safety Assurance and Safety Foundation

According to the calculation method in Sect. 3.2.2, the index value of risk management, safety assurance and safety foundation in 2015 are obtained, as shown in Table 9.

Table 9. Index value of risk management, safety assurance and safety foundation

	Flying fleet 1	Flying fleet 2	Flying fleet 3	Flying fleet 4	Flying fleet 5
Risk management	90.00	98.68	97.43	96.09	98.68
Safety assurance	97.27	90.36	94.90	96.80	90.00
Safety foundation	100.00	95.71	97.14	100.00	100.00

4.4   Safety Performance Evaluation Results

Radar Chart. Based on the calculation results above, five dimensions of safety result, operation quality, risk management, safety assurance and safety foundation for each flying fleet can be presented in the form of radar chart. Take the data in 2015 as an example to illustrate, as shown in Fig. 4. This way of result presentation can directly see the safety performance of each fleet in different dimensions, and it is convenient to analyze the differences and reasons of the safety performance.

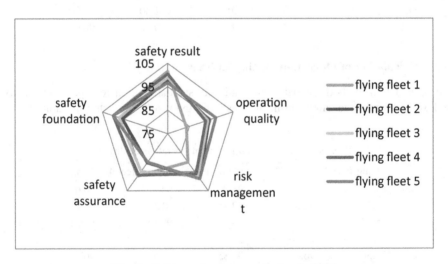

Fig. 4. Safety performance evaluation in 2015

- Flying fleet 1: although the safety result indexes show good results, but because of the risk management indexes are at low level, which reflect the critical risk control effect is not very good, and affecting the operation quality indexes. The follow-up work should strengthen the critical risk control.
- Flying fleet 2: The safety foundation is poor, and safety assurance indexes are not satisfied, which reflect the implementation and effect of the safety management work is not good. The follow-up work should strengthen the implementation and effect of safety management.

- Flying fleet 3 and 4: all types of safety performance indexes are in the middle level, and operation quality can be further enhanced. The follow-up work can enhance the operation technical conditions.
- Flying fleet 5: the performance of safety assurance index is poor, which directly affects the safety result indexes. The follow-up work should continue to improve safety management.

Comprehensive Evaluation Results. In addition to comparing fleet safety performance from five dimensions respectively, airline management level also need to understand the results of comprehensive evaluation of safety performance. Subjective and objective combined weights method mentioned in Sect. 3.2.4 is used to calculate the weights of each type of safety performance indexes, as listed in Table 10. And the comprehensive evaluation of safety performance for each flying fleet is shown in Table 11.

Table 10. Weights of safety performance indexes

	Safety result	Operation quality	Risk management	Safety assurance	Safety foundation
Weights	0.25	0.35	0.15	0.15	0.1

Table 11. Comprehensive evaluation results

	Flying fleet 1	Flying fleet 2	Flying fleet 3	Flying fleet 4	Flying fleet 5
Evaluation results	92.72	95.33	96.00	96.37	96.42

As can be seen from the tables, the company is more concerned about the process indexes and management indexes. Therefore, despite the safety results of flying fleet 1 is the best performance, due to its poor operation quality and unsatisfactory risk management, the overall evaluation of its safety performance ranks last.

5 Conclusion

Based on the idea of Reason's model, safety performance index system which can integrally reflect airline's safety state is established. And based on improved efficacy coefficient method, the airline safety performance evaluation model is presented. Some conclusions are given as follows.

- The safety performance index system based on Reason's model can reflect the airline's safety state from 5 dimensions of safety result, operation quality, risk management, safety assurance and safety foundation. The establishment of the index system has a theoretical basis, and is more comprehensive.
- Compared with the commonly used safety performance comprehensive evaluation methods, the evaluation model established in this paper has smaller computation

cost, doesn't rely much on expert experience, and the evaluation results is consistent with the subjective cognition of the management level.

- Safety performance evaluation model established in this paper could compare fleet safety performance from five dimensions respectively, as well as obtain the results of comprehensive evaluation of safety performance for each fleet. So it helps to further analyze the safety performance level and causes, and make work improvement plan.
- Safety management should pay attention to the process, not just focus on the results. Therefore the flying fleet which has worse process management also has lower evaluation result of safety performance.

References

1. International Civil Aviation Organization: ICAO Doc 9859 Safety Management Manual, 3rd edn. International Civil Aviation Organization, Montreal (2012)
2. Zhang, P.P.: Studies on Safety Performance Evaluation for Airlines. Civil Aviation University of China, Tianjin (2008)
3. Wang, Y.G., Wang, Y.W.: Goal oriented decomposition study of the airport safety and security based on the risk management. J. Saf. Environ. **12**(6) (2012)
4. Shyur, H.J.: A quantitative model for aviation safety risk assessment. Comput. Ind. Eng. **54**, 34–44 (2008)
5. Reason, J.: Human Error. Cambridge University Press, New York (1990)
6. Huang, X.X., Wang, R.H., Zhou, Y.R., et al.: Application of method of combined weights in comprehensive evaluation on inhabitants' health status. J. Math. Med. **19**(4) (2006)

Deciphering Workers' Safety Attitudes by Sensing Gait Patterns

Cenfei Sun, Changbum R. Ahn[✉], Kanghyeok Yang, Terry Stentz, and Hyunsoo Kim

Charles Durham School of Architectural Engineering and Construction, University of Nebraska-Lincoln, Lincoln, NE, USA
{csun, kyang12}@huskers.unl.edu,
{cahn2, tstentz1, hkim13}@unl.edu

Abstract. Workers' unsafe behaviors are a top cause of safety accidents in construction. In practice, the industry relies on training and education at the group level to correct or prevent unsafe behaviors of workers. However, evidence shows that some individuals were identified to be showing risky behavior repeatedly and have a high rate to be involved in accidents and current safety training approach at the group level may not be effective for those workers. A worker's evaluation of a hazard (risk perception) and tendency to take/avoid risks (risk propensity) determines how they respond to a hazard and identifying those workers with biased risk perceptions and high risk propensity can thus provide an opportunity to prevent behavior-based injuries and fatalities in the workplace. However, as risk perception and propensity are influenced not only by inherited personal traits (e.g. locus of control) but also by specific situational factors (e.g. mood and stress level), existing approaches relying on surveys are not sufficient when measuring workers' risk perception and propensity continuously in day-to-day operations. In this context, this study examines the potential of ambulatory and continuous gait monitoring in the workplace as a means of identifying workers' risk perception and propensity. Two experiments simulating construction work environments were conducted and subjects' gait patterns in hazard zones were assessed with inertial measurement unit (IMU) data. The experimental results demonstrate changes in gait patterns at pre-hazard zones for most of the subjects. However, the results fail to identify the relationship between gait pattern changes at pre-hazard zones and risk propensities assessed using the Accident Locus of Control Scale.

Keywords: Behavioral adaptation · Human risk propensity · Gait Abnormality · Safety management

1 Introduction

Unsafe behavior on the part of construction workers is one of the main reasons for accidents in the construction industry [1]. Current practices to prevent and correct workers' unsafe behavior rely mostly on training and education conducted at the group level. However, substantial evidence indicates some people tend to be involved in workplace accidents more often than others [2] and training or education at the group

© Springer International Publishing AG 2017
V.G. Duffy (Ed.): DHM 2017, Part II, LNCS 10287, pp. 397–405, 2017.
DOI: 10.1007/978-3-319-58466-9_35

level may not be effective in preventing individual risky behavior [3–5]. Such differences in accident rates are mainly due to individual differences in perception and/or attitudes towards safety risks [6]. Self-reported interviews [7–9] and biological components [10] confirmed the existence of these individual differences in perception and/or attitudes towards safety risks [11, 12]. Measuring and understanding individual workers' risk perception and propensity (risk taking tendency) [13] is thus critical in identifying risk-prone workers and providing appropriate individualized interventions to prevent their risky behavior.

Many studies that have attempted to measure workers' risk perception and propensity mostly rely on questionnaires and surveys [14–16]. However, social desirability bias leads to inaccuracy in reports, which means people tend to over-report good behavior and under-report bad behavior [17]. Moreover, risk perception and propensity are often affected by situational-specific factors (e.g. temporary mood and goal imminence) [18, 19], and existing approaches cannot continuously capture such changes in workers' attitudes toward risks in day-to-day operations.

In a high-risk workplace where a worker repeatedly encounters multiple safety hazards, such as a construction site, a worker's risk perception and propensity determines how they detect and prepare for potential hazard risks (risk preparedness). Observing and measuring workers' behavioral changes upon encountering hazards (behavioral adaptation) may provide an opportunity to decipher workers' risk perceptions and propensities. This study examines the potential in assessing workers' gait patterns as measurable behavioral markers of individual workers' responses to hazards. Specifically, this study investigates whether workers' gait patterns manifest their behavior adaptations when interacting with hazards and how observed changes in gait patterns can be related to individual differences in risk perception and/or propensity. Two experiments that exposed subjects to various pre-defined hazard zones were designed and conducted to answer these research questions.

2   Assessment of the Gait Adaptation upon Hazards

2.1   Purpose and Experimental Setup

Experiment 1 examined whether workers' gait patterns measured by a wearable inertial measurement unit (IMU) reflected behavior adaptations developed through interacting with hazards. This laboratory experiment was designed to simulate the working environment of ironworkers, providing a simple testbed to easily estimate subjects' locations and control subjects' movement trajectories toward hazards. Eight healthy naïve subjects were recruited and asked to wear safety boots, safety harnesses and a safety helmet, with an IMU sensor on the right ankle. Two types of hazards were tested in the experiment: obstacles that may cause trip accidents and slippery surfaces that may cause slip accidents. The subjects were asked to walk at a comfortable speed on an elevated I-beam (4 inches in width and 80 ft in length) in four different conditions: (1) and (2) an obstacle located at 30 ft and 50 ft from the starting point of the I-beam; and (3) and (4) a slippery surface located at 30 ft and 50 ft from the starting point of the I-beam. The subjects then underwent ten trials with each condition. Figure 1 shows the experiment setting and subject participant. Details of the experiment can be found in [20].

Fig. 1. Laboratory experiment environment. (a) Slippery surface, (b) obstacle, (c) subject participating in the experiment.

2.2   Gait Pattern Assessment

IMU data was used to assess workers' gait patterns. In order to observe how a worker generated different gait patterns in order to adapt to the risk of hazards, we assessed the abnormalities between observed gait cycles as compared to workers' normal gait patterns. We thus used the IMU-based Gait Abnormality Score (I-GAS) developed by Yang et al. [21] with computed gait features (e.g., stride time, stride length). In this approach, the authors estimated the abnormality of gait and the gait features were computed into one score to measure the deviation of a subject's momentary gait stride from their normal gait strides. The I-GAS was calculated as follows:

$$I - GAS = \sqrt{(x - \bar{y})C^{-1}(x - \bar{y})^{T}} \tag{1}$$

In this equation, x represents the vector of the observed samples and the computed gait features, $\bar{y}$ represents the vector of the mean value of referenced samples and the computed gait features, and C^{-1} is the inverse covariance matrix of reference data.

2.3   Results

We selected the gait where the subject encounters the hazard as the reference point (Gait 0) and calculated I-GAS values of ten steps from Gait −5 (five steps before Gait 0) to Gait +5 (five steps after Gait 0). Figure 2a illustrates the I-GAS values of one subject. Each line within Fig. 2a represents the average I-GAS values of one subject through ten trials in four different hazard conditions. The I-GAS score peaks at Gait 0, when encountered hazards (e.g., stepping on obstacles) significantly affected gait patterns. However, Gait −1 also showed relatively high values compared to other gaits. This pattern was observed across all four hazard conditions, which indicates that such changes may not be a random alteration due to human movement variability [22] and may instead result from behavioral adaptations mitigating the risk of the hazards.

Figure 2b presents average I-GAS values for eight subjects from Gait −5 to Gait −1. The similar pattern of high I-GAS values in Gait −1 was also observed in most

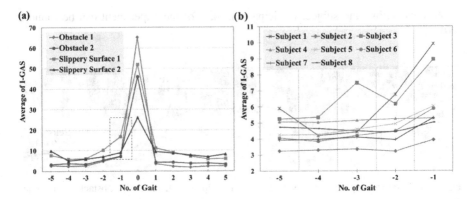

Fig. 2. Results of Experiment 1: (a) a subject's I-GAS values in different experimental conditions, (b) average I-GAS values of different subjects.

subjects. The t-test results confirmed the difference between I-GAS values at Gait −1 compared to previous gaits in most of the subjects (Table 1). This indicates the potential of using I-GAS values upon encountering hazards (e.g., Gait −1) as measurable behavioral markers of individual workers' responses to hazards. Individual differences in such patterns are also observed. For example, some subjects (Subject 1 and 3) were observed to present high I-GAS values at earlier gaits (Gait −2), while Subject 4 does not present much change in I-GAS values from Gait −5 to Gait −1.

Table 1. T-test results of eight subjects

	Gait −3 and Gait −1		Gait −2 and Gait −1	
	Mean difference	t	Mean difference	t
Subject 1	5.48	−5.41***	3.16	−2.68**
Subject 2	1.20	−2.95**	1.36	−3.54***
Subject 3	1.69	−2.48**	1.34	−2.06*
Subject 4	1.43	−2.11*	1.11	−1.58
Subject 5	0.62	−1.22	0.71	−1.68*
Subject 6	−0.10	0.11	−0.51	0.57
Subject 7	1.47	−0.48	2.78	−1.12
Subject 8	1.00	−1.14	1.08	−1.24

* $p < .05$, **$p < .01$, ***$p < .001$

3 Gait Adaptation and Risk Propensity

3.1 Purpose and Risk Propensity Measurement

Experiment 2 was designed and conducted to further investigate whether individual differences in gait adaptations are related to subjects' attitudes toward risks (risk propensity). To measure subjects' risk propensities the Accident Locus of Control Scale (ALCS) was used in this experiment.

Psychologists often use scales based on surveyed personal traits to measure human risk propensity because such personal traits are considered a strong influencer of risk behavior [23]. However, risk propensity differs markedly across contexts, meaning it is possible that an individual is risk seeking in some areas, like health, but risk averse in others, like finance [23]. Locus of control is a personal cognition concept reflecting an individual's belief about who or what controls their life events [24]. Individuals with an internal locus of control perceive that they can exert control over the outcome of a situation, while individuals with an external locus of control attribute outcomes to external factors, such as luck, the environment or others' behavior. In the domain of safety, people with internal locus of control are likely to be more safety conscious than those with external locus of control [25], and individuals with specific training or more experience tended to be more internal orientation [26]. The internal-external locus of control theory, developed by Rotter [24], has been used successfully as a means of predicting involvement in accidents [27–29]. The ALCS is a 24-item questionnaire developed by modifying the general locus of control scale to fit job hazards and risk at work [26]. Each item includes two statements representing situations of internal and external locus of control, subjects were asked to select the one they believe is more true. Subjects who choose the external viewpoint score 1, with a higher score indicating a more external locus of control and a higher likelihood of taking risks. Janicak has used this scale to successfully predict workers' involvement in accidents [26].

Subjects' ALCS scores were compared to their gait adaptions observed in the below experiment.

3.2   Experimental Setup

This experiment was designed to simulate bricklaying work at a construction site in an open indoor space. Subjects were required to walk and lay bricks at selected working areas. Six types of hazards were installed along the anticipated paths taken by the subjects (Fig. 3). A survey area was established next to the operation area in order to minimize time variation when measuring risk propensity in the experiment. Subjects were asked to complete a survey using a tablet computer and then start the experiment immediately. 32 subjects participated in this experiment, with 25 having previous experience in construction. During the experiment the subjects were required to wear (1) an IMU sensor on the right ankle, (2) a safety helmet with a localization sensor and (3) safety shoes and vests. Their gait features were recorded by IMUs and the entire experiment was video-recorded to provide reference data for further analysis.

3.3   Results

Subjects with high ALCS scores are assumed to have a tendency to take/ignore risks compared to subjects with low ALCS scores, who have a tendency to avoid risks. It was thus hypothesized that subjects with high ALCS scores have smaller gait

Fig. 3. Hazards installed for the experiment: (a) unavoidable obstacle, (b) unstacked pipes, (c) warning sign for falling object, (d) unorganized wire, (e) avoidable obstacle, (f) slippery surface.

adaptations (less risk preparedness) compared to subjects with low ALCS scores. Data analysis of Experiment 2 was guided by this hypothesis.

ALCS includes 24 items, yielding a score ranging from 0 to 24 in total; a score of zero indicates a subject has a completely internal locus of control, while a score of 24 indicates that a subject has a completely external locus of control. Table 2 lists the ALCS scores of all 32 subjects.

Table 2. Accident locus of control scale scores for 32 subjects

	Accident locus of control scale score								
	0	1	2	3	4	5	7	9	10
No. of subjects	6	2	4	3	7	3	3	2	2

We can see from these results that all subjects involved in the experiment tended to have lower ALCS scores. Two subjects have the highest score of 10 and six subjects have the lowest, 0. We thus compared gait adaptation values between these two groups. Based on the result from Experiment 1, I-GAS values of Gait −1 (one gait before hazard zone) were computed to represent gait adaptation values for the two groups.

A subject's first three encounters with each type of hazards (out of a total of eighteen encounters) were included to assess gait adaptations, as gait adaptations in subjects tend to decrease with each following encounter. In addition, two avoidable hazard types, including the falling object warning sign (Fig. 3c) and the avoidable object (Fig. 3e), were excluded in computing gait adaptations. Most of the subjects avoided these hazards by changing their paths and did not present any significant gait adaptations when encountering these hazards.

Figure 4a illustrates average I-GAS values for each type of hazard, while Fig. 4b represents I-GAS distributions for each subject. Subjects with score 0 are shown in blue

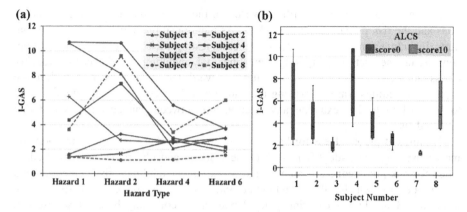

Fig. 4. Results of Experiment 2: (a) average I-GAS values for different hazards, (b) I-GAS distributions of individual subjects with ALCS scores 0 and 10. (Color figure online)

(blue solid lines in Fig. 4a and blue boxplots in Fig. 4b) and subjects with a score of 10 are shown in green (green dashed lines in Fig. 4a and green boxplots in Fig. 4b).

These results shown in Fig. 4 do not demonstrate any clear difference between the two groups. In particular, two subjects with score 10 show completely different patterns of gait adaptations. For example, Subject 7 tends to have smaller gait adaptations and their variance is small, while Subject 8 has larger gait adaptations with significantly different magnitudes across the hazards. Consequently, these results are not sufficient to confirm any relationship between ALCS scores and gait adaptations.

Although the experiment results fail to provide any meaningful evidence on how gait adaptations to hazards are related to subjects' attitudes toward risks, there are several points that should be considered. First, Subject 8, part of the group with an ALCS score of 10, is the only female subject included in the two comparison groups, and female subjects (3 out of 32 subjects) tend to have higher gait adaptations compared to male subjects. Thus gender needs to be considered and controlled as an independent variable in future experiment designs. In addition, the subjects recruited were university students. While most of them have field experience, the entire subject group has relatively lower ALCS scores. Thus there is a high chance that the difference of risk propensities between the two selected groups may not present differing observable behaviors within the experiments.

4 Conclusions

This study investigates whether workers' gait patterns can represent their behavioral adaptations developed to mitigate the risks of hazards. Laboratory experiments were designed and conducted to assess changes in subjects' gait patterns upon encountering simulated workplace hazards. The results indicate that subjects tend to modify their gait patterns even before encountering hazards and individual differences exist in such changes in gait patterns. However, the experimental results fail to confirm any relationship between gait adaptations and risk propensities assessed by ALCS.

Future research needs to further investigate the relationship between gait adaptations and the risk preparedness of workers. As mentioned previously, various personal traits, including gender, should be considered in testing such relationships. In addition, considering the fact that any single existing tool, including ALCS, cannot reliably assess subjects' perceptions and attitudes toward the risks presented within the experiment settings, various existing tools to assess risk perception and attitudes need to be used to further examine any relationship between gait adaptations and risk preparedness.

Insufficient preparedness for hazard of risk-prone workers on the construction site may cause accidents. Identifying risk-prone workers and observing behavioral adaptation for risk preparedness is an effective way to understand their risk perception and risk propensity which allows individual intervention to correct their risk taking behavior. Meanwhile, measuring gait adaptation by collecting bodily response can continuously detect insufficient risk preparedness during construction workers' day-to-day working operation in order to prevent injuries on site and enhance construction safety performance.

References

1. Bohm, J., Harris, D.: Risk perception and risk-taking behavior of construction site dumper drivers. Int. J. Occup. Saf. Ergon. **16**, 55–67 (2010). doi:10.1080/10803548.2010.11076829
2. Mayer, D.L., Jones, S.F., Laughery, K.R.: Accident proneness in the industrial setting. Proc. Hum. Factors Soc. Annu. Meet. **31**, 196–199 (1987). doi:10.1177/154193128703100213
3. Cooper, M.D.: Behavioral safety interventions: a review of process design factors. Prof. Saf. **54**, 36 (2009)
4. Sulzer-Azaroff, B.: Does BBS work? Prof. Saf. **45**, 19 (2000)
5. Tharaldsen, J.-E., Haukelid, K.: Culture and behavioural perspectives on safety – towards a balanced approach. J. Risk Res. **12**, 375–388 (2009). doi:10.1080/13669870902757252
6. Mckenna, F.P.: Accident proneness: a conceptual analysis. Accid. Anal. Prev. **15**, 65–71 (1983). doi:10.1016/0001-4575(83)90008-8
7. Arnett, J.: Sensation seeking: a new conceptualization and a new scale. Pers. Individ. Differ. **16**, 289–296 (1994). doi:10.1016/0191-8869(94)90165-1
8. Bradley, G., Wildman, K.: Psychosocial predictors of emerging adults' risk and reckless behaviors. J. Youth Adolesc. **31**, 253–265 (2002). doi:10.1023/A:1015441300026
9. Heino, A.: Risk taking in car driving; perceptions, individual differences and effects of safety incentives (1996)
10. Zuckerman, M.: Behavioral Expressions and Biosocial Bases of Sensation Seeking. Cambridge University Press, Cambridge (1994)
11. Zhang, M., Fang, D.: A continuous behavior-based safety strategy for persistent safety improvement in construction industry. Autom. Constr. **34**, 101–107 (2013). doi:10.1016/j.autcon.2012.10.019
12. Geller, E.S.: Behavior-based safety and occupational risk management. Behav. Modif. **29**, 539–561 (2005). doi:10.1177/0145445504273287
13. Landeweerd, J.A., Urlings, I.J.M., De Jong, A.H.J., et al.: Risk taking tendency among construction workers. J. Occup. Accid. **11**, 183–196 (1990). doi:10.1016/0376-6349(90)90028-T

14. Namian, M., Albert, A., Zuluaga, C.M., Behm, M.: Role of safety training: impact on hazard recognition and safety risk perception. J. Constr. Eng. Manag. **142**, 04016073 (2016). doi:10.1061/(ASCE)CO.1943-7862.0001198
15. Rodríguez Garzón, I., Lucas-Ruiz, V., Martínez Fiestas, M., Delgado Padial, A.: Association between perceived risk and training in the construction industry. J. Constr. Eng. Manag. (2015). doi:10.1061/(ASCE)CO.1943-7862.0000960
16. Rodríguez-Garzón, I., Martínez-Fiestas, M., Delgado-Padial, A., Lucas-Ruiz, V.: An exploratory analysis of perceived risk among construction workers in three spanish-speaking countries. J. Constr. Eng. Manag. **142**, 04016066 (2016). doi:10.1061/(ASCE)CO.1943-7862.0001187
17. Fisher, R.J.: Social desirability bias and the validity of indirect questioning. J. Consum. Res. **20**, 303–315 (1993). doi:10.1086/209351
18. Mishra, S., Lalumière, M.L., Williams, R.J.: Gambling as a form of risk-taking: individual differences in personality, risk-accepting attitudes, and behavioral preferences for risk. Pers. Individ. Differ. **49**, 616–621 (2010). doi:10.1016/j.paid.2010.05.032
19. Mishra, S., Lalumière, M.L.: You can't always get what you want: the motivational effect of need on risk-sensitive decision-making. J. Exp. Soc. Psychol. **46**, 605–611 (2010). doi:10.1016/j.jesp.2009.12.009
20. Kim, H., Ahn, C.R., Yang, K.: Identifying safety hazards using collective bodily responses of workers. J. Constr. Eng. Manag. **143**, 04016090 (2017). doi:10.1061/(ASCE)CO.1943-7862.0001220
21. Yang, K., Ahn, C.R., Vuran, M.C., Kim, H.: Sensing workers gait abnormality for safety hazard identification. In: 2016 Proceedings of the 33rd ISARC, Auburn, USA, pp. 957–965 (2016)
22. Stergiou, N., Harbourne, R., Cavanaugh, J.: Optimal movement variability: a new theoretical perspective for neurologic physical therapy. J. Neurol. Phys. Ther. JNPT **30**, 120–129 (2006)
23. Nicholson, N., Soane, E., Fenton-O'Creevy, M., Willman, P.: Personality and domain-specific risk taking. J. Risk Res. **8**, 157–176 (2005). doi:10.1080/1366987032000123856
24. Rotter, J.B.: Generalized expectancies for internal versus external control of reinforcement. Psychol. Monogr. Gen. Appl. **80**, 1–28 (1966). doi:10.1037/h0092976
25. Loosemore, M., Lam, A.S.Y.: The locus of control: a determinant of opportunistic behaviour in construction health and safety. Constr. Manag. Econ. **22**, 385–394 (2004). doi:10.1080/0144619042000239997
26. Janicak, C.A.: Predicting accidents at work with measures of locus of control and job hazards. Psychol. Rep. **78**, 115–121 (1996). doi:10.2466/pr0.1996.78.1.115
27. Wuebker, L.J.: Safety locus of control as a predictor of industrial accidents and injuries. J. Bus. Psychol. **1**, 19–30 (1986)
28. Jones, J.W., Wuebker, L.: Development and validation of the safety locus of control scale. Percept. Motor Skills **61**, 151–161 (1985). doi:10.2466/pms.1985.61.1.151
29. Guastello, S.J., Guastello, D.D.: The relation between the locus of control construct and involvement in traffic accidents. J. Psychol. **120**, 293–297 (1986). doi:10.1080/00223980.1986.10545255

Driving Process' Analysis and HUD Design Based on Conditional Autonomous Traffic Safety

Jian-min Wang$^{(\boxtimes)}$, Lu-lu Qian, and Yu-jia Wang

School of Arts and Media, Tongji University, Shanghai, China
wangjianmin@tongji.edu.cn

Abstract. With the rapid increasing of car quantity, traffic safety problem has become more and more serious. Traffic crash is also a major world public health problem; hence, it has become a topic of interest among màny scholars. This study intends to analyze the factors that affect driving safety under different driving scenarios. The results of this study are based on conditional autonomous driving. The context-aware conditional autonomous safety driving process and the relationships among three elements, namely, the environment, the driver and the car, are analyzed based on the Haddon matrix and the system attribution model. The vehicle used is a conditional autonomous car capable of context awareness; it can send useful information as feedback to the driver and interact with driver behavior. Afterward, the results are applied in parking scenario and lane changing scenario, and the factors that influence safety during parking and lane changing are analyzed. Then, the obtained information is validated based on driver perspective, and a design concept for head-up display is proposed. This design is expected to assist drivers in parking and lane changing without accident.

Keywords: Conditional autonomous · Traffic safety · Driving process · HUD

1 Introduction

With the continuous development of society, cars have become the most common transportation in our daily life. With the rapid increasing of car quantity, traffic safety problem has become more and more serious. Traffic crash is a major world public health problem [1]; hence, it has become a topic of interest among many scholars. An increasing number of vehicles are currently equipped with advanced driver assistance systems (ADAS), which improve car autonomy in terms of specific driving functions [2]. Automation is a very popular topic in the field of automobile and SAE International's On-Road Automated Vehicle Standards Committee has defined six levels of driving automation [3]: 0 (no automation), 1 (driver assistance), 2 (partial automation), 3 (conditional automation), 4 (high automation), and 5 (full automation). Among them, in 0–2 levels, human driver monitors the driving environment and in 3–5 levels, automated driving system monitors the driving environment. In 3 (conditional automation) level, system executes the steering and acceleration/deceleration and monitors the driving environment. Human driver performs when getting the dynamic

© Springer International Publishing AG 2017
V.G. Duffy (Ed.): DHM 2017, Part II, LNCS 10287, pp. 406–418, 2017.
DOI: 10.1007/978-3-319-58466-9_36

driving task. According to BASt level, 3 level is equivalent to highly automated and to NHTSA level, it is equivalent to 3 level. Considering practical applications, this study chooses 3 (conditional automation) level as the research object.

In the field of safety driving, many theories, some of which are universal, have been applied. For example, scholars have proposed driver models to describe driver performance. Many vehicle driving models are based on either cybernetics or control theory, cognitive psychology as information processing or a mix thereof [4]. Explaining how control can be achieved in a driving situation has been the main objective of driver models [5]. The contextual control model (COCOM) by Hollnagel in 1993 provides a framework for examining control in different contexts, whereas the extended control model (ECOM) in 2003 aims to describe driving control at high levels [4]. These models share the single driver perspective, or in some cases, the driver-vehicle system, in approaching the task of driving. Another theory or model that aims to explain the process of driving is the accident-causing theory [5]. This theory is an accident model that corresponds to the main component of the principium of safety and is an important part of accident theory. It temporarily avoids the concrete characteristics of hazard sources and contents as well as accident modes. Instead, it abstractly considers the person, machine, goods and environment in the system under study, and consequently, identifies accident causes, processes, and results in nature.

Although many methods and models have been presented in the field of safety driving, no method has yet been established for analyzing the process of conditional autonomous driving. This study intends to bridge this research gap. It proposes the process of conditional autonomous driving and the relationships among three elements based on several theories, including the Haddon matrix [6]. A conditional autonomous car is capable of context-awareness; thus, it can send useful information to driver and interact with driver behavior. Finally, the findings of this study are applied in a parking scenario, and a design concept for head-up display (HUD) is formulated based on the results.

2 Analysis of Context-Aware Conditional Autonomous Driving Process

Two theories are used to analyze the conditional autonomous driving process. The first theory is the Haddon matrix [6], which is the most commonly used paradigm in the injury prevention field. This matrix considers factors related to personal, vector or agent, and environmental attributes before, during, and after an injury or death. The relative importance of different factors and design interventions can be evaluated using this framework. We propose three elements involved once the driver take action, namely, the driver, the environment and the car, based on the Haddon matrix. The second theory is system attribution model, which is the last stage of accident model development. This model theoretically shows the importance of multiple-factor interaction in accident evolution. It presents the notion that the human factor is not the only consideration that must be analyzed in the context of entire system in a driving scenario. Thus, this study analyzes both the relationships among the three elements and process of individual driving behavior based on semi-autonomous driving.

A driving scenario is highly complex, and driving behavior is influenced by many factors. Therefore, this study presents certain assumptions as follows.

- The scenario is simple. This research focuses on a single scenario with a specific task, such as parking or lane changing.
- The object is unique. Only one car or one driver is present in a particular scenario, and other cars and drivers are included in the environment. Communication between drivers or cars is disregarded, and only communication among environment, driver, and car is considered.
- The driving scenario is safe. Only the appropriate processes and normal relationships are considered.
- The vehicle is conditional automation. It quantifies and obtains the environmental and driver information. The vehicle can determine which information the driver requires and provide such data after filtering.
- The driver is willing to comply with the recommendations of the car.

We analyze the processes and relationships among the three elements by considering these prerequisites (Fig. 1).

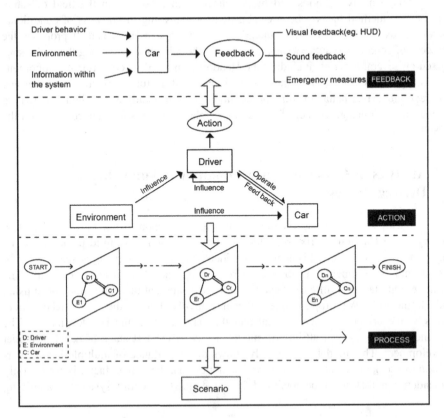

Fig. 1. Driving process and relationships among environment, driver, and car

Figure 1 includes three aspects of information as follows.

- **Driving process:** The driving process is composed of several step-by-step actions. Each scenario involves its own task and process and requires several actions to achieve the task. The order of such actions influences driving safety.
- **Relationships among the environment, the driver, and the car:** The environment can influence both the driver and the car. The driver operates the car, whereas the car provides feedback to the driver. The driver can also influence himself/herself. Both the basic information and conditions of the driver can affect his/her behavior. Environmental factors can be roughly divided into internal and external factors. The internal factors can then be divided into passenger diversity, electronic devices (e.g., mobile phone), internal environment (e.g., air quality and seat size), and car feedback. External factors can be mainly divided into five categories: road conditions, motor vehicle conditions, nonmotor vehicle conditions, road signs, and natural environment.
- **Car feedback:** The vehicle is conditional automation. Feedback is multiple. It includes visual feedback, sound feedback, and emergency measures. Feedback and driver's actions are interactional. Car's feedback can also be included in the internal environmental factors.

3 Research on Parking Scenario

In this section, we choose the parking scenario as an example and use the aforementioned result for analysis. Then, we formulate a design concept for HUD [7] that assists drivers during parking. Parking situations include back parking, parallel parking, and oblique parking. Parallel parking is a general and complex parking situation. Thus, we choose parallel parking as an example for analysis.

3.1 Parallel Parking Process

The parallel parking process can be divided into three stages (Fig. 2): preparation, parking and tail-in work. In the first stage, the main work involves selecting a parking area and preparing to park. During parking, the driver switches on the turn signal, changes gears, and turns the steering wheel several times. During this stage, the driver should pay attention to the surroundings. If other vehicles and pedestrians are passing by, then the driver should avoid scraping them. During the final stage (tail-in work), the driver should turn off the turn signal and change to parking gear. If the driver cannot park in the selected area in a single attempt, then he/she should adjust until he/she has parked completely. After analyzing the parallel parking process, we identify factors that can influence the success rate of parking. These factors include the position and size of the parking area, the start position of reverse, the timing of gear change, the timing of turning the steering wheel, and the distance from other vehicles.

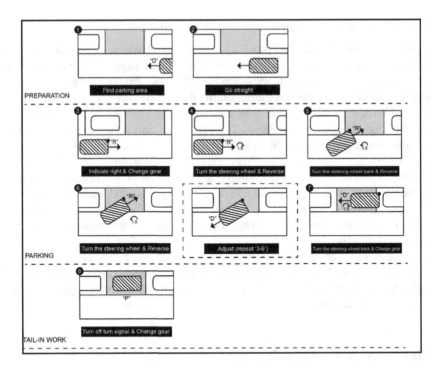

Fig. 2. The process of parallel parking

3.2 Relationships Among the Environment, the Driver, and the Car

In this section, we analyze environmental and driver factors that influence safety during parking. The environmental factors in a parking scenario can be divided into five types: road conditions, motor vehicle conditions, pedestrians, road signs, and natural environment. In this study, road conditions refer to whether the road is crowded or open. Motor vehicle conditions mainly correspond to the presence of any passing vehicle. Road signs comprise parking signs as well as the size and location of the parking area. Natural environment includes poor weather conditions and lighting in an outdoor parking lot. For a parking garage, the natural environment is the main source of light. As mentioned earlier, driver factors can be divided into basic information and driver conditions. Considering the parallel parking scenario, we propose specific factors related to drivers, namely, parking skills, driver confidence, and the ability to estimate vehicle body size. Parking skills include knowledge of the correct parking process and control of speed and distance. Driver confidence is based on the age, experience, and other basic information of the driver.

3.3 Car Feedback

In a parking scenario, feedback from the car can be divided into visual feedback on HUD, sound warning, and emergency measures. The information shown on HUD is based on driver demand. After analysis, we find the position where the driver stops to reserve and how the steering wheel should be turned are important to a driver during parking. Finally, we conclude that the essential information consists of the parking route, key point, real-time position, next operation, gear, positions of the steering wheel and the wheel, and revised parking route. Sound feedback includes lane-departure warning, vehicle distance warning and voice reminders. Emergency measures include emergency brake and protection measures for both drivers and passengers in case of collisions.

Based on Fig. 1, we organize all the information above and conclude them in Fig. 3.

Figure 3 includes the parallel parking process, the relationships among environment, driver, and car and the car's feedback during parallel parking.

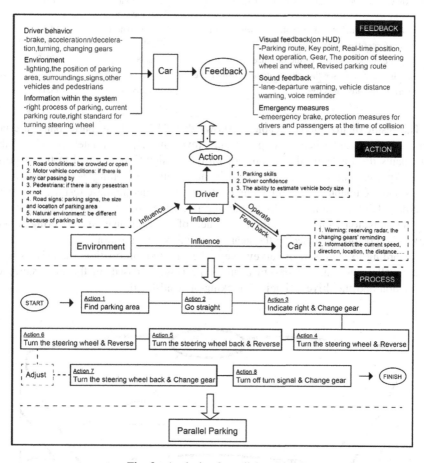

Fig. 3. Analysis of parallel parking

3.4   Design on HUD

We validate the obtained information and select HUD as the platform. We adopt the windshield as a display platform using the shadow casting technique. Hence, we can display the information on the windshield. The driver only has to watch the windshield to improve safety while driving. We perform a questionnaire survey to confirm whether the previously cited requirements are actually those needed by the driver and to sort the importance of information. The number of participants is 19. The result of questionnaire is showed in Table 1.

Table 1. Result of questionnaire

Question	The corresponding information	Probability
Don't know where and when to stop and start reversing	Parking route Point location	16/19
Don't know how much should the steering wheel turn	Steering wheel	14/19
Sometimes forget the wheels' direction	Wheel	12/19
Can't open the door because of the distance	Distance	10/19
Collision because can't see the whole situation behind the car	Rear view camera	8/19
Can't park in the area directly	Corrective route	17/19

The result of the survey (Table 1) shows that 84.2% of the participants are not aware of where and when to stop and start reversing. Approximately 73.7% of the participants do not know the number of turns that should be applied to the steering wheel. Approximately 63.2% of the participants admit to forgetting the direction of the wheels and are unable to park in a single attempt. Considering these results, we obtain the order of information as follows: parking route (key point, revised parking route, real-time position) > next operation (manner of gear change and steering wheel turn) > the position of wheel = the gear = steering wheel position.

According to the result of survey, we make sure the information that drivers need when parallel parking. We design a prototype (Fig. 4) based on the importance of information and the drivers' habit of looking at windshield.

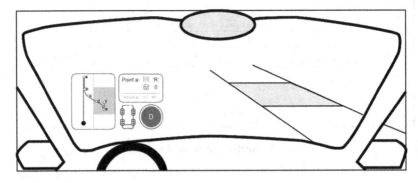

Fig. 4. HUD prototype in parking scenario

The main information in prototype (Fig. 4) includes the parking route, the point location, the steering wheel, the wheel and the distance between car and point. When the driver turns "R" gear, the information will be displayed in RVC. If drivers can not park in one time, here will be the corrective route displayed on HUD.

4 Research on Lane Changing Scenario

4.1 Lane Changing Process

In the process of driving, the frequency of lane changing scenario is high, but also more likely to cause traffic accidents scene. Therefore, it is very meaningful to design the assistance device for the safe driving behavior of lane changing. Depending on the weather and the brightness differences, we found that the driver's lane changes were more difficult due to the poor visibility at night, rainy days and haze days. However, there is a common lane changing regardless of the environment, as shown in Fig. 5. First of all is the normal driving. Secondly, according to the lane will be changing the vehicle speed and vehicle distance to determine whether changing lane. If it is suitable for lane changing, then open the lane changing lights. According to vehicle speed inside line, adjust themselves speed, acceleration or deceleration, or uniform, until a lane changing safety area appeared. At this point, immediately turn the steering wheel, change to the target lane. If changing lane succeed, turn back to the lights. If failed, return to the original lane immediately, and to find the next changing opportunity.

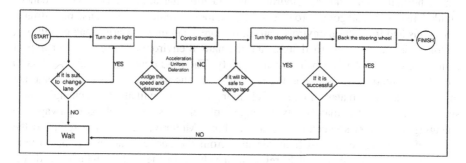

Fig. 5. The process of lane changing

As the vehicles in different situations of lane changing, the drivers' throttle control is not the same. In normal daytime weather conditions, there are five main situations for lane changing (Fig. 6):

(a) The right front vehicle speed is slower, take the action like acceleration or uniform. And maintain a safe distance with after car then change lane.
(b) The right front of the vehicle speed is faster, take the action like deceleration. And maintain a safe distance with after car then change lane.
(c) The right rear of the vehicle speed is faster, take the action like deceleration until overtake that car. And maintain a safe distance with after car then change lane.

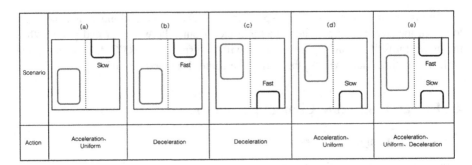

Fig. 6. Five main situations for lane changing

(d) The right rear of the vehicle speed is slower, take the action like acceleration or uniform until overtake that car. And maintain a safe distance with after car then change lane.

(e) The right rear of the vehicle speed is slower, take the action like acceleration, uniform or deceleration. And maintain a safe distance with before and after cars then change lane

4.2   Relationships Among the Environment, the Driver, and the Car

Under normal circumstances, environmental factors that affect driving safety can be divided into five categories: road conditions, motor vehicle conditions, pedestrians, road signs and the natural environment. In the lane changing scenario, road conditions, motor vehicle conditions, road signs and the natural environment are a greater impact factors on drivers' driving behavior and safety. The road conditions, mainly refers to whether the road is crowded and the type of road. The more vehicles on the road, the more crowded, the greater difficulty of changing lanes, and will affect the changing lane speed; type of road is mainly having impact of vehicle speed, such as highway lane changing, the driver's speed can relatively high. Motor vehicle mainly refers to the speed of other vehicles, and their distance from the car and the upcoming driving behavior. Here, the other vehicle refers to a vehicle in the lane in which the driver wants to change the lane and a vehicle that wants to change lane to the current lane. Road signs will mainly affect whether the driver is suitable for lane changing and whether the lane should be changed, in addition to lane does not allow lane change, overtaking, if the driver wants to turn right at the junction must change lanes to allow the right lane. Natural environment mainly includes two aspects, one day/night, on the other hand is bad weather, such as rain, haze days, snow days and so on, these natural environments will affect the driving environment and the driver's line of sight, in different environments, the driver needs to set aside the safety lane change will not be the same. Pedestrians of this factor in the lane scene of the impact of the other four factors are not large, lane changing scenario generally occur at a certain speed on the road, and pedestrian contact opportunities less, so pedestrians in this scenario factors can be ignored.

In lane changing scenario, the drivers' personal factors will also affect the safety of vehicles, mainly including the following aspects: the driver's personal skills, personal driving habits and personal basic information. Personal skills mainly refer to the driver of the other vehicle speed and vehicle distance of the ability to judge; personal habits mainly refer to the process of lane changing to see mirror habit, turning lights time, the speed of the habit, etc. Personal basic information, including the driver's character and driving experience, timid or self-confidence, driving experience much or little will affect the safety of lane change process.

Finally, the factors on the vehicle itself, in the lane changing scenario mainly refers to the speed of their vehicles, their speed will affect the relative speed of other vehicles, and in different speeds, lane changing safety distance will be different, these determine the appropriate time to lane change, and ultimately affect the lane change security.

4.3   Car Feedback

In lane change scenario, the feedback information to the driver after obtaining the relevant information about the driver and the environment can be divided into three main aspects: visual feedback (HUD display), sound feedback and emergency measures. Visual feedback mainly presents information that requires the driver to determine whether or not it is suitable for lane changes by personal judgment. Compared with the subjective judgment of the driver, after obtaining the information of the vehicle itself, the driver and the environment, the vehicle can show more rational information after the calculation and screening, which can help the driver avoid the safety accident caused by the mistake of subjective judgment. After analysis, the final decision on the information presented in the HUD has the following parts: the current vehicle speed, the proposed driving behavior (acceleration/constant speed/deceleration), the current environment is suitable for lane (whether with other vehicles to maintain a safe lane distance), real-time vehicle conditions within the safety range (if other vehicles appear? What's situation of their speed and distance?), and turn signal lights.

There are two types of sound feedback, voice prompts and alarm tones. Under normal circumstances, in order to avoid distracting the driver's attention, we will minimize the voice prompts to simple and necessary alarm sound as an adjunct to help the driver in the driving process to avoid dangerous situations. In the course of the lane change, the sound feedback appears mainly in two situations, the vehicle distance detection and the lane departure detection, when the vehicle is too close or the vehicle deviates from the lane there will appear an alarm tone.

The final emergency measures are not very different in different scenarios. This feature mainly considers the extreme case where the car's pre-set protection system replaces the driver's behavior in extreme danger, as well as the driver and the car in a dangerous situation Protection of passengers within the measures.

Based on Fig. 1, we organize all the information above and conclude them in Fig. 7.

Figure 7 includes the lane changing process, the relationships among environment, driver, and car and the car's feedback during lane changing.

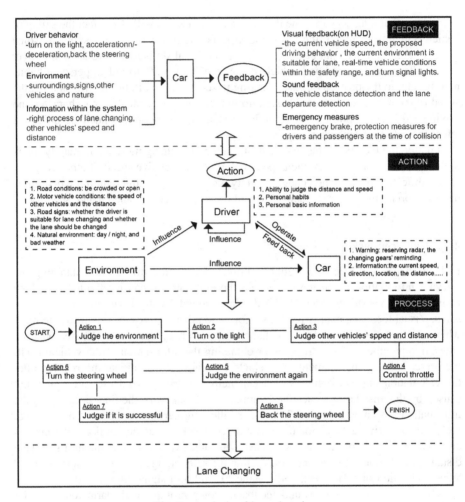

Fig. 7. Analysis of lane changing

4.4 Design

According to the result of analysis, we make sure the information that drivers need when lane changing. We design a prototype (Fig. 8) based on the importance of information and the drivers' habit of looking at windshield.

The main information in prototype (Fig. 8) includes the current vehicle speed, the proposed driving behavior (acceleration/constant speed/deceleration), the current environment is suitable for lane, real-time vehicle conditions within the safety range, and turn signal lights.

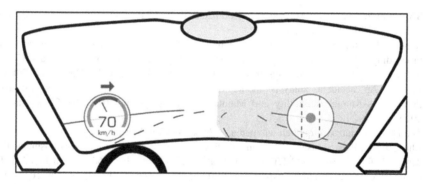

Fig. 8. HUD prototype in lane changing scenario

5 Conclusion and Future Work

This paper aims to analyze the process of conditional autonomous driving and the relationships among elements based on context-aware safety driving. We propose three elements involved in a single action, namely, the environment, the driver, and the car, based on the Haddon matrix. We analyze the relationships among the three elements and the process involved in a single driving scenario using the system attribution model, which is the last stage in accident model development. The driving is highly complex, and driving behavior is influenced by many factors. Hence, we initially make certain assumptions, such as the involvement of a simple scenario, a unique object, a safe driving scenario, a semi-autonomous car, and a compliant driver who follows the recommendations of the car. Considering these prerequisites, we propose the process involved and the relationships among the environment, the driver, and the car in a single driving scenario. To adopted car is conditional automation and capable of context awareness, and thus, it can send useful information as feedback to the driver and interact with driver behavior. Then, we choose parallel parking scenario and lane changing scenario to apply the obtained results. We analyze the parallel parking process and lane changing process, environmental and driver factors that influence safety driving, and car feedback. Finally, we develop a design concept for a parking and lane changing assistance device on HUD.

Acknowledgements. We thank all the volunteers, and all publications support and staff, who wrote and provided helpful comments on previous versions of this document.

References

1. Liu, Y.F., Wang, Y.M., Li, W.S., Xu, W.Q., Gui, J.S.: Improve driver performance by experience of driver cognitive behavior model's practice. In: 2009 IEEE Intelligent Vehicles Symposium, pp. 475–480, 3–5 June 2009
2. Rödel, C., Stadler, S., Meschtscherjakov, A., Tscheligi, M.: Towards autonomous cars: the effect of autonomy levels on acceptance and user experience. In: Proceedings of the 6th International Conference on Automotive User Interfaces and Interactive Vehicular Applications (AutomotiveUI 2014), article 11, 8 p. ACM, New York (2014)

3. SAE. http://www.sae.org/servlets/pressRoom?OBJECT_TYPE=PressReleases&PAGE=show
Release&RELEASE_ID=3544
4. Renner, L., Johansson, B.: Driver coordination in complex traffic environments. In:
Proceedings of the 13th Eurpoean Conference on Cognitive Ergonomics: Trust and Control
in Complex Socio-Technical Systems (ECCE 2006), pp. 35–40. ACM, New York (2006)
5. Li, X.: An accident analysis model oriented to complex tasks process. In: 2010
Proceedings-Annual Reliability and Maintainability Symposium (RAMS), 25–28 January
2010
6. The Haddon Matrix. https://en.wikipedia.org/wiki/Haddon_Matrix
7. Charissis, V., Papanastasiou, S., Chan, W., Peytchev, E.: Evolution of a full-windshield HUD
designed for current VANET communication standards. In: 16th International IEEE
Conference on Intelligent Transportation Systems (ITSC 2013), The Hague, pp. 1637–1643
(2013)

ECG Identification Based on PCA-RPROP

Jinrun Yu[1], Yujuan Si[1,2(✉)], Xin Liu[1], Dunwei Wen[3], Tengfei Luo[1],
and Liuqi Lang[2]

[1] College of Communication Engineering, Jilin University,
Changchun 130012, China
yujinrun@qq.com, siyj@jlu.edu.cn
[2] Zhuhai College of Jilin University, Zhuhai 519041, China
[3] School of Computing and Information Systems, Athabasca University,
Alberta, Canada
dunweiw@athabascau.ca

Abstract. With the quick development of information technology, people pay more and more attention to information security and property safety, where identity is one of the most important aspects of information security. Compared with the traditional means of identification, biometrics recognition technology offers greater security and convenience. Among which, electrocardiogram (ECG) human identification has been attracted great attention in recent years. As a new type of biometric feature authentication technology, the feature selection and classification of ECG has become a focus of the research community. However, there exist some problems that can impair the efficiency and accuracy of ECG identification, including information redundancy and high dimensionality in feature extraction, and insufficient stability in classification. In order to solve the problems, in this paper, we propose a recognition method based on PCA-RPROP. In this method, firstly, only R points are located to get the original single-cycle waveforms. Then, PCA and whitening are used to process original data, where whitening is to make the input less redundant and PCA is to reduce its dimensionality. Finally, the resilient propagation (RPROP) algorithm is used to optimize the neural network and establish a complete recognition model. In order to evaluate the effectiveness of the algorithm, we compared the PCA feature with the wavelet decomposition and multi-point localization features in an ECG-ID database, and also compared RPROP with traditional BP algorithm, SVM and KNN. The experimental results show that this method can improve the performance compared with other classifiers, and simultaneously reduce the complexity of localization and the redundancy of features. It is superior to the other methods both speed and accuracy in recognition, especially when compared with the traditional BP. It can solve the problems of traditional BP with 2.4% higher recognition accuracy than LIBSVM, and 14 s faster than KNN in terms of time efficiency. Therefore, it is an efficient, simple and practical recognition algorithm.

Keywords: ECG · Identity recognition · Whitening · PCA dimensionality reduction · Neural network · RPROP

© Springer International Publishing AG 2017
V.G. Duffy (Ed.): DHM 2017, Part II, LNCS 10287, pp. 419–432, 2017.
DOI: 10.1007/978-3-319-58466-9_37

1 Introduction

Electrocardiogram (ECG) is one of the most common physiological signals of human and its signal waveform has obvious regularity. While heart beat recognition technology has been well advanced since Einthoven invented the ECG in 1903, it is limited to medical diagnosis. In 2001, Biel [1] first proposed the ECG identity recognition technology. In recent years, with the impact of the Internet boom and the rapid development of information technology, people pay more attention to information security and property safety, as identity is the most important aspect of information security. Compared with traditional identification technology, biometrics-based recognition is more secure and convenient, but the existing biometric identification techniques such as fingerprint identification, iris identification, face identification, have their own shortcomings. For instance, in fingerprint identification fingers are susceptible to wear, expose, and inverted copy, and this results in instability and risk. Iris recognition requires stringent illumination condition, and also its cost is high. In face identification, faces can be easily copied, and the difference after cosmetic surgery is obvious. Therefore, we need a kind of identification technology that has strong security and satisfies various indicators of biometrics.

The identification technology based on ECG can meet the requirements. Produced by the human heart with a weak voltage signal, ECG is the most common physiological signal of human body. It contains a lot of biological information, which can be utilized for different purposes, more than just in clinical diagnostic tools. The difference of individual ECG signals provides a theoretical basis for ECG signal feature extraction and identification. Also, ECG can be collected at low computational cost and low acquisition cost, and cannot be lost or stolen. Compared with the above commonly identification technology, ECG is a signal generated by the heart of the human body, and is more secure than the other identification techniques mentioned above that reply on exposed biometrics outside of the body.

At present, there are two kinds of common feature extraction algorithms used in ECG identification, namely reference point extraction and non-reference point extraction. Reference point extraction mainly extracts several characteristic points in signal, which includes the morphological information of individual waveforms. In [2], QRS segments are extracted from heart beats, and five feature points and one morphology factor are selected. In [3], peak points are determined by a local curvature minimum method. As the extraction of reference points from ECG signal is too dependent on the location accuracy of each reference point, the stability of the system is greatly affected and the accuracy of recognition is reduced.

Non-reference point extraction does not need to locate feature points. In [4], autocorrelation coefficient and cosine transform are used to extract the feature parameters of ECG signals. But the data acquisition time is long, and the storage capacity is large. It is difficult to make full use of the differences in individual signals, and this causes a lot of information loss. Thus it is not conducive to effective classification.

Regarding classification, k-Nearest-Neighbor (KNN), Support Vector Machine (SVM), Lib-linear and Naive Bayes are classic classification or supervised learning models. But the adaptability of these algorithms is not as good as Neural Networks (NN). For example, KNN is not a regularized category scoring method and prone to skew when applied to unbalanced data. Although SVM has good performance, it is sensitive to missing data, and the choice of kernel function needs to be made with caution.

Based on the above problems, this paper presents a new feature extraction and classification algorithm, which combines principal component analysis (PCA) and whitening with resilient propagation (RPROP). First, we obtain complete heart beats through R points, then use whitening to eliminate the correlation between the heart beats and use PCA to transform the multidimensional features into low dimensional features. By eliminating feature redundancy, the new features can retain more than 90% of the useful information. Finally a neural network is used to replace the traditional supervised classifier. We use RPROP algorithm to optimize the gradient of the neural network, and combine PCA whitening feature with RPROP algorithm to improve the classification efficiency of neural networks. Experimental results show that the feature extraction is simple to perform and the classifier optimization is significant, which can greatly improve the training speed and identification precision.

In Sect. 2, we briefly describe the PCA whitening technology and the characteristics of RPROP. In Sect. 3, we discuss the flow of our algorithm from three modules: Preprocessing, Feature Extraction and Classification. Section 4 introduces the experimental steps and discusses the results. Finally, in Sect. 5, we summarize this paper.

2 PCA Whitening and RPROP

2.1 PCA Whitening

The PCA whitening is a multivariate statistical method to investigate the correlation between multiple variables [5]. By means of an orthogonal transformation, PCA whitening transforms original random vectors with relevant components into new random vectors with irrelevant components. The covariance structure of multivariate is then expressed by a few principal components, so that the data samples are reduced from original n dimensions to k dimensions ($k < n$), achieving a transformation into a low dimensional system with a high precision. Because of the temporal correlation between the heart beats, we use whitening to remove the correlation and use PCA technology to process the data. It not only reduces the amount of the data, but also highlights their characteristics. These features often retain the most important aspects of the data, and significantly reduce the complexity of the classification system.

2.2 RPROP

The classical gradient descent based back-propagation (BP) algorithm has laid a solid foundation for the development of neural networks. However, it has uncertain computational complexity and slow convergence rate in practice. It is also easy to fall into the local minimum, and hard to converge once caught in a flat region. Many optimized algorithms including the prominent Levenberg-Marquardt (L-M) method [6] have been proposed, but they adjust the weights of the network based on the amount of the gradients, and thus the local minimum problem is not well handled.

Due to the complexity of the error hypersurface, it is difficult to obtain much heuristic information from its global region. We should use a local adaptive strategy, where a different adaptive learning rate is used for each weight, which generally requires less specific information. RPROP method [7] is a good local adaptive method for classification in ECG identification. Regardless of the amount of the gradients, RPROP method is based on the direction of the gradients to determine the direction of weight adjustments. So, the algorithm is not much affected by bad gradient values from unforeseen disturbances. In addition to the gradient calculation, the weight adjustments only depend on the resilient update values, so the calculation is much less than many other algorithms. The RPROP algorithm also has the same learning ability at different layers of neural network, without being affected by the distance from the output layer.

3 Our Approach

3.1 Preprocessing

• Denoising

In this paper, we focus on feature extraction and classification optimization of ECG Identification. Therefore, we prefer to choose ECG heart beats as the initial data sets because they are less susceptible to interference [8]. Before the extraction of the initial features, we firstly need to denoise the signal, i.e., reducing the noises such as baseline drift, electromyographical interference and power frequency interference. ECG signal frequency ranges between 0.05 Hz–100 Hz, covering the above three kinds of noise. We use a median filter to remove baseline drift, and use discrete wavelet transform to remove power frequency interference and electromyographical interference [9].

• R Point Location

In fact, locating multiple feature points in ECG signal processing is difficult because many people's ECG waveform is different from the ideal ECG waveform, which may include no P waves, 'Camel Hump' T waves and inverted T waves etc. Thus we extract complete heart beats by locating R points alone [10]. The specific steps are as follows:

1. Locate R points
   We apply dyadic spline 4-layer wavelets transform to denoised ECG signals. Because the R wave is prominent in the 3-layer detail coefficients, R points can be easily detected by maximum-minimum method with 3-layer coefficients.
2. Compensate for drift
   There is a drift phenomenon between the 3-layer detail coefficients and the corresponding position of the original signal in the process of wavelet transform, so the drift compensation is needed.

3. Undetected and wrong-detected R points

In some cases, R points may be undetected and wrong-detected. We detect the distance from adjacent R points. When the distance between adjacent R points is less than 0.5 mean (RR), the R points with small values are removed; when the distance between adjacent R points is more than 1.5 mean (RR), find a maximum of extreme points between the two R-R points and locate the R point. The effect of R point location is shown in Fig. 1.

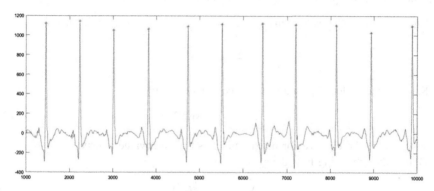

Fig. 1. R point location

- **Heart Beats Segmentation**

Find two adjacent R points, resampling the waveform between the R-R, then splicing the two adjacent waveforms to obtain a complete heart beat. Standardizing the number of sample points as 250, we randomly intercepted the two groups of heart beats, as shown in Fig. 2.

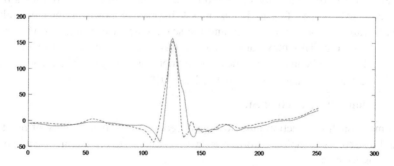

Fig. 2. Heart beat segmentation

3.2 Feature Extraction

Based on whitening and PCA, the initial heart beats correlation is removed, and the dimensionality of heart beats is reduced from 250 to 30. Assuming heart beats

$X \in R^{m \times n}$, where m is the number of beats, n is the dimensionality of the heart beats, all heart beats are aligned with the start and end points. Each heart beat has 250 points and the length is the same [11].

- **Whitening Step**

Whitening eliminates the correlation between ECG data and allows further analysis to be focused on higher order statistics, which can lead to a significant increase in subsequent processing speed. The specific steps are as follows.

1. Calculate the covariance matrix:

$$\Sigma = \frac{1}{m} X X^T \tag{1}$$

2. Singular value decomposition of the covariance matrix:

$$[U, S, V] = svd(\Sigma) \tag{2}$$

where U is the eigenvector matrix and S is the eigenvalue matrix.
3. Obtain the whitening beat data:

$$X_{\text{white}} = S^{-\frac{1}{2}} U^T X \tag{3}$$

where $S^{-\frac{1}{2}}$ is equivalent to the data on each spindle to do a scaling. Scaling factor is divided by the corresponding square root of the eigenvalue; $U^T X$ is the original data in the principal component axis projection.
4. Substitute the result of Step 3 into covariance matrix:

$$\sum\nolimits_{\text{white}} = \frac{1}{m} X_{\text{white}} X_{\text{white}}^T = I \tag{4}$$

The obtained covariance matrix is a unit matrix, each dimension becomes uncorrelated, and the variance of each dimension is 1. In practice, however, the eigenvalue of the heart beats may be close to zero, and the scaling step will result in dividing by a value close to zero. This may cause data overflow, so we introduce a regularization term that adds a small constant ε to the denominator of the eigenvalue matrix S to avoid affecting the feature. When X is normalized, $\varepsilon = 10^{-5}$.

- **Dimensionality Reduction Step**

PCA dimensionality reduction aims to greatly reduce the dimensionality of heart beat data and to express complete information with minimal feature quantity. The specific steps are as follows.

1. The heart beat data is organized in the form of $m * n$ matrices to form a data set

$$X_{ij} = \begin{bmatrix} x_{11}, x_{12}, \ldots, x_{1n} \\ x_{21}, x_{22}, \ldots, x_{2n} \\ \ldots \\ x_{m1}, x_{m2}, \ldots, x_{mn} \end{bmatrix}, \text{ the set is normalized:}$$

$$Z_{ij} = \frac{X_{ij} - \overline{X}_j}{S_j} \quad \begin{array}{l} i = 1, 2, \ldots, n \\ j = 1, 2, \ldots, m \end{array} \tag{5}$$

where $\overline{X}_j = \dfrac{\sum\limits_{i=1}^{n} X_{ij}}{n}$ is the mean and $S_j = \sqrt{\dfrac{\sum\limits_{i=1}^{n} (X_{ij} - \overline{X}_j)^2}{n-1}}$ is the standard deviation.

2. Calculate the eigenvalues of the correlation coefficient matrix and obtain m eigenvalues:

$$R = \frac{Z^T Z}{n - 1} \tag{6}$$

3. Determine the p value:

$$\frac{\sum\limits_{j=1}^{p} \lambda_j}{\sum\limits_{j=1}^{m} \lambda_j} \geq a \tag{7}$$

where a is the contribution rate of the components, usually more than 90%. For each eigenvalue λ_j, solving $Rd = \lambda_j d$ obtains unit eigenvector d_j^o.

4. Conversion to the main components:

$$Y_j = Z_i^T d_j^o \tag{8}$$

In general, only the first few variables are the main components, we should calculate whether the contribution rate meets the requirements.

3.3   Classification

According to the principle of RPROP algorithm, the learning rate is changed by the gradient direction according to the local adaptive strategy, which makes the convergence stable, fast and not easy to fall into the local minimum. The specific steps are as follows.

① Similar to the traditional BP algorithm, the number of neurons in each layer was set on the basis of heart beat samples, PCA feature dimensionality and the number of classes. Let i, j, k be the number of neurons in the input layer, hidden layer and output layer, respectively.

② Initialize the variable speed $\Delta_{ji}^{(0)}$, variable speed factor v, lower threshold Δ_{min} and upper threshold Δ_{max}.

③ Calculate the error between actual output and expected output:
$E(t) = \frac{1}{2} \sum\limits_{k=1}^{n} (o_{1k} - o_{2k})^2$, where o_{1k} is the actual output, o_{2k} is the desired output.

④ Judge the relationship between the value of $\frac{\partial E^{(k-1)}}{\partial W_{ji}} * \frac{\partial E^{(k)}}{\partial W_{ji}}$ and 0. If the value is equal to 0, go to step ⑤; if greater than 0, go to step ⑥; if less than 0, go to step ⑦.

⑤ Weight update item $\Delta_{ji}^{(k)} = \Delta_{ji}^{(k-1)}$ needs no change.

⑥ Weight update item $\Delta_{ji}^{(k)} = \min(\Delta_{ji}^{(k-1)} \cdot v^+, \Delta_{max})$, for increasing the update value. We take $v^+ = 1.2$ generally.

⑦ Weight update item $\Delta_{ji}^{(k)} = \max(\Delta_{ji}^{(k-1)} \cdot v^-, \Delta_{min})$, for reducing the update value. We take $v^- = 0.5$ generally.

⑧ According to the above steps, adjust the weight $W_{ji}^{(k)} = W_{ji}^{(k-1)} - \text{sgn}(\frac{\partial E^{(k)}}{\partial W_{ji}})\Delta_{ji}^{(k)}$.

⑨ Take the minimum gradient of 1.0-e7, limit the iteration times to 500, and judge if the error E reaches the setting value, and if not, back to step ③; if so, end the training process, save the training model, and record the training time.

By this method, we optimize the classifier of ECG identification and improve the classification stability.

3.4 Identification

The principle of hierarchical voting is applied in identification, which uses the resulting confusion matrix obtained by the above classification algorithm as the voting data source. The registration database and the identification database are then compared one by one, and the majority of voting is used as the final recognition result. Figure 3 is the complete flow chart of ECG identification.

4 Experiments and Results

4.1 Database

This data is obtained from the ECG-ID database in PhysioNet (www.physionet.org), which contains the ECG signals of 88 persons, 20 s per person on average, with a digital frequency of 500 Hz and a resolution of 12 bits. Everyone has no less than two sets of signals collected at different times, all signals can be obtained freely from the website. The experiment goal is to identify the 88 persons. The identification process is shown in Fig. 4.

4.2 Preprocessing and NN Model Setting

Select two different times from the database of the heart beats, about 20 s each time, from a total of 88 people. After denoising, locating R points and obtaining individual heart beats, we resample 250 points from the beats and align the start and end points. We then perform PCA whitening, extract PCA feature, and reduce the dimensionality to 30. We take 2055 beats at time A as the training set and 2103 at time B as the testing

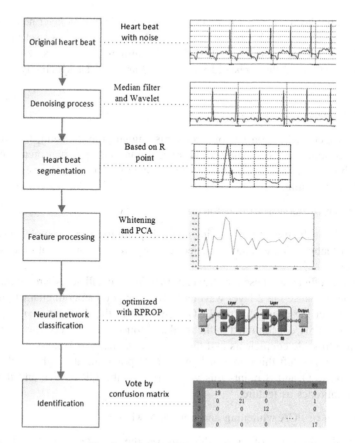

Fig. 3. ECG identification flow chart

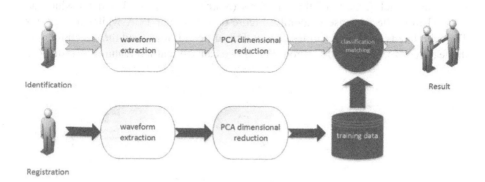

Fig. 4. Recognition process

set for neural networks training and testing respectively. The number of neurons in the output layer is the number of people. We set the number of neurons in the hidden layer based on the classical formula $a = \sqrt{b+c} + r$ (b is the number of input layers, c is the number of output layers, r = 1–10), and this forms a single hidden layer neural network classification model of 30-20-88 neurons. For RPROP algorithm, we set the iteration times as 500, the error standard as 0.0005, the minimum gradient as 1e-7, the initial shift value as 0.07, and the threshold values as 50 and 0.001 respectively.

4.3   Experiment

A complete ECG system consists of three parts: signal preprocessing, feature extraction, classification. We have denoised the ECG signal during signal preprocessing as described above, and now the focus of the experiment will be on feature extraction and classification algorithm.

• Comparison of initial feature extraction:

This paper adopts the method of locating single R point to extract complete heart beats as the initial features. To evaluate its effectiveness, we compare it with the following two methods.

Wavelet coefficients: Discrete wavelet transform coefficients are extracted for identification. Because the 2-layer wavelet (DB2) has good smooth characteristic, it is suitable to detect the change of the ECG signal. Also, the different frequency of the heart beats is mainly concentrated in the third and fourth scales. Therefore, we take the third and fourth scale coefficients and the detail coefficients as feature.

QRS wave: The left third pole of R point is Q point and the right third pole is S point. We locate Q and S points this way, and take the QRS wave and the points' intervals, amplitudes as feature.

• Comparison of PCA whitening and non-PCA whitening:

Because of the influence of PCA whitening on the efficiency of classification, we separate the initial features into PCA whitening and non-PCA whitening. Figure 5 shows the initial features of three persons (represented by A, B and C) which are selected from the database randomly. Figure 6 shows their PCA whitening features. The solid line is the features of tester A at three different times, and the dotted lines are the features of tester B and C. From Fig. 6, we can see that the features of tester A at

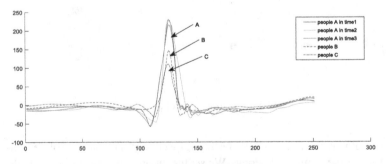

Fig. 5. Initial features of heart beat

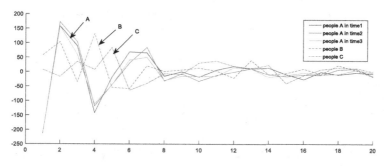

Fig. 6. PCA whitening feature

different times almost coincide, but different from others. Therefore, the PCA whitening features of ECG signals have obvious advantages over ECG identification.

- Comparison of classifiers:

We use PCA to reduce the feature dimensionality from 250 to 30, yet the 30 principal components can still provide 98.75% contribution. As shown in Fig. 7, the first 10 principal components can actually reach a comprehensive contribution of close to 90%. Under the same standard, we take the heart beats of the same person in different times as training set and test set. The accuracy and efficiency of KNN, SVM, traditional BP and RPROP algorithm are compared respectively. Figure 8 shows the error convergence of RPROP algorithm and L-M algorithm under the same set. As one can see, compared with L-M algorithm (based on amount of gradient), the RPROP (based on the direction of gradient) has a faster and smoother convergence.

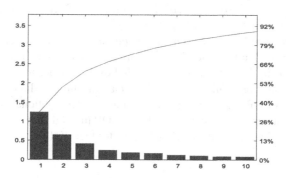

Fig. 7. Principal component contribution rate

4.4   Results and Analysis

The classification accuracy of three initial features with LIBSVM [12] is shown in Table 1.

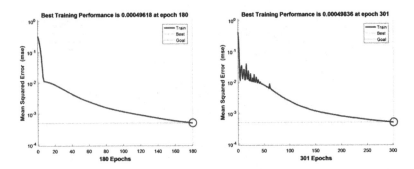

Fig. 8. Error convergence curve of RPROP and L-M

Table 1. Accuracy of different initial features (%)

Feature	Accuracy (SVM)
Wavelet coefficient	90.9
QRS wave	86.4
Complete beat	93.2

Table 1 is shows that the effective information of our complete beat feature extraction method is higher than QRS wave and wavelet coefficient. Given that location only involves R points, our method of extracting the initial features is simple and more efficient.

In order to save test time in experiment, we compared the time consumed by using PCA whitening data and the results are shown in Table 2. We compared the feature of PCA with that of non-PCA in each classifier to test the effect of PCA whitening. The results of classification are shown in Fig. 9.

Table 2 shows that the our RPROP based approach only takes about 10 s, which is much more efficient than the other three classifiers. It can be seen from Fig. 8 that the features processed by PCA whitening yield slightly higher accuracy than the unprocessed feature. Compared with the other three classification methods, the recognition accuracy of our RPROP approach is obviously higher than traditional BP algorithm. In terms of PCA whitening, the accuracy of the RPROP method is 96.6%, which is 2.4% higher than SVM. The time efficiency is 14 s faster than KNN.

Table 2. The training time of different classifiers

Classifier	Training time
KNN	24 s
SVM	3200 s
Traditional BP	240 s
Our approach	10 s

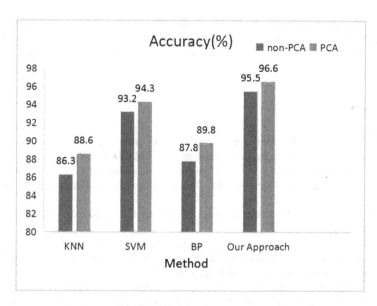

Fig. 9. Classification accuracy

5 Conclusion

In order to improve the accuracy and efficiency of ECG identification, we conducted an experimental study in feature extraction, classification and recognition. By comparing a series of methods, the information integrity of the proposed complete heart beat features is seen to be superior to the features through other methods such as wavelet coefficient, QRS wave, and the classification accuracy also higher than the other features under LIBSVM. The complexity and redundancy of proposed features are significantly reduced by PCA whitening. The paper selected the optimal features as input to the neural network that is further optimized by RPROP algorithm for classification. The accuracy of the PCA-RPROP algorithm is higher than KNN, SVM and BP, reaching 96.6%. This demonstrates the validity of PCA-RPROP algorithm for ECG identification. Because of its obvious time efficiency in recognition, it can be used as a core algorithm for engineering a complete ID system.

ECG signals are frequently applied in monitoring patient's heart rate status and adjuvant therapy. Likewise, simple and effective ECG identification can be widely used in identity recognition in a variety of applications, such as drug use management, privacy protection, medical treatment recording and other remote medical identification without additional data.

Acknowledgment. We thank all the volunteers and colleagues provided helpful comments on previous versions of the manuscript. This work was supported by the Science and Technology Development projects funded by Jilin Government (20150204039GX, 20170414017GH), Science and Technology Development Special Funded by Guangdong Government (2016A030313658), and Key Scientific and Technological Special Fund Project supported by

Changchun Government under Grant No. 14KG064. This work was also supported by Premier-Discipline Enhancement Scheme Supported by Zhuhai Government and Premier Key-Discipline Enhancement Scheme Supported by Guangdong Government Funds.

References

1. Biel, L., Pettersson, O., Philipson, L., et al.: ECG analysis: a new approach in human identification. IEEE Trans. Instrum. Meas. **50**, 808–812 (2001)
2. Palaniappan, R., Krishnan, S.M.: Identifying individuals using ECG beats. In: International Conference on Signal Processing and Communications, Bangalore, India, pp. 569–572 (2005)
3. Israel, S.A., Irvine, J.M., Cheng, A., et al.: ECG to identify individuals. Pattern Recogn. **38**, 133–142 (2005)
4. Plataniotis, K.N., Hatzinakos, D., Lee, J.K.M.: ECG biometric recognition without fiducial detection. In: Biometric Consortium Conference, 2006 Biometrics Symposium: Special Session on Research, Baltimore, MD, pp. 1–6 (2006)
5. Jégou, H., Chum, O.: Negative evidences and co-occurrences in image retrieval: the benefit of PCA and whitening. In: Fitzgibbon, A., Lazebnik, S., Perona, P., Sato, Y., Schmid, C. (eds.) ECCV 2012. LNCS, pp. 774–787. Springer, Heidelberg (2012). doi:10.1007/978-3-642-33709-3_55
6. Moré, J.J.: The Levenberg-Marquardt algorithm: implementation and theory. In: Watson, G. A. (ed.) Numerical Analysis. LNM, vol. 630, pp. 105–116. Springer, Heidelberg (1978). doi:10.1007/BFb0067700
7. Riedmiller, M., Braun, H.: A direct adaptive method for faster backpropagation learning: the RPROP algorithm. In: IEEE International Conference on Neural Networks, San Francisco, CA, vol. 1, pp. 586–591 (1993)
8. Saxena, S.C., Kumar, V., Hamde, S.T.: Feature extraction from ECG signals using wavelet transforms for disease diagnostics. Int. J. Syst. Sci. **33**, 1073–1085 (2002)
9. Han, X.U., Wang, D.D., Jiang, T.B.: Research on the ECG signal denoising algorithm based on wavelet transform and the median filter. Autom. Instrum. (2012)
10. Sadhukhan, D., Mitra, M.: R-peak detection algorithm for ECG using double difference and RR interval processing. Procedia Technol. **4**, 873–877 (2012)
11. Marrtis, R.J., Acharya, U.R., Min, L.C.: ECG beat classification using PCA, LDA, ICA and discrete wavelet transform. Biomed. Signal Process. Control **8**, 437–448 (2013)
12. Chang, C.C., Lin, C.J.: LIBSVM: a library for support vector machines. ACM Trans. Intell. Syst. Technol. **2**, 27 (2011)

Author Index

Printed in the United States
By Bookmasters